OXFORD MONOGRAPHS IN
INTERNATIONAL LAW

General Editor: Professor Ian Brownlie QC, DCL, FBA
*Chichele Professor of Public International Law at the University of
Oxford and Fellow of All Souls College, Oxford*

THE JURIDICAL BAY

OXFORD MONOGRAPHS IN
INTERNATIONAL LAW

This new series of monographs will publish important and
original pieces of research on all aspects of public international law. Topics which will be given particular prominence
are those which, while of interest to the academic lawyer, also
have important bearings on issues which touch the actual conduct of international relations. Nonetheless, the series is
intended to be wide in scope and thus will include the history
and philosophical foundations of international law.

ALSO IN THIS SERIES

The Exclusive Economic Zone in International Law
DAVID ATTARD

Judicial Remedies in International Law
CHRISTINE GRAY

Occupation, Resistance and Law
ADAM ROBERTS

The Legality of Non-Forcible Counter-Measures
in International Law
OMER ELAGAB

The Shatt-Al-Arab Boundary Question:
A Legal Re-appraisal

KAIYAN KAIKOBAD

THE
Juridical Bay

GAYL S. WESTERMAN

Oxford University Press · New York
Clarendon Press · Oxford
1987

Oxford University Press

Oxford   New York   Toronto
Delhi   Bombay   Calcutta   Madras   Karachi
Petaling Jaya   Singapore   Hong Kong   Tokyo
Nairobi   Dar es Salaam   Cape Town
Melbourne   Auckland

and associated companies in
Beirut   Berlin   Ibadan   Nicosia

Library of Congress Cataloging-in-Publication Data
Westerman, Gayl.
The juridical bay.
(Oxford monographs in international law)
Bibliography: p.   Includes index.
1. Bays (International law)   I. Title.   II. Series.
JX4137.W47   1987   341.4'48   87-1712
ISBN 0-19-503998-X

1 3 5 7 9 8 6 4 2

Printed in the United States of America
on acid-free paper

Law

Editor's Preface

While the delimitation of bays for purposes of international law is not a new subject, it is one of those classical aspects of the law of the sea which has not only remained significant but, as a result of the higher levels of oil and gas development, has become increasingly relevant.

Professor Westerman has produced a well-structured account of the difficult problems involved in the application of the formulation in Article 7 of the 1958 Geneva Convention on the Territorial Sea and Contiguous Zone. The fine analytical approach is accompanied by reference to State practice and the particularly important experience of the United States Courts in respect of federal–state maritime boundary disputes. The subject matter does not lend itself to fluent exposition, but Professor Westerman has a lively and engagingly disputatious pen, and the result is a treatment characterized by readability and vigor.

Oxford
November 1986

Ian Brownlie

Author's Foreword

The special problem of identifying the juridical nature of coastal indentations, lying ambiguously within the land territory of the littoral state and yet exposed to the open sea, is but one aspect of a more fundamental problem: that of accommodating the legitimate exclusive interests of individual coastal states in maximizing wealth, power, and national security with the inclusive interests of the community of states in maximizing freedom of the seas.

Throughout historical cycles of free and closed seas, this fundamental accommodation has remained the central focus of man's interest in the oceans. Even today, after thoroughgoing codification efforts in 1958 and 1982, the law of the sea remains in transition. Many fear a return to a period of mare clausum as states struggle to determine what constitutes a reasonable accommodation between the exclusive and inclusive interests of states in the context of a technological and societal reordering which daily increases the capacity of certain states to exploit the resources of more extensive areas of the earth's waters, seabed, and subsoil. After several centuries of development in the international law of the sea, the central question remains, what, in light of today's reality, are the most equitable and yet the most productive uses of ocean space?

Within this context, the international rules pertaining to coastal indentations, which have remained surprisingly constant over time, have also entered a period of uncertain application. Faced with the prospect of an unreasonable expansion of internal waters by coastal states, the world community adopted Article 7 of the *Geneva Convention on the Territorial Sea and the Contiguous Zone,* which struck a historic procedural and evidentiary compromise between the exclusive and inclusive interests of states. In effect, once an indentation has been characterized as a juridical bay within the parameters defined by Article 7, an irrebuttable presumption is raised that the claimant state owns those waters as a matter of right against all states. In turn, an extraordinarily high standard of proof is required for a state to lay claim to indentations which cannot be characterized as a bay under Article 7 criteria.

Well drafted and remarkably unambiguous, Article 7 would seem to have resolved, for some time at least, the issue of unreasonably expansive bay claims. However, the adoption of Article 4 within the same convention has led to an early derogation of the accommodation principle announced in Article 7. Designed as an exception to the normal low-water baseline rule of Article 3, Article 4 allows a coastal state the option of drawing a straight baseline along a deeply indented coastline or one fringed with islands if warranted by the economics of the region. Unfortunately, this option has been seized upon as the normal method of baseline measurement by many states, whether possessed of deeply indented coastlines or not, if such delimitation can conceivably be justified by the presence of offshore islands. As a result, many coastal indentations which would have been subject to analysis under Article 7 have been subsumed within this promiscuous use of Article 4.

Within this context, one may well ask whether the mandatory regime imposed by Article 7 for the designation and delimitation of a juridical bay has continuing relevance; and, if not, why then a book on the juridical bay? The answers to these questions are twofold. First, within states, such as the United States, which have not adopted Article 4 for baseline measurement purposes under any circumstances, Article 7 remains the authoritative basis for bay delimitation. The U.S. Supreme Court has held that Article 7 of the Territorial Sea Convention is the best and most workable definition available for defining inland waters such as bays and is, therefore, to be used exclusively for bay delimitation purposes in order that the United States may establish a single coastline under both international and domestic law. Thus incorporated into domestic law in the United States, and potentially in certain other federal states, Article 7 retains tremendous importance in the resolution of federal-state maritime boundary conflicts. Second, in the international arena, the importance of Article 7 is only in temporary eclipse. States have made extensive and arguably impermissible use of Article 4 to draw straight baselines in situations never envisioned by convention drafters. As these expansive claims are tested by courts and arbitral tribunals in the next several years, it seems inevitable that many extravagant baselines will be disallowed, and the regime mandated for bay delimitation under Article 7 will once again become the authoritative basis for the enclosure of coastal indentations.

I would like to express my profound appreciation to W. Michael Reisman, Myres S. McDougal, and Charles L. Black, Jr., all of Yale Law School, without whose supervision, guidance, and wisdom this work could never have come into being; to J. Patrick Ovington, of Pace University School of Law, without whose studious assistance this work could never have been completed; and to my husband, Lawrence C. Olin, who prepared the original artwork included herein and without whose support this project could never have been sustained. A debt of gratitude is also owed to Joseph Saccomano and William Sunkle, student research assistants at Pace Law School, who helped me to shepherd the book through its various publication processes; to my daughter, Kara Westerman, whose proofreading, indexing, and moral support throughout the project proved invaluable; to Professors William Burke and Ian Brownlie, whose editorial suggestions so enriched my work; and to the libraries and librarians of the Pace, Columbia, and Yale law schools, whose assistance to scholars so enriches our profession.

New Haven   G.S.W.
March 1987

Contents

THE JURIDICAL BAY

I

Introduction

History reveals[1] that from earliest times, the inhabitants of coastal lands settled near small, protected indentations in the coastal littoral. The land surrounding the indentation sheltered it from the full force of nature while man labored to extract benefit from a thus protected arm of the sea. In its provision of an easily obtained and abundant food supply, of an efficient transportation system for persons and goods, and of easily protected coastal boundaries, this sheltered sea area contributed even more than the surrounding land mass or the open sea to man's basic requirements for food, security, services, and goods.

Throughout centuries of fluctuating international norms in regard to the sea as a whole,[2] these indentations lying within the land mass of a single state and variously termed bays, gulfs, locks, firths, estuaries, and the like, were perceived by coastal states as so vitally entwined with life on shore as to be valid components

---

1. *See infra*, Chapter III, *The Historical Treatment of Bays*, for discussion of historic practices in regard to coastal indentations.
2. *See infra*, Chapter II, *Fundamental Purposes, Principles, and Policies*, for discussion of the development of international norms in regard to the sea in general and bays in particular. *See also, infra*, Chapter III.

of their own territory. For the most part, this perception was shared by the world community as part of a broader effort to accommodate the exclusive interests of individual states in preserving their respective shares of natural resources and the security of their borders with the inclusive interests of the community as a whole in resource exploitation and navigation. Within this equation, the exclusive interests of a given state were seen to attach most particularly to waters lying *inter fauces terrae,* literally within the jaws of the land.

This fragile equilibrium, supported by various legal constructs, was easily destabilized in the nineteenth and twentieth centuries as population growth, improved communications and technology, and ever-fluctuating shifts in the power and economic well-being of both older and newly emergent nation states created an intense international competition for world resources. As each new technology has made the vast economic potential of the oceans more realizable, the sea, which since the sixteenth century[3] has been subject to an international regime which has allocated the major share of its riches for the common use of all, has become one of the major battlefields of this competition.

States, depending on their natural allocation of sea wealth, on the particular path which they have chosen for their economic development, and most particularly on their degree of maritime power, have tended either vigorously to defend the principle of maximum freedom of the seas or to advocate the expansion of exclusive territorial sovereignty over adjacent waters.[4] Regardless of a given state's principled posture, however, as international competition for scarce resources has intensified, all states have

3. It is generally recognized that the sixteenth century marks the point at which the principle of *mare clausum* began to be gradually superseded by the principle of *mare liberum.* *See* the Reply of the United Kingdom in the Anglo-Norwegian Fisheries Case (U.K. v. Nor.), 1951 I.C.J. Pleadings 312.

4. It should not be inferred that because a state has persistently supported the principle of *mare liberum,* that state has acted wholly on the basis of beneficent concern for the common good. If the open sea is declared free to all, and narrow limits are set for the territorial sea and other water areas susceptible of exclusive control, such as bays, those maritime states best equipped to exploit the oceans for fishing, commerce, and freedom of movement during hostilities may control the seas even more effectively than might be possible by claiming large ocean areas as private property under the theory of *mare clausum.* *See* S. SWARZTRAUBER, THE THREE MILE LIMIT OF TERRITORIAL SEAS 1–2 (1972).

endeavored through a variety of strategies to increase sovereign possession and control over as much of their coastal waters and resources as possible, given espoused national policies.[5]

Because the closing line[6] of a bay has been generally recognized in international law as a maritime boundary enclosing internal waters, carrying with it the exclusive authority which that term implies, many states have declared sovereignty over bays of increasing size as one strategy for maximizing national control over waters previously considered high seas. Naturally, such expanded claims have often led to conflict, either between a state whose economic well-being depends upon maximum open sea areas and one whose livelihood is primarily derived from the resources of its adjacent waters,[7] or between two or more states who claim the sovereign right to exploit the same area within their adjacent waters.[8]

Since the early part of the nineteenth century, courts of law,

---

5. For example, in 1959 Peter the Great Bay, which is 115 miles across at its mouth, was declared to be inland waters by the U.S.S.R., a nation which in general has favored the extension of territorial sovereignty over wider sea areas. The United States, which has vigorously defended the policy of maximum freedom of the seas, protested this claim. 38 DEP'T ST. BULL. 461(1958). On the other hand, the United States has continuously asserted exclusive authority over the resources lying on and within the continental shelf and has for many years been embroiled in conflict with her own states for the rights to coastal resources. The United States sees no conflict in these positions due to the fact that exclusive authority over the resources of the continental shelf does not in any way compromise freedom of the surface water for navigation, fishing and other inclusive community purposes. *See* Outer Continental Shelf Lands Act, Pub. L. No. 212, 67 Stat. 462 (1953); Submerged Lands Act, Pub. L. No. 31, 67 Stat. 29 (1953); Exec. Proclamation No. 2667 (Truman Proclamation on the Continental Shelf), *reprinted in* 59 Stat. 884 (1945).

6. A closing line is the imaginary line drawn across the mouth of a bay for boundary delimitation purposes. In modern doctrine and practice, and international law now valid, once a coastal indentation has been designated as a bay under either juridical or historical standards, the waters of the bay are indisputably recognized as internal waters of the coastal state. This classification confers upon a given state certain competences, such as the exclusive right to exploit the resources (i.e., fisheries and oil) within the bay, as well as the competence to arbitrarily deny access to foreign vessels, whereas innocent passage must be allowed through the territorial sea. Gihl, *The Baseline of the Territorial Sea*, in SCANDINAVIAN STUDIES IN LAW 137 (1967).

7. *See* Anglo-Norwegian Fisheries Case (U.K. v. Nor.), 1951 I.C.J. 116; Icelandic Fisheries Case (U.K. v. Ice.), 1974 I.C.J. 3.

8. *See* North Atlantic Coast Fisheries Case (Gr. Brit. v. U.S.), Hague Ct. Rep. (Scott) 141 (Perm. Ct. Arb. 1910); North Sea Continental Shelf Case, 1969 I.C.J. 12 (Judgment); Delimitation of the Maritime Boundary in the Gulf of Maine Area (Can. v. U.S.) (I.C.J., Judgment of Oct. 12, 1984).

arbitral tribunals, and international conventions alike have sought to concretize the international rules on bays in order to define the proper basis for conflict resolution in a given controversy. As late as 1910, the Tribunal in the North Atlantic Coast Fisheries Arbitration found it difficult to define a bay conclusively, stating that they were "unable to understand the term 'bays' . . . in other than its geographical sense, by which a bay is to be considered as an indentation of a coast bearing a configuration of a particular character easy to determine specifically, but difficult to describe generally."[9] Not only has it proven difficult and often impossible for decision makers to determine the positive international law of bays applicable to a given controversy, but alternative efforts to transport concepts of equity and comparative justice from the municipal law of states into international decisions has proven unsuccessful on the whole, both in resolving conflict and in offering a reliable guide to future state action.[10]

Nor has the problem of bay definition and delimitation been confined to the international arena. For over thirty years, the U.S. government and her maritime states have been embroiled in a legal struggle for the possession and control of coastal resources.[11] Most of these controversies have addressed, *inter*

9. North Atlantic Coast Fisheries Case (Gr. Brit. v. U.S.), Hague Ct. Rep. (Scott) 141, 187 (Perm. Ct. Arb. 1910).
10. The Court in the Anglo-Norwegian Fisheries Case, 1951 I.C.J. 116, having attempted unsuccessfully to determine the applicable rules of positive or customary international law, settled instead for bringing to light "certain criteria" which might provide courts with an adequate basis for decisions in dealing with coastlines fringed with islands and marked by indentations: 1) that the drawing of baselines must not depart to *any appreciable extent* from the *general direction* of the coast; 2) that *certain sea areas* lying within these lines should be *sufficiently closely linked to the land domain* to be subject to the regime of internal waters; and 3) that *certain economic interests peculiar to a region*, the *reality and importance* of which are clearly evidenced by long usage, *might* be considered in issuing a decree. The italicized phrases indicate major points of imprecision which cause the judgment to fail utterly to provide clear guidelines for state action or future judicial decision. When the judgment was announced in 1951, many in the world community feared that whatever international agreement *had* been reached on bays over two centuries had been vitiated by the Court's reliance on vague municipal notions of equity and surrounding circumstances.
11. *See, e.g.,* United States v. California, 447 U.S. 1 (1980); United States v. Louisiana, 446 U.S. 253 (1980); United States v. Florida, 425 U.S. 791 (1976); United States v. Alaska, 422 U.S. 184 (1975); United States v. Maine, 420 U.S. 515 (1974); United States v. Louisiana, 404 U.S. 388 (1971); United States v. Louisiana (Texas Boundary Case), 394 U.S. 836 (1969); United States v. Louisiana (Louisiana Boundary Case),

alia, the issue of whether a given coastal indentation such as Monterey Bay in California or Ascension Bay in Louisiana, long recognized as part of the internal waters of the named state, might be stripped of its bay designation, thus placing the resources beneath the bay under federal control. The U.S. Supreme Court has at times treated this question as a sub-issue of federalism and at other times as a foreign policy issue deserving of wide judicial deference to the executive.[12] Not surprisingly, this approach has resulted generally in decisions favoring the U.S. government position to the detriment of the maritime states.[13]

In both the international and federal-state arenas, this fundamental question must inevitably arise: by what criteria are we to determine that a given indentation in a state's coastline is of such a character and size as to give it the juridical status of internal waters? In the absence of an international prescriptive power capable of providing a conclusive answer to this and other vital

---

394 U.S. 11 (1969); United States v. Louisiana (Texas Boundary Case), 394 U.S. 1 (1969); United States v. Louisiana, 389 U.S. 155 (1967); United States v. California, 382 U.S. 448 (1966); United States v. Louisiana, 382 U.S. 288 (1965); United States v. California, 381 U.S. 139 (1965); United States v. California, 342 U.S. 891 (1951); United States v. Texas, 339 U.S. 707 (1950); United States v. California, 332 U.S. 19 (1947). *See infra,* Chapter V, *Current State Practice,* for discussion of the resolution of federal-state controversies under U.S. law.

12. *See* Note, *A Jurisprudential Problem in the Submerged Lands Cases: International Law in a Domestic Dispute,* 90 YALE L. J. 1651, 1652 (1981).

13. Two such federal-state controversies have just been decided at the time of this writing. Under the continuing jurisdiction of the Supreme Court in United States v. Maine, the federal government is attempting to define the maritime boundaries of the states along the eastern seaboard in such a way as to favor federal interests. In one such case, Unites States v. Maine et al. (Rhode Island and New York Boundary Case), 469 U.S. 504, 105 S.Ct. 992, 83 L. Ed. 2d 998 (1985), the government makes the claim that the waters of Long Island Sound and Block Island Sound may not legally be classified as a bay and thus that the federal government rather than the states has the right to the resources beneath a portion of those waters. In another case, United States v. Louisiana (Alabama & Mississippi Boundary Case), 470 U.S. 93, 105 S.Ct. 1074, 84 L. Ed. 2d 73 (1985), the government seeks to prove that the waters of Mississippi Sound are not legally classifiable as a bay and therefore may not be treated as internal waters by Mississippi and Alabama. As in the New York and Rhode Island case above, such a determination would wrest control of the resources beneath the bay from the states and place it in federal hands. In both cases, the water areas have long been claimed by the respective states as internal waters; and in both cases the major issue is whether or not the disputed waters can be legally defined as "bays." The Special Master's Report in each case will be discussed *infra* in Chapter V, *Current State Practice.* The final decision by the Supreme Court in each case will also be noted.

maritime questions, a momentum grew after World War II for a formal codification of the international law of the sea. Building upon many years of preparatory work, first by the Hague Codification Conference of 1930 and then by the International Law Commission in the years 1949 to 1958, the first United Nations Conference on the Law of the Sea convened in Geneva, and on April 29, 1958, four major international agreements were signed:

1. The Geneva Convention on the Territorial Sea and the Contiguous Zone.[14]
2. The Geneva Convention on the Continental Shelf.[15]
3. The Geneva Convention on the High Seas.[16]
4. The Geneva Convention on Fishing and Conservation of Living Resources of the High Seas.[17]

The adoption of four international conventions by substantial majorities marked a significant advance in the codification of the law of the sea. Conflicting interests between states were partially reconciled to achieve accord on substantive matters including the right to the use of the high seas, the right of passage through international straits and the territorial sea, and the right to the resources of the continental shelf. In the Territorial Sea Convention agreement was reached on objective criteria for drawing both normal and special baselines,[18] and in Article 7 (Bays), for determining the juridical status of coastal indentations.

These accords, though binding on signatory states only, have been widely accepted as the most authoritative restatement of the

14. Geneva Convention on the Territorial Sea and the Contiguous Zone, Apr. 29, 1958, 15 U.S.T. 1606, T.I.A.S. No. 5639, 516 U.N.T.S. 205 (entered into force for the United States Sept. 10, 1964) [hereinafter cited without cross reference as Territorial Sea Convention].

15. Geneva Convention on the Continental Shelf, Apr. 29, 1958, 15 U.S.T. 471, T.I.A.S. No. 5578, 449 U.N.T.S. 311 (entered into force for the United States June 10, 1964).

16. Geneva Convention on the High Seas, Apr. 29, 1958, 13 U.S.T. 2312, T.I.A.S. No. 5200, 450 U.N.T.S. 82 (entered into force for the United States Sept. 30, 1962).

17. Geneva Convention on Fishing and Conservation of Living Resources of the High Seas, Apr. 29, 1958, 17 U.S.T. 138, T.I.A.S. No. 5969, 559 U.N.T.S. 285 (entered into force for the United States Mar. 20, 1966).

18. The baseline, or legal coastline, of a state is that point from which the territorial sea and all succeeding maritime zones are measured. The baseline also marks the limit of a state's internal waters, separating these waters from the territorial sea. United States v. California, 382 U.S. 448, 450 (1966). *See* Chapter II, *infra* at notes 2–11, for full discussion of maritime boundaries.

international law of the sea[19] and have had a major impact on both international and domestic controversies. But like most Conventions, the rules prescribed are in the nature of general parameters which in many cases are not susceptible of application to the complex coastal configurations likely to be encountered, without further clarification and interpretation.[20]

Vattel's famous first principle, that "it is not permissible to interpret what has no need of interpretation,"[21] has been rejected

19. On Dec. 17, 1970, the General Assembly of the United Nations adopted resolution 2750 C (XXV) wherein it decided "to convene, in 1973, a Conference on the Law of the Sea which would deal with the establishment of an equitable international regime—including an international machinery—for the area and the resources of the sea-bed and ocean floor, and the subsoil thereof, beyond the limits of national jurisdiction . . . ." Introduction to Draft Final Act of the Third United Nations Conference on the Law of the Sea, U.N. Doc. A/CONF. 62/121, at 2 (1982). The Conference was mandated to produce a precise definition of that area, and because it was felt that the problems of ocean space were closely interrelated and needed to be considered as a whole, the Conference was also directed to consider a broad range of related issues which had been partially resolved in the 1958 Conventions, namely the regimes of the high seas, the continental shelf, the territorial sea and contiguous zone, fishing and conservation of the living resources of the high seas, the preservation of the marine environment, and scientific reseach. *Id.* In all, eleven sessions of the Conference were held between December, 1973, and September, 1982. *Id.,* at 4–5. After a decade of intense negotiation and controversy, the United Nations Convention on the Law of the Sea (U.N. Doc. A/CONF. 62/122) [hereinafter cited without cross reference as UNCLOS] was adopted by the Conference Oct. 7, 1982, and was concluded Dec. 10, 1982, at Montego Bay, Jamaica. Although the 1982 Convention contains some revision of 1958 Convention Articles, as well as new law on many issues, numerous 1958 Articles remain virtually unchanged. Article 7 (Bays) of the Territorial Sea Convention has become Article 10 of the United Nations Convention on the Law of the Sea (See U.N. Doc. A/CONF. 62/122, at 5); but except for the addition of "nautical" to clarify any reference to "miles," the language of the two Articles is identical. *See infra,* Chapter IV, note 10. Because the 1982 Convention has only just been concluded at this writing and because there is substantial doubt as to who the eventual signatories will be (the United States being the most glaring absentee at present), the 1958 Conventions remain in force. Therefore, reference will be made throughout this study to Article 7 of the Territorial Sea Convention as the most authoritative statement of positive international law on the subject of bays. Where significant differences exist between other relevant 1958 Convention sections and UNCLOS, these differences will be noted. The caveat must be repeated, however, that although UNCLOS certainly reveals trends in the law, the treaty has not yet entered into force and most of the provisions of the 1958 Conventions remain valid.

20. A. Shalowitz, Shore and Sea Boundaries, xxiii, 209 (1962).

21. E. Vattel, The Law of Nations 199 (Fenwick trans. 1758 ed. 1916). As to his phrase "no need of interpretation," Vattel clarified: "When a deed is worded in clear and precise terms, when its meaning is evident and leads to no absurdity, there is no ground for refusing to accept the meaning which the deed naturally presents." *Id.*

by most modern scholars and decision makers[22] in favor of the
view that some interpretation is always necessary in the application and policing of international agreements.[23] No sequence of
words can be arranged to designate in concrete detail all mean-
ings understood by the parties to an agreement, although these
can be approximated by reasonably careful drafting, as is more
probable in the case of international agreements negotiated
intensely over a span of years. However, even objective criteria,
from the ruthlessly simple to the unintelligibly complex, can only
serve as guidelines to prevent excessively wide or narrow interpretations of the intent of the drafters by courts, tribunals, or
other decision makers.[24] A valid examination of this intent, therefore, must involve the task of interpretation, including a thorough analysis of the text and context of an agreement, in order
to ascertain as fully as possible the genuine shared expectations
of the parties and the compatibility of those expectations with

22. Many scholars have criticized Vattel's principle as a tautology in that the determination of what does or does not require interpretation is in itself an act of interpretation. Thus, Dean Wigmore criticized Vattel: "Instead of the fallacious notion that
'there should be interpretation only when it is needed,' the fact is that there must
always be interpretation." 9 J. WIGMORE, A TREATISE ON THE ANGLO-AMERICAN SYSTEM
OF EVIDENCE IN TRIALS AT COMMON LAW §2470 at 227 (3d ed. 1940) (quoting from
Hartford Iron Mining Co. v. Cambria Mining Co., 80 Mich. 491, 499, 45 N.W. 351,
353 (1890)). In like manner, Sir Hersch Lauterpacht noted the "decisive drawback"
to the Vattel principle: "it often assumes as a fact what has still to be proved . . . it
proceeds not from the starting point of the inquiry but from what is normally the
result of it." H. LAUTERPACHT, THE DEVELOPMENT OF INTERNATIONAL LAW BY THE INTER-
NATIONAL COURT 52 (1958). Oppenheim commented that Vattel's maxim could be
regarded as a preliminary rule but one which "often begs the question." L. OPPEN-
HEIM, INTERNATIONAL LAW 858 n.1 (H. Lauterpacht, 7th ed. 1948). And Fitzmaurice
observed: "[T]he conclusion that the meaning of a text is clear . . . involves itself a
process of interpretation, the result of which might have been different if the records
had in fact been consulted." Fitzmaurice, *The Law and Procedure of the International
Court of Justice: Treaty Interpretation and Certain Other Treaty Points,* 28 BRIT. Y. B. INT'L
L. 1, 5 (1951). McDougal, Lasswell and Miller conclude that the most critical flaw in
Vattel's first principle is that it may encourage a foreshortened view of the interpret-
er's task and lead to the belief that some decision-making situations are not worthy
of full contextual analysis. M. MCDOUGAL, H. LASSWELL & J. MILLER, THE INTERPRE-
TATION OF AGREEMENTS AND WORLD PUBLIC ORDER 39 (1967).
23. M. MCDOUGAL, H. LASSWELL & J. MILLER, *supra* note 22, at 82.
24. P. BEAZLEY, MARITIME LIMITS AND BASELINES §2.1 (The Hydrographic Society, Special
Publication No. 2, n.d.).

broader community policies and applicable norms of international law.[25]

It has been said that the foresight of the parties to an agreement is seldom adequate to anticipate, and provide in minute

---

25. This interpretive approach, widely espoused by decision makers and scholars in this century, has been codified in the Vienna Convention on the Law of Treaties, U.N. Doc. A/CONF. 39/27 (1969), *reprinted in* 8 I.L.M. 679 (1969), *and in* B. WESTON, R. FALK, & A. D'AMATO, BASIC DOCUMENTS IN INTERNATIONAL LAW AND WORLD ORDER 59 (1980). As of June, 1983, this Convention, which entered into force Jan. 27, 1980, has been ratified by forty-three nations. Even in states such as the United States, which have signed but not yet ratified the treaty, most of its terms arguably have the force of customary law. The relevant sections are set out in full below:

Part III: OBSERVATION, APPLICATION AND INTERPRETATION OF TREATIES

Section 3. Interpretation of Treaties

Article 31. General Rule of Interpretation
(1) A treaty shall be interpreted in good faith in accordance with the ordinary meaning to be given the *terms* of the treaty in their *context* and in the light of its object and purpose.
(2) The *context* for the purpose of the interpretation of a treaty shall comprise, in addition to the text, including its preamble and annexes:
   (a) any *agreement* relating to the treaty which was made between all the parties in connexion with the conclusion of the treaty;
   (b) any *instrument* which was made by one or more parties in connexion with the conclusion of the treaty and accepted by the other parties as an instrument related to the treaty.
(3) There *shall* be taken into account, together with the context:
   (a) any *subsequent agreement* between the parties regarding the interpretation of the treaty or the application of its provisions;
   (b) any *subsequent practice* in the application of the treaty which establishes the agreement of the parties regarding its application;
   (c) any *relevant rules of international law* applicable in the relations between the parties.
(4) A special meaning shall be given to a term if it is established that the parties so intended.

Article 32. Supplementary Means of Interpretation
Recourse may be had to supplementary means of interpretation, including the *preparatory work* of the treaty and the *circumstances* of its conclusion, in order to *confirm* the meaning resulting from the application of article 31, or to determine the meaning when the interpretation according to article 31:
   (a) leaves the meaning ambiguous or obscure; *or*
   (b) leads to a result which is manifestly absurd or unreasonable.

detail for, the evolving future.[26] Thus it is that although Article 7 of the 1958 Territorial Sea Convention offers a more precise and objective method for the determination of a juridical bay, and has in fact been accepted by judicial bodies including the United States Supreme Court as the authoritative basis for such determinations,[27] the actual language of Article 7 has not ended but merely narrowed the scope of controversy. Many questions remain unanswered, and a more thorough interpretation of Article 7 is required in order to prevent controversies over sea

---

Part V: INVALIDITY, TERMINATION AND SUSPENSION OF THE OPERATION OF TREATIES

Section 2. Invalidity of Treaties

Article 53. Treaties Conflicting with a Peremptory Norm of General International Law (Jus Cogens)

A treaty is void if, at the time of its conclusion, it conflicts with a *peremptory norm* of general international law. For the purposes of the present Convention a peremptory norm . . . is a norm accepted and recognized by the international community of States as a whole as a *norm from which no derogation is permitted* and which can be modified only by a subsequent norm of general international law having the same character.

Section 3. Termination and Suspension of Operation of Treaties

Article 64. Emergence of a New Peremptory Norm of General International Law (Jus Cogens)

If a new *peremptory norm* of general international law emerges, any existing treaty which is in conflict with that norm becomes void and terminates.

B. Weston, R. Falk & A. D'Amato, *supra* at 65–73 (emphasis added).

For a thoughtful and detailed explication of substantive and procedural principles of interpretation, *see also* M. McDougal, H. Lasswell & J. Miller, *supra* note 22, at 35–77.

26. M. McDougal, H. Lasswell & J. Miller, *supra* note 22, at 39.

27. *See* United States v. California, 381 U.S. 139, 161–67 (1965); United States v. Louisiana, 394 U.S. 11, 17–35 (1969). *See also* Re Dominion Coal Co. Ltd. v. County of Cape Breton, 40 D.L.R. 2d 593 (1963), wherein the Supreme Court of Nova Scotia refers to Article 7 as authority to decide whether the waters of Spanish Bay are to be classified as internal or territorial. *See also* European Fisheries Convention, Art. 6; Post Office v. Estuary Radio, Ltd., 2 Q.B. 740, 3 All E. R. 663 (1967).

28. One need only refer to note 11, *supra,* to observe that although only three federal-state maritime boundary controversies were decided in the United States before the Territorial Sea Convention was adopted, twelve have been adjudicated since 1958 with no end in sight.

29. The recent and potentially violent confrontations between American and Libyan warplanes over the Gulf of Sidra, the shots fired between British and Icelandic fishing fleets in disputed Icelandic waters, and the injuries resulting from French firings on Spanish vessels fishing in European Community waters are timely reminders that the problems of maritime delimitation are not abstract and, left unresolved, may pose a significant threat to world order.

boundaries from spawning endless litigation[28] or actual armed conflict.[29]

In the years since its adoption in 1958, Article 7 has failed to receive the thorough analysis necessary to provide a reliable basis for conflict resolution in cases involving complex coastal configurations. The purpose of this study of the juridical bay, therefore, will be to interpret, in the light of general community principles and policies of the law of the sea and the historical development of the international law of bays, the text and context of Article 7 of the Territorial Sea Convention. With the assistance of the legislative history of the convention, the previous work of legal scholars, and evidence suggested by current state practice, reasoned solutions will be offered to some of the interpretative problems which continue to serve as sources of national and international conflict.

II

Fundamental Purposes, Principles, and Policies Underlying the International Law of Bays

When the modern concept of a marginal belt of territorial waters around the shore of a coastal state developed in the eighteenth and nineteenth centuries, the distances claimed were usually modest, the baseline for measuring the marginal waters was generally accepted to be the shoreline, and those affected by such delimitation were for the most part fishermen, smugglers, and the warships of belligerent nations.[1] The boundary of the territorial sea was close enough to the shore for a mariner to determine his position easily, and no great precision nor expertise was or could be required of either the delimitation method or the delimitator.

In the twentieth century, however, as increasing requirements for protein, oil, and other ocean resources led to expansive national claims to areas of the sea and seabed previously held to be *res communes,* a need emerged, where none had previously existed, to determine boundaries with precision and to develop a body of rules capable of making sophisticated differentiations between various zones of national and international jurisdiction.

1. P. BEAZLEY, *supra,* Chapter I, note 24, §1.2.

Both the 1958 Geneva Conventions[2] and the recently completed United Nations Convention on the Law of the Sea (UNCLOS)[3] codify community recognition of a series of sea zones which extend landward and seaward of a state's "baseline."[4] The delimitation of this baseline is fundamental to the determination of all other sea boundaries, for it is this line which marks the seaward limit of a state's internal waters as well as the landward limit of the territorial sea. It is from this baseline that every sea zone extending from the coast of a given state is measured.

Within each zone, different coastal competences are honored. All waters landward of the baseline are *internal* or *inland waters*,[5] over which a coastal state may exercise exclusive control, identical to that exercised over its land territory.[6] This sovereign authority includes the right to exploit the resources of the surface waters, the seabed, and the subsoil, as well as the right to arbitrarily deny access to foreign vessels. Directly seaward from the baseline lies the *territorial sea*,[7] over which the coastal state may exercise some

2. *See supra*, Chapter I, notes 14–17 and accompanying text.
3. *See supra*, Chapter I, note 19.
4. The Territorial Sea Convention, Article 3, provides that "the normal baseline for measuring the breadth of the territorial sea is the low-water line along the coast . . . " This rule remains unchanged in UNCLOS, Article 5, at 3. These provisions reflect community agreement that a baseline should follow the sinuosities of the coastline, except where there are islands, rocks, bays, rivers and other special features to the coast, where special rules apply. The closing line of a bay is recognized as part of this system of baseline delimitation.
5. The term "internal waters" embraces those waters which actually lie within the land mass of the coastal state, such as lakes, rivers, harbors, certain bays and estuaries, and waters enclosed by island fringes through which straight baselines have been drawn. Within these areas the domestic authority of the coastal state is supreme, except in the case of sea areas previously classified as high seas which are made internal by the use of the straight baseline system of Article 4 of the Territorial Sea Convention, where a right of innocent passage still exists. P. BEAZLEY, *supra*, Chapter I, note 24, §3.2. *See also* S. SWARZTRAUBER, *supra*, Chapter I, note 4, §4.6.
6. Pearcy, *Geographical Aspects of the Law of the Sea*, 49 A. AM. GEOGRAPHERS 1, 14 (1959).
7. Historically, states have claimed sovereignty over territorial waters of varying breadths. *See Synopsis Table*, drawn up by the U.N. Secretariat for the 1958 Conference, U.N. Doc. A/CONF. 13/c.1/L.n/Rev.1 (as amended by Corr. 1 and 2), 3 Apr. 1958. Agreement could not be reached in the Territorial Sea Convention on a single width for territorial waters. Although UNCLOS now specifies a maximum twelve-mile territorial sea (*See* UNCLOS, Article 3, at 3), some states, including the United States, adhere to a three-mile limit at this writing. *See also* S. SWARZTRAUBER, *supra*, Chapter I, note 4, for an excellent discussion of the historical development of the three-mile limit for the territorial sea in international law.

of the attributes of sovereignty, such as the preservation of fish-ery resources for its own nationals, but through which must be allowed the innocent passage of foreign vessels.[8] Overlapping with the territorial sea and extending twelve miles seaward from the baseline lies the *contiguous zone,* wherein the coastal state enjoys extraterritorial jurisdiction to enforce its own customs, tax, sanitary, and pollution laws, but no sovereign power to deny access to foreign vessels outside the territorial limit. As one pro-ceeds further seaward through the *continental shelf,* and today, the newly conceived *exclusive economic zone,*[9] the state may lay claim to various ocean resources but must increasingly compromise its interests with those of other states. The last zone, the *high seas,* lies beyond the reach of any exclusive regime[10] and is open to all. Of critical importance to this system of competences is the loca-tion of the baseline, for whatever the width of the territorial sea claimed by the littoral state, any movement of the baseline land-

8. Although the coastal state must ordinarily allow innocent marine transit through the territorial sea, flight over these waters may be lawfully prohibited and access for for-eign vessels can be regulated and absolutely prohibited in certain circumstances. *See* M. McDougal & W. Burke, Public Order of the Oceans 317 (1962).

9. *See* UNCLOS, Part V: Exclusive Economic Zone. This section creates an exclusive economic zone of 200 nautical miles from the baseline from which the territorial sea is measured. *Id.,* art. 57, at 23. Within this zone, the coastal state has jurisdiction for the purpose of "exploring and exploiting, conserving and managing the natural resources, whether living or non-living, of the waters superjacent to the sea-bed and of the sea-bed and its subsoil, and with regard to other activities for the economic exploitation and exploration of the zone, such as the production of energy from the water, currents and winds." *Id.,* art. 56(1)(a), at 22. Other states retain the freedoms of navigation, overflight, the laying of submarine cables and pipelines, and other internationally lawful uses of the sea related to these freedoms. *Id.,* art. 58(1), at 23. In essence, this new competence zone grants to a coastal state exploitation rights in an area roughly corresponding to the continental shelf, which comprises "the sea-bed and subsoil of the submarine areas that extend beyond its territorial sea throughout the natural prolongation of its land territory to the outer edge of the continental margin, or to a distance of 200 nautical miles from the baselines. . . . " *Id.,* art. 76(1), at 33; *see* Convention on the Continental Shelf, *supra,* Chapter I, note 15, Article 1. Most states have now claimed an EEZ of 200 miles. In the United States, such a zone was proclaimed by Presidential decree, Mar. 10, 1983.

10. Except for occasional exclusive competence claimed for limited purposes. *See* M. McDougal & W. Burke, *supra* note 8, at 565–729. It should be noted that the fun-damental community policy favoring freedom of the high seas has been considerably diluted by the expansion of national jurisdiction over ocean space under UNCLOS. (*See supra,* Chapter I, note 19 and *supra* note 9; *infra* notes 18, 28, 29, and Chapter III, note 45. The new "freedom of the seas" is very different from the traditional concept in terms of the utility of its exercise.

ward or seaward affects the limits of that state's exclusive authority.[11]

The most significant effect of a *seaward* extension of this crucial boundary line is to increase the area of ocean space over which the littoral state may exercise the most comprehensive control and thereby to decrease the total sea area over which all states share inclusive authority and use.[12] Because what is ultimately at stake is the distribution of authority over the use of the oceans, the issue of baseline delimitation poses a classic conflict between the legitimate interests of an individual state in obtaining as large a share of ocean space as is deemed necessary to pursue wealth, power, and national security, and the wider interests of the community of states in preserving the maximum sea area possible for navigation, communication, fishing, and other inclusive pursuits. This conflict of interest must inevitably involve the espousal of two firmly established principles of international law: freedom of the seas and territorial sovereignty.

The *mare liberum* or free seas principle entered the law of nations as a reaction against broad claims to territorial sovereignty over vast sea areas put forward by major sea powers in the sixteenth and seventeenth centuries.[13] It is familiar history[14] that common interests eventually triumphed over monopoly; and that until the present, most states have, to a greater or lesser degree, shared the conviction that the greatest production of community values can be achieved by permitting and protecting the widest possible sharing of ocean space. Professor McDougal has expressed the basis for this conviction thusly:

11. *See* Pearcy, *supra* note 6, at 5; 1 A. SHALOWITZ, *supra*, Chapter I, note 20, at 28. *See also* Territorial Sea Convention, art. 6.

12. The effect on inclusive community interests can be even more dramatic when extensive internal waters are created by extending the baseline than when the width of the territorial sea is increased. This is due to the fact that when a state enlarges its internal waters, it extends its comprehensive authority seaward not only with respect to maintaining exclusive fisheries but also to retaining complete discretion to deny access to foreign vessels engaged in navigation, resource exploitation, or scientific research. M. MCDOUGAL & W. BURKE, *supra* note 8, at 333.

13. *See* McDougal & Schlei, *The Hydrogen Bomb Tests in Perspective: Lawful Measures for Security,* 64 YALE L. J. 648, 661 (1955).

14. *See infra,* Chapter III, for full discussion of the historical development of principles underlying the law of the sea.

The sea—in much higher degree than the land masses—is an easily sharable resource. It is tremendously vast. . . . Most of its resources . . . are renewable, flow resources. . . . [W]here one ship has just been, another, with proper rules of accommodation, can soon come. There are tremendous numbers of the peoples in the world . . . capable of exploiting this resource, peoples who have the skills and other bases of power to make an effective contribution. There is a great range of objectives that can be satisfied from the exploitation of the seas. . . . The strategy in the use of this resource may be co-operative, non-competitive: what one gets, others may also get. For three centuries the important outcome of this co-operative enjoyment of the oceans has been a tremendous production of goods and services for distribution to the whole of mankind.[15]

Despite intense international competition for resources and increasing demand for national ownership of ever larger areas of the oceans, the freedom of the seas principle has not disappeared from international prescription. Both the 1958 Geneva Convention on the High Seas[16] and UNCLOS[17] preserve the freedom of

15. M.McDougal, *International Law and the Law of the Sea,* in The Law of the Sea: Off-shore Boundaries and Zones 15 (1967).
16. Article 2 of the 1958 Geneva Convention on the High Seas, *see supra,* Chapter I, note 16, provides:
   The high seas being open to all nations, no State may validly purport to subject any part of them to its sovereignty. Freedom of the high seas is exercised under the conditions laid down by these articles and by the other rules of international law. It comprises, *inter alia,* both for coastal and non-coastal states:
      (1) Freedom of navigation;
      (2) Freedom of fishing;
      (3) Freedom to lay submarine cables and pipelines;
      (4) Freedom to fly over the high seas.
   These freedoms, and others which are recognized by the general principles of international law, shall be exercised by all States with reasonable regard to the interests of other States in their exercise of the freedom of the high seas.
17. Article 87 of UNCLOS provides:
      1. The high seas are open to all States, whether coastal or land-locked. Freedom of the high seas is exercised under the conditions laid down by this Convention and by other rules of international law. It comprises, *inter alia,* both for coastal and land-locked States:
         (a) freedom of navigation;
         (b) freedom of overflight;
         (c) freedom to lay submarine cables and pipelines,subject to Part VI;
         (d) freedom to construct artificial islands and other installations permitted under international law, subject to Part VI;
         (e) freedom of fishing, subject to the conditions laid down in section 2;
         (f) freedom of scientific research, subject to Parts VI and XIII.

all states in the use of the high seas for navigation, fishing, over-flight, the laying of submarine cables and pipelines, and specifi-cally in UNCLOS, for scientific research and the construction of artificial islands.

Yet, these freedoms can in no sense be termed absolute. Although the world community has a vital, continuing interest in preserving the greatest practicable freedom of navigation, fish-ing, and scientific research, other compelling inclusive interests in pollution control and fishery conservation must occasionally take precedence if ocean resources are to be truly preserved to the common good of all.[18] Nor can it be inferred that the wide-spread acceptance of the free seas principle absolutely precludes all claims to exclusive authority and use. Individual states are rou-tinely granted permission for special uses of ocean space which only temporarily affect community access.[19] More controversy is a certainty, however, when a state lays claim to permanent and exclusive use of expanded water areas under the principle of ter-ritorial sovereignty.

---

2. These freedoms shall be exercised by all States with due regard for the interests of other States in their exercise of the freedom of the high seas, and also with due regard for the rights under the Convention with respect to activities in the Area.

Although Article 89 of UNCLOS reaffirms the 1958 proscription that "No State may validly purport to subject any part of the high seas to its sovereignty," it must be noted that the most valuable ocean resources are to be found in ocean areas which are no longer considered high seas and which are now subject to exclusive coastal state control. *See supra,* Note 9; *infra* notes 28, 29, Chapter III, note 45 and Chapter V, notes 10, 11, 12.

18. Whereas the basic freedoms of the high seas were stated in somewhat absolute terms subject only to general conditions in 1958 (*see supra,* note 16), the language of the new UNCLOS treaty (*see supra,* note 17) makes clear that the freedom of fishing granted under the conservation and management of the living resources of the high seas and the freedom of scientific research, the freedom to lay submarine cables and pipelines, and the freedom to construct artificial islands and other permitted instal-lations are granted subject to strict regard for the exclusive interests of other states and the inclusive interests of the community at large.

19. The world community usually recognizes as consistent with international law and sub-stantial freedom of access a claim to set aside areas of the high seas for a given time in order to conduct naval maneuvers, space-flight splashdowns and other temporary, non-destructive operations. There has been widespread opposition, however, to potentially harmful uses such as nuclear weapons testing. *See, e.g.,* Nuclear Tests Case (Austl. v. Fr.) 1973 I.C.J. 98 (Interim Protection Order of June 22); and again, 1974 I.C.J. 252, 257 (Judgment of Dec. 20); Treaty Banning Nuclear Weapon Tests in the Atmosphere, in Outer Space and Underwater. 14 U.S.T. 1313, T.I.A.S. No. 5433, 480 U.N.T.S. 43 (1963); McDougal & Schlei, *supra,* note 13, at 690–710.

Under both positive and customary international law now valid, the sovereignty of a given state extends to its land territory and its internal waters, to the belt of territorial sea adjacent to its coast, including the bed and subsoil thereof, and to the superjacent air space.[20] Within this territory, each state may exercise the rights inherent in the concept of sovereignty, which include, *inter alia,* the right to defend its territorial integrity and political independence, to provide for its preservation and prosperity, to choose and develop its political, social, economic, cultural, and legal systems as it sees fit, to legislate concerning its interests, to administer its services, to enforce its laws and regulations, and to determine the jurisdiction and competence of its courts.[21]

When a given state, citing its sovereign right to provide for the security, prosperity, and sustenance of its inhabitants, asserts a claim to extend its territory to include waters previously considered *res communes,* those in the community of states who fear encroachment on their right to freely utilize these waters for their own pursuits must forcefully object.[22] Faced with a conflict

20. *See* Territorial Sea Convention, Articles 1 and 2. *See also* UNCLOS, Article 2, which extends territorial jurisdiction in the case of an archipelagic state to its archipelagic waters.

21. Many formulations and codifications of the sovereign rights of states exist. *See, e.g.,* Ch. IV of Charter of the Organization of American States, Apr. 30, 1948, 2 U.S.T. 2394, T.I.A.S. No. 2361, 119 U.N.T.S. 3, Protocol of Amendment, Feb. 27, 1967, 21 U.S.T. 607, T.I.A.S. No. 6847, *reprinted in* B. WESTON, R. FALK & A. D'AMATO, *supra,* Chapter I, note 25, at 32; Final Act of the Conference on Security and Co-operation in Europe (the "Helsinki Accords"), Aug. 1, 1975, art. I, VIII, *reprinted in* 14 I.L.M. 1292 (1975), *and in* B. WESTON, R. FALK & A. D'AMATO, *supra,* Chapter I, note 25, at 81; Declaration Concerning Friendly Relations and Co-operation, Preamble, Part 1, G.A. Res. 2625 (XXV), 25 U.N. GAOR, Supp. (No. 28) at 121, U.N. Doc. A/8028 (1971), *reprinted in* 9 I.L.M. 1292 (1970), *and in* B. WESTON, R. FALK & A. D'AMATO, *supra,* Chapter I, note 25, at 75.

22. An extraordinarily large claim such as the Soviet attempt to enclose Peter the Great Bay with a closing line of over one hundred miles has considerable impact on the enterprises of neighboring states, in particular the Japanese fishing industry. Similar controversies commonly erupt between states which are heavily dependent upon their adjacent waters for sustenance and livelihood, such as Iceland, Sweden, Norway, Greenland, Mexico, Chile, and Peru, and states with long-range fishing fleets such as the United Kingdom, the Soviet Union, Japan, and the United States. *See supra,* Chapter I, notes 4 & 6–7. *See also Note of Protest, United States to Mexico,* Jan. 14, 1948, in 1948 U.S. NAV. WAR COL. 481–82; *Note Between Sweden and the Soviet Union,* July 18, Aug. 21, 1951, in *Id.,* at 496–500. *See also* von Cleve, *The Economic and Scientific Basis of the Principle of Abstention,* 1 United Nations Conference on the Law of the Sea, Geneva, 1958: *Official Records,* U.N. Doc. A/CONF. 13/3, at 55–59.

between two fundamental principles of international law, as well as vital yet mutually exclusive state interests, community policy has taken the form of a strong presumption in favor of inclusive authority and use of the oceans, balanced with the recognition that a certain degree of exclusivity is essential if each state is to thrive within the community of states and the companion realization that community interests are as well served by a policy which encourages the existence of independent nation-states, secure in their own borders and economically viable, as by maximum open seas.

This community policy has been effectuated both by ad hoc decision makers, balancing the interests of the parties in a live controversy,[23] and by international agreement makers, attempting to narrow the scope of controversy by defining and delimiting the areas of ocean space within which the inclusive and exclusive interests of states may be given appropriate weight. In both lawmaking arenas, there has been consistent recognition that it is the land-sea relationship of the waters in question that must constitute the proper basis for a decision that presumptively preeminent community interests in navigation and fishing may be infringed and the waters incorporated within a state's domain.[24]

For example, it is presumed that all states have an overriding interest in maintaining the widest possible freedom of navigation. However, because it is obvious on balance that the economic and defense[25] interests of a coastal state are much stronger in

23. *See* Anglo-Norwegian Fisheries Case (U.K. v. Nor.), 1951 I.C.J. 116; Icelandic Fisheries Case, 1974 I.C.J. 3 (Judgment of July 25); North Atlantic Coast Fisheries Case (Gr. Brit. v. U.S.), Hague Ct. Rep. (Scott) 141 (Perm. Ct. Arb. 1910); Re Dominion Coal Co. Ltd. v. County of Cape Breton, 40 D.L.R. 2d 593 (1963); Delimitation of the Maritime Boundary in the Gulf of Maine Area (Can. v. U.S.) (I.C.J., Judgment of Oct. 12, 1984).

24. In the Anglo-Norwegian Fisheries case, 1951 I.C.J. 116, 133, the Court referred to the close connection between sea areas and the land domain as being "at the basis of the *rules* relating to bays." Waldock, *The Anglo-Norwegian Fisheries Case,* 28 BRIT. Y.B. INT'L L. 112, 141 (1951). *See also,* R. HODGSON & L. ALEXANDER, TOWARDS AN OBJEC-TIVE ANALYSIS OF SPECIAL CIRCUMSTANCES 2 (1972).

25. Although one of the earliest rationales for the closing of internal waters and the extension of the seaward boundary of the territorial sea was the need to better defend the land territory from attack, advances in technology and weaponry since World War II have made all distances on the ocean somewhat irrelevant, at least as far as those states possessing long-range weapons capability are concerned. For more prosaic threats such as smuggling, arms running, illegal immigration, pollution, and piracy, a coastal state is adequately protected by the combination of competences granted in

waters which penetrate into the land mass than in waters which extend seaward from the coast and because the interest of foreign vessels is much weaker in these landlocked waters, which by and large do not encompass major navigation routes,[26] it has been widely accepted that a littoral state may exercise exclusive authority over its internal waters.[27] But because state interests diminish as the land-sea relationship diminishes and communal interests become more prominent, a state must allow innocent passage through the territorial sea and cannot in general restrict passage of any kind on the high seas.

A similar balancing of interests has been performed in regard to the allocation of water resources. There is general and intense community interest in maintaining maximum freedom of the seas for fishing; and because the richest fishing grounds are most frequently located within a short distance of the coast,[28] the enclosure of wide areas of coastal waters for the exclusive use of coastal inhabitants causes a much more significant deprivation to foreign fishermen, particularly those who have historically enjoyed co-use of the waters, than one might think, considering the seeming vastness of the oceans. Nonetheless, even given the presumption in favor of inclusive use, the maritime state's interest in and, in many areas, dependence upon coastal waters to pro-

---

internal, territorial, and contiguous waters. M. McDougal & W. Burke, *supra*, note 8, at 335. Nonetheless, military and neutrality considerations have not been entirely bypassed, and there is yet some value in permitting the coastal state to arbitrarily refuse access to either hostile or professedly friendly foreign "observers."

26. This latter factor is often adduced as the rationale for restricting the application of Article 7 of the Territorial Sea Convention to bays lying within the territory of a single state. *See* Article 7(1). When a baseline encloses an area so related to the surrounding land mass that vessels would have to divert their course to enter, the inclusive interest in navigation is relatively slight and coastal interests are more significant. If, however, two or more states share the coastline of an indentation, and major sea lanes therefore extend between those two countries as well as to the outside world, inclusive interests in navigation are much stronger, and the likelihood of the bay having been exclusively incorporated into the lives and processes of a given state is relatively slight. *See* M. McDougal & W. Burke, *supra* note 8, at 333–34; Gihl, *supra*, Chapter I, note 6, at 138.

27. *See* Territorial Sea Convention, arts. 1, 4, 7; UNCLOS, arts. 8, 9, 10.

28. Alexander has cited the concern, in reference to all resources, that not only does the areal extent of national claims continue to diminish the area of free seas left to community use, but more importantly, the marginal seas to which these claims are advanced are often of greater economic or strategic value than are areas of commensurate size in mid-ocean. Alexander, *Offshore Claims of the World*, in The Law of the Sea 76 (1967).

vide a livelihood for its inhabitants as well as an easily accessible, renewable, and protein-rich food source at relatively low labor and capital cost has been seen as justifying the exclusive access of the coastal state to the fish resources in both its internal and territorial surface waters.[29] In regard to the living and nonliving resources of the seabed and subsoil, the community at large has concluded that the interests of the coastal state must in general outweigh inclusive community interests in these resources in all but the high seas.[30]

The community policy in regard to internal waters has been based upon the recognition that the exclusive interests of states attach most fundamentally to waters which penetrate into the land mass. A coastal state has a pronounced interest in assuring that water areas which are so intimately and strategically related to its land territory are not used to the disservice of the local population. Enclosure of these waters, therefore, is not perceived as an unreasonable infringement on the free use of the seas as long as the penetration of water area into the littoral is significant enough to evoke the reasonable concern of the coastal state and to suggest a balancing in favor of exclusive use.

This concern is clearly warranted in the case of rivers, lakes, and inland seas, and opposition rarely accompanies the enclosure of these wholly internal waters.[31] In the case of bays, however, which lie both within the land and yet exposed to the open sea, and which may vary widely in both size and configuration, the

29. UNCLOS represents a tremendous expansion of territorial rights over fish resources. With the creation of the Exclusive Economic Zone, (*see supra* note 9) exclusive state control is extended to all resources in a 200-mile-wide belt of ocean space measured from the baseline of the territorial sea. It is probably safe to say that this extension of resource jurisdiction will become customary international law, even if the treaty itself does not receive the formal approval of the major maritime states. *See infra*, Chapter V, *Current State Practice.*

30. *See* Convention on the Continental Shelf, *supra*, Chapter I, note 15, arts. 1, 2. *See also* UNCLOS, pt. XI, at 51–85, for a description of the controversial regime designed to guarantee the participation of all states in the exploitation of the resources of the high seas.

31. There are exceptions of course, as where a great river such as the Mississippi empties into the sea through a wide delta area which in itself may encompass many smaller indentations, channels, and streams, or numerous land formations, such as islands, which may form a portico or extend seaward many miles, leading to extensive national claims and wide community opposition. *See, e.g.*, The Anna, 165 Eng. Rep. 809, 815 (1805).

potential impact of such an enclosure on community interests is very great, and foreign opposition, therefore, much more likely. Community policy in regard to bays has, therefore, been more difficult to concretize.

In general principle, when "nature has lodged a bay in the very bosom of a maritime state,"[32] she has encouraged that state to claim the bay as its own and other states to respect that claim. Such a claim has two effects: first, to appropriate waters and internalize them; and second, to reinforce the notion that it is appropriate to do so. In that sense, the claim is constitutive. In practice, individual states have enjoyed wide latitude in determining which coastal indentations may be regarded as a part of their national domain. This latitude has been granted partly because a bay, even of relatively wide expanse, may be effectively occupied, utilized, and controlled by the territorial sovereign[33] and partly because these indentations do not ordinarily serve as channels of transportation and communication which the maritime state seeks to keep open but merely as means of access to points within the bay.[34] The intimate geographical relationship of the water to the surrounding land has generally been seen as the decisive factor in justifying an assertion of territorial sovereignty and discouraging foreign opposition.

As international economic competition has intensified and technological advancement has made the exploitation of adjacent waters more profitable, however, states have at times laid claim to indentations which are perceived by other states as either too slight an indentation to be geographically interrelated with life on

---

32. 1 C. HYDE, INTERNATIONAL LAW CHIEFLY AS INTERPRETED AND APPLIED BY THE UNITED STATES 468 (1945).

33. It is frequently suggested that the imposition of sovereignty over a bay by the littoral state is analogous to perfecting a right of dominion by prescription, but this assertion does not comport with the theory on which maritime states have traditionally acted. A prescriptive right is one which grows out of conduct which is deemed wrongful in its initial stages by the state against which the act is undertaken. No prescriptive claim begins to run that may not be opposed by the possessor of a legal right of which the assertion is defiant. In the case of bays, it is doubtful that a state, making a claim to a water area geographically within its land territory, assumes that it is engaging in wrongful conduct. Generally, the configuration of the bay in relation to the land territory of the claimant state has constituted a rough test of the legal quality of the claim. *Id.*, at 468–69.

34. *See* Charteris, *Territorial Jurisdiction in Wide Bays,* Int'l Law Assoc. Proceedings, in Report of the 23rd Conference 103, 107 (1906).

shore or too large to be clearly outside of major shipping routes or to be easily recognized by mariners as closed to foreign access.[35] In either case, the impact on inclusive community use is significant and the latitude granted to coastal states far more restricted. The thrust of law-making efforts for the better part of a century[36] has been toward defining community policy regarding such claims and prescribing rules to insure that indentations into the coast are both large enough and yet not too large to justify a deviation from normal baseline rules and their enclosure behind water-crossing baselines.

The attempt by a coastal state to incorporate a slight indentation of the coast into its internal waters, with the consequent seaward extension of the baseline and all succeeding sea zones which that act entails, may constitute a significant derogation of the free seas principle. Since slight indentations appear along the entire coastline of the earth, routine enclosure of these areas could result in the carving out of a large portion of the high seas which had previously been accessible to navigation, fishing, scientific research, and overflight. Balanced with this deprivation of community interests, the interests of a coastal state in a slight indentation of its coast are not perceived to be any greater than those which attach to waters adjacent to a nonindented shoreline. Unlike a bay which penetrates significantly into the littoral and serves to focus the activities of the coastal inhabitants on the land-locked waters, a slight curvature ordinarily lacks this quality of geographical interrelationship. Nor do the waters of a mere curvature pose any greater threat to life on shore from the entry of foreign vessels than if the coast were without indentation at that point.

35. Boggs has suggested that if the baseline is to be delimited in a way to occasion the least interference with navigation, it is necessary to assume the viewpoint of one who is on the sea and wishes to know where territorial waters begin. Difficulties have arisen, he asserts, largely from the fact that the problem of bay delimitation has been considered from the viewpoint of man on the land. Since the legal rights of coastal states and foreign states differ greatly in adjacent sea zones, it is vitally important that navigators, fishermen, and others on the sea be able to determine with certainty whether or not a vessel is on the high seas, in territorial waters, or entering the internal waters of the coastal state. Boggs, *Delimitation of the Territorial Sea: The Method of Delimitation Proposed by the Delegation of the United States at the Hague Conference for the Codification of International Law*, 24 Am. J. Int'l Law 541, 543 (1930).

36. *See infra*, Chapter III.

Historically, when a state claim to exclusive authority would result in substantial deprivation to community use without compensating benefit to coastal interests, the balance has been struck in favor of the inclusive interests of states.[37] Community policy regarding claims to slight coastal indentations, therefore, can be stated quite categorically: a mere curvature of the coast does not warrant the extension of coastal authority over wider sea areas, and a significant penetration of the coast is necessary to justify a shift from a normal baseline at the low-water mark to a closing line across the mouth of the indentation. This policy now finds expression in Article 7(2) of the Territorial Sea Convention, which defines a bay as "a well-marked indentation whose penetration is in such proportion to the width of its mouth as to contain landlocked waters and constitute more than a mere curvature of the coast."[38]

Although there has been an almost universal agreement on the issue of mere curvatures of the coast, and community policy has therefore proven comparatively easy to formulate, states, courts, legal scholars, and international bodies have for several centuries[39] struggled to reach agreement on this question: How wide may the mouth of an indentation be before the indentation is perceived as too large to justify its classification as internal waters? Even though an indentation may be more than a mere curvature, community interests may be severely prejudiced by a state claim to exclusive authority if the proposed closing line of the bay is so wide that mariners approaching from the sea cannot clearly determine when they have left the safety of the high seas and have come dangerously within coastal jurisdiction.[40] Inclusive interests suffer an even greater derogation if international trade routes crisscross the bay or if the fishing fleets of neighboring states have historically enjoyed co-use of its waters. Yet, because

37. *See* M. McDougal & W. Burke, *supra* note 8, at 330–35.
38. This language remains materially unchanged in UNCLOS, art. 10(2) at 5. Article 7(3)–(5) prescribes rules for making the discrimination between landlocked waters and a mere curvature of the coast. *See infra,* Chapter IV, for full textual analysis.
39. *See infra,* Chapter III, for more detailed discussion of the historical development of community policy on the maximum width of bays.
40. This danger has been considerably diminished since the advent of increasingly sophisticated navigational aids and sailing directions. *See infra,* Chapter IV, note 24, and accompanying text.

of the intimate location of the bay within the land mass, vital economic and security interests of the littoral state may be compromised by disallowing a claim of exclusive sovereignty, thus exposing the interior to foreign exploitation. The history of the international law of bays has been dominated by the search for a reasonable accommodation of these legitimate and competing interests.

Early delimitation theories, derived primarily from security considerations, held that an indentation might be regarded as *inter fauces terrae* only if a man could see from headland to headland across the mouth of the indentation. Other theories held that the width of the mouth should not exceed the reach of shore batteries, and later, that the maximum width should not exceed twice the distance claimed for the territorial sea.[41] The notion that a state could effectively control only those waters which could be seen with the naked eye or defended with cannon was rapidly overcome in the nineteenth century by technological advances in hydrographic equipment and weaponry;[42] and states, depending on the widths claimed for their respective territorial seas and their policies regarding the use of ocean space, posited bay closing lines of from three to fifteen miles as reasonable under international law.

The so-called ten-mile rule had many adherents[43] and was proposed as a basis for discussion at the Hague Codification Conference in 1930. Although some limitation was perceived as necessary, delegates failed to agree that the ten-mile rule, or in fact any rule concerning the maximum width of bay closing lines, had become customary in international law.[44] As late as 1951, the Court in the *Anglo-Norwegian Fisheries Case* was forced to conclude:

41. *See* P. Jessup, The Law of Territorial Waters and Maritime Jurisdiction 355–58 (1927); *see also,* Gihl, *supra,* Chapter I, note 6, at 142–44.
42. *See* M. Strohl, The International Law of Bays 139–43, 174–75 (1963). *See also infra,* Chapter III, notes 58–73 and accompanying text for more detailed discussion of the gradual transition from the use of cannon-shot or line-of-sight measurements to more objective, specific dimensions for limiting both the width of the territorial sea and, later, the width of bay closing lines.
43. Great Britain introduced the ten-mile rule into bilateral fishery conventions with France in 1839 and into the multilateral North Sea Convention in 1882. These treaties provided for a territorial sea of three miles and a bay closing line of ten miles. Gihl, *supra,* Chapter I, note 6, at 142.
44. *Id.*

In these circumstances the Court deems it necessary to point out that although the ten-mile rule has been adopted by certain states both in their national law and in their treaties and conventions, and although certain arbitral decisions have applied it as between these States, other States have adopted a different limit. Consequently, the ten-mile rule has not acquired the authority of a general rule of international law.[45]

Even though no community consensus could be reached on an exact dimension for bay closing lines, most states agreed in general on the necessity for some limitation; and this trend toward a maximum width doctrine led over time to the parallel development of the entirely new concept of an historic bay.[46] Before a limitation on the width of bay closing lines was perceived as necessary to prevent expansive claims to internal waters, bays now

45. Anglo-Norwegian Fisheries Case (U.K. v. Nor.), 1951 I.C.J. 116.
46. The term "historic bay" is used to designate a bay which is treated as internal waters but which would not have that character were it not for the existence of an historic title. In order to establish that a body of water is an historic bay, a coastal nation must have "traditionally asserted and maintained dominion with the acquiescence of foreign nations." United States v. California, 381 U.S. 139, 172 (1965). At least three factors are significant in the determination of historic bay status: (1) the claiming nation must have exercised authority over the area; (2) that exercise must have been continuous; and (3) foreign states must have acquiesced in the exercise of authority. United States v. Louisiana, 394 U.S. 11, 23, 24, 24 at note 27, 75 (1968). In United States v. Alaska, the Court stated that as to factor (1) above, the exercise of sovereignty must have been an assertion of power to exclude all foreign vessels and navigation, and that the authority exercised must have been commensurate in scope with the nature of the title claimed. 422 U.S. 184, 197 (1975). In order to satisfy factor (3), the Alaska Court further held that something more than the mere failure of a foreign nation to object must be shown. "The failure of other countries to protest is meaningless unless it is shown that the governments of those countries knew or reasonably should have known of the authority being asserted." 422 U.S. at 200. The recent holding of the U.S. Supreme Court in United States v. Louisiana (Alabama and Mississippi Boundary Case),—U.S.—(No. 9, Original. Argued Nov. 26, 1984; decided Feb. 26, 1985) may have significantly softened the harshness of the Alaska holding in this regard. See Chapter V, note 182. In a U.S. case in which the federal government has previously disclaimed historic title to the body of water in question, an affected state may override the disclaimer by evidence "clear beyond doubt" establishing historic title under the factors cited above. See United States v. California, 381 U.S. at 175; United States v. Louisiana, 394 U.S. at 77. The recent holding in the Alabama and Mississippi Boundary case cited above makes clear, however, that if the federal government has traditionally claimed historic title to the waters in question and then disavows such a claim with an eye toward federal-state litigation, such a disclaimer will not be countenanced. *See also Juridical Regime of Historic Waters, Including Historic Bays*, 2 Y.B. I.L.C. 23, U.N. Doc. A/CN.4/143 (1962).

regarded as historic were in no way distinguished from other bays. All bays which were not too open and large (this concept not being precisely defined) were recognized as part of the territory of the coastal state.[47] When the maximum width doctrine began to gain recognition, in theory if not in specifics, it became clear that many bays which had traditionally been enclosed and utilized as internal waters were so wide at their entrance that they would fall outside all proposed limitations and would therefore become open sea beyond the territorial margin. Such a result, in the face of long established patterns of usage, was seen as an unreasonable deprivation of the exclusive interests of coastal states. Yet it could not be denied that some limitation on the width of bay closing lines was necessary to prevent excessive bay claims from arising in the future, further partitioning the oceans into a mosaic of national zones of control.

This political and legal controversy culminated in 1958 when the exclusive and inclusive interests of states were compromised by a community policy in the form of a procedural and evidentiary innovation introduced into international prescription by Article 7 of the Territorial Sea Convention,[48] which provides in essence that if an indentation meets the geographical and mathematical criteria set out in Article 7(1)–(3), and if the distance between natural entrance points is no more than twenty-four miles,[49] then a deviation from the normal low-water baseline rule[50] is justified, a closing line may be drawn across the entrance of the bay, and the waters enclosed thereby may be considered internal waters.[51] In effect, once an indentation has been characterized as a bay under Article 7, an irrebuttable presumption is raised that the littoral state may assert absolute sovereignty over the waters so characterized against the claims of all states.

If, however, the distance between natural entrance points exceeds twenty-four miles, a state has two options under Article

47. 1 C. HYDE *supra* note 32, at 465–70.
48. *See infra,* Chapter IV, for full text and discussion of Article 7.
49. The "twenty-four-mile rule" was new in 1958, having no precedent in previously existing international law. UNCLOS has retained the limitation but has changed it to read "24 nautical miles." *See* UNCLOS, art. 10(4), at 5.
50. *See* Territorial Sea Convention, art. 3; UNCLOS, art. 5.
51. *See* Territorial Sea Convention, art. 7(4); UNCLOS, art. 10(4).

7.[52] It may move inland within the bay to a point at which the distance from shore to shore does not exceed twenty-four miles and enclose as internal the maximum area of water possible with a line of that length.[53] Alternatively, it may claim that because of historic patterns of exclusive use, authority, and control, the rules set out in Article 7 do not in fact apply to the waters in question because they constitute an "historic" bay, a sea area which the world community has excluded from the application of Article 7.[54] At that point, the burden shifts to the claimant state to prove historic usage, a burden which can only be carried by an extraordinarily high standard of proof.[55]

Community policy on the issue of the maximum width of bay closing lines has thus been concretized via the procedural and evidentiary scheme established under Article 7, a very successful artifact of the 1958 Convention. Most indentations previously considered historic bays have become juridical bays under the generosity of the twenty-four-mile rule. Coastal states may lay claim to such bays as a presumptive right. Exclusive authority over bays which exceed that limitation may be retained only if a state can justify the claim by historic usage.[56]

In the development of principles and policies governing the use of the oceans in general and bays in particular, the world community has sought to serve the basic purposes of the law of the sea: to define the rights of the parties, to reduce the likeli-

---

52. *See* Territorial Sea Convention, arts. 7(5) and 7(6); UNCLOS, arts. 10(5) and 10(6).
53. *See* Territorial Sea Convention, art. 7(5); UNCLOS, art. 10(5).
54. Article 7(6) of the Territorial Sea Convention makes clear that "[t]he foregoing provisions shall not apply to so-called 'historic' bays." UNCLOS, art. 10(6). Although many states pressed for the inclusion of a regime for historic bays in both the 1958 Convention and UNCLOS (*see infra,* Chapter IV, notes 275–280 and accompanying text), no agreement could be reached. The term itself remains undefined in international prescription at this writing.
55. States laying claim to bay waters under this theory ordinarily prevail only if they are able to prove that they have traditionally asserted and maintained dominion with the acquiescence of foreign nations. *See supra* note 46.
56. *See, e.g.,* United States v. California, 381 U.S. 139, 172 (1965); United States v. Alaska, 422 U.S. 184, 189 (1975); Anglo-Norwegian Fisheries Case, (U.K. v. Nor.) 1951 I.C.J. 116. For the most recent discussion of historic claims at this writing, *see* Report of the Special Master, United States v. Louisiana, Texas, Mississippi, Alabama & Florida (Mississippi Boundary Case), No. 9, Original, October 1979, (preliminary draft issued February 1984), and the recent Supreme Court decision in this case, United States v. Louisiana (Alabama & Mississippi Boundary Case),—U.S.— (No. 9, Original. Argued Nov. 26, 1984; decided Feb. 26, 1985).

hood of conflict, to provide clear guidelines for mariners, thereby ensuring that those who use the oceans for navigation and fishing can with certainty determine their location with respect to the reach of coastal power, and to make an equitable allocation of ocean space and resources which may serve both the exclusive and inclusive interests of all states. Perhaps no single accommodation effort has so fully and successfully served all these purposes than that embodied in Article 7 of the Territorial Sea Convention, which has served to concretize the international law of bays.

III

The Historical Treatment
of Bays

The special problem presented by internal waters in general and bays in particular is but a single aspect of a more fundamental problem, i.e., the constant and nearly universal struggle between those who defend the principle of freedom of the seas and those, sometimes the same parties in a different context, who espouse enlarging the exclusive sovereignty of states over coastal waters.[1] This conflict between the inclusive and exclusive interests of states in regard to ocean use is one of the oldest in recorded history, and the development of international rules of law to accommodate these legitimate interests is a fascinating study in itself.[2]

1. Reply of the United Kingdom, Anglo-Norwegian Fisheries Case (U.K. v. Nor.), 1951 I.C.J. Pleadings 416.
2. It is beyond the scope and purpose of this work to detail this development. Many excellent resources exist on the topic. Particularly useful treatments of ancient sea practices are to be found in H. MAINE, ANCIENT LAW (1906); H. MAINE, DISSERTATIONS ON EARLY LAW AND CUSTOM (1886); H. MAINE, EARLY HISTORY OF INSTITUTIONS (1875); H. ORMEROD, PIRACY IN THE ANCIENT WORLD (1924); C. PHILLIPSON, THE INTERNATIONAL LAW AND CUSTOM OF ANCIENT GREECE AND ROME (1911); P. POTTER, THE FREEDOM OF THE SEAS IN HISTORY, LAW, AND POLITICS (1924). *See also* D. AZUNI, DROIT MARITIME DE L'EUROPE (1805); T. FULTON, THE SOVEREIGNTY OF THE SEAS (1911); Fenn, *Justinian and the Freedom of the Sea*, 19 AM. J. INT'L L. 716–727 (1925). M. STROHL, *supra*, Chapter II,

The limited purpose of this section, however, is to establish—through a brief historical review—the fact that the claim of sovereignty over bays and other inland waters has been a well-established state practice from antiquity and that, despite widely fluctuating norms in regard to the sea as a whole, the historical treatment of bays locked within the littoral of a single state has remained surprisingly constant over time. In every era, bays and other internal waters have been generally recognized as so vitally interconnected with the economic and security interests of shore inhabitants as to become natural extensions of the land itself and thus susceptible to claims of exclusive authority by the littoral state. Every era has also witnessed opposition to such claims when it was feared that, carried to excess, they would impinge upon communal uses of the oceans. Only within the last quarter century, after several failed attempts at codification, have the parameters of such claims been established through the development of an international regime for the delimitation of the juridical bay.

Ancient Practice

Although many early writers spoke of the sea as originally belonging to all men in common and as insusceptible of exclusive ownership,[3] it appears that the use of water as a medium of transport dates from the earliest beginnings of agriculture and that in fact

---

note 42, at 3–31, 95–131, cites an extensive array of ancient and modern sources for the further study of the historical development of the law of the sea, including the development of marine architecture and navigational aids. Another excellent collection of historical resources on the law of the sea may be found in the accompanying documents to United States v. Maine, 420 U.S. 515 (1975), many of which will be cited separately below.

3. Grotius's theories, set forth in florid style in *Mare Liberum* in 1609, are by now familiar reading: "There is here no question of an interior sea of scarcely the width of a river, but of the ocean itself to which antiquity gave the names of the infinite, the father of things, the limits of heaven; which feeds by its never ending vapor, not only springs, rivers, and seas, but the clouds and according to the belief of the ancients, the stars themselves; which, finally, encompassing the earth as it does and penetrating the land with its humidity, cannot be enclosed or restrained, and instead of being possessed, is the real possessor." (Tr. in 1 C. CALVO, LE DROIT INTERNATIONAL THEORIQUE ET PRATIQUE 476 (5th ed., 1896). *See also* the work of VON MARTENS, A COMPENDIUM OF THE LAW OF NATIONS 160 (W. Cabbett trans. 1802); J. BLUNTSCHLI, LE DROIT INTERNATIONAL CODIFIE, §304 (5th rev. ed. 1895); 1 E. CAUCHY, LE DROIT MARITIME INTERNATIONAL 37 (1862).

man first began to take a proprietary attitude toward the sea with the emergence of water-borne commerce and the communal development of ports.[4]

The earliest creations of positive law regarding the use of the sea appear to have stemmed from the desire of ancient peoples to protect their vulnerable coastal communities and commercial enterprises from the marauding of neighboring communities and pirates. Within this context, ports became a place of refuge and protection, and their usual location within sheltered arms of the sea such as bays, estuaries, and rivers led to early laws restricting the entrance to these sea areas and the consequent notion, well established before Greek and Roman times, that it was possible to create and maintain dominion and control over a sea area comparable to that exercised on the land.[5] Although the Court in the *Anglo-Norwegian Fisheries Case* takes note of a difference of opinion among authorities as to whether the regimes of territorial and internal waters are truncated relics of far greater pretensions to sea sovereignty or rather represent a more recent encroachment upon sea areas always considered *res nullius*,[6] there seems to be little doubt that the exercise of authority by the littoral community over protected inland waters was recognized by early seafaring communities as a matter of ownership and right,[7] and that claims of exclusive control over these inland waters were established, and by and large accepted, long before the advent of claims to more extensive water areas seaward from the coast.[8]

As to claims of sovereignty over areas of open sea, most authorities cite the rampant abuse of the oceans by major sea powers in the sixteenth and seventeenth centuries, but historical evidence suggests that attempts to lay claim to waters beyond the coastal littoral were made at least 3000 years before the English, Spanish, Dutch, and Portuguese attempted to divide the seas among themselves. It is generally agreed that the Kingdom of Minos in Crete made the first claim to dominion over the high seas, creating a

4. Strohl reveals that the port of Patala in what is now Hyderabad was in operation 7000 years before the Christian era and the port of Ur in Asia Minor is said to have been in existence as early as 2250 B.C. M. STROHL, *supra*, Chapter II, note 42, at 10.
5. *See id.*, at 11; 2 C. PHILLIPSON, *supra* note 2, at 367; P. POTTER, *supra* note 2, at 11.
6. *See* 1951 I.C.J. Pleadings at 309.
7. *See* H. ORMEROD, *supra* note 2, at 154.
8. *See* M. STROHL, *supra*, Chapter II, note 42, at 13; Gihl, *supra*, Chapter I, note 6, at 129.

sea empire which flourished fifteen centuries before Christ. A succession of rulers in Tyre and Greece likewise claimed dominion over portions of the waters in the eastern Mediterranean and the Levant.[9] Historical evidence also suggests that fledgling attempts were made by the Greeks and others to develop a primitive "international" law of sorts claiming dominion over their surrounding seas.[10]

It must be noted, however, that the term "dominion" was never adequately defined, and some authorities contend that the word did not connote complete ownership but rather "a temporary supremacy or predominating influence."[11] It is well known that early peoples sailed long distances on the open sea but rarely out of the sight of land due to the lack of seaworthy vessels and reliable navigational aids. Because of this natural restriction, ancient claims to open sea areas were consequently constrained, and Strohl concludes that "the purported dominion over the sea finds its modern day counterpart in the geopolitical concept of sea power, or command of the sea"[12] rather than ownership in the strict sense.

This was not the prevailing attitude, however, in regard to waters *within* the coastal littoral. A clear distinction was made by early societies between the waters of bays, ports, rivers, and other sheltered inland waters and those of the open sea; and separate concepts of control derived from this distinction. Because sea traffic took place along the coastal perimeter, a natural difference developed between bays and the waters beyond their outer limits where maritime traffic took place.[13] Seafarers had no reason to enter a bay unless in distress or headed for a port therein. Even

---

9. *See* M. STROHL, *supra*, Chapter II, note 42, at 13. *See also* P. POTTER,, *supra*, note 2, at 12-14, for a full listing of Levantian peoples who asserted dominion over the sea.

10. The first recorded example of the creation of positive law establishing dominion over the high seas appears to be a treaty concluded between the Greeks and the Persians after a decisive naval battle in approximately 494–467 B.C., wherein Xerxes, king of the Persians, agreed to come no closer to the coast of Greece than a "horse's course" and that none of his ships should appear between the Cyanean and Chalidonean isles. P. POTTER, *supra* note 2, at 18, citing Plutarch, *Cimon*, XIII, 4. *See also* P. POTTER, at 15-19.

11. *See* 2 C. PHILLIPSON, *supra* note 2, at 376. *See also* P. POTTER, *supra* note 2, at 14–19, for a thorough discussion of Greek, particularly Athenian, attitudes in regard to the sea.

12. M. STROHL, *supra*, Chapter II, note 42, at 18.

13. *See* Gihl, *supra*, Chapter I, note 6, at 129.

then, entry was not always permitted. Access to internal waters was often forbidden to foreign vessels[14] based on the clear perception of the port or bay as a discernible part of the land territory and therefore susceptible of ownership by the littoral community.

Roman Practice

Because at its height the Roman Empire extended along the entire coast of the Mediterranean, the Romans treated it as their private sea, as had the Phoenicians and Carthaginians before them.[15] One may not consider this an exercise of territorial sovereignty in the modern sense, however, as there were few other "states" against which such a claim could be maintained.[16] Rome's major interest was the maintenance of an open sea for conquest, commerce, and colonization among regions of her far-flung empire. Thus, she made no formal claims to sovereignty over the seas, and the Roman *Institutes* and *Digests* are replete with references which declare the sea to be free to all,[17] declarations which led Bracton and other writers influenced by Roman law to conclude that the sea had been regarded as free from antiquity. Historical evidence indicates, however, that in actuality the Romans exercised exclusive authority over their sea routes and assumed special and absolute control over rivers, ports, and the approaches to inland waters[18] in keeping with the practices of earlier societies.

14. Pirates and other marauding invaders continued to be the most pressing concern of coastal communities. Carthage and other early city states made a practice of sinking any ships which ventured into their internal waters. H. Ormerod, *supra* note 2, at 140.
15. J. Bluntschli, *supra* note 3, §305.
16. There is some evidence that a treaty may have been concluded or at least contemplated between Rome and Carthage which set a boundary between their respective sea areas and provided for free entry into one another's ports. *See* M. Strohl, *supra*, Chapter II, note 42, at 19.
17. *See* M. Strohl, *supra*, Chapter II, note 42, at 19–20; Fenn, *supra* note 2, at 716–27. *See also* Report of Special Master Albert B. Maris, in United States v. Maine, 420 U.S. 515 (1975), at 26, reproduced on microfiche by Government Printing Office, card 1, at 18 [hereinafter cited without cross reference as *Report of the Special Master*].
18. M. Strohl, *supra*, Chapter II, note 42, at 20 n.157, cites Roman *Digest* XLIII, at 3 and 8, to show that such authority was assumed under the principle of public use and in the collective interest. As Potter carefully documents, the seeming discrepancy between the free seas language of the *Institutes* and *Digests* and the actual Roman

Modern Practice through the Nineteenth Century

While ports, harbors, and the small bays which sheltered them were recognized as subject to littoral ownership and control from earliest times, it was not until significant advances in navigational and shipbuilding techniques[19] enabled mariners to sail out of the sight of land that expansive claims could be made to the open sea. After the collapse of the Western Roman Empire, pirates swarmed the sea lanes and coastal communities were again vulnerable to depredation. Associations of merchants and, later, of maritime states began to police neighboring seas in an exercise of protective admiralty jurisdiction. By the thirteenth century, this activity had become a prerogative of sovereign power.[20] The early Italian republics claimed and controlled much of the Adriatic, Ligurian, and Tyrrhenian seas,[21] apparently basing their claims in part on primitive notions of property.[22] These assertions of exclusive control over open sea areas merely reinforced the long-held claims of coastal states to absolute sovereignty over ports, bays, and other inland waters.

With the emergence of major sea powers in the fifteenth and sixteenth centuries, even more vast claims to open sea were advanced. The attempts by the Spanish and Portuguese in the sixteenth century to divide the great oceans of the East and West Indies between them based on voyages of exploration, priority of discovery, and papal grant are well known to every school child, but these claims were by no means singular. Denmark,[23] Norway,

---

practice of dominion may be explained by the fact that the rules were never intended as statements of international law. Rather, they refer solely to the right of *Roman* citizens to the free, common, or public use of the sea and seashore. P. POTTER, *supra* note 2, at 32.

19. Strohl details these advances in most interesting fashion, M. STROHL, *supra*, Chapter II, note 42, at 31–47, 95–110.

20. Venice demanded fees beginning in 1269 from all vessels sailing in the Adriatic, maintaining control over that ocean space until the sixteenth century. S. SWARZTRAUBER, *supra*, Chapter I, note 4, at 11. *See also Report of the Special Master, supra,* card 1, at 18.

21. *See* P. POTTER, *supra* note 2, at 36–37.

22. The Genoese claim to the Ligurian Sea and the Venetian claim to the Adriatic were based on the ceremony of Bucentaure during which each year the Doge advanced into the water, threw out a ring, and married the sea. *See* 2 G. CARNAZZA-AMARI, TRAITE DE DROIT INTERNATIONAL PUBLIC EN TEMPS DE PAIX 41 (1880–1881), translated in H. CROCKER, THE EXTENT OF THE MARGINAL SEA (1919).

23. J. BLUNTSCHLI, *supra* note 3, §305.

Sweden, and Poland all laid claim to parts of the North Sea and the Baltic.[24] Turkey claimed ownership of the Red Sea, and Russia asserted the right to exclude all states from the Black Sea.[25]

Perhaps the most audacious claims were advanced by the English, who from the tenth century claimed territorial sovereignty over increasing areas of the high seas.[26] Although there exists a continuing controversy over the legal content of the term sovereignty as applied to the oceans, many early statutes, proclamations, documents and treatises indicate that from the time of Edgar through the seventeenth century, English kings considered themselves sovereign in their surrounding seas, at one time claiming much of the North Sea, the English Channel, and eventually that portion of the North Atlantic between Great Britian and her North American colonies as British seas.[27]

Within varying portions of these waters, English monarchs exercised many of the attributes of sovereignty, including the right to claim flotsam, jetsam, lagan, wreck,[28] and treasure trove;

24. *See* S. SWARZTRAUBER, *supra*, Chapter I, note 4, at 11–15. *See also Report of the Special Master, supra,* card 1, at 18.
25. J. BLUNTSCHLI, *supra* note 3, §305.
26. The first recorded claim of English kings to sea sovereignty is to be found in the tenth century when Edgar the Peaceful styled himself "Sovereign of the Britannic Ocean" and "King . . . of the ocean lying round about Britian." *See Supplemental Brief of the Common Counsel States,* at 8–9, United States v. Maine, 420 U.S. 515 (1975), reproduced on microfiche by Government Printing Office, card 4 [hereinafter cited without cross reference as *Supplemental Brief*] citing C. COLOMBOS, THE INTERNATIONAL LAW OF THE SEA 48 (6th rev. ed.). *See also* P. POTTER, *supra* note 2, at 38–41.
27. For excellent and detailed source materials on English claims to sovereignty, see the following documents, all submitted as part of the United States v. Maine adjudication (420 U.S. 515): *Exceptions and Brief of the Common Counsel States,* reproduced on microfiche by Government Printing Office, card 2, at 7–67, [hereinafter cited without cross reference as *Exceptions and Brief*]; *Appendix to Exceptions and Brief of the Common Counsel States,* Vol. I. (Testimony of Morton J. Horowitz, David H. Flaherty, Joseph H. Smith, Lyman B. Kirkpatrick, and Phillip C. Jessup) reproduced as above [hereinafter cited without cross reference as *Appendix to Exceptions and Brief*]; *see also Supplemental Brief, supra,* cards 4–6 at 10–226; *Report of the Special Master, supra,* card 1, at 1–27. The Court in United States v. Maine commended all parties on the exceptional quality of their historical research.
28. To constitute a legal wreck, goods must come to the shore. Jetsam refers to goods which are cast into the sea and then sink and remain underwater. Flotsam continues to float on the surface of the water. Lagan refers to goods which are sunk in the sea but are tied to a cork or buoy in order to be found again. Stat. 17 Edw. 2, c. 11 provided that "the king shall have the wreck of the sea throughout the realm." There has been a continuing controversy over whether the seas were considered part of the realm of England, and the Statute of 1389, 13 Rich. 2, c. 5, which holds that the

as well as to reap the benefits of derelict or emerged lands[29] and of the royal fish[30] catch. The crown demanded and received the flag salute from foreign ships,[31] regulated fisheries,[32] granted pat-

---

admiral should "not meddle from henceforth with anything done within the realm, *but only* of a thing done upon the sea" (emphasis added), is often cited to prove that the seas were not so considered. More careful translation of the words "but only" (from the Latin *nisi solomordo*) reveals, however, that the words were used in the sense of "except only with respect to." The French transcription of the Latin text also confirms this meaning, indicating an opposite conclusion, i.e., that admiralty jurisdiction was confined to crimes committed in that part of the realm which was on the seas. *See Supplemental Brief, supra,* card 4, at 14–18. *See also Appendix to Exceptions and Brief, supra,* card 9, at 49–51, wherein Horowitz explains that the reference to admiralty jurisdiction as being "outside the Realm" had a different connotation in the seventeenth century and was understood to mean "out of the body of a county of the Realm."

29. Contrary to Roman law which held the seabed to be *res nullius,* English law held that a new island rising from the sea belonged to the Crown based on the principle that the Crown had owned the land while still under water. *See Exceptions and Brief, supra,* card 2, at 33. *See also* The King v. Oldsworth, Hillary 12 Charles I (1636–37), which upheld the Crown's right to derelict lands because the soil under the water "needs be of the same propriety as it is when it is covered with water. If the soil of the Sea, while it is coverd with water, be the King's, it cannot become the subjects' because the water hath left it."

30. *See infra* note 32.

31. The requirement that foreign ships strike their flag to English ships on English seas was considered an attribute of sovereignty and had its origin in a King John ordinance dated 1201. *See, e.g., Supplemental Brief, supra,* card 4, at 13.

32. Crown regulation of fisheries dates back at least to the Magna Carta, which included a provision against the erection of new weirs. One of the recognized causes of action in medieval common law, for which forms are provided in the law books, is action for trespass on an exclusive fishery. In Scotland as early as David I (1124–1153), Scots and foreigners were prohibited from fishing at the mouth of the Firth of Fourth without paying tithes or obtaining licenses. *Supplemental Brief, supra,* card 4, at 19–23. Tolls for sea fishing were routinely imposed and collected. Richard II, by an act of Parliament, imposed a tax on every ship, British or foreign, passing through British seas or fishing therein. Edward IV prohibited all foreigners from fishing in the Irish Sea without a license. James I's fishing proclamation of 1609 described the fishing "regalities" (royalties) to be assessed in English seas and prohibited foreigners from fishing without license. In 1610 the Privy Council, well aware of the civil law rule reflected in Bracton that all fisheries are held in common, expressly declared the common law of England to be contrary and that the king had exclusive rights to fish as part of his prerogative. *See* In the Case of the Royal Fishery of the Banne, 80 Eng. Rep. 540 (1610). The proclamation of Charles I in 1636, made with the advice of the Privy Council, asserted sovereign rights over "the coasts and seas of Great Britain, Ireland, and the rest of the isles adjacent." *See also The Charter of the Royal Fishery of England,* Patent Rolls, 29 Car. 2 pt. X (1688). By the seventeenth century, fishing rights in English seas could be categorically summarized: Prima facie, the Crown owned the sea fisheries as one of its principal royalties. Their ownership of royal fish, certain large fish caught in adjacent waters, was full. English subjects had a common

ents, monoplies, and charters, enabling grantees of the Crown to exploit the riches of the sea and seabed,[33] and exercised extensive admiralty jurisdiction over their marginal waters.[34]

In the early exercise of territorial sovereignty over their surrounding seas, the English by and large obtained, not always by peaceful means, the acquiescence of other states;[35] and whatever

---

law right to take lesser fish except where this right had been superseded by royal grant of an exclusive fishery. Foreigners had no right to fish in English seas except by license. *See Supplemental Brief, supra,* card 5, at 74–92, citing cases, Acts of Parliament, Royal Proclamations, pronouncements, treatises and treaties indicating the seventeenth-century implementation of Crown ownership of fisheries throughout the English seas.

33. The Crown granted subjects the right to "myne undersea treasures," which included both oysters and other live seabed resources as well as coal. The earliest example of undersea mining was commenced about 1588 at Culross, Perthshire, Scotland, by Sir George Bruce. In 1729, a coal mine, partially underwater, was constructed by Sir James Lowther at Whitehaven, Cumberland, England. By 1765, shafts had been extended as much as a mile under sea. All such ventures operated under royal charter. *See Appendix to Exceptions and Brief, supra,* card 10, at 95–98. During the colonial period, charters granted to groups seeking to explore and exploit the New World regularly included a transfer of rights to both the land and the surrounding sea areas discovered and claimed. Many of the colonial charters are similar to the Second Virginia Charter which conveys " . . . all lands, countries, territories . . . all the islands lying within 100 miles along the coast of both seas . . . together with all soils and grounds, havens, and ports, mines as well. . . . Rivers, waters, fishings, commodities . . . within said territories . . . and thereto and thereabouts both by Sea and Land." For further information regarding colonial grants, *see Exceptions and Brief, supra,* card 2, at 34, 38, 64–89; *Appendix to Exceptions and Brief, supra,* card 11, at 239–351, and card 13 at 354–488; *Supplemental Brief, supra,* cards 5–6, at 140–177.

34. Admiralty jurisdiction was regarded by the English as an attribute of sovereignty and, contrary to some opinion that it was applied only to British subjects and pirates (*see Report of the Special Master, supra,* card 7, at 31–32), historical evidence suggests that the jurisdiction of the Admiral extended to foreigners while in English waters, at least during the seventeenth and eighteenth centuries and perhaps as early as 1300. The record of an admiralty inquisition held in 1376 illustrates the comprehensive range of criminal offenses with which the jurisdiction was concerned. Far from being limited to flag salute violations and acts of piracy, the list includes murder, manslaughter, petty felony, aiding the enemy, exporting goods without license, false weights and measures, unauthorized claim of royal wreck, and sedentary fishing violations. *See Supplemental Brief, supra,* card 4, text 25–30. There is considerable evidence from the seventeenth century confirming the general power of Admiralty courts to try foreigners for crimes within English waters. A 1681 Statute of Scotland grants the High Admiral jurisdiction "in maritime and seafaring causes, foreign and domestic . . . within this realm . . . both to natives and strangers." *See also, Appendix to Exceptions and Brief, supra,* at 55 (testimony of M. Horowitz on direct examination).

35. There is considerable evidence to suggest that other nations submitted to the licensing of their fishermen by English authorities. When the Dutch requested and received permission to fish off Scottish waters in 1594, it was agreed that they would not come within sight of shore. *Appendix to Exceptions and Brief, supra,* card 9, at 39.

powers the English kings claimed in their own seas, they by and large accorded to other sovereigns in theirs.[36] However, during the era of great commercial and colonial expansion, which began during the reign of Elizabeth I and continued through the seventeenth century, European powers vied for trade routes in every sea, claims to sovereignty over ocean space reached extravagant proportions,[37] and hostilities between major sea powers seeking to enforce their claims became endemic.[38] Within this context, the bays of both the mother countries and their colonies became essential havens in which ships might seek shelter from the privateers of other nations and fleets might anchor in anticipation of ocean battle. Ports and harbors were fortified, sovereignty over bays was declared and defended, and various laws in all states forbade entry to foreign ships.[39] Overshadowed somewhat by immense pretensions to sovereignty over the high seas, these exclusive claims to vulnerable internal waters continued to be rec-

36. By treaty in 1490 and 1523, England acknowledged the sovereignty of Denmark in its northern waters and agreed to take out licenses for fishing therein. *Supplemental Brief, supra,* card 4, at 23. In another treaty between Great Britain and Denmark, signed at Whitehall in 1661, England recognized the duty of English ships to pay tolls for passage "through the sound appertaining to the king of Denmark and Norway." *Id.,* card 5, at 72.

37. English claims became particularly excessive during the reign of Charles I (1625–49), who claimed absolute sovereignty over all foreign fleets and men of war on the high seas from the coast of England to the Continent. He asserted that the seas were under his protection as Lord of the Seas. *See* H. SMITH, THE LAW AND CUSTOM OF THE SEA 59 (3d. ed. 1959); I. BROWNLIE, PRINCIPLES OF PUBLIC INTERNATIONAL LAW 208 (1966).

38. In 1637, after decades of protracted sea warfare, Spain expressly recognized English sovereignty in English seas. *Supplemental Brief, supra,* card 5, at 72. Between 1652 and 1674, three wars were fought by the English and the Dutch, against whom most of the Stuart fishery proclamations were directed. The English insistence that the Dutch pay arrears in tolls due for fishing in British waters after the passage of the Navigation Act in 1651 was one of the causes of the first Anglo-Dutch war. *Id.,* at 77. Charles II's declaration of war on the Dutch in 1672 was based primarily on Dutch refusal to recognize English dominion over English seas. That war ended in 1674, giving the Dutch the right to continue to fish the rich herring fisheries of the North Sea unimpeded by English authorities. *Report of the Special Master, supra,* card 1, at 30. William III's declaration of war on France in 1689 had two main causes: French violations of the flag salute and French encroachment on the Newfoundland fisheries in the American seas. *Supplemental brief, supra,* card 4, at 60.

39. Harbors and bays were defended by forts as well as guard ships in part to protect the convoys which remained for long periods within the bays of their sovereign. In 1579, Spain enacted a law applicable to all Spanish Indies ports, which held that no ship might enter or leave under cover of darkness without being fired upon. *See* M. STROHL, *supra,* Chapter II, note 42, at 10 n. 23. Similar laws were enacted by most maritime states during this period.

ognized throughout this period as a corollary of territorial sovereignty and to be opposed when their excessive nature threatened the claims and interests of other states.[40]

Although the right of the sovereign to assert exclusive control over internal waters had been recognized from earliest times based on the proximate relationship of the waters to the land territory, no such logical foundation underlay the claim of waters seaward from the coast. Unlike bays, whose location within the land mass so obviously determined the extent of coastal claims, the open sea had no natural limitation and thus was subject to vast assertions of sovereignty and control. Power alone determined whether or not these assertions could be maintained against foreign opposition. Realizing the fragility of such claims, sovereigns and their legal advisors began as early as Elizabethan times to actively seek and construct legal arguments either to justify or to oppose claims to sovereignty over sea and seabed beyond the coast.[41] This doctrinal contest between major sea

40. Wide opposition attended the attempt of James I to delimit water areas of enormous size, sometimes referred to as the "King's Chambers," along the coasts of England as neutral areas within which the hostile acts of belligerents could be prohibited and over which the Crown might exercise exclusive authority as Protector of the Oceans. *See Report of the Special Master, supra,* card 1, at 30.

41. Albert Gentili, an Italian lawyer who was much influenced by the earlier writings of Bartolus and Baldus and who wrote in defense of both English and Spanish maritime claims during the reign of Elizabeth I, appears to be the first to apply the term "territorium" to the adjacent seas, and his usage is said to be the origin of the term "territorial sea." *See* A. Gentili, De Jure Belli Libre Tres 384 (1598); *See also* S. Swarztrauber, *supra,* Chapter I, note 4, at 16–17, 24; *Supplemental Brief, supra,* card 4, at 35. The term became commonly used to refer to a belt of surrounding seas of undefined width over which the coastal state might assert some degree of authority in order to forward the economic, defense, and neutrality interests of its inhabitants. By 1689, Sir Philip Medows confirmed this doctrinal uncertainty by writing that although all might agree that each state was sovereign in its adjacent sea by virtue of its sovereignty over the land, the difficulty lay in determining how far the so-called territorial sea might extend. *Id.,* card 5, at 68. It was also during Elizabeth's reign that the companion doctrine of Crown ownership of the seabed was first articulated (in Thomas Digges's treatise of 1568 or 1569), although many scholars seeking to justify English claims maintain that assertions of ownership over seabed resources date from a much earlier period. *E.g.,* S. Moore, A History of the Foreshore 481 and n.1. (3rd ed., 1888); *see* Codlerington, His Majesties Propriety and Dominion of the British Seas Asserted (1665); Elder, the Royal Fishing Companies of the Seventeenth Century; P. Medows, Observations Concerning Dominion and Sovereignty of the Seas (1689); Molloy, De Jure Maritime et Navali (1665); *Supplemental Brief, supra,* card 4, at 36; *Appendix to Exceptions and Brief,supra,* card 9, at 26–30, card 10, at 98. *See also* Coke's *Fourth Institute* 142–45 (1644), reproducing a proclamation of

powers reached its climax in the seventeenth century when the Dutch legal scholar Grotius wrote *Mare Liberum,* ostensibly to defend the concept of freedom of the seas,[42] followed in 1618 by the publication of *Mare Clausum,* written by the eminent English scholar John Selden to defend English claims of sovereignty over surrounding seas and seabed.[43] Both works exerted a profound influence on the development of the modern law of the sea, *Mare Clausum* becoming an authoritative "lawbook" to which genera-

---

Edward I, dated 1299, which asserts English sovereignty over the English seas and seabed, and the office of Admiral. The phrase "sovereignty of the sea" is expressed in documents of the period as "superioritas," "custodia," or "Admirallatus Maxis." *See* 1 SELECT PLEAS IN THE COURT OF ADMIRALTY (R. Marsden ed.).

42. In essence a brief for the Dutch East India Company, *Mare Liberum* (1609) was written to combat the Portuguese claims to exclusive control of the Indian Ocean and the English claims to exclusive fisheries. *See Supplemental Brief, supra,* card 10, at 113–114 (testimony of P. Jessup); C. CALVO, *supra* note 3, §350, at 472. In his now familiar work, Grotius argued that all property rights are grounded upon occupation, which requires that movables shall be seized and that immovables shall be enclosed and whatever cannot be so seized and enclosed is incapable of being made the subject of property. The vagrant waters of the oceans are thus necessarily free. The right of occupation rests upon the fact that most things become exhausted by promiscuous use, but this is not the case with the sea, which cannot be exhausted by its two most common uses, fishing and navigation. Grotius declares that if exclusive ownership is unjust in certain cases, it is barbarous and inhuman in regard to the sea. The doctrine was repeated in *De Jure Belli* (lib. ii, cap. ii, §3). For an interesting discussion of the political context within which *Mare Liberum,* the full title of which translates as "The Freedom of the Seas or the Right which Belongs to the Dutch to Take Part in the East Indian Trade," was written, *see* S. SWARZTRAUBER, *supra,* Chapter I, note 4, at 18–20. *See also* W. HALL, A TREATISE ON INTERNATIONAL LAW (7th ed. 1917), translated in H. CROCKER, *supra* note 22, at 67; J. BLUNTSCHLI, *supra* note 3, §§304 and 305; C. CALVO, *supra* note 3, §350. Even Grotius was not consistent throughout his life, however. After leaving Dutch service for the Swedish, he never opposed Sweden's extensive claims in the Baltic and is said to have written on the publication of Selden's *Mare Clausum* that he had written *Mare Liberum* as a Hollander and was "exceedingly glad to see the contrary proved." *See Supplemental Brief, supra,* card 7, at 276.

43. Selden conceived of the sea as part of the territory of the Crown, susceptible of ownership in the same manner as the land itself and neighboring isles, and limited in scope only by vague notions of the "Four Seas" in and around England. In answer to Grotius's argument that the resources of the sea should be held in common because inexhaustible, Selden argued that there must be exclusive ownership of the seabed precisely because its products are not inexhaustible. Analogizing pearls and coral to undersea mines, he states that both lessen every hour "when their Treasures and Fruits are taken away." *See Appendix to Exceptions and Brief, supra,* card 9, at 35 (testimony of M. Horowitz). Selden concludes that in accord with natural law and the law of nations, the sea as well as the land may be occupied and, therefore, the king of England has an incontestible right to exclusive dominion over the British seas, which Selden asserts might extend from the coasts of England to the ports and coasts of neighboring states. *See* C. CALVO, *supra* note 3, §351.

tions of scholars, lawyers, and jurists, primarily but not exclusively English, referred to support the concept of territorial sovereignty over the oceans,[44] and *Mare Liberum* being even more widely relied upon to refute the excessive nature of such claims.

It has become commonplace to summarize the outcome of this key doctrinal struggle somewhat simplistically in terms of an eventual triumph of good (i.e., Grotius's concept of freedom of the seas) over evil (i.e., Selden's notion that the seas could be possessed and controlled by the coastal state). It would seem more realistic to conclude, certainly in the face of ever increasing claims to exclusive authority over ocean space and resources in the present, that this fundamental struggle is far from over and that although over three centuries a community consensus has evolved favoring inclusive use of the oceans as most productive of values for all mankind, this policy applies only to the high seas, an area of ocean space which by all accounts appears to be shrinking at an alarming rate.[45] The outcome of the controversy raised

44. Although more scholarly and thorough than Grotius, Selden drew authority primarily from the past and was at the distinct disadvantage of supporting the status quo at a time when public attitudes toward claims of sovereignty over vast ocean areas were in transition. Nonetheless, Selden's writings provided the basis for English policy for over one hundred years. S. SWARZTRAUBER, *supra*, Chapter I, note 4, at 20–22. Selden's work was preceded and followed by several other treatises, all commissioned to serve royal interests in the sea and seabed. The Thomas Digges treatise, written to justify Elizabeth I's expansive sea claims, has been mentioned. *See supra* note 41. Welwood, writing before Selden in AN ABRIDGEMENT OF ALL SEA LAWS 67 (1613), asserted English sovereignty in adjacent seas and like Selden claimed that the rules for acquiring title to the sea were the same as those for acquiring title to land. James I and Charles I commissioned extensive legal research prior to issuing their fishery proclamations. *See supra* note 32. The first of those ordered by Charles I was completed in 1633 by Sir John Boroughs who, drawing heavily on Selden, claimed full maritime territorial sovereignty for the Crown, including lawmaking power, criminal and civil jurisdiction, and ownership of the resources of both the surface waters and the seabed. By 1637, Selden's work was regularly cited as authority not only in the international context but in municipal cases attempting to challenge royal authority. *The Ship Money Case* (Rex v. Hampden) and Rex v. Oldsworth, both decided in 1637 and relying heavily on Selden's writings, are but two cases of that period which declare that by the fundamental laws and policy of England, the sole interest and property of the sea is in the King. *Supplemental Brief, supra*, card 4, at 49–54; card 5, at 75. In 1652, Parliament adopted a resolution requesting the Council of State to prepare a declaration asserting the right of England to full sovereignty over her claimed seas. The Council's response was to order the translation and republication of Selden's *Mare Clausum. Id.*, card 4, at 55.
45. One need only glance at a map of sea zones claimed by states under the Geneva Conventions and even more alarmingly under UNCLOS to conclude that today's balance

by the work of Grotius, Selden, and others who preceded and followed them[46] might therefore be more accurately summarized in terms of an eventual melding of the principles of freedom of the seas and exclusive maritime sovereignty into an international regime of the oceans which recognizes and delimits discrete zones of ocean space within which the inclusive and exclusive interests of states may be accorded appropriate weight.[47]

Throughout two and one-half centuries of gradual compromise and accommodation of these interests in the development of an international law of the sea, the recognition of bays, ports, harbors, rivers, and other internal waters as susceptible of exclusive ownership and control by the coastal state has remained constant. Even Grotius excused from his doctrine of freedom of the seas "inland seas, bays, straits, and as large a sea as can be sighted from land."[48] In *De Jure Belli et Pacis* (1625) he reiterated that a bay or strait may be occupied by the state which owns the land on both sides unless the bay is so large in relation to the surrounding land mass that it cannot be considered a part of it.[49] A succession of writers after Grotius[50] reinforced the view that

---

is increasingly being weighed in favor of exclusive state interests. *See, e.g., McBryde's Map*, World Oceans and Seas (1982) (available through Transemantics, Washington, D.C.), which, by accurately projecting ocean space rather than land mass, graphically illustrates the limited area now recognized as high seas after national claims to exclusive economic zones and territorial waters have been subtracted. When one reflects on the fact that the most valuable and realizable ocean resources lie in water areas closest to shore, the impact of expansive national claims is even more significant. *See also infra*, Chapter V, *Current State Practice.*

46. Writers who maintained the right of state sovereignty over great seas included Gentilus, Pacius (Julius), Gotsfredus, Paolo Sarpi, Burgus, Rivius, Marisoltus, Schookius, Coringius, Jenkinson (Lord Liverpool), de Fretas, Heineccius, and Borough. Defenders of freedom of the seas included Pufendorf, Graswinkell, Huberus, Graverus, Groeningius, Pontanus, Bynkershoek, Lucchesi, Palli, Hübner, Azuni, Galliani, Hautefeuille, Klüber, Martens, Wheaton, and all other international law authorities since 1880. *See* CARNAZZA-AMARI, *supra* note 22, at 35.

47. *See supra*, Chapter II, notes 5–11 and accompanying text.

48. "In hoc autem oceano non de sinu aut freto, nec de omni guidem so quod e litore conspici potest controversia est." *See* Gihl, *supra*, Chapter I, note 6, at 136.

49. *See id. See also* W. HALL, *supra* note 42, at 67.

50. *See* in particular the following, all translated in H. CROCKER, *supra* note 22: D. AZUNI, DROIT MARITIME DE L'EUROPE §17, at 254 (1805); J. BLUNTSCHLI, *supra* note 3, §309; H. BONFILS, MANUEL DE DROIT INTERNATIONAL PUBLIC (7th ed. 1914); C. CALVO, *supra* note 3, §367; G. CARNAZZA-AMARI, *supra* note 22, §11, at 53; 1 CAUCHY, LE DROIT MARITIME DES NATIONS §41, at 97 (1862); E. CREASY, FIRST PLATFORM OF INTERNATIONAL LAW 232–240 (1876); F. DECUSSY, PHASES ET CAUSES CELEBRES DU DROIT MAR-

when the sea penetrates the land and "becomes almost confused with it,"[51] the reasons upon which the freedom of the open sea is founded no longer apply and the social, economic, and defense interests of the coastal state become paramount.

ITIME DES NATIONS §41, at 97 (1856); F. DESPAGNET, COURS DE DROIT INTERNATIONAL PUBLIC §402, at 608 (1910); H. HALLECK, INTERNATIONAL LAW §13, at 167 (4th ed. 1908); J. KLÜBER, DROIT DES GENS MODERNE DE L'EUROPE §130, at 180 (2d. Fr. ed. 1874); T. LAWRENCE, THE PRINCIPLES OF INTERNATIONAL LAW §72, at 140 (5th ed. 1913); F. VON LISZT, DAS VOLKERRECHT §9, at 86–91 (5th ed. 1907); A. NUGER, DES DROITS DE L'ETAT SUR LA MER TERRITORIALE 190–95 (1887); 1 E. NYS, LE DROIT INTER-NATIONAL 441 (1904); J. ORTOLAN, REGLES INTERNATIONALES ET DIPLOMATIE DE LA MER 156 (2d ed. 1893); R. PIEDELIEVRE, PRECIS DE DROIT INTERNATIONAL PUBLIC OU DROIT DES GENS §417 at 363 (1894); P. PRADIER-FODERE, TRAITE DE DROIT INTERNATIONAL PUBLIC §634 (1885); E. VATTEL, *supra*, Chapter I, note 21, §291; J. WESTLAKE, INTER-NATIONAL LAW PART I 187 (2d. ed. 1910); H. WHEATON, ELEMENTS OF INTERNATIONAL LAW §177, at 255 (8th ed. 1866); de Lapradelle, *The Right of the State Over the Terri-torial Sea*, in 5 REVUE GENERALE DE DROIT INTERNATIONAL PUBLIC 264 (1898); Martens, *Le Tribunal d'Arbitrage de Paris et la Mer Territoriale*, in 1 REVUE GENERALE DE DROIT INTERNATIONAL PUBLIC 39 (1894).

51. E. CAUCHY, *supra* note 3, at 37, concisely summarizes the doctrinal basis for an inter-national law of bays:

> The very nature of the sea resists the domain of man and being inexhaustible in its use, lacks the one characteristic which legally could justify exclusive pos-session. Therefore, one concludes that a state of liberty, of free navigation, of common and indivisible enjoyment is the normal, natural, and actual status of the sea just as private possession, cultivation, or division constitutes the natu-ral, normal, or actual state of the land. But this first principle of maritime law is transformed and modified where *the sea approaches the land and becomes almost confused with it*. Reasons upon which liberty of the open sea is founded no longer apply with the same force to either bays or gulfs by which *the sea pene-trates into the land*. If it is true that the mass of waters of which the open sea is composed escapes domination, the same waters, divided into *stretches of small extent* become susceptible of public or even private property. In the case of a bay or gulf *communicating with the ocean by an opening more or less wide*, it becomes sea in its turn, but it is one of those seas which publicists call interior or territorial seas to show that *they still retain more the nature of the territory than the open sea. The sovereign of adjacent land may establish ports and roadsteads in such waters, may defend its access, and make himself absolute master of these waters so intimately connected with his domain* (emphasis added).

Cauchy also uses exhaustion of resources as a justification for exclusive control of internal waters:

> Whereas ... fishing could justly be considered inexhaustible in the ocean whose wealth and depth we do not know, the same cannot be said for gulfs and bays which are constantly plowed by fishing vessels, all parts of which have been explored by the sounding lead, where the abundance and rarity of fish and quality, taste, and size are known in advance and thus become more or less exhaustible of an industry especially adapted to the inhabitants of the shores. *Id.*

The earliest writers, however, did not speculate on the juridical nature of bays and other internal waters beyond reinforcing the right of the coastal state to assume dominion and control access. Nor was there any attempt made until well into the nineteenth century to distinguish such waters from the belt of open sea, variously termed "territorial," "littoral," or "jurisdictional," which lay adjacent to but seaward from the coast and which gradually gained recognition as susceptible of possession by the coastal state.[52] Because it had been assumed from antiquity that bays were relatively small arms of the sea which sheltered ports and harbors and were intimately connected with the processes of life on shore, early writers felt no necessity to place limits on the size of bays which might be controlled by the coastal state beyond the vague parameters suggested by Grotius, i.e., those bays, straits, or seas the extent of which could be sighted from shore to shore and which were not so large in relation to the surrounding land mass that they could not be considered a part of it.[53] However, as claims to territorial waters beyond the coast grew excessive, publicists began to posit various doctrinal bases for limiting such claims; and it is within this context that more precise limitations on the size of bays were first established and fine distinctions between the juridical nature of internal and territorial waters were first drawn.

The doctrine of territorial waters developed in response to the need to justify state sovereignty over a portion of the waters beyond the coast as well as the need to place a reasonable limit on the extent of such claims. When the doctrine gained ascendancy in the sixteenth century,[54] it became commonplace for coastal states to claim sovereignty over territorial seas of enormous proportions. These claims were by and large supported by

---

52. As we have seen, the doctrine of the territoriality of bays long predated the doctrine of the territorial sea. *See* Gihl, *supra,* Chapter I, note 6, at 136–37; Hurst, *The Territoriality of Bays,* 3 Brit. Y.B. Int'l L. 42, 43–53 (1922–23).

53. *See supra* text accompanying notes 46–49. The principle enunciated by Lord Hale in De Jure Maris (at 1, c. 4) and quoted with approval in many judicial decisions is often cited to epitomize early limitations on bay size: "That arm or branch of the sea which lies within the fauces terrae where a man may reasonably discern between shore and shore is . . . within the body of a county and therefore within the jurisdiction of the sheriff or coroner." This is often cited as the "reasonable discernment" test of Lord Hale.

54. *See supra* note 41.

early authorities,[55] and exclusive national claims extending as far
as 100 miles from the coast were memorialized in international
treaties and municipal laws of the sixteenth, seventeenth, and
eighteenth centuries.[56] Various so-called narrow limit rules[57] were

55. As early as the fourteenth century, the jurist Bartolus proposed a 100-mile limit for
    territorial jurisdiction over wider seas, and Baldus appears to have been the first to
    propose a 60-mile limit. *See Supplemental Brief, supra,* card 7, at 276–77. As the doc-
    trine became firmly entrenched in the sixteenth and seventeenth centuries, Bodin,
    Selden, Pacius, Welwood, Casaregis, and Abreu justified claims extending 60 to 100
    miles into the open sea. Others, such as Loccenius and Hieronymous of Brescia based
    the limit on a two-day voyage, whereas Sarpi gave the adjacent state "all that it
    needed" (presumably referring to economic and defense interests), and Valin
    accorded territorial sovereignty to all that portion of the sea in which a bottom could
    be found. Rayneval justified claims to the actual horizon. *See* H. CROCKER, *supra* note
    22, at 11–15. One notable exception among jurists who supported wide sovereignty
    over coastal waters was the distinguished sixteenth-century Spanish lawyer and pub-
    licist Francisco Vitoria, who vigorously challenged the papal grants authorizing Span-
    ish claims in the New World. Grotius later referred to Vitoria as authority for his
    concept of *mare liberum. See* S. SWARZTRAUBER, *supra,* Chapter I, note 4, at 14.
56. Historical evidence indicates that wide territorial sovereignty was claimed and exer-
    cised by the majority of nations bordering on the sea and that international law by
    and large affirmatively countenanced such claims. *See Supplemental Brief, supra,* card
    7, at 261–65. The Scots bitterly opposed any intrusion by foreigners into their
    "reserved waters" and major sea battles in the fifteenth and sixteenth centuries were
    fought to vindicate that right. Such "reserved waters" extended to a "land-kenning,"
    i.e., the distance from which land could be seen from the top of a mast, usually
    defined as either 14 or 18 miles. The English Charter granted for Nova Scotia in 1662
    expressly established a 30-league territorial sea, a limit frequently cited by interna-
    tional law scholars as appropriate for exclusive fisheries. (Thirty English marine
    leagues is equal to 90 nautical miles, which in turn is equal to 103.5 statute miles.)
    This limit was memorialized in the Treaty of Utrecht between England and France in
    1713. The Treaty of Paris in 1765 (by which France ceded Canada to England) con-
    firmed the Utrecht 100-mile territorial limit. Most of the colonial charters granted by
    the English included a grant of territorial seas extending 100 miles from the coast of
    North America. A 20-league (60-mile) limit was established for the maritime bound-
    ary of the United States by the Treaty of Paris of 1783. Documents drawn during the
    negotiation period compare the Treaty of Utrecht and Treaty of Paris boundary lines
    and record a 20-league (60-mile) boundary line for the entire length of the American
    coast. *See Exceptions and Brief, supra,* card 3, at 99–100. In 1790, Britain agreed by
    treaty with Spain that British subjects would not navigate or fish within 10 leagues
    (30 miles) of the Pacific coast occupied by Spain. The only nation to have denied the
    existence of a territorial sea was the Netherlands which did not wish to be excluded
    from North Sea herring fisheries. It would appear that whereas territorial sovereignty
    out to 100 miles was routinely claimed throughout the sixteenth and seventeenth cen-
    turies, a gradual retreat to a 60- or 30-mile limitation took place in the eighteenth
    century when freedom of navigation theories began to gain wide acceptance. *Supple-
    mental Brief, supra,* card 7, at 263–336; *Exceptions and Brief, supra,* card 2, at 49–50.
57. "Narrow limit" rules include, *inter alia,* the range-of-vision or line-of-sight doctrine,
    the cannon-shot rule, the one-league, two-league, three-league, three-mile limits, and
    other specific but less common limitations.

developed by states during this period, but these were utilized primarily for neutrality purposes and not as overall limitations on territorial waters.[58]

Although some early claims to *neutral waters* were based on the distance one could see from the shore, reality dictated that since a given state could only prevent hostilities as far from the shore as her cannon could carry, this then should be the limit of neutral waters. Writing in 1702, Cornelius Van Bynkershoek, the publicist most commonly associated with the so-called cannon-shot rule, criticized the extensive maritime claims then commonplace among nations as well as the attempts by some to limit sovereignty to that distance which might be seen from the shore.[59] Bynkershoek argued instead:

> The possession of a maritime belt ought to be regarded as extending just as far as it can be held in subjugation to the mainland, for in that way, although it is not navigated perpetually, still the possession acquired by law is properly defined and maintained; for there can be no question that he possesses a thing continuously who so holds it that another cannot hold it against his will . . . wherefore on the whole it seems a better rule that the control of

58. Nations could and did establish much more modest limits for neutrality (that distance into the sea wherein the coastal state assumed the right and duty to prevent belligerant ships from attacking one another) than for any other aspects of sovereignty and dominion. Indeed, coastal states were quite inclined to do so, since neutrality limits imposed onerous obligations upon them without any corresponding benefit, except that of preventing hostilities so close to shore as to endanger the land territory. Powerful maritime nations had a further incentive to limit neutral waters in their desire to minimize those areas of the sea where their weaker enemies could find sanctuary in time of war. *Supplemental Brief, supra,* card 7, at 278.

59. Bynkershoek was critical of the approach taken by King Phillip II of Spain in the Nautical Laws given to the Netherlanders in 1563 in which it was held that since foreigners could not attack their enemies within sight of land (the Spanish neutrality limit), this limitation should also apply to the width of the territorial sea. Bynkershoek considered the range of vision rule too indefinite and variable, comprehending as it might the distance any man could see, including one aided by the newly invented telescope or one with extremely keen eyesight such as Pliny describes in *Natural History* who could see all the way from Sicily to Carthage. Writing in DE DOMINIO MARIS at 42–43, Bynkershoek asserted: "You may see that the early jurists who ventured to recognize dominion over a maritime belt wander about in great uncertainty in regulating its limits. . . . Some authorities extend it to a hundred miles, some to sixty . . . others set various other limits. . . . But no one could easily approve the reasoning on which all these rules are based, or that reasoning either by which it is accepted that dominion over the sea extends as far as the eye can reach."

the land [over the sea] extends as far as cannon will carry; for that is as far as we seem to have both command and possession.[60]

Many writers after Bynkershoek interpreted his writings as recommending the application of the cannon-shot rule to the determination of the seaward limit of the territorial sea. It seems more likely, however, considering evidence provided by the later writings of Bynkershoek,[61] the work of publicists such as Carasegi, Wolff, Vattel, Abreu, and Valin, and the general practice of states throughout the eighteenth century,[62] that the cannon-shot rule was intended and indeed primarily applied for purposes of neutrality and prize law.[63]

---

60. (Terrae potestas finitur ubi finitur amorum vis.) BYNKERSHOEK, DE DOMINIO MARIS (1702), translated in C. CROCKER, *supra* note 22, at 15. The cannon-shot rule was a practical doctrine which had the virtue of flexibility. The extent of seaward boundaries could increase along with increases in the force of arms, without necessitating a doctrinal change. Cannon range was approximately one mile when DE DOMINIO MARIS was published in 1702. This range had been extended to two miles by the end of the eighteenth century, and to three miles by the end of the Napoleonic wars. *See* S. SWARZTRAUBER, *supra*, Chapter I, note 4, at 34–35.

61. In his later work, QUESTIONUM JURIS PUBLICI LIBRI DUO (Question of Public Law) at 54, 57, Bynkershoek writes: " . . . for I hold that the territorial domain ends where the power of weapons terminates. . . . Following this principle, it is not permitted to begin a battle on the seas so near land that it is within reach of the cannon of the forts. . . . " *See* S. SWARZTRAUBER, *supra*, Chapter I, note 4, at 29–30, who concludes, citing the work of Walker and Brierly, that Bynkershoek was merely recording the current practice of certain states, notably Holland and France (*Id.*, at 24–28), in recognizing the protection afforded to belligerent ships by the series of coastal "safe havens" within firing range of actual guns in forts on the shore. Although it is evident from state practice as early as the seventeenth century that Bynkershoek did not invent the cannon-shot rule as some writers have suggested, there seems to be little doubt that he was the first publicist to record and recommend it and, in so doing, to popularize its use among states. *Id.*, at 25–27, 30.

62. *See* S. SWARZTRAUBER, *supra*, Chapter I, note 4, at 30–33.

63. *Id.*, at 32. To say that the cannon-shot rule was first applied primarily as a limit on neutral waters is not to say that this is the only rule that *was* so applied, though it does appear to have been the most common among maritime powers other than the Scandinavian states. In 1758, King Adolph Frederick of Sweden adopted a three-mile limit for neutrality purposes, but the Swedish mile is thought to have been equal to twelve-eighteen nautical miles in actuality. *Supplemental Brief, supra*, card 7, at 271. By a letter of Nov. 8, 1793, President Jefferson fixed a provisional distance of three miles for neutrality purposes off the U.S. Atlantic coast, apparently the first clear use of such a limit in history. Seven months later, the three-mile limit was inacted into law by the Congress, making the United States the first nation to incorporate the three-mile limit into its domestic laws. S. SWARZTRAUBER, *supra*, Chapter I, note 4, at 56–58. Somewhat inexplicably, this enactment did not lead to uniform practice. A U.S. treaty with Great Britain in 1794 established the cannon-shot, not the three-mile

These narrow limitations on neutral waters were established during a period when states still routinely claimed sovereignty over territorial seas of thirty to sixty miles for fishing, national security and other exclusive purposes.[64] In time, however, considerations militating in favor of a gradual retrenchment from excessive maritime claims to the high seas, i.e., the natural capacity of the sea to be used by all nations in common, the seeming inexhaustibility of ocean fishery resources, the growing influence of freedom of navigation theories espoused by Grotius and others, and the gradual realization by principal maritime powers that such theories best served their own interests,[65] led to a retrenchment in claims to territorial waters as well. At this point, the various narrow limit rules which had been used to define the extent of neutral waters were proposed and utilized for delimiting the territorial sea.

The range-of-vision or line-of-sight doctrine, so deplored by Bynkershoek,[66] was used by many states to establish a continuous protective security belt around the coastal littoral.[67] Like the cannon-shot rule which produced boundaries of varying distances depending upon the force of cannon, the range-of-vision doctrine justified boundaries of three to fifty miles depending upon

---

limit, as the measure of neutral waters. In 1806, Secretary of State Madison proposed four leagues as the width of neutral waters in the Gulf of Mexico. In an unratified treaty of 1806, the United States agreed to extend her neutral waters to five miles. *See Supplemental Brief, supra,* card 8, at 392–96.

64. *See supra* note 55.
65. *See supra*, Chapter I, note 4.
66. *See supra* note 60 and accompanying text.
67. The line-of-sight doctrine was occasionally used in connection with customs and neutrality zones as above, but the most common purpose, reflected in state documents and the writings of publicists of the seventeenth and eighteenth centuries, was that of protection. *See* S. SWARZTRAUBER, *supra*, Chapter I, note 4, at 33–43. In treaties with Tripoli, Algiers, and Tunis between 1676 and 1751, Great Britain sought to protect her interests in Tangier, Minorca, and Gibraltar with treaty provisions which typify those used by many states to establish a protective margin:

   Article VIII. That none of the ships or other smaller vessles of Tripoli shall remain cruising near His Majesty's city and garrison of Tangier, *or in sight of it*, nor [in any] other way disturb the peace and commerce of that place.

Great Britain and Tripoli, "Treaty of Peace and Commerce, Mar. 5, 1676," *British & Foreign State Papers,* vol. I, pt. I, at 715 (emphasis added), cited in S. SWARZTRAUBER, *supra*, Chapter I, note 4, at 37.

one's geographical perspective.[68] The Scandinavian states were
the first to translate range of vision directly into a linear measurement. Establishing a protective zone within sight of the coasts
of Norway and Jutland in 1691, the Dano-Norwegian monarchy
computed the phrase "within sight of our coasts" as "four or five
leagues . . . from the outlying rocks."[69] Following the Scandinavian lead, many states in the late seventeenth and eighteenth centuries rejected the variable range-of-vision and cannon-shot rules
in favor of more objective linear measurements to define boundaries for security purposes.[70] Boundaries claimed to protect other

68. Swarztrauber relates that a man standing on the beach at sea level can see approximately three nautical miles seaward. A man standing ten meters above sea level has a
horizon of six nautical miles. A man atop a 500 foot beach cliff can see twenty-six
miles. A ship with a 100 foot mast can be seen eleven miles further at sea by all three
men. In sum, on a clear day the distance things can be sighted at sea depends on the
height of the viewer and the height of the object viewed. S. SWARZTRAUBER, *supra*,
Chapter I, note 4, at 40–41.
69. King of Denmark, "King's Order in Council Regarding Maritime Prizes, June 13,
1691," cited in S. SWARZTRAUBER, *supra*, Chapter I, note 4, at 37. Four or five Scandinavian leagues were approximately equal to sixteen or twenty nautical miles, the
distance on a clear day that the uppermost parts of the rigging of a large ship would
first appear to an observer on the shore. *Id.*, at 38 and n. 8. This use of leagues rather
than miles to measure distances on the territorial margin was not without precedent.
An earlier Danish ordinance in 1598 ordered the seizure of any English ships hovering or fishing within two leagues of the coast. *Id.*, at 16. Thereafter, with few exceptions, Scandinavian states measured their territorial sea boundaries in leagues. By the
nineteenth century, France, England, Holland, Spain, the United States, Germany,
and others had begun to use the *marine league* to define various limits of their territorial seas. Unfortunately for generations of scholars, the Scandinavian league measured roughly four nautical miles, whereas the marine league used by the majority of
other states measured three nautical miles, an inconsistency which has led to difficulty
in reconciling scholarly texts. *Id.*, at 45–48.
70. The three-mile limit was one of the linear measurements which came into vogue
among certain states in the eighteenth century, and there has been much scholarly
debate on its origin. Some have claimed that the three-mile limit derived from the
range of the cannon-shot which, at the time the three-mile limit came into use, is often
said to have been three miles. Although it is fair to say that some connection was made
between the two measurements in diplomatic documents and scholarly texts of the
eighteenth century (*See* S. SWARZTRAUBER, *supra*, Chapter I, note 4, at 54–56), it is
also clear that cannon range was approximately one mile in 1704 when one of the
first three-mile limits was imposed in the British hovering acts (*Id.*, at 51) and had
only increased to two miles when Galliani first publicized the three-mile limit in 1782.
(*Id.*, at 54–55.) The range of the cannon shot had only reached three miles at the end
of the Napoleonic Wars. By that time, the three-mile limit had been used for various
purposes for well over one hundred years.
    Others argue that the three-mile limit had its genesis in the range-of-vision test,
since in any era, a man standing at sea level can see roughly three miles seaward on

exclusive interests such as fishing remained more extensive until well into the nineteenth century.[71] Eventually, the majority of states adopted a narrow limit of specific, if not uniform, linear dimensions to delimit their seaward boundaries for all purposes—neutrality, security, jurisdiction, and at last, fishing.[72]

---

a clear day. *See* S. SWARZTRAUBER, *supra*, Chapter I, note 4, at 40; B. BRITTIN, INTERNATIONAL LAW FOR SEAGOING OFFICERS 54 (1956). *See also* A. RAESTAD, LA MER TERRITORIALE (1913); Walker, *Territorial Waters: The Cannon Shot Rule,* 22 BRIT. Y.B. INT'L L. 210 (1945). Yet another theory holds that the three-mile limit derived from the one-league limit adopted by the Scandinavians in 1745 (which unfortunately for precision's sake measured four miles), or the three-mile marine league. Neither of these measurements, however, can claim a much longer lineage than the three-mile limit. Rather, they appear to have been expressions of the same desire to set narrow sea boundaries of definite length.

The truth of the foregoing claims to origin has been muddied perhaps most irremediably by early-nineteenth-century court decisions. The British High Court of Admiralty wrote in 1805 in the case of the Anna:

> We all know that the rule of law on this subject is *"terrae dominium finitur, ubi finitur armorum vis,"* and since the introduction of firearms, that distance has usually been recognized to be about three miles from the shore. . . .

See The Anna (La Porte, Master), 5 C. Robinson 373 (1805), in FENWICK, INTERNATIONAL LAW, at 482–83 (emphasis added). The hand of a legal historian is even less in evidence in the first major three-mile limit case in the United States, The Brig Ann, wherein the U.S. Circuit Court of Massacusetts wrote in 1812:

> As the Ann arrived off Newburyport, and within *three miles* of the shore, it is clear she was within the acknowledged jurisdiction of the United States. All the writers upon public law agree that every nation has exclusive jurisdiction to the *distance of a cannon shot,* or *marine league,* over the waters adjacent to its shore.

See The Brig Ann, I Gollison 62 (1812), in U.S. Government, 1 *The Federal Cases* 926–28 (emphasis added). Scholary debate has as yet provided no clear-cut answers to the question of origin. It *is* known that President Jefferson considered the cannon-shot rule, the line-of-sight doctrine, and the marine-league limitation specifically before selecting a provisional three-mile limit for neutral waters in 1793. *See* S. SWARZTRAUBER, *supra*, Chapter I, note 4, at 58. Perhaps such evidence supports an inference that the three-mile limit was but the last in a succession of narrow-limit rules, none of which gained universal acceptance but all of which were traceable to the growing acceptance among states of the *mare liberum* concept and, therefore, of the need to establish more reasonable and enforceable maritime boundaries.

71. A Dano-Norwegian fifteen-league fishing zone around Greenland, the fifteen-league fishing zone established by the Treaty of Paris between France and England in 1763, and the thirty-mile territorial sea established against Moroccan vessels in the Franco-Morrocan Treaty of Peace and Commerce in 1767 are but a few examples of extensive fishery zones established at a time when narrow neutrality and security limits were becoming commonplace. *See* S. SWARZTRAUBER, *supra*, Chapter I, note 4, at 44–50.

72. The three-mile limit was widely utilized by states, but it cannot be said to have been universally adopted as a rule of international law. Riesenfeld, writing in PROTECTION OF COASTAL FISHERIES UNDER INTERNATIONAL LAW in 1942, made an exhaustive survey

Precise limitations on the dimensions of bays appear to have evolved within this larger context of restricting the extent of the territorial sea. During the seventeenth and eighteenth centuries, it would have been impossible for a mariner to have determined his position on the sea with such precision that he could orient himself to an imaginary line laid down beyond the vision of coastal landmarks. A host of improved navigation techniques in the nineteenth century, and most particularly the invention of the gyrocompass in the early twentieth century, made such determinations possible.[73] As technological capacity grew, the earlier natural restrictions on bay size, which had resulted from the obvious geographical relationship of a bay to the surrounding land mass and the ability of a mariner to perceive this geographical reality with his naked eye (and thus avoid illegal entry), were rendered obsolete. In order to prevent exclusive national claims to wider bays than might be comprehended from shore to shore, and in keeping with the freedom of navigation theories which had led to the gradual limitation of territorial sea claims and the development of international rules of conduct in regard to the sea as a whole, two general groups emerged with differing approaches to bay delimitation. One group held that the actual geographical relationship of the land to the sea must determine a bay's status as internal waters, while the second contended that a more precise, technical delimitation method was needed in order to prevent abuse by coastal states.

Members of the first group, linear descendants of Grotius and

---

of the literature on the three-mile limit and found that of 114 writers who had dealt with the issue between 1900 and 1942, 41 believed the three-mile rule to be obligatory under international law, 21 favored different rules, and 52 believed that no limitation had achieved the status of a binding rule. Riesenfeld concluded, *Id.*, at 278–82, that no obligatory rule was then in force to delimit the territorial sea. His conclusion is lent force by the fact that no consensus on limitation could be reached at either the Hague Conference in 1930 (where limits of three, four, and six miles were found to be common among states) or the Geneva Conference in 1958. Whatever vogue a three-mile limit for the territorial sea may have enjoyed prior to 1982, UNCLOS establishes the right of each state to claim a maximum territorial sea of twelve miles. *See* UNCLOS, art. 3, at 3. Some states, including the United States, continue to recognize a three-mile territorial sea at this writing.

73. There is an implicit assumption that if a mariner can fix his position for navigation purposes, he can do so for jurisdictional purposes as well. *See* M. STROHL, *supra*, Chapter II, note 42, at 139–43 for an illuminating discussion of navigational techniques and technological advancements during this period.

the "reasonable discernment" test of Lord Hale, maintained that it was the geographical location of a bay *inter fauces terrae,* literally within the jaws of the land, which justified the inclusion of the bay within the territorial sovereignty of the littoral state. Such a bay, the theory continued, lying as it did within the land mass, was naturally interrelated to the processes of life on shore. Because bays of enormous dimension would not ordinarily share this interrelationship with the land, no more precise limitation was necessary to restrict excessive claims. The normative power of the actual, i.e., the relationship *in fact* of the bay to the land, must logically determine its juridical status.

Several writers of the nineteenth century typified this approach. Azuni, writing in 1805, asserts:

> It is already established among polished [sic] nations that in places *where the land by its curve forms a bay* . . . we must suppose a line to be drawn from one point to the other . . . and that the whole of this bay or gulf is to be considered as territorial sea[74] even though the center may be in some places at a greater distance than 3 miles from either shore.[75]

Creasy, writing near the end of the century in 1876, graphically exemplifies the geographical approach:

> Those portions of the sea, which are *landlocked, and almost enclosed within the territories of a State,* which are *inter fauces terrae* . . . are clearly within the exclusive territorial jurisdiction of the state *whose lands gird them round.* In the case also of bays, or portions of the sea not so completely enclosed, but which *lie within a clear and well-defined concave curve,* the base of which is a line drawn from one promontory or *other excrescence of land*[76] to another, the State whose territories *thus clasp these oceanic waters,* claims and exercises jurisdiction over them.[77]

74. No distinction was made in the early nineteenth century between the juridical nature of "territorial" and "internal" waters. Territorial in this context is used in the sense of "within the territorial jurisdiction of the coastal state." Note, however, that by this time the concept had emerged that a bay could be "closed" by an imaginary line drawn headland to headland (footnote added).

75. D. Azuni, *supra* note 2, §17, at 254 (emphasis added).

76. Presumably, this phrase includes the possibility of islands serving as headlands (footnote added). *See infra,* Chapter IV, at notes 113, 135–136 and accompanying text.

77. E. Creasy, *supra* note 50, at 232–240 (emphasis added).

The same approach is taken by Nuger in 1887, who reflects the growing awareness of a difference between the juridical nature of internal and territorial waters:

> Certain parts of the sea closer to land and *partaking so to speak of its condition* must be considered in a different light. The territorial sea is not of a nature to be owned, while one thinks on the contrary that the *indentations of small extent formed by encroachments of the sea into the land* and known as ports, harbors, roadsteads, and small bays may be possessed by the bordering state.[78]

Calvo reflects the same view in 1896, and adds even more content to the juridical nature of internal waters:

> They [bays] belong of right to the nation inhabiting the adjacent coasts. This ownership, a *natural consequence of the geographical position of States* . . . is sanctioned by international law as indisputable. . . . Sovereign possession . . . gives to nations which enjoy it the right to declare them closed, open, or free, and freely to impose . . . on foreign ships and merchandise such taxes or such internal regulations as it may deem appropriate to its interests.[79]

Many English and American decisions of the period appear to have adopted the theory that the geographical relationship of a bay to the surrounding land mass of a single state should govern its inclusion within national territory.[80]

78. A. NUGER, *supra* note 50, at 190–95 (emphasis added).
79. C. CALVO, *supra* note 3, §366 (emphasis added).
80. *See* Regina v. Cunningham, Ball's C.C. 86 (1859), which declares Bristol Channel to be under exclusive British authority; Direct U.S. Cable Co. v. Anglo-American Telegraph Co., 2 App. Cas. 394 (1877), which declares Conception Bay in Newfoundland to be within national territory; Mowatt v. McFee, 5 S.C.R. 66 (Can. 1880), which holds the Bay of Chaleurs to be within the territory of the Dominion; Stetson v. United States (the Case of the Alleganean), Ct. of Commissioners of Alabama Claims, 4 Moore's Int'l Arbitration 4333, Scott's Cases of Int'l Law, at 143, which holds Chesapeake Bay to be within the territory of the United States. This case relied in part on an earlier opinion by Attorney General Randolph, May 14, 1793, 1 Am. State Pap., For. Rel., at 148, which, relying on the fact that the United States was proprietor of the lands on both sides of the Delaware from its head to its entrance into the sea, declared Delaware Bay to be within U.S. territory. *See also* Dunham v. Lamphere, 69 Mass. (3 Gray) 268 (1855), which, like the foregoing cases, works back to the principle that waters *inter fauces terrae* could be claimed as internal waters of the coastal state. The question of whether or not such a rule might apply regardless of bay size remained ambiguous.

The second group of commentators concerned with bay delimitation agreed with the first that the landlocked character of the bay and the factual interrelationship of bay and land mass provided the fundamental basis for a claim of exclusive authority by the coastal state; but they feared that these factors alone would not provide a sufficient test which would serve to prevent states from laying claim to bays of increasing size, thus endangering freedom of navigation. Members of this group argued that since general agreement had been reached on a more or less precise limit for territorial waters, the rules developed for this delimitation should logically be applied to bays as well. DeCussy, writing in 1856, reflects the concern of many nineteenth century authorities who feared that without precise limits, bays of enormous size would be removed from inclusive use:

> All gulfs and straits cannot belong, throughout their entire extent, to the territorial sea of the State whose coasts they wash. State sovereignty is limited to the range of cannon shot from shore. . . . Beyond this point the center of the gulf or channel is assimilated to the open sea and its use is free to all nations.[81]

The underlying basis for this theory is perhaps best summarized by Phillimore, writing in 1879:

> With respect to bays and gulfs, there seems to be no reason or authority for the limitation suggested by . . . Grotius. . . . The real question is as Gunther says whether the area is within the physical competence of the adjacent nation to exclude other nations.[82]

The same protective view is espoused by many other writers,[83] including Ortolan who states in 1893:

> We must classify under the same heading as roadsteads and ports, gulfs and bays and all other identations. . . . When these identations made in the land of a single state do not exceed in width the double range of cannon or when the entrance may be controlled

---

81. F. DeCussy, *supra* note 50, §41, at 97.
82. R. Phillimore, Commentaries upon International Law §cc.
83. *See* R. Piedelievre, *supra* note 50, §417, at 363; C. Calvo, *supra* note 3, §365; G. Martens, *supra* note 50, at 39.

by artillery or when it is naturally defended by islands, banks, or rocks . . . these identations or bays are within the power of the State which is mistress of the territory which surrounds them.[84]

The problem in applying the cannon shot rule to bays, however, was identical to that which arose in delimiting the territorial sea by cannon shot, i.e., as the force of arms increases so must the limit of state sovereignty.[85] Thus, when more precise linear measurements evolved for the territorial sea,[86] these limits were applied to bays as well, under the theory that state sovereignty should be limited to bays whose width did not exceed twice the distance claimed for the territorial sea. As this distance was often, but not exclusively, set at three miles, it became common to limit the exclusive claims of states to those bays whose openings did not exceed six miles. As Westlake wrote in 1912, "the inner part of a bay belongs to the coastal state if the mouth is no more than six miles across and access can only be gained through territorial waters."[87] Under this conception, if the width of the bay opening exceeded six miles, states were once again limited to a three-mile territorial belt around the shore, leaving the center of the bay free for fishing and navigation.[88] This so-called "2 x 3" rule was espoused by several authorities in the late nineteenth and early twentieth centuries[89] and found its way into several judicial and administrative decisions of the same period.[90]

Another branch of the "precise limitation" school maintained that since distances claimed for the territorial sea varied greatly

84. J. ORTOLAN, *supra* note 50, at 156.
85. Both Cauchy and Martens questioned whether such a limit could become a lasting rule for bay delimitation due to daily improvements in the "formidable art of artillery." *See* 1 E. CAUCHY, *supra* note 3, at 37; Martens, *supra* note 51, at 264.
86. *See supra* notes 58–73 and accompanying text.
87. J. WESTLAKE, *supra* note 50, at 189–191.
88. P. JESSUP, *supra*, Chapter II, note 41, at 356.
89. In particular, *see* T. LAWRENCE, *supra* note 50, §72, at 140; E. VATTEL, *supra*, Chapter I, note 21, §291.
90. *See* Manchester v. Massachusetts, 139 U.S. 240, 258 (1891): "We think it must be regarded as established that, as between nations, the minimum limit of the territorial jurisdiction of a nation over the tide-waters is a marine league [three miles] from its coast; that bays wholly within its territory not exceeding two marine leagues [six miles] in width at the mouth are within this limit." *See also* 169 Parl. Deb. (4th ser.) 989 (1907) (remarks to Commons by a representative of the British Foreign Office indicating that all departments of government then currently applied the six-mile rule for bays).

from state to state, a delimitation criterion should be adopted which in fact had no relation whatever to the territorial sea but which could be accepted by most states as reasonable. This compromise between the exclusive interests of the coastal state and the inclusive interests of the community at large had many advocates,[91] not all of whom agreed on the same arbitrary limit.

John Basset Moore commented upon the reasonableness of adopting a ten-mile limitation:

> Since you observe that there does not appear to be any convincing reason to prefer the ten mile line . . . to that of double three miles, I may say that there have been supposed to exist reasons both of convenience and of safety. The ten mile line has been adopted in the cases referred to . . . as a practical rule. The transgression of an encroachment upon territorial waters by fishing vessels is generally a grave offense, involving in many instances the forfeiture of the offending vessel and it is obvious that the narrower the space in which it is permissible to fish the more likely the offense is to be committed. In order therefore that fishing may be both practicable and safe and not constantly attended with the risk of violating territorial waters, it has been thought . . . expedient not to allow it where the extent of free waters, between the three mile line drawn on each side of the bay, is less than 4 miles. [3 miles + 3 miles + 4 miles = 10 miles.] This is the reason of the ten mile line. Its intention is not to hamper or restrict the right to fish but to render its exercise practicable and safe.[92]

The ten-mile limitation for bays found its way into many treaties, conventions, and the municipal laws of the time.[93] The content of the rule as expressed during this period is typified by Article 2 of the North Sea Fisheries Convention of 1882:

91. *See* H. Bonfils, *supra* note 50, §516; J. Latour, La Mer Territoriale 48 (1889); E. Nys, *supra* note 50, at 443; F. Perels, Manuel de Droit Maritime International 42 (Arendt trans. 1884); 1 A. Rivier, Principes du Droit des Gens 153 (1896).

92. *See* the letter to Mr. Bradley, cited in 13 Annuaire de L'Institut de Droit International 146 (1894–95); P. Jessup, *supra* note 70, at 356.

93. *See* the Anglo-French Fishery Convention of 1839; regulations between the same countries of 1843; the Anglo-French Fishery Conventions of 1859 (unratified) and 1867; and the Anglo-Dutch Fishery Convention of 1901, 5 Hertslet, Treaties and Conventions 89; 6 Hertslet, *supra* at 416; 33 Hertslet, Commercial Treaties 425. *See also* French municipal law of Mar. 1, 1888, regulating fisheries, noted in 18 Hertslet, Commercial Treaties 398.

> The fishermen of each country shall enjoy the right of fishery within a distance of 3 miles from the low water mark along the whole extent of the coasts of their resepctive countries as well as of the dependent islands and banks. . . . As regards bays, the distance of 3 miles shall be measured from a straight line drawn across the bay in the part nearest the entrance at the first point where the width does not exceed 10 miles.[94]

The legislative history of this Convention makes clear, however, that the framers were not attempting to lay down a general rule of international law nor declaring an existing rule in Article 2. Rather, Convention drafters sought only to define the exclusive fishery limits in the North Sea by one of the several bay delimitation rules then in vogue.[95]

Although popular, the ten-mile limit was never universally recognized as a binding rule. The Institute of International Law first attempted to develop a regime of territorial waters during their Lausanne session of 1888. Influenced by the work of many scholars and publicists who had addressed the topic, the Institute attempted to formulate a code reconciling the work of these experts and the practice of states.[96] The Institute met again in Paris in 1894, where a heated debate arose between those members who wished to set a ten-mile closing line for bays and those who supported a twelve-mile limitation, representing a distance of twice the six-mile width adopted for the territorial sea at the Paris session. Those who supported the ten-mile limit argued that the very essence of the rule lay in the fact that a bay-closing line had *no* relationship to the territorial sea. Nonetheless, the Institute adopted the following resolution by a wide majority at the 1894 session:

> For bays, the territorial sea follows the sinuosities of the coast, except that it [the coast] is measured from a straight line drawn across the bay at its narrowest part toward the sea, where the distance between the 2 shores of the bay is 12 marine miles, unless continuous and established usage shall have sanctioned a greater width.[97]

94. *See* 1887 For. Rel. U.S. 439.
95. *See* Proces Verbaux of the Convention, *Parl. Papers*, Commercial No. 24, 1882 (Cd. 3238).
96. M. STROHL, *supra*, Chapter II, note 42, at 195.
97. *See* Article 3, 12 ANNUAIRE DE L'INSTITUT DE DROIT INTERNATIONAL 325, 329 (1894–95).

The International Law Association,[98] meeting in Brussels in 1895, adopted many of the Institute's resolutions in regard to the territorial sea but substituted ten marine miles for the width of bay-closing lines.[99] The same rule was recommended in the Report to the Third Commission of the Second Hague Peace Conference in 1907.[100] One may conclude that by the end of the nineteenth century, many variations on the precise limitation theme had been promulgated with bay-closing lines of six miles, ten miles, and twelve miles recognized as reasonable under international law.

Twentieth-Century Practice

Although earlier writers had made no distinction between the juridical nature of territorial and internal waters and some had in fact denied the right of the coastal state to assume absolute sovereignty over bays,[101] by the early twentieth century a clear juridical distinction had been made between these water areas. Article 3, adopted by the Institute of International Law at its Paris session of 1894[102] unequivocally states that territorial waters are to be measured seaward from a closing line drawn between bay headlands and that landward waters are not to be included within the "territorial" designation. De Lapradelle and others suggested that internal waters might be better classified as "national" seas, expressing the idea that waters which penetrate closely into the land are associated with it in forming the internal boundaries of the state.[103] There was general agreement that coastal states might assume unlimited sovereignty over their bays, whereas their rights in regard to the waters seaward from the coast were best seen as a series of jurisdictional servitudes which gave a coastal state lim-

98. Founded in 1873 as the Association for the Reform and Codification of the Law of Nations, the Association is open to members who, unlike the Institute membership, are not international law experts.
99. The International Law Association, *Report of the Seventeenth Conference*, Brussels, 102 (1896). *See also* Transactions 1873–1924, at 223.
100. J. Scott, *Reports to the Hague Conference of 1899 and 1907*, at 664.
101. Both Carnazza-Amari and Bluntschli maintained that although the exclusive possession of bays is necessary to riparian peoples, no property rights attach to these waters, only the rights of surveillance and jurisdiction. 2 G. CARNAZZA-AMARI, *supra* note 22, §11, at 53; J. BLUNTSCHLI, *supra* note 3, §§309, 310, 322 and 772.
102. *See* 12 ANNUAIRE DE L'INSTITUT DE DROIT INTERNATIONAL 324–29 (1894–95).
103. *See* A. De Lapradelle, *supra* note 50, at 264.

ited powers over fishing, defense, customs, sanitary regulations and other matters, but accorded to foreign states the right of innocent passage.[104]

No such consensus had been reached, however, on the issue of bay delimitation. The doctrinal conflict noted above between "geographical relationship" and "precise limitation" adherents, and indeed among the various permutations of the latter group, continued into the twentieth century and had reached full flower by the time of the North Atlantic Coast Fisheries Arbitration in 1910.

The roots of this Anglo-American controversy may be traced to the economic consequences of the American Revolution. Prior to 1776, American fishermen had enjoyed the right of British subjects to fish the Grand Banks and to dry their catch on the shores of Canada and Newfoundland. One of the major interests of the New England colonies during the treaty negotiations of 1781–1783 lay in retaining these fishing rights as newly independent Americans. The Treaty of Paris of 1783 granted previous rights in full, but the English refused to renew these rights under the treaty ending the War of 1812 unless the United States would grant reciprocal rights to British fishermen in American coastal waters. The United States was unwilling to grant this demand, and by a treaty concluded October 20, 1818, renounced any previously held "liberty" to "take, dry, or cure fish, on or within three marine miles of any of the coasts, bays, creeks or harbours, of his Britannic Majesty's dominions in America. . . . "[105]

The term "bay" was left undefined in the treaty, and this omission became a continuing source of conflict as Americans sought to defy British fishery regulations.[106] After almost 100 years of

104. *See* 1 E. Nys, *supra* note 50, at 441; F. Von Liszt, *supra* note 50, §9, at 86; H. Halleck, *supra* note 50, §13, at 167; E. Vattel, *supra,* Chapter I, note 21, §291; F. Despagnet, *supra* note 50, §402, at 608; J. Westlake, *supra* note 50, at 187. Bonfils preferred to use the term "littoral" or "jurisdictional" for the territorial sea, the latter term expressing more correctly the legal status of those waters as opposed to waters landward from the coast where absolute sovereignty could be claimed. H. Bonfils, *supra* note 50, §491, at 322.

105. *See* Convention with Great Britain, Article I, 8 Stat. 248, 249 (1818); 2 H. Miller, Treaties and Other International Acts of the United States 658 (1930).

106. Three hundred American fishing vessels were seized between 1818 and 1838. M. Strohl, *supra,* Chapter II, note 42, at 165.

economic warfare in adjacent waters, the parties referred the matter to a tribunal selected from the panel of the Permanent Court of Arbitration at the Hague. This tribunal was asked to determine, *inter alia,* how the three-mile fishery limit agreed to by the parties in Article I of the 1818 Convention was to be measured at bays.

Utilizing the geographical relationship theory, Great Britain argued that Article I should be read to exclude American fishermen from all bays, regardless of size. The British contended that the word "bays" had been used in 1818 in its purely geographical sense and that all bodies of water marked on maps as bays were included within the proscription. The three-mile limitation, therefore, should be measured from a line drawn from headland to headland across the entrance of each Canadian bay, whether formally claimed or not.[107]

The position of the United States[108] was that the word "bays" in the 1818 treaty referred only to small indentations similar to creeks or harbors. In the American view, Article I represented no more than a renunciation of a previous right to fish in British territorial waters. Reflecting one of the precise limitation theories extant in 1910, the United States argued that bays more than six miles wide (i.e., twice the three-mile distance claimed for the territorial sea) were not "territorial" and therefore not within the renunciation clause.[109]

After lengthy and detailed presentations by both parties, the majority of the Tribunal seemingly rejected the United States' "precise limitation" position and adopted the geographical relationship theory of bays argued by Great Britain. The Court focused on what in view of all the evidence was in the minds of the negotiators in 1818 and, concluding that all descriptions of the coast were expressed in purely geographical terms, said in part:

107. *Proceedings,* 1 North Atlantic Coast Fisheries Arbitration 94, Senate Doc. No. 870, 61st Cong., 3d Sess. (1909); *See* Special Agreement Between United States and Great Britain Relating to North Atlantic Coast Fisheries, Jan. 27, 1909, 36 Stat. 2141, 2142, T.S. No. 521.

108. Argued by Elihu Root and printed in full in *North Atlantic Coast Fisheries Arbitration at the Hague: Argument on Behalf of the United States by Elihu Root* (R. Bacon & J. Scott eds. 1917).

109. *See North Atlantic Coast Fisheries Case,* Hague Ct. Rep. (Scott) 141, 183.

The tribunal is unable to understand the term 'bays' . . . in other than its geographical sense, by which a bay is to be considered as an indentation of the coast, bearing a configuration of a particular character easy to determine specifically, but difficult to describe generally. . . . [110]

and thus held:

In case of bays the three marine miles are to be measured from a straight line drawn across the body of water at the place where it ceases to have the configuration and characteristics of a bay.[111]

Justifying the exclusion of bays from the general rule of the tidemark, the Tribunal stressed the exclusive interests of states implicated by the location of a bay within the land mass:

[A]dmittedly the geographical character of a bay contains conditions which concern the interests of the territorial sovereign to a more intimate and important extent than do those connected with the open coast. Thus conditions of national and territorial integrity, of defense, of commerce and of industry are all vitally concerned with the control of bays penetrating the national coast line. This interest varies, speaking generally in proportion to the penetration inland of the bay.[112]

The Tribunal also emphasized the importance of delimiting bays in a manner that will not cause confusion to mariners. Again relying on geographic cues, the majority asserted:

[W]here the configuration of the coast and the local climate conditions are such that foreign fishermen when within the geographic headlands might reasonably and *bona fide* believe themselves on the high seas, the limits of exclusion shall be drawn in each case between the headlands hereinafter specified as being those at and within which such fishermen might be reasonably expected to recognize the bay under average conditions.[113]

110. *Id.*, at 187. This now-famous statement by the Tribunal may be roughly translated as "I can't define a bay with precision but I know one when I see one," perhaps a precursor of Justice Potter Stewart's obscenity theory.
111. *Id.*, at 187–88.
112. *Id.*, at 183.
113. *Id.*, at 189.

However, apparently dissatisfied with the vagueness of a purely geographical configuration approach, the Tribunal suggested that in light of the geographical importance of bays to the interests of the coastal state, those interpreting the term "bays" under the treaty might take into account "all the individual circumstances which for any one of the different bays are to be appreciated,"[114] including the relationship of its width to the length of penetration,[115] the possibility and necessity of its being defended,[116] the special value which it has for the industry of the shore inhabitants,[117] the distance which it is secluded from the highways of nations on the open sea,[118] and, reaching the height of ambiguity, "other circumstances not possible to enumerate in general."[119]

Although in theory the Tribunal appears to have adopted the geographical relationship argument advanced by the British, the potpourri of bay delimitation doctrines also alluded to in the opinion could not possibly serve as a reliable guide to future state action. Recognizing that their decision, though perhaps correct in principle, was not entirely satisfactory in terms of its practical applicability, the Tribunal included with its decision, though not a part of it, a series of "recommendations" designed to assist the parties in the actual process of bay delimitation. Having failed to find evidence of specific limitations intended by the parties in 1818,[120] the majority nonetheless felt that the so-called ten-mile limit was representative of the practice of enough states in 1910 to warrant its use as a delimitation *guideline,* if not a rule. After specifically delimiting two groups of bays by name, the Tribunal suggested the following approach for all other bays in dispute:

> In every bay not hereinafter specifically provided for the limits of exclusion shall be drawn three miles seaward from a straight line across the bay in the part nearest the entrance at the first point where the width does not exceed ten miles.[121]

114. *Id.,* at 187.
115. A geographic criterion.
116. A variation of the cannon-shot rule.
117. A precursor of the economic interests theory advanced in the later *Anglo-Norwegian Fisheries Case* and in Geneva Convention negotiations. *See infra,* Chapter IV.
118. Another geographic criterion.
119. *North Atlantic Coast Fisheries Case,* Hague Ct. Rep. (Scott) at 187.
120. *See id.,* at 184.
121. *Id.,* at 188. Note that the wording here is identical to that used in the North Seas Fishery Convention of 1882. *See supra* note 94 and accompanying text.

The Award and Recommendations of the Tribunal were sub-
stantially accepted by the parties and were adopted by treaty, July
20, 1912.[122] The net effect of the *Fisheries* decision was to give
weight to the ten-mile rule, if only in recommendation form,[123]
but to leave unsettled the question of which indentations in fact
possess the "configuration and characteristics of a bay" and to
leave unanswered whether this important question is to be settled
by geographical or mathematical criteria.

Proof that the award failed to provide a reliable guide for
future state action in regard to bays may be found in the variety
of state practice which followed. Because it had been specifically
rejected by the Tribunal, the six-mile limit for bay closing lines
fell into disuse, whereas the use of precise closing line limitations
of ten and twelve miles remained common. The ten-mile rule was
adopted in an Italian law of June 16, 1912, regulating the passage
of merchant vessels,[124] and was reflected in the neutrality proclamations of many states during the Russo-Japanese and First
World wars.[125] In 1913, the Naval War College, noting the necessity to move beyond ancient and anachronistic delimitation measures such as the range of cannon, and being undoubtedly influenced by the codification efforts of the Institute of International
Law in 1894,[126] recommended a six-mile limit for the territorial
sea and a corresponding twelve-mile limit for bay closing lines.[127]
The group of distinguished professors, lawyers, and jurists, organized to propose draft rules for the First League of Nations Con-

---

122. 37 Stat. 1634, T.S. No. 572.
123. Dr. Luis M. Drago dissented vigorously from the majority opinion on the basis of
     his opinion that the award lacked a suitable guiding principle. He argued for the
     inclusion of the ten-mile rule into the body of the Award so that it might obtain the
     force of a binding rule of law. *North Atlantic Coast Fisheries Case*, Hague Ct. Rep.
     (Scott), at 206–07 (Drago, dissenting).
124. H. CROCKER, *supra* note 22, at 603.
125. See for example the Dutch neutrality proclamation issued during the Russo-Japa-
     nese War (1913 U.S. NAV. WAR COL. 37); the Dutch neutrality proclamation of Aug.
     5, 1914 (1916 U.S. NAV. WAR COL. 61, 63); the Uruguayan neutrality proclamation
     of Aug. 4, 1914 (1916 U.S. NAV. WAR COL. 105, 107).
126. *See supra* notes 96–97 and accompanying text.
127. 1913 U.S. NAV. WAR COL. 11. First published in 1901, the Naval War College "Blue
     Books" summarize aspects of international law thought to be of particular interest
     to naval officers. Their twelve-mile recommendation in 1913 was based on the per-
     ception of the twelve-mile limit as a broad principle "coming to be generally rec-
     ognized in regard to maritime jurisdiction in time of war." *Id.*, at 52.

ference on the Codification of International Law, recommended the use of a ten-mile limit.[128] Yet, in spite of serious prescriptive efforts by jurists and informal codification bodies, no precise closing line limitation achieved the status of an obligatory rule of law. In actual practice, most states, on the eve of the Hague Codification Conference of 1930, continued to use the geographic location of a given bay within their land territory as the primary justification for the assertion of sovereignty and agreed to more precise limitations in treaties and conventions only when it served their purposes to do so.

The International Conference for the Codification of International Law, the first official body to address maritime delimitation rules, was called together by the League of Nations and met at The Hague from March 13 to April 12, 1930. Prior to this gathering, the League directed a Committee of Experts to prepare an agenda of international law topics that seemed ripe for codification. After soliciting responses from governments, the Committee concluded that a regime of territorial waters appeared realizable, with codification of the international rules for bays an integral part of that regime.

It was generally recognized that community agreement on three major issues would be necessary in order to develop an international regime for bays:

1. Agreement on claims already made by States to particular bays regardless of size (i.e., historic bays).
2. Agreement on the permissible width of closing lines for those bays not within the reserved class above.
3. Agreement on a method of measurement to determine which indentations justified the use of a water-crossing baseline for the territorial sea.[129]

In answer to the first question, the Committee of Experts recommended the establishment of an Internal Waters Office to serve as a registry for all present and future claims to sovereignty over internal waters. The Committee proposed that all present claims to historic bays be duly registered and honored, but that

128. *See Harvard Law School Research in International Law*, 23 Am. J. Int'l L., at 265–74 (Special Supp. April, 1929).
129. 1 C. Hyde, *supra*, Chapter II, note 32, at 478.

no further historic rights be susceptible of acquisition.[130] The Internal Waters Office concept was eventually abandoned by the Committee, although the general approach to historic waters was approved by most states.[131]

As to the second issue, the original draft article on bay-closing lines developed by the Committee of Experts read as follows:

> In the case of bays which are bordered by the territory of a single state, the territorial sea shall follow the sinuosities of the coast, except that it [the coast] shall be measured from a straight line drawn across the sea, where the distance between the two shores of the bay is *12 marine miles,* unless a greater distance has been established by continuous and immemorial usage.[132]

After heated debate in subcommittee,[133] the original draft was amended to include another precise limitation variant, the ten-mile closing line for bays. In spite of strong support from many states,[134] neither the ten-mile rule nor the twelve-mile rule nor

---

130. M. STROHL, *supra,* Chapter II, note 42, at 203.

131. *See* 2 League of Nations Conference for the Codification of International Law, 39–45 (1930). The U.S. delegation proposed a simplified solution to the problem based on the doctrine of uti possidetis at the time of agreement, i.e., "waters, whether called bays, sounds, straits or by some other name, which have been under the jurisdiction of the coastal state as part of its interior waters, are deemed to continue a part thereof. Charts indicating the line drawn in such cases shall be communicated to the other parties thereto." *See* H. Miller, *The Hague Codification Conference,* 24 AM. J. INT'L L. 674–90 (1936). *See also Report of the Second Committee* (Territorial Sea), M. François, Rapporteur, League of Nations Doc. C. 230. M. 117. (1930), at 5. The question of whether future claims to historic waters might be established was not formally resolved, but was left to customary law. *See supra,* Chapter II, note 46 and accompanying text for current approach to historic inland waters under international law and the domestic law of the United States.

132. *See* Codification Committee Report, at 14 (emphasis added).

133. *See* Report of the Sub-Committee, No. II, Ann. II to Report of the Second Committee, Territorial Sea, League of Nations Doc. C. 230. M. 177. (1930).

134. In support of the ten-mile rule at The Hague, *see* Article 4 of *Draft Convention* drawn up by Dr. Shucking, Rapporteur of the Committee of Experts for the Progressive Codification of International Law, League of Nations Doc. C. 74. M. 39. (1929), at 193; P. JESSUP, *supra,* Chapter II, note 41, at 481; Observations of the Preparatory Committee for the Hague Codification Conference of 1930. League of Nations Bases of Discussion, II, Territorial Waters—C. 74. M. 39. (1929), at 44–45. Denmark replied to Basis of Discussion 6, Point IV(b) (how the breadth of territorial waters in front of bays is to be measured): "Bays not exceeding 10 nautical miles in width at the entrances or having islands more than 10 nautical miles apart at the entrance are considered national waters." 2 League of Nations Conference on the

any other precise limit on closing lines gained the consensus necessary to be adopted as a binding rule of international law.[135]

As to the bay delimitation issue, no other aspect of the baseline delimitation problem has caused as much controversy as the attempt to develop an objective method by which states may determine which indentations will be deemed to constitute internal waters and which will remain territorial and/or open sea.[136] Alluding to the nebulous nature of the test derived from the *North Atlantic Coast Fisheries* decision, S. Whittemore Boggs, Geographer of the U.S. Department of State, declared in 1930:

> There is as yet . . . no established rule by which to determine what bodies of water "have the configuration and characteristics of a bay." It is admitted that when an indentation of the coast is regarded as a *bona fide* bay, it ceases to have the configuration of a bay at its outer headlands.[137]

Codification of International Law 40 (1930). Estonia, France, Japan, and the Netherlands concurred in the ten-mile limit. *Id.*, at 40, 41, 42, 43. Many states did not support a ten-mile restriction, however. Great Britain replied that although in favor of a six-mile limit, she would consider the ten-mile limit embodied in many fishery conventions to which she was a party. However, South Africa, Germany, and Australia supported a six-mile closing line. *Id.*, at 39. Belgium and Finland supported a line equal to two times the territorial sea. *Id.*, at 40–41. Latvia, Poland, and Sweden favored a twelve-mile line. *Id.*, at 43–44. Portugal argued for a closing line equal to three times the territorial sea, *id.*, at 43, and Norway claimed all bays regardless of size whether formed by the mainland or part of the Skjaergard. *Id.*, at 42–43. The U.S. response curiously referred to previous cases declaring large bays such as the Delaware and Chesapeake as American waters. *Id.*, at 40–41. Needless to say, it could not be maintained that the ten-mile rule had become customary in 1930.

135. The variety of opinion among states is referenced in notes 125 and 134 *supra*. Many scholars believe that it is most unfortunate that agreement on a ten-mile closing line could not be reached in 1930. *See, e.g.,* Gihl, *supra*, Chapter I, note 6, at 122–24. When the issue was raised again after World War II, the complement of states had altered drastically, with many newly emergent states as well as the United States in favor of wider state sovereignty over sea and seabed resources. Defenders of freedom of the seas lost ground in Geneva in 1958, and suffered even more serious setbacks within UNCLOS.

136. The problem of baseline determination was well understood at both the Hague and Geneva Conferences. Thirteen of the eighteen bases of discussion drawn up by the Preparatory Committee for the Hague Conference (2 LEAGUE OF NATIONS, ACTS OF THE CONFERENCE FOR THE CODIFICATION OF INTERNATIONAL LAW, BASES OF DISCUSSION, TERRITORIAL WATERS, C. 74. M. 39 (1929), at 35–64) and eleven of thirty-two articles of the Territorial Sea Convention addressed the topic of bay delimitation.

137. Boggs, 5 *Delimitation of the Territorial Sea: The Method of Delimitation Proposed by the Delegation of the United States at the Hague Conference for the Codification of International Law*, 24 AM. J. INT'L L. 541, 549 (1930).

Once again at The Hague, conflict arose between those delegates who believed that a bay determination was best founded on
geographical criteria alone and those who believed that a precise
limitation formula was necessary to insure that coastal states
could not validly claim mere curvatures of the coast or bays of
excessive width at the entrance as internal waters. The geographical approach was typified by the British who, during preparatory
work for The Hague Conference in 1930, expressed the view that
for a bay to constitute a part of the baseline for the territorial
sea, it must be "something more pronounced than a mere curvature of the coast. There must be a distinct and well-defined
inlet, moderate in size and long in proportion to its width."[138]

A vastly different approach was taken by the French and American delegations who proposed highly technical delimitation
methods. Boggs, chief of the U.S. delegation at The Hague, presented the U.S. proposal and asserted that it represented an
attempt to set forth a body of rules both simple in application and
definite in result.[139] Boggs argued that since states cannot choose
their coasts but must take them as they find them, the limit of the
territorial sea must be a line derived from the coastline in an
automatic manner except where special configurations or existing agreements justify an exception.[140] In response to the special
situation created by the presence of bays, the United States
argued that the Conference should avoid defining a bay in vague
geographical (i.e., subjective) terms, and instead determine the
question of when the size of an indentation is sufficiently great to
warrant its inclusion within national waters on a purely geometric
(hence objective) basis.

To this end, the United States proposed the "envelope of the
arcs of circles" method, which mandated the following
procedure:

1. Draw a line across the opening of the bay or within the bay at
   a point which is equal to ten miles.

138. 2 League of Nations, Conference for the Codification of International Law 41
     (1930). The British adopted the same approach before the I.C.J. in the *Anglo-Nor-
     wegian Fisheries Case*, to wit: "a bay for this purpose is any well-marked indentation
     of the coast whose penetration inland bears a reasonable proportion to the width of
     its mouth."
139. Boggs, *supra* note 137, at 541.
140. *Id.*

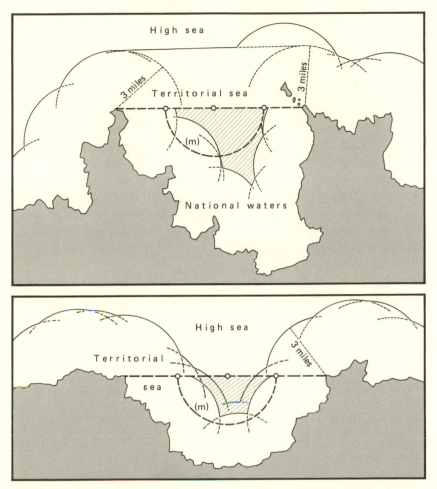

High sea

3 miles

Territorial sea

3 miles

(m)

National waters

High sea

Territorial

3 miles

sea

(m)

Figure 1. The Boggs Method presented at the Hague Codification Conference, 1930.

2. Take one-fourth of the length of that line and throw arcs of that length from all points along the sinuosities of the coast-line, thus creating an "envelope" of waters within the bay. (See Figure 1.)

3. Compare the water area *not* included within the envelope with the area enclosed by a semicircle drawn on a line one-half the length of the closing line.

4. If the area of water not included in the envelope exceeds the area of the semicircle, it may be classified as a bay and

enclosed as internal waters. If not, then use the line of arcs
around the shoreline of the bay as the limit of the territorial
sea.

Figure 1 is the graphic representation of the envelope of the
arcs of circles method proposed by the United States:[141]

Boggs maintained that the envelopes method would simplify
and objectify delimitation procedures and provide a foolproof
way for navigators to determine the limits of territorial waters,
thus obviating the need to indicate such boundaries on charts or
to define them in "sailing directions" or "pilot books."[142] Despite
these and other advantages cited and recognized by many delegates as deriving from a more objective delimitation approach,
neither the U.S. proposal nor the French proposal[143] could command a consensus at The Hague.

Thus, the three basic issues upon which agreement was necessary in order to codify the international rules related to bays were
left unresolved in 1930: historic bay claims remained, then as
now, amorphously circumscribed; no consensus had been
reached on a precise limit for bay closing lines; and no objective
method had been accepted by which it could be determined that
an indentation merited the juridical status of internal waters.
Because of this failure to reach consensus on central issues, the
rigorous efforts at codification put forward at The Hague did not
result in an international regime for bays but merely laid a foundation for the consensus ultimately achieved in Geneva.

141. Unless otherwise noted, all drawings have been rendered by Lawrence C. Olin,
     B.C.E. In this case, the rendering is reproduced from Boggs, *supra* note 137, at 547.
142. This is a time-consuming and complicated task not completed to this day. *Id.*, at 555.
     Another advantage of the envelopes method was that delimitors only had to measure
     a small water area, uncomplicated by subsidiary bays and adjoining rivers. *See infra*,
     Chapter IV, text accompanying note 67. The major disadvantage of the proposed
     method, aside from its highly technical appearance, was that it tended to generalize
     the shape and area of the bay, and it was feared that this might affect bay determi-
     nations. In order to determine the effect of the U.S. proposal on existing bay claims,
     several countries submitted their coastal charts for analysis during the conference.
     It was determined that application of the envelopes method would result in identical
     bay claims in some cases and negligible differences in others. Boggs, *supra* note 137,
     at 554.
143. The French proposal was similar in approach but not identical to that proposed by
     the United States. *See* M. STROHL, *supra*, Chapter II, note 42, at 213.

Nor were courts and tribunals better able to determine applicable rules of international law in the interim. The conflict between the geographical relationship and precise limitation proponents continued unabated, with the Court in the *Anglo-Norwegian Fisheries Case* holding as late as 1951:

> Although the ten-mile rule has been adopted by certain states both in their national law and in their treaties and conventions, and although certain arbitral decisions have applied it as between states, other states have adopted a different limit. Consequently the ten-mile rule has not acquired the authority of a general rule of international law.[144]

The Court declared further that "geographic realities"[145] must dictate whether or not a sea area is sufficiently closely linked to the mainland to be subject to the regime of internal waters, thereby offering little more assistance in the matter than had the North Atlantic Coast Fisheries Tribunal in their ambiguous 1910 decision.

This doctrinal conflict was not resolved until states again addressed the issue in Geneva in 1958[146] and agreed that the geographical relationship test alone with its heavy reliance on the intimate relationship of the bay to the social processes of the surrounding land mass was too open-ended to prevent ever-widening claims to internal waters in response to technological advancement. In order to accommodate the exclusive interests of coastal states with the inclusive interests of the community at large, an international regime for bay determination and delimitation was at last approved, which in essence grants presumptive juridical status to a bay of a given geographic and geometric configuration that is no more than twenty-four miles wide at its entrance. In order to justify a claim to a bay which exceeds this

144. Anglo-Norwegian Fisheries Case (U.K. v. Nor.) 1951 I.C.J. 116, 131.
145. *Id.*, at 128.
146. There is some evidence to suggest that, at best, only a reluctant compromise was reached between the "geographic reality" and "precise limitation" theorists in Geneva, and that in fact controversy continues to brew between those experts who maintain that the semicircle rule adopted in Article 7 is unnecessary if states will fully enforce the landlocked requirement, and others who maintain as forcefully that the semicircle rule has rendered the geographical requirements of Article 7, section 2, mere anachronisms. *See infra,* Chapter IV, text accompanying notes 46, 57.

twenty-four-mile statutory cap, a state may argue on the basis of the intimate geographical relationship of the waters to the surrounding land mass but must prove continuous historic usage with the acquiescence of foreign states.

Summary

On the basis of historical evidence, it may be concluded that bays have from earliest times been recognized as so intimately connected to the social, economic, and security interests of the coastal state that they by right may be claimed as part of the land territory which encloses them. The geographical reality of their existence within the land mass of states has primarily dictated the scope of such claims. As technological advancement has rendered wider claims both possible and profitable, efforts have been made to limit state sovereignty over bays by more objective criteria, often analogized from theories devised to restrict claims to waters beyond the territorial margin. In our century, a compromise has been struck between those who espouse wider sovereignty over the seas and those who purport to support free, inclusive use of the oceans. In the case of bays, this compromise is embodied in Article 7 of the Geneva Convention on the Territorial Sea and the Contiguous Zone, which sets forth an international regime for the designation and delimitation of a juridical bay.

IV

Textual and Contextual Analysis of Article 7

Article 7 of the 1958 Geneva Convention on the Territorial Sea and the Contiguous Zone[1] provides a self-executing, mandatory procedure for the designation and delimitation of a juridical bay. As contrasted with other geographical indentations or irregularities, a juridical bay is a coastal indentation, the location, size, configuration, and use of which warrant its inclusion within the internal waters, and hence the exclusive authority, of the coastal state under the rules prescribed by Article 7.[2] To fully understand Article 7, it is necessary to place it within the context of the Territorial Sea Convention as a whole.

Having firmly established, in Articles 1 and 2, the sovereignty

---

1. *See supra,* Chapter I, note 14 [hereinafter cited without cross reference as the Territorial Sea Convention]. *See supra,* Chapter I, note 19 for discussion of the relationship between the 1958 Geneva Conventions and the recently-concluded United Nations Convention on the Law of the Sea (UNCLOS).
2. Because Article 7 establishes a legal construct and does not attempt to define a bay in its purely geographical sense, it follows that an indentation having been historically labeled a "bay" has little bearing on whether or not it will be deemed a juridical bay under Article 7. Enormous identations such as Hudson Bay in Canada will most certainly fail to meet Article 7 criteria. P. BEAZLEY, *supra,* Chapter I, note 24, §6.2, at 12.

of a state over its land territory, its internal waters, and the belt of sea adjacent to its coast known as the territorial sea, including the seabed, subsoil, and superjacent airspace thereof, the Territorial Sea Convention establishes, in Articles 3 through 13, procedures for the delimitation of the baseline of the territorial sea. Article 3 sets out the normal method of baseline delimitation:

> Except where otherwise provided in these articles, the normal baseline for measuring the breadth of the territorial sea is the low-water line along the coast as marked on large-scale charts officially recognized by the coastal State.[3]

Article 5 provides that waters on the *landward* side of the baseline of the territorial sea form part of the internal waters of the state, and Article 6 establishes the *seaward* limit of the territorial sea as that line every point of which is at a distance from the nearest point of the baseline equal to the breadth of the territorial sea claimed by that state.[4]

If all coasts were composed of regular geographical features, Articles 3, 5, and 6 read together would provide the only framework necessary for baseline delimitation, restricting each state to a belt of territorial waters following the sinuosities of its coastline. Coastal reality, however, displays a wide variance from the normal, and such natural and artificial irregularities as rivers, indentations, rocks, coastal islands, harbor works, ports, and buoys regularly appear.[5] The world community has traditionally made allowances for special circumstances;[6] and Articles 4 through 13 of the Territorial Sea Convention represent lex speciali which treat coastal irregularities as exceptions to the normal baseline

---

3. Territorial Sea Convention, Article 3. The language of Article 3 is virtually identical to that embodied in UNCLOS, Article 5, where the only change has been the replacement of the words "these articles" with "this Convention."
4. This delimitation system is unchanged by UNCLOS except that every state is given the right to establish a territorial sea not exceeding twelve nautical miles in breadth. UNCLOS, Article 3, at 3.
5. M. MCDOUGAL & W. BURKE, *supra*, Chapter II, note 8, at 307. See the *Anglo-Norwegian Fisheries Case, Annexes, Maps*, for an excellent illustration of the complexity of coastal configurations.
6. *See* R. HODGSON & L. ALEXANDER, TOWARDS AN OBJECTIVE ANALYSIS OF SPECIAL CIRCUMSTANCES 1 (1972).

rule of Article 3.[7] Even with delimitation rules designed to cover complex coastal configurations, however, the establishment of a baseline in cases of special circumstances can be very problematic.

The basic rationale for claims arising under one of the "exceptions" articles is not to extend the territorial sea of the coastal state,[8] but rather to include within the internal waters of the state areas of the sea which are closely dependent upon and which intensely affect the land regime. It has become increasingly clear to maritime nations that, inasmuch as the highest degree of state sovereignty can be exercised in these inland water areas, it is within their national security and economic interests to increase the area of such waters if possible. In virtually every instance, an artificial baseline must be provided to "close" these special waters. Resetting a baseline seaward in this fashion accomplishes a dual purpose: (1) additional sea areas come within the exclusive authority of the coastal state, and (2) the seaward limit of all sea zones is extended proportionately, thus extending a state's jurisdiction over additional areas of high seas.[9]

Within this context, Article 7 can best be understood as a lex specialis which sets forth a mandatory procedure to be used in the determination of the existence of a juridical bay and in the delimitation of its baseline. Article 7 is designed to make more explicit the customary international practice of allowing a coastal state reasonable sovereignty over sea areas closely related to the land, while at the same time preserving maximum areas of high seas to community use.

The text of Article 7 reads:

---

7. *See* Territorial Sea Convention, Article 4 (the straight baseline rule for deeply indented coastlines); Article 7 (bays); Article 8 (harbor works); Article 9 (roadsteads); Article 10 (islands); Article 11 (low tide elevations); Article 13 (rivers). UNCLOS, Article 6, has added special delimitation rules for reefs.

8. This can much more easily be accomplished by extending the *breadth* of the territorial sea, as many states have done. R. HODGSON & L. ALEXANDER, *supra* note 6, at 2.

9. Since such attempts intrude upon the fundamental community policy favoring freedom of the seas, resistance to many such attempts is predictable. The hand of an expert is usually required to draw an equitable baseline which can survive the attacks of foreign states. Pearcy, *supra*, Chapter II, note 6, at 5–6. As noted, *supra*, Chapter II, note 10, the "fundamental policy" favoring freedom of the seas has been diluted under UNCLOS.

1. This article relates only to bays the coasts of which belong to a single State.
2. For the purpose of these articles, a bay is a well-marked indentation whose penetration is in such proportion to the width of its mouth as to contain landlocked waters and constitute more than a mere curvature of the coast. An indentation shall not, however, be regarded as a bay unless its area is as large as, or larger than, that of the semi-circle whose diameter is a line drawn across the mouth of that indentation.
3. For the purpose of measurement, the area of an indentation is that lying between the low-water mark around the shore of the indentation and a line joining the low-water marks of its natural entrance points. Where, because of the presence of islands, an indentation has more than one mouth, the semi-circle shall be drawn on a line as long as the sum total of the lengths of the lines across the different mouths. Islands within an indentation shall be included as if they were part of the water area of the indentation.
4. If the distance between the low-water marks of the natural entrance points of a bay does not exceed twenty-four miles, a closing line may be drawn between these two low-water marks, and the waters enclosed thereby shall be considered as internal waters.
5. Where the distance between the low-water marks of the natural entrance points of a bay exceeds twenty-four miles, a straight baseline of twenty-four miles shall be drawn within the bay in such a manner as to enclose the maximum area of water that is possible with a line of that length.
6. The foregoing provisions shall not apply to so-called "historic" bays, or in any case where the straight baseline system provided for in article 4 is applied.[10]

Paragraph One: The Scope of Article 7

Article 7 sets out two limitations[11] on its overal applicability. The first is embodied in paragraph one which codifies the customary

---

10. Territorial Sea Convention, Article 7. The text of Article 7 was left virtually intact in Article 10 of UNCLOS. *See supra,* Chapter I, note 19. The only change is the insertion of the word "nautical" to clarify any reference to "miles" in subsections 4 and 5. *See* UNCLOS, Article 10, at 5.
11. The second limitation is embodied in paragraph 6, which is discussed separately in this section.

rule in international law that an exception from the low-water baseline norm will only be made for bays the coasts of which belong to a single state. This statement is unequivocal[12] and is necessary in to order to prevent large bodies of water such as the Mediterranean or Baltic seas from technically becoming juridical bays under Article 7.[13]

Paragraph Two: Bay Designation

In preparing this important paragraph, the International Law Commission and its Committee of Experts strove to add substantive content and mathematical objectivity to the definition of a juridical bay. The paragraph can best be understood in two parts: (1) the first sentence sets out the *geographical* criteria which must be met in order to enclose an indentation as a juridical bay; (2) the second sentence contains a *mathematical* formula to be used as a check to be sure that the geographical requirements are met and to define with more certainty those indentations which are truly inland and not mere curvatures of the coast.

Before turning to the actual language of the paragraph, a preliminary point must be made. Water areas may be classified in several different ways, two of the most important classifications for these purposes being juridical and geographical. From the purely geographical point of view, there exist only two types of waters: those enclosed within the land, and thus "inland" or "internal," and those lying without the land and thus, in the geo-

---

12. One judicial exception to this rule is the Gulf of Fonesca which was adjudged by the Central American Court of Justice to be under the co-ownership of El Salvador, Nicaragua, and Honduras as successor states to the Crown of Castile, P. BEAZLEY, *supra*, Chapter I, note 24, at 10 n. 3.

13. There is no regime under international law for bays which lie within the littoral of two or more states. Although states may in such circumstances use Article 7 to formulate their boundary agreements, there is no requirement that the regime established must conform to Article 7 in any way. M. STROHL, *supra*, Chapter II, note 42, at 55. Even by agreement, bordering states which share access to a bay cannot close off these waters to deny access to foreign states. Fitzmaurice, *Some Results of the Geneva Conference on the Law of the Sea*, 8 INT'L & COMP. L. Q. 78, 82–83 (1959). A specific proposal made by the Chairman of the ILC, contemplating the Gulf of Fonesca situation (*see supra* note 12) to the effect that in the case of bays whose coasts were shared by more than one state, those states might by agreement consider waters within a joint closing line as internal waters, was specifically rejected by the ILC in prepartory work for the Convention. [1956] 1 Y.B. INT'L L. COMM'N 192, para. 59.

graphic sense, "open" seas. Juridically, however, these two natural classifications have been further subdivided into internal
waters, the territorial sea, the contiguous zone, and so on, until
we reach the high seas,[14] each classification implying significant
differences in coastal authority and control. The territorial sea,
the contiguous zone, the high seas, and the newly conceived
exclusive economic zone, are purely juridical concepts, derived
not from natural geographic boundaries but rather from man-
imposed regimes. Delimitation of these zones, therefore, may be
done in a rather arbitrary fashion, based solely on those distances
from the shore which the world community currently considers
as necessary to regulate coastal passage, to enforce pollution, customs, and sanitary regulations, and to protect and exploit
national resources.

"Internal waters," however, is a term which is at once both
geographical *and* juridical, with the consequence that any attempt
to design a juridical regime for bays under international law must
of necessity be highly dependent upon the actual geographical
relationship of the waters to the land. It is the bay's existence
locked within the land mass which distinguishes it from a mere
curvature of the coast and leads to the juridical determination
that within a bay there exists no right of passage for foreign vessels, the most important distinction between internal waters and
the territorial sea.[15] It is this intimate interrelationship of the bay
with the processes of life on shore that determines whether it may
be legally assimilated to the land. It is important, therefore, while
analyzing the technical formulae imposed by Article 7, to retain
this overview: international rules concerning bays are not linked
to the name or concept of a bay[16] but to the bay's character as
internal waters in the geographical sense. It is the landlocked

---

14. Torsten Gihl suggests the use of a different juridical label for open or high seas, i.e.,
"free seas," which would more clearly reflect its status under the law. Gihl, *supra*,
Chapter I, note 6, at 136–137. *See* Chapter II for discussion of the various maritime
zones recognized under both the Geneva Conventions and UNCLOS, and the exclusive and inclusive competences honored therein.

15. Gihl, *supra*, Chapter I, note 6, at 138–139.

16. Explorers have often applied the term "bay" to parts of coasts which were merely
gentle curvatures. This was likely due to the fact that the name was given by an individual unfamiliar with the strict geographical meaning of the term or that the word
in the namer's language included such curvatures. *See* M. Strohl, *supra*, Chapter II,
note 42, at 55.

character of the bay which justifies extending the exclusive authority of the land regime to its governance.[17]

The obvious consequence of the foregoing for international law purposes is that an area of water must fulfill certain geographical criteria in order to be considered a bay, with all the juridical consequences that flow from that determination. For that reason, the Convention places the geographical considerations in the first sentence of paragraph two, without any limitation as to bay size. If a body of water fails to meet the geographical criteria which identify it as internal waters, there is absolutely no need to move further in Article 7.

Paragraph Two, Sentence One: Geographical Criteria

The first sentence of paragraph two contains two separate geographical criteria, which may or may not be related. First, it is specified that a bay must be a *well-marked indentation.* Secondly, it is required that the depth [18] of the penetration must be in such proportion to the width of the mouth as to contain *landlocked waters,* not a *mere curvature of the coast.*

The well-marked indentation requirement has received scant attention from scholars and judicial bodies. If the language is treated at all, it is usually merged into the landlocked waters requirement or referred to as the opposite of a mere curvature of the coast.[19] The legislative history is silent on the point as well.[20]

---

17. Gihl, *supra,* Chapter I, note 6, at 144.
18. Depth here refers to the extent of a bay's intrusion into the land, not the depth of the water. From the language of the Convention and the earlier *Report of the Committee of Experts* (U.N. Doc. A/CN. 4/61/Add. 1, 18 May 1953: International Law Commission Fifth Session, Addendum to *Second Report of the Regime of the Territorial Sea* by J. P. A. François, Special Rapporteur) [hereinafter cited as *Report of the Committee of Experts* (1953)], it seems clear that bays are two-dimensional phenomena. The depth of the water contained within the bay is irrelevant, as is its navigability, R. HODGSON & L. ALEXANDER, *supra* note 6, at 3, except as to the issue of whether or not the waters of an indentation are truly landlocked. That is to say, if the waters are very shallow or to some extent unnavigable, they are unlikely to support international maritime traffic and more likely to be related to the land regime.
19. *See* P. BEAZLEY, *supra,* Chapter I, note 24, at 12; R. HODGSON & L. ALEXANDER, *supra* note 6, at 4–8; 1 A. SHALOWITZ, *supra,* Chapter I, note 20, at 218–19; M. STROHL, *supra,* Chapter II, note 42, at 55–56.
20. Although the Report of the Committee of Experts and the International Law Commission's draft articles of Article 7 in 1953 and 1954 take a purely mathematical approach to bay definition, i.e., "a bay is a bay in the juridical sense if its area is as

Yet, one must assume that the drafters chose their language with care. They did not require a "well-defined" indentation or a "significant" or a "pronounced" one. They required a "well-marked" indentation. To properly interpret this phrase, it is necessary to understand the function of section II of the *Convention,* as well as the place of Article 7 within the whole.

Section II of the Territorial Sea Convention, in which Articles 3 through 13 appear, is entitled: *Limits of the Territorial Sea.* The purposes served by these limitation articles are identical to the major purposes of the law of the sea as a whole, i.e., to define the rights of parties, to reduce the likelihood of conflict, to equitably allocate ocean space and resources, and to define baselines with enough precision that those actually moving on the sea may know with some certainty whether they are within another state's jurisdiction or on the high seas.

In some cases, charts exist which assist the mariner in making these discriminations. Article 3, which sets forth the normal baseline rules, requires that the territorial sea be measured from the low-water line "as marked on large-scale charts officially recognized by the coastal State." Article 4, which sets forth a straight baseline system for deeply indented coasts or those fringed with islands, requires the coastal state to indicate these baselines clearly on charts and to publicize them. However, even these publication requirements fail to take note of various reality problems which exist in regard to charts. First, not all states have officially adopted large scale charts of their own. In addition, many of the

---

large as, or larger than that of a semi-circle drawn on the entrance to that bay" (*see* U.N. Doc. A/CN. 4/61 Add. 1; U.N. Doc. A/3159, at 3; U.N. Doc. A/CN. 4/77, at 10), later replies by governments indicated some desire to retain the more familiar geographical norms (*see supra* Chapter III, notes 74–100 and accompanying text). Thus, the 1955 draft article of Article 7 reflects a compromise approach, i.e., "For the purpose of these regulations, a bay is a well-marked indentation whose penetration inland is in such proportion to the width of its mouth as to contain landlocked waters and constitute more than a mere curvature of the coast. An indentation shall not, however, be regarded as a bay unless its area is as large as, or larger than that of a semi-circle drawn on the entrance of that indentation." This language was adopted by the International Law Commission at its seventh session in 1955, without any explanation in the Commentary for the shift in approach. (*See* U.N. 6.A.O. Rec. 10th Session, supp. to 9 A/2934, at 17.) This version of bay definition was modified slightly (*see* full text of Article 7, *supra,* accompanying note 10) and eventually adopted as Article 7 (2) of the *Territorial Sea Convention.*

so-called official charts of major maritime states have used different tidal levels for delimiting coastal baselines.[21] Charts may be based on several different types of projections as well. In fact, for the vast majority of the world's coasts, few reliable charts exist. This creates a major problem for mariners who, lacking precise knowledge of normal baselines and special closing lines, may violate the territorial waters or, far worse, the internal waters of a foreign state.

This problem is even more acute in regard to coastal indentations because Article 7 has promulgated *no* charting or publication requirement for bay closing lines.[22] Thus, even if a reliable chart does exist for a particular section of coast line, it is quite possible that the closing lines of bays will not be recorded thereon. It is within this context that the well-marked requirement obtains relevance, for a correct interpretation would seem to require a second inquiry, i.e., "well marked *to whom?*" Clearly, an indentation should be well marked in such a way that a mariner, approaching the indentation from the sea and equipped with charts which may hold no clue as to the official boundary line, may yet perceive the indentation as clearly lying within the boundaries of the coastal state and therefore not subject to his passage.

What, then, "marks" an indentation so that a mariner may avoid illegal entry? Early mariners made such discriminations visually; and some may suggest that because a twenty-four-mile bay entrance is no longer visually comprehensible from the sea, the well-marked requirement has no continuing relevance. But, of course, a mariner could not *visually* comprehend the limits of a ten-mile entrance or a twelve-mile entrance or any other entrance limit in use at the time Article 7 was adopted. In fact, the use of coastal charts and improved navigational instruments had replaced purely visual identification methods for at least 100 years, while states and scholars still spoke in terms of distinct or

21. In some areas such as the United Kingdom and the U.S. Pacific Coast, *low* low-water is indicated on hydrographic charts. In other areas, such as the U.S. Atlantic and Gulf Coasts, *mean* low-water is the criterion for recording soundings. Similar variations exist worldwide. Pearcy, *supra,* Chapter II, note 6, at 6.
22. There is a charting and publication requirement for bays under UNCLOS, Art. 16. However, UNCLOS is not yet in force, and states have not in general complied with the obligation to deposit such charts with the U.N. Secretary General at this writing.

well-defined or clearly identifiable indentations.[23] It is highly
unlikely, therefore, that the drafters were thinking in purely
visual terms when they imposed the well-marked requirement
along with a twenty-four-mile cap on bay entrances.

Others suggest that because several hydrographers, including
Boggs, Beazley, and Alexander, took an active role in the drafting
process, the term "well-marked" must, therefore, have been used
in the familiar hydrographic sense of being conspicuously marked
with a lighthouse, entranceway, or other navigational aid. To read
this highly specific denotation into the Convention would, of
course, mean that any coastal indentation without such a navigational signal could not obtain juridical bay status under Article
7. When one reflects on the enormous number of coastal indentations worldwide which may have little if any commercial significance and, therefore, in all likelihood are not so marked, one
may only conclude that such a meaning could not have been
intended by the drafters, certainly not without further express
notification to states.

It has also been suggested that the well-marked requirement
has been reduced to an anachronism altogether by the reality of
modern navigation which has made inadvertent entry into the
internal waters of a coastal state virtually impossible. Today's
mariner, the argument proceeds, approaches a given section of
coastline with highly sophisticated instrumentation and detailed
sailing directions from many sources, and is in constant radio
contact with his shore agent who may provide him with the most
up-to-date restrictions. This characterization is no doubt accurate
if one limits the application of Article 7 to those significant commercial harbors for which detailed instructions exist or to those
vessels which are equipped with the most sophisticated instruments and are assisted by on-shore personnel. Many, and perhaps
most, ships worldwide are not so equipped and assisted, however,
and even those which are must occasionally find themselves in

---

23. *See e.g.,* E. CREASY, *supra,* Chapter III, note 50, at 232–240. *See also* the view of the
United Kingdom, expressed during the preparatory work at The Hague, that a bay
must be "a distinct and well-defined inlet . . . ," 2 LEAGUE OF NATIONS, CONFERENCE
FOR THE CODIFICATION OF INTERNATIONAL LAW 41 (1930). *See also* the British pleadings
in the *Anglo-Norweigian Fisheries* case, which state that " . . . a bay for this purpose is
any well-marked indentation in the coast . . . ," (U.K. v. Nor.), (1951) I.C.J. Pleadings.

areas of the world for which few reliable charts, let alone sailing directions, exist. The well-marked requirement retains relevance in just such circumstances as these.

The reality of life upon the sea is such that a given mariner, regardless of the sophistication of his navigational equipment, must determine his position while approaching a particular section of coastline and must then transfer this information to his coastal chart.[24] When an indentation appears, it must be identified. If the sailing directions reveal the limits of coastal authority, or if those limits are marked with a buoy, light, or other navigational aid, so much the better. In the absence of any such external assistance, however, the mariner must rely on the two-dimensional configuration of the indentation on his chart; and it must be *geographically obvious* to the mariner that internal waters are likely to be enclosed, even if no official boundary line has been recorded by the coastal state, if he is to avoid illegal entry. It is this quality of geographical obviousness, i.e., the existence of a coastal indentation lying behind identifiable entrance points and having the general configuration of a bay, which is sufficient to put the mariner on notice and which, at last, lends content to the well-marked requirement of paragraph two, sentence one.

The second geographical criterion of paragraph two, sentence one, requires that the penetration of the indentation lie in such proportion to the width of its mouth as to contain *landlocked waters* and not constitute a mere curvature of the coast. The term "landlocked" by itself is lacking in precise meaning, but the clause read as a whole does effectuate the traditional community policy favoring exclusive state control over waters which are so closely related to the land, its interests, and the enjoyment of its peoples and so separated from major navigational routes due to their geographical location inland as to be more like the land than the open sea.

Several scholars have reflected on the correct interpretation of the term "landlocked." Commander Beazley maintains that to a seaman, the term implies that there shall be land in all but one direction and that the land shall be close enough to all points to provide the mariner with shelter. He states that a bay with a

---

24. *See* M. STROHL, *supra*, Chapter II, note 42, at 31–47 for an excellent discussion of navigation problems and techniques.

twenty-four-mile entrance has already exceeded the sort of distances that would be considered small enough to provide such shelter, and implies that as a consequence, the term "landlocked" is something of an anachronism.[25]

Beazley cites no authority for the shelter component which he reads into landlocked, although, as is documented above in Chapter III, ports, harbors, and the bays and rivers which enclosed them were historically perceived as places of refuge or shelter from the threats of nature and predation. Hodgson and Alexander are more excessive, however, when they maintain that "the bay, in a practical sense, must be *usefully sheltered* and *isolated* from the sea. *Isolation or detachment from the sea* must be considered the key factor."[26] "Usefully sheltered" is a term without precedent in international prescription, and the phrase "isolation and detachment from the sea" seems to prove too much. Historically, as noted, states have tended to view these waters as essentially inland and separate from major maritime traffic, but it is difficult to conceive of a bay as isolated or detached from the sea when by its very nature it is open to the sea on perhaps its longest axis and provides the coastal inhabitants with their major access *to* the sea. Hodgson and Alexander seem more in keeping with the language and intent of this section when they read the landlocked requirement to mean that "[b]asically the character of the bay must lead to its being perceived as part of the land rather than of the sea."[27]

Strohl[28] has suggested that the term "landlocked" is hard to reconcile with the shape of most of the water bodies which would otherwise qualify as juridical bays. Relying on a definition credited to Renee de Kerchove,[29] Strohl contends that landlocked technically means "surrounded by land." Reading this restrictive definition into the landlocked requirement would mean that to be truly landlocked, a bay would have to be entered from the sea through a narrow access channel, a configuration shared by only

25. P. BEAZLEY, *supra,* Chapter I, note 24, §6.5, at 13.
26. R. HODGSON & L. ALEXANDER, *supra* note 6, at 8 (emphasis added).
27. *Id.,* at 8.
28. M. STROHL, *supra,* Chapter II, note 42, at 56.
29. R. KERCHOVE, INTERNATIONAL MARITIME DICTIONARY 396 (1948).

a handful of bays worldwide.[30] Strohl concludes that with so few concrete examples, a strict construction of the landlocked requirement would severely reduce the general applicability of Article 7, which could not have been the intent of the drafters. It might be argued further that such a restricted configuration is more appropriately called an inland sea[31] than a bay; and although such a water area would certainly fall within a state's internal waters, it is not what has been perceived historically as a coastal indentation, which by definition has open access to the sea on one side. One must conclude that there is no basis for such a restrictive definition within the actual language of paragraph two, sentence one.

Strohl maintains that the interpretation of "landlocked" which best serves the intent of the rule, and which would result in reasonably wide community use, would require the depth of the bay from the closing line to the furthest penetration point to be equal to or exceed the width of the mouth, thus producing an indentation which of necessity would be landlocked on three sides.[32] This construction escapes plausibility, however, for several reasons. First, on the basis of logic and geometry alone, a minimum width-depth ratio of 1:1 is neither the only nor even the minimum proportion which will produce waters surrounded on three "sides" by land.[33] Secondly, several earlier attempts to define landlocked in relation to a precise width-depth ratio were expressly rejected by The Hague Codification Conference, by the International Court of Justice, and most relevant, by the International Law Commission in the process of drafting the landlocked requirement;[34] and therefore, such a construction could not have been intended by the drafters of Article 7.

30. Purvis Bay in the British Solomon Islands, the Gulf of Corinth in Greece, Trondheimfjord in Norway, Galveston Bay in Texas, the North Gulf of Evvoia in Greece, Port Philip Bay in Australia, Lake Maracaibo in Venezuela, and Hudson Bay in Canada fall within this restrictive interpretation. M. STROHL, *supra*, Chapter II, note 42, at 56.

31. *See* UNCLOS, Article 122, at 48 for the definition of an enclosed or semi-enclosed sea.

32. M. STROHL, *supra*, Chapter II, note 42, at 56–57.

33. *See, e.g.,* map of Monterey Bay, California *infra* Figure 2.

34. In its reply to the request for information made by the Preparatory Committee for the 1930 Codification Conference at The Hague, the United Kingdom proposed that definitionally, a bay "must be a distinct and well-defined inlet, moderate in size, and

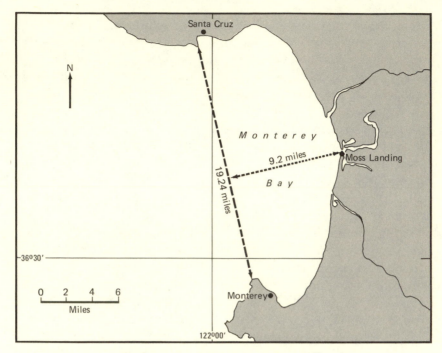

Figure 2. Monterey Bay, California.[35]

Finally, if the width-depth ratio proposed by Strohl were to become widely accepted as a landlocked test, an indentation such as Monterey Bay in California, measuring 19.24 miles across the entrance but penetrating only 9.2 miles into the coast, would fail to qualify as a juridical bay, even though its waters are clearly well marked and landlocked, as can be seen in Figure 2, and its area meets the semi-circle test prescribed in Article 7, paragraph two, sentence two.[36] It seems highly unlikely that such a result could

---

long in proportion to its width." This definition, widely criticized as too vague, was rejected by the Codification Conference; and a later attempt by the United Kingdom to forward the same definition during arguments in the *Anglo-Norwegian Fisheries* dispute was likewise rejected by the International Court of Justice. The Committee of Experts assisting the International Law Commission in drafting proposals for the 1958 Convention suggested that, roughly speaking, the width of a bay must be at least half its length. A/CN. 4/61/Add. 1, Annex, at 2. The International Law Commission, however, expressly rejected the use of a width-depth ratio as a landlocked requireent. *See* [1956] 1 Y.B. INT'L L. COMM'N 190.

35. Figure 2 is reproduced from *United States v. California*, 381 U.S. 139, Appendix B to opinion of Black, J., dissenting (1965).

36. The United States Supreme Court has declared Monterey Bay to be a juridical bay

have been intended by the same drafters who expressly rejected the use of a precise width-depth ratio in 1956.

It must be conceded that the drafters have muddied the waters of their intent to some extent by their reference to proportion in paragraph one, sentence one.[37] However, it seems clear from the linguistic structure of sentence one, read in light of the legislative history[38] and in light of the effort of the drafters throughout Article 7 to refocus attention on the nature of the *waters* enclosed, that, although the relationship between the width and depth of an indentation is intended as a factor to be considered in bay designation, well-marked indentations of *varying* proportions may gain bay status as long as they contain *landlocked waters.*

The fallacy of the Strohl approach lies in the fact that the depth of an indentation may well equal or exceed the width of its entrance and yet, unless one looks at "landlocked" in purely two-dimensional terms, such an indentation may still fail to enclose waters which are factually landlocked, i.e., not only geographically proximate to the surrounding land mass but intimately related to the processes of life on shore and thus of vital interest to shore inhabitants. It is the fact that such waters are more related to life on the land than to the open sea, not that they conform to a given *shape*, which justifies the extension of exclusive coastal sovereignty. To fully implement the mandate of the landlocked requirement, therefore, it is not necessary to devise and impose an extra-textual geometric test to which the proportions of all indentations must conform. Rather it is necessary to give content to the second basic test imposed by sentence one, *landlocked waters.*

When a phrase has been left undefined in an international

---

under the tests prescribed by the 1958 Convention. *See* United States v. California, 381 U.S. 139, 170 (1965).

37. "For the purposes of these articles, a bay is a well-marked indentation *whose penetration is in such proportion to the width of its mouth* as to contain landlocked waters. . . . " Territorial Sea Convention, Article 7(2) (emphasis added). *See supra,* full text of Article 7 accompanying note 10.

38. It is evident from the legislative record of the 1958 Convention that no specific ratio was intended to be attached to the general proportional terms of paragraph two, sentence one (such a ratio was in fact specifically rejected), and that the drafters opted instead for the more precise areal test of the landlocked requirement provided by the semi-circle rule in paragraph two, sentence two. *See* [1956] 1 Y.B. INT'L L. COMM'N 190. *See also supra* note 34.

treaty, accepted canons of construction require that the phrase be interpreted in good faith in accordance with the ordinary meaning of the terms in their context and in light of the object and purpose of the treaty itself, in order to ascertain as fully as possible the genuine shared expectations of the parties and the compatibility of those expectations with broader community policies and applicable norms of international law.[39] One of the fundamental purposes underlying the development of an international law of bays has been to accommodate the exclusive interests of coastal states on the one hand with the inclusive interests of international users of the oceans on the other. Any decision to remove an area of water from common use and place it within the absolute control of the coastal sovereign, therefore, both implies and requires a balancing of these competing interests.

Within this context, the use of the phrase *landlocked waters* in paragraph two, sentence one of Article 7 may be best understood as a *legal conclusion,* in essence a shortened form if you will of this longer sentence: *we have carefully evaluated the interests of the coastal state in this water area as well as the interests of the community as a whole and have concluded on balance that the interests of the coastal state are paramount.*[40]

In order to reach this legal conclusion, many purely geographical factors, i.e. the depth-width ratio, the depth of surface waters, etc., have traditionally been considered as relevant; but because they are seemingly disparate, one may easily lose track of

---

39. *See* Vienna Convention on the Law of Treaties, *supra,* Chapter I, note 25, Articles 31, 32, 53, 64. *See also* M. McDougal, H. Lasswell & J. Miller, *supra,* Chapter I, note 22, at 35–77.

40. Historically, the term "inter fauces terrae," literally "within the jaws of the land," was likewise used as a shortened version of this longer conclusory sentence. Like "landlocked," "inter fauces terrae" was a legal conclusion reached on the basis of the common perception that waters lying within clearly defined coastal headlands (points at which the coast abruptly changed direction and moved landward away from the sea, causing the land to become "locked" within the littoral) were more like the land than the open sea in their vital relationship to state interests, and therefore more susceptible of exclusive state control. Because this was obvious to coastal users and international users alike, community recognition of a coastal state's claim to sovereignty over such waters long predated recognition of a coastal state's right to claim sovereignty over a marginal belt lying seaward from the natural coastline. *See* Gihl, *supra* Chapter I, note 6, at 128–130. *See also supra,* Chapter II, notes 31–47 and accompanying text; Chapter III, notes 3–14, and accompanying text.

the fundamental question being asked, i.e., are the waters of this indentation so closely related to coastal interests that a conclusion may be reached favoring those interests? Every geographical factor taken into account in reaching the conclusion that an indentation does in fact contain landlocked waters is directly related to this basic inquiry. Thus, the language of paragraph two, sentence one directs decision makers to consider the relationship between the width of the mouth of an indentation and the depth of its penetration into the coast *not* because by measuring this geographical relationship against an absolute standard one may find the true path to "bayness," but rather because the world community over several hundred years[41] has recognized that the more deeply an indentation penetrates the coastal littoral, the more likely it is that the security interests of the coastal state are affected; the more likely it is that the economic, political, and social processes of life on shore have become entwined with the waters; the more likely it is that the waters have special value for the industry of shore inhabitants; and the less likely it is that the international users of the oceans have habitually used the waters as a route of commerce and navigation.

Other geographical factors, such as the actual depth of the surface waters throughout the indentation and the number and accessibility of outlets to the sea, are considered as relevant to the inquiry only because they offer further evidence as to the likely patterns of human use. Clearly, waters of comparatively shallow depth are not likely to support international traffic, and waters which lead only to inland shorepoints or other inland waters of the coastal state are more likely to be used by coastal inhabitants and mariners bound for inland ports than by international users of the oceans.

Thus, perhaps one might best envision the landlocked requirement of paragraph two, sentence one as a legal conclusion, to be reached via a two-part analysis:

1. When a body of water moves landward away from the sea behind well-marked entrance points, the geographical configuration created by water and land mass alone may be such as to raise a presumption regarding the landlocked nature of the

---

41. *See supra,* Chapters II and III.

waters. The more deeply the waters penetrate the land, the more shallow the depth of those waters, the more constricted the outlets to the open sea, the more compelling the inference that coastal interests in those waters are paramount. The less intimate the geographical relationship, the more compelling the inference that a decision favoring coastal interests will infringe, perhaps impermissibly, on the interests of international users. In some instances, the geographical configuration may be *so* compelling that a legal conclusion that the waters are landlocked may be reached on that basis alone; and if left unchallenged, will stand.

2. In other cases, preliminary inferences drawn from geographical configuration will not be determinative and must then be confirmed or rebutted by *actual* patterns of human use. (In the end, of course, it is the *use* of the waters which must be evaluated in order to correctly weigh the competing interests of the *users.*) That is to say, in marginal cases one may not be able to accurately determine use from geographical factors alone and must instead seek factual evidence of the use of the waters by coastal inhabitants and others. *Do* international trade routes criss-cross these waters? *Are* coastal inhabitants the primary users, and if so, what are these uses? *Do* foreign ships regularly enter these waters for reasons other than reaching an inland port? *Are* security installations located along the coast? All these questions and more are important to the extent that they enable us to answer the fundamental question posed above: Are the waters of this indentation so closely related to the interests of coastal inhabitants that a legal conclusion may be reached favoring those interests?

If, either on the basis of geographical configuration alone or on the basis of that configuration and actual patterns of use, this question may be answered affirmatively, then the legal conclusion may be drawn that the waters are in fact landlocked. If the answer to the question posed is "no", then the waters have failed the landlocked requirement and there is no reason to move further in Article 7.[42]

---

42. *See supra* full text of Article 7 accompanying note 10.

If the waters of an indentation *are* deemed "landlocked," one further requirement must be met before the indentation may obtain bay status: the indentation must pass the semicircle test imposed by paragraph two, sentence two. Failing this test, even a well-marked, landlocked indentation may not be enclosed as internal waters by the coastal state.[43]

Paragraph Two, Sentence Two: The Semi-circle Test

Without the semi-circle test imposed by paragraph two, sentence two,[44] endless discussion of the various configurations which might meet the "well-marked" and "landlocked" requirements of sentence one would doubtless have continued unabated by the adoption of the Convention. Anticipating such difficulties and building on proposals introduced at The Hague Codification Conference of 1930,[45] the drafters inserted a mathematical/geometric formula into the paragraph to serve as a final check on the well-marked and landlocked requirements above, namely, that regardless of configuration, *no* indentation shall be regarded as a bay unless its *area* is as large as, or larger than, that of a semicircle whose diameter is a line drawn across the mouth of the indentation. Figure 3 illustrates the application of the semicircle rule to coastal indentations.

In its totality, Article 7, paragraph two represents a somewhat uneasy marriage between the general configuration requirements of sentence one and the highly specific mathematical requirements of sentence two. The former lead to subjective analyses of configuration and use whereas the latter lead to objective comparisons of water *area*. Reading the paragraph together as a whole, two constructions seem possible:

1. The addition of the semi-circle test has rendered the subjective requirements of sentence one mere anachronisms.[46]

---

43. *See infra* notes 46–47 and accompanying text.
44. Paragraph two, sentence two, reads: "An indentation shall not, however, be regarded as a bay unless its area is as large as, or larger than, that of the semi-circle whose diameter is a line across the mouth of that indentation." *Territorial Sea Convention*, Article 7(2). *See supra* full text of Article 7 accompanying note 10.
45. *See* Chapter III, text accompanying notes 125–28, for discussion of previous codification efforts.
46. Beazley and others have forwarded such a view. *See supra* text accompanying note 25.

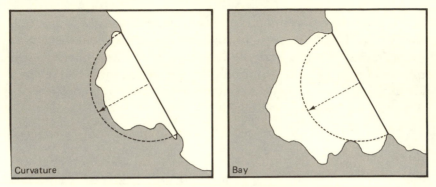

Figure 3. The application of the semicircle test.

2. The two sentences of paragraph two represent separate empirical tests. Sentence one contains the configuration requirements which must be met before a first order decision on bay designation can be made. Sentence two places an absolute areal limit on such designations.

The linguistic structure of paragraph two[47] would seem to indicate that an indentation which is well-marked and landlocked may nonetheless fail to meet the juridical standard of Article 7 if its area does not conform to the semi-circle rule. The opposite result, however, is not indicated by the structure of the paragraph, the language of which in no way suggests that an indentation which passes the semi-circle test might be refused juridical status because it is not landlocked or well-marked.

Most authorities appear to believe that a bay which meets the semi-circle test is by definition landlocked and well-marked.[48] This

47. The well-marked and landlocked configuration requirements in sentence one are followed immediately in sentence two with, "[a]n indentation shall *not, however,* be regarded as a bay *unless* . . . " suggesting that an indentation which is both well marked and landlocked may fail to become a bay *unless* it passes the semicircle test. Territorial Sea Convention, Article 7(2) (emphasis added). *See supra* full text of Article 7 accompanying note 10.

48. *See* P. BEAZLEY, *supra,* Chapter I, note 24, at 12–13; R. HODGSON & L. ALEXANDER, *supra* note 6, at 6; Pearcy, *supra* Chapter II, note 6, at 7. Shalowitz maintains that by itself, paragraph two, sentence one, is little better than the "configuration and characteristics of a bay" language promulgated by the North Atlantic Coast Fisheries Tribunal and without the semicircle rules, establishes no criteria for determining how landlocked a bay must be to remove it from the category of a mere curvature. 1 A. SHALOWITZ, *supra,* Chapter I, note 20, at 219.

conclusion has been firmly rejected, however, by the United States Supreme Court in *United States v. Louisiana* which holds that an "indentation must by its own features qualify as a bay."[49] As the Court makes clear:

> We cannot accept Louisiana's argument that an indentation which satisfies the semicircle test *ipso facto* qualifies as a bay under the Convention. Such a construction would fly in the face of Article 7(2), which plainly treats the semicircle test as a minimum requirement.[50]

The Court did not, however, attempt to explain how an indentation which met the semi-circle test might fail to meet the well-marked and landlocked requirements of sentence one.

The historical record provides little unambiguous guidance on this issue. It is clear that for many years prior to the Geneva Convention, legal and maritime experts, including the developers of the French and American proposals to The Hague Codification Conference in 1930, had argued that some sort of mathematical formula should eventually replace the vague geographical norms which had so defied judicial and scholarly definition.[51] The legislative history of the Geneva Convention reveals that although the addition of a technical, geometric formula to paragraph two did not go unopposed,[52] the majority of delegates agreed that a precise objective test was necessary to determine the proper configuration of a juridical bay. This consensus is clearly indicated in the following Commission *Commentary* to Article 7:

> 3. The Commission discussed at length the question of the conditions under which the waters of a bay can be regarded as internal waters. The majority considered that it was not sufficient to lay down that the waters must be closely linked to the land domain by reason of the depth of the penetration of the bay into the mainland, or otherwise by its configuration, or by

49. United States v. Louisiana (Louisiana Boundary Case), 394 U.S. 11, 54 (1969).
50. *Id.*
51. Boggs, *supra*, Chapter III, note 137, at 551.
52. Brazil was joined by several other delegations in issuing a strong denunciation of paragraph two as establishing a bay definition which was unnecessarily complicated, too difficult for a jurist to follow, and expressive of a rule which had not yet been formulated in international practice. *See* [1956] 1 Y.B. INT'L L. COMM'N 190–197.

reason of the utility the bay might have from the point of view
of the economic needs of the country. These criteria lack legal
precision.[53]

The Commission comments further that "in adopting this provision [paragraph two] the Commission repaired the omission to
which attention had already been drawn by The Hague Codification Conference of 1930 and which the International Court of
Justice again pointed out in its judgment in the [Anglo-
Norwegian] Fisheries Case,"[54] namely the failure to adopt an
objective test which could provide a reliable guide to future state
action in regard to bays. Although this evidence indicates that the
geographical norms in and of themselves were considered an
inadequate basis for bay definition, the record is silent on the
issue of whether the semi-circle test was meant to supplant the
norms or to supplement them by placing a final areal limit on bays
which meet the norms.

Do the well-marked and landlocked requirements have independent validity under paragraph two? Is there any reason to
retain somewhat imprecise geographical norms in the face of a
geometric formula? These questions do not admit of easy answer.
If the areal comparison mandated by sentence two will suffice to
make a bay determination then the whole of sentence one is ren-

53. INT'L L. COMM'N REPORTS (1956), Supp. No. 9, at 15. *See* [1956] 1 Y.B. INT'L L.
    COMM'N 190–197, for a record of the introduction and eventual rejection of several
    amendments proposing use of the imprecise norms noted by the Commission in its
    Commentary.
54. INT'L L. COMM'N REPORTS (1956), Supp. No. 9 at 15, para. 1. Further motivation for
    the inclusion of the semi-circle test is suggested by the Commission's comment that
    such a test was necessary "in order to prevent the system of straight baselines from
    being applied to coasts whose configuration does not justify it, on the pretext of
    applying the rules for bays." *Id.* That is to say, the Commission feared that an inden-
    tation might arguably meet the general configuration requirements of sentence one,
    and yet not contain enough water area to actually be considered a bay. If a given state
    were permitted to enclose all such indentations under the pretext of applying Article
    7, it would be achieving an Article 4 straight baseline on a coast which in reality was
    not deeply indented enough to qualify for the application of Article 4. The Commis-
    sion was greatly concerned at that time that Article 4 would be applied to coastlines
    which did not really justify a straight baseline, thus greatly impinging on inclusive
    community use of the oceans. The concern was justified, as that has been one result
    of the Territorial Sea Convention, regardless of the inclusion of the semicircle test to
    limit Article 7.

dered superfluous, an unapproved construction in treaty interpretation. On the other hand, international conventions are
often the product of compromise, and Beazley has suggested that
the paradox of paragraph two is the result of the blending of a
single objective test submitted by the Committee of Experts advising the International Law Commission and a subjective test which
was drafted to satisfy the demands of semi-circle opponents and
lawyers for a "simple" definition.[55]

It would seem more reasonable to conclude, on the basis of the
language and structure of paragraph two read in conjunction
with the historical effort to provide a final, objective limit on traditional methods of bay designation, that the second construction
posited above, i.e., that an indentation must first pass the empirical tests imposed by the well-marked and landlocked requirements of sentence one before moving on to the semi-circle test
of paragraph two,[56] best effectuates the intent of the drafters.
Having been deemed both well-marked and landlocked, an indentation is in the running for bay status. It is only when the final
test imposed by the semi-circle rule has been passed, however,
that the indentation can unequivocally be designated as a bay.

Further weight is lent to this construction of paragraph two by
consideration of the reality of life on the sea as well as the context
in which most bay claims will be made. Even without sophisticated
delimitation methods and accurate charts, the mariner must navigate the seas without incident. In many instances, geographical
cues will retain primary significance.[57] Paragraph two, sentence
one, embodies those geographical requirements which the world
community has traditionally imposed before coastal indentations
may be enclosed as internal waters. In the vast majority of cases,
bays are most likely to be claimed and recognized on the basis of
these norms alone. It is only when a claim must be justified

55. P. BEAZLEY, *supra*, Chapter I, note 24, at 12.
56. This is the approach adopted by the United States Supreme Court in United States
v. Louisiana, 394 U.S. 11, 54 (1969).
57. *See supra* notes 19–24 and accompanying text. It is interesting to note that Strohl
argues forcefully for the retention of the landlocked requirement and the deletion of
the semi-circle rule. He claims that such a formula is needed only if the landlocked
requirement is ignored or given too liberal an interpretation. M. STROHL, *supra*,
Chapter II, note 42, at 57. But *see supra* notes 28–30 and accompanying text for
Strohl's own method of placing a limit on "landlocked."

against opposition that the semi-circle test is likely to be used to any great extent outside of academia. The geographical criteria, therefore, will form the basis for most first-order decisions as to whether or not a given indentation is part of the internal waters of the coastal state. Within this context, it seems the better part of wisdom to retain in the actual words of the Convention those geographical norms which the semi-circle test is meant to concretize.

Another equally compelling reason to retain the geographical norms is that in certain cases the precise mathematical requirements of the semi-circle test are relaxed, as for example where, because of the presence of islands, an indentation has more than one mouth.[58] In these circumstances, the well-marked and landlocked requirements will assume even greater importance in making the determination of a juridical bay.

To summarize, then, the definition set forth by Article 7, paragraph two: An indentation which is well-marked and landlocked qualifies as a bay only if its *area* equals or exceeds the *area* of a semi-circle whose diameter is measured by the width of the entrance. Once this determination has been made by the delimitation methods described in paragraph three which follows, a bay exists under international law. The only remaining question is how much of the waters of the bay may be claimed as internal, a question answered by the baseline rules set forth in paragraphs four and five.

Paragraph Three: Bay Delimitation

Article 7, paragraph 3[59] sets out the rules for the *areal measurement* of a coastal indentation. Some commentators convey the notion that "[p]aragraph 3 continues the statement of requirements to be fulfilled in determining the existence of a 'bay.'"[60] This is a somewhat misleading characterization. The introductory words of paragraph two signal its purpose: "For the purposes of these articles *a bay is* . . . . " These words indicate clearly that paragraph two has been designed to set out the *definitional* cri-

---

58. *See* discussion of paragraph three, *infra* this section.
59. For the full text of Article 7, paragraph 3, *see supra* text accompanying note 10.
60. *See, e.g.,* P. BEAZLEY, *supra,* Chapter I, note 24, §6.8, at 14.

teria which must be met before a bay may be deemed to exist. The purpose of paragraph three is also indicated in its initial wording: "For the purpose of *measurement, the area* of an indentation is . . . . " Because the semi-circle rule in paragraph two has set forth an areal standard, it follows that in some cases it will be necessary to measure the areas specified in order to make a proper comparison. Paragraph three provides rules for such measurement but does not embody further definitional requirements for a juridical bay.

It should also be noted that in most instances, the areal comparison mandated by paragraph two can be done in a relatively simple manner with proper maps. Most bays are not "borderline" in their relation to the area of the semi-circle, and a sufficient comparison may often be made by merely drawing a semi-circle on the map using the line joining the natural entrance points of the indentation as the diameter, and making a visual comparison between semi-circle and indentation.[61] If simple methods are not decisive, then more complicated geographic and hydrographic measures may be employed, using the measurement rules of paragraph three.[62] But as Strohl has noted,

> Judging from the study made of the coasts of the world . . . it is this author's opinion that there would be very few borderline situations which would require geodetic and hydrographic surveys to establish the juridical quality of indentations or to establish exact[ly] the extent of internal waters in bays.[63]

Discussion below as to the interpretative difficulties which may arise under this paragraph should be seen within this context. In all likelihood, exacting measurement will only be necessary as part of a potential or actual challenge to the coastal state's assertion of territorial sovereignty over borderline water areas.

Paragraph three is composed of the three major sections. *Sentence one* states the general rule that the *area* of an indentation is that lying between the low-water marks around the shore and a

61. P. HODGSON & L. ALEXANDER, *supra* note 6, at 5. *See also supra* Fig. 1.
62. *See* M. STROHL, *supra*, Chapter II, note 42, at 88–92, for excellent discussion of such techniques.
63. *Id.*, at 92.

line joining the low-water marks of its natural entrance points.[64] This is the same line which will serve as the diameter of the semi-circle with which the area of the indentation is to be compared. The sequence of this comparison would seem to be as follows:

1. Determine the natural entrance points of the indentation and locate their low-water marks.
2. Measure the distance between these low-water marks.
3. Draw a semi-circle on a diameter line of that length.
4. Measure the area of the semicircle.
5. Locate the low-water mark around the shore of the indentation and measure the area of the indentation.
6. Compare areas four and five above. If the area of the indentation (5) equals or exceeds the area of the semi-circle (4), then a bay exists under Article 7; and one proceeds to paragraphs four and five to determine how much of the waters of the bay may be enclosed as internal. If the area of the indentation does *not* exceed that of the semi-circle, then no bay exists and there is no need to move further within Article 7.

As can be easily deduced, in order to complete the six-step process outlined above one must first ascertain the location of the low-water mark around the shore as well as the natural entrance points of the indentation.

Low-Water Mark

For the purpose of definition, a *low-water mark* is the point of intersection of the plane of mean low-water with the shore.[65] The *plane of mean-low water,* in turn, is the average of all tides and serves as the average or reference plane from which the depth of water is indicated on nautical charts. Reference planes, however,

---

64. One must note that at this point in Article 7, there is no limitation on the length of this line, nor is it as yet referred to as a "closing" line. A closing line will be drawn only when the amount of water which may be enclosed as internal waters has been determined under paragraphs four and five below.
65. *Report of the Second Committee (Territorial Sea), Annex 2,* 24 AM. J. INT'L LAW, SUPPLE-MENT 247, 248 (1930); 1937 U.S. NAV. WAR COL. at 128. "Shore" is used here in its widest sense, including not only that of the mainland but also of islands, low-tide elevations, and the like.

vary with the agency or country constructing the chart,[66] which may of course result in an interesting battle of the hydrographers in cases where areal measurement is challenged.

In general, the location of the low-water marks around the shore of an indentation is easily accomplished. However, two questions may arise in defining the *low-water mark* of an indentation which contains special features:

1. What is to be done about harbor works lying within the indentation?
2. What is to be done about subsidiary waters which are enclosed within the indentation?

Article 8 of the Territorial Sea Convention provides that for the purpose of delimiting the territorial sea, the outermost permanent harbor works which form an integral part of the harbor system shall be regarded as forming part of the *coast*.[67] This article is designed to benefit the coastal state by making the waters surrounding and within harbor works internal waters of the state, the territorial sea therefore being measured from the outermost perimeter of such facilities.[68] The problem arises when one attempts to reconcile Article 8 with the Article 7 low-water mark measurement rule. The question presented is, since Article 8 stipulates that the outermost perimeter of harbor works are deemed to be the *coast*, and the area of an indentation is to be measured from the low-water mark around the *shore*, are the terms *coast* and *shore* sufficiently synonymous to require that, when a harbor facility is located within an indentation, the waters in and around the harbor works must be excluded from the areal measurement of

66. Mean low-water is the reference plane for nearly all charts prepared by the U.S. Navy Hydrographic Office from its own survey. Mean lower low-water, the average of the lower of the two daily tides, is the plane used on the U.S. Pacific Coast, Hawaii, Alaska, and the Phillipines. Mean low-water springs, the average low-water at spring tides, is the reference plane for most British Admiralty charts. Where there is a large tidal range, the reference plane chosen can be quite significant. M. STROHL, *supra*, Chapter II, note 42, at 70.
67. Territorial Sea Convention, Article 8. The term "harbor works" has been defined by Shalowitz as "[s]tructures erected along the seacoast at inlets or rivers for protective purposes, or for enclosing sea areas adjacent to the coast to provide anchorage and shelter." 1 A. SHALOWITZ, *supra*, Chapter I, note 20, at 292.
68. M. STROHL, *supra*, Chapter II, note 42, at 59.

the indentation under paragraphs three, sentence one? In borderline cases, the water area substracted due to the existence of harbor works extending from the shore of the indentation might conceivably lead to the failure of that indentation to qualify as a juridical bay.

One might argue that the drafters purposely used the word "shore" in paragraph three rather than "coast" in order to differentiate Article 7 from Article 8 and to indicate that the area of an indentation is to be measured from the precise point where the land meets the sea, regardless of what man-made structures might extend from the shore. However, the word "coast" has *also* been defined by some experts as "the edge of terra firma in immediate contact with the sea."[69] The distinction between the terms coast and shore might, therefore, seem a bit thin to have been intended as a key differentiation, and no such conclusions may be drawn from the legislative history. Reading the text and context of the Convention as a whole, however, one must conclude that the word "coast" is indeed a technical term, consistently utilized in other than its ordinary sense[70] to denote that point along the shore at which the baseline is delimited and from which the territorial sea and other sea zones are measured. The location of the "coast" is, therefore, the last step in the baseline delimitation process.

Applying this analysis to Article 7, until the determination has been made under paragraphs two and three that a given indentation is indeed a bay, there is no "coast" within the indentation, even though there is a "shoreline." Once a bay has been deemed to exist, under paragraphs two and three, the *coast* of the bay is delimited by drawing a closing line across the entrance, and the internal waters around interior harbor works are subsumed within the internal waters of the bay. If *no* bay is found to exist under paragraphs two and three, then the *coast* of the indentation recedes to the low-water mark around the interior shore line as prescribed by Article 3. In that context, the special allowance provided for coastal states under Article 8, to enclose the waters

---

69. Bencker, *Maritime Geographical Terminology Relating to Various Hydrographic Subdivisions of the Globe,* 29 INT'L HYDROGRAPHIC REV. at 60–74 (1942).

70. *See Vienna Convention on the Law of Treaties, supra,* Chapter I, note 25, Article 31(4): A special meaning shall be given to a term if it is established that the parties so intended.

in and around harbor works as internal waters, once again becomes relevant; and it cannot be maintained that the special allowance granted to benefit coastal states under Article 8 should be construed to their detriment under Article 7. It must be concluded, therefore, that for areal measurement purposes under paragraph three, the low-water mark around the shore of an indentation is to be measured at that point at which the land would naturally meet the sea regardless of harbor works which happen to extend from the shore.

The second question raised by paragraph three, sentence one, is even more problematic: what is to be done about subsidiary waters in locating the low-water mark around the shore of an indentation? Neither the language of Article 7 nor the legislative history provides assistance on this point, and commentators vary widely in their approaches.

In applying the semi-circle rule to an indentation containing tributary waterways such as rivers or subsidiary bays, Shalowitz maintains that the entire identation including all tributary water areas should be included in areal measurement. If the area of the indentation meets the semi-circle test based on this comparison, the entire area may be enclosed as internal waters.[71] Shalowitz cites no authority for this interpretation, but claims it is reasonable based on the concept of a bay as inland waters. Because the indentation is situated within the body of land, any tributary waterway also situated within the land should also have the character of inland waters.

The fallacy inherent in such an approach is that some tributary waters such as rivers are *already* recognized as internal waters and therefore have little relevance in determining whether or not the bay itself may be so recognized. Serious problems may result from such an interpretation in cases where tributaries extend far from the bay into the land mass, as in the case of rivers, and one must then determine how far into the land one may go and still be measuring the indentation. Shalowitz suggests two solutions for such cases:

1. Establish an additional rule under Article 7 limiting the width of a waterway, such as a river, beyond which it would not be considered part of the primary indentation; or

71. 1 A. Shalowitz, *supra*, Chapter I, note 20, at 219–20.

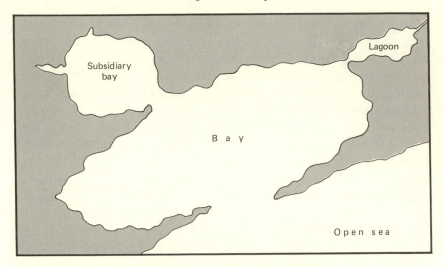

Figure 4. Subsidiary water areas.

2. First apply the semi-circle test to the tributary. If it becomes
   internal waters under that test in and of itself, close off that
   waterway and measure the primary indentation alone. If the
   tributary does *not* fulfill the semi-circle test alone, then include
   its area as part of the main indentation in making the areal
   comparison.[72]

Although the second approach has some merit when applied to
water areas such as subsidiary bays, coves, and lagoons extending
directly from the main indentation, even in those cases the order
of measurement seems misguided. It is the existence of a well-
marked, landlocked coastal indentation which warrants the application of Article 7. It is, therefore, the nature of this primary
indentation which must be first determined. If other baylike
waters extend directly from it, as in Figure 4, it would seem that
each should be included within the initial areal measurement, as
all are a part of those water areas landlocked within the littoral.[73]

72. *Id.*, at 220 n. 28. Again it must be noted that the tributary waters such as rivers are
    already by definition "internal" and need no application of an Article 7 test to so
    designate them.

73. This is the approach adopted by the U.S. Geographer in *Sovereignty of the Sea*, 3
    United States State Department Geographic Bulletin 11 (1965): "The water of bays
    within bays may be included as water surface of the outer bay in determining the
    dimensions of any coastal indentation."

If the area of the main indentation thus measured fails to meet the semicircle test, the "coast" would then move inward to the low-water line around the internal shore of the major indentation. Any subsidiary bay would then become a coastal indentation in itself, and might be measured against the various definitional and measurement rules of paragraphs two and three to determine whether it alone may obtain juridical status.

Beazley takes yet another approach. He reports that there are numerous situations worldwide where a major indentation of the coast is itself divided into a number of smaller indentations. In answer to the question of whether secondary indentations may be considered if the major indentation fails to meet juridical bay standards, Beazley argues that since cases such as *United States v. Louisiana*,[74] and *Post Office v. Estuary Radio, Ltd.*,[75] make clear that subsidiary bays may exist along the shore of a larger indentation, it would be clearly absurd to deny the possibility that each subsidiary indentation might obtain bay status. According to Beazley, that would be tantamount to saying that no juridical bay could be found to exist anywhere along a concave coastline unless that concavity itself conformed to the definitional requirements of paragraph two.[76] One might add that such a conclusion would be impermissible in light of community policy which favors the assertion of coastal sovereignty over waters that extend into the land territory, thus implicating the vital economic and security interests of the coastal state. Subsidiary bays located along the shore of a larger indentaion are arguably even more landlocked than those which indent the outer coastline. Just because the larger curvature fails to meet the tests imposed under paragraphs two and three, is no reason to deny juridical status to a secondary indentation which independently meets those requirements. Beazley would argue as this writer has, however, that secondary bay determinations should be made only after the entire indentation has failed to meet the bay criteria imposed by Article 7.

Beazley also discusses another issue which may arise when a primary indentation is found to be a bay under paragraphs two and three, but its entrance exceeds the twenty-four-mile limitation of

74.   394 U.S. 11, 48–53 (1969).
75.   [1968] 2 Q.B. 740,756.
76.   P. BEAZLEY, *supra,* Chapter I, note 24, at 15.

paragraph four; and consequently, a twenty-four-mile closing line must be drawn within the bay as required by paragraph five. In certain circumstances, this process may leave smaller bays within the larger bay but *seaward* of the twenty-four-mile closing line. The question then arises, may these indentations be treated as bays in their own right?

Some argue that in doing so, a coastal state is trying to have "two bites at the cherry," since the waters of the subsidiary indentation will have already been included as part of the initial areal measurement of the bay. Beazley maintains that if in fact the area of the smaller indentation was used in calculating the total water area of the bay, in all fairness it should not be claimed as a bay on its own. If the area was not used in the original determination or if that determination is unaffected by deleting the area of the subsidiary waters, then the indentation should be allowed to pass the paragraph two requirements on its own, and if successful, to be claimed as a bay in its own right.[77]

The fairness principle seems irrelevant here. One could argue with equal force that in such cases, overall community policies as well as the policies and purposes of Article 7 must govern. If a smaller bay is left exposed by either a negative bay determination on the primary indentation or the drawing of a twenty-four-mile closing line landward of its location on the shore, the subsidiary bay should be judged as if it existed alone on the coastline. If such an area lies within the land territory of the coastal state, if it is well-marked from the sea and landlocked so as to be obviously outside major navigational routes, and if its area conforms to the semi-circle rule, it should be treated as any other bay because it falls within that category of water area which has been traditionally seen as best governed by a regime of exclusive state control. Whether its area has been used in making the original bay determination or not, once the subsidiary bay has been "set free" by that determination, it must be judged on its own merits. To proceed otherwise would lead to the anomalous creation of territorial waters or perhaps even high seas within an indentation which would obviously have enclosed internal waters were it not part of a larger bay.

Even more troublesome issues are raised by Shalowitz's sug-

77. *Id.*, at 15.

gestion that rivers which flow into an indentation should also be included in its areal measurement.[78] Hodgson and Alexander point out that only bays are included within the language of Article 7, and no mention whatever is made of subsidiary features or tributary waterways. If these waterways are included in the areal evaluation, vast river systems and interconnected inland lakes, clearly unrelated to the bay itself, might be added to the area of an indentation in order to assure its meeting the semi-circle test. These authors argue, therefore, that only a true bay area, i.e., an indentation of the coast, should be measured to meet the areal requirement. All water surfaces which do not conform to the general configuration of a bay should be geographically detached from the bay before measurement.[79]

Beazley would argue, however, that since one is dealing with an arm of the sea, the true measurement point is that at which the water of a tributary ceases to be sea water. This rule would eliminate the problem set out in the worst case analysis of Hodgson and Alexander, i.e., that vast inland water systems might be included within the area of the bay. Beazley concludes that "one should interpret 'shore of the indentation' as including all waters as far as the tide runs to the extent that the navigational chart clearly depicts a low-water line. When the tide ceases to run, there is no low-water line."[80]

Although this is a plausible suggestion based on somewhat verifiable hydrographic data, it does not address the actual problem of assessing tidal action and salt water flow in rivers. Documents received from the Army Corps of Engineers' San Francisco Bay Model reveal that the tidal action of San Francisco Bay actually extends sixty to seventy miles up the Sacramento and San Joachin Rivers as far inland as Sacramento and Stockton. See Figure 5.[81] In addition, the salt water of the Pacific flows into San Francisco Bay and through the subsidiary waters of San Pablo Bay, the Carquines Strait, and Suisun Bay, into and at times beyond the junction of the Sacramento and San Joachin Rivers, sometimes mix-

78. *See supra* this section, text accompanying notes 71–72.
79. R. HODGSON & L. ALEXANDER, *supra* note 6, at 4–6.
80. P. BEAZLEY, *supra*, Chapter I, note 24, §6.15, at 15. The author cites the case in which New Zealand enclosed Palliser Bay by relying on the area of the tidal Onoke Lake.
81. Figure 5 reproduced through the courtesy of the Department of the Army, San Francisco District U.S. Army Corps of Engineers.

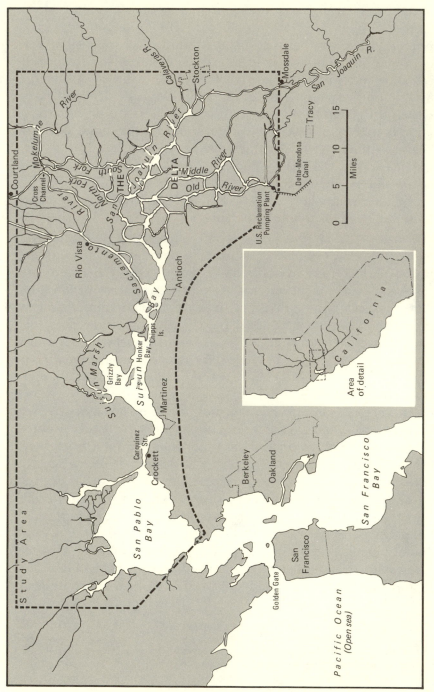

Figure 5. *San Francisco Bay estuarial system.*

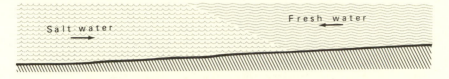

Figure 6. The salt wedge.

ing with fresh river waters and sometimes forming a "salt wedge" which sinks to the bottom of the river, flowing upstream as fresh water flows downward over the wedge to San Francisco Bay. See Figure 6.[82]

The actual point at which salt water ceases to flow in this dynamic estuarial system varies from season to season and from year to year.[83] In a year of heavy rains and snows, the fresh water run-off from the Sierra Nevadas changes the hydraulic balance of

82. As fresh water flow from upland rivers meets the bay's salt waters, a rather distinct boundary materializes. Turbulent eddies result as the two masses of water converge. The salt wedge is a phenomenon common to most estuaries or other areas where salt and fresh water meet. *See* EXPLORE 5; THE CALIFORNIA COASTLINE: SAN FRANCISCO BAY, a Bulletin of the San Francisco District U.S. Army Corps of Engineers, undated, published in keeping with President Carter's declaration of 1980 as "the Year of the Coast."

83. The analysis of salinity intrusion into tidal estuaries is closely linked to the prediction of turbulence generation and energy dissipation throughout the length of the water system. Local salinities are the result of the complex interaction of horizontal and vertical convection of salinity by the transient and turbulent tidal shear flows, of the convective currents generated by the density gradients, and of the seaward convective velocities resulting from the fresh water flow into the estuary. Depending on the relative strength of these currents, the characteristics of the salinity intrusion are usually described in terms of the observed salinity distribution as follows:
   a. The *unmixed* or *completely stratified case* with a fairly well-defined interface or discontinuity in salinity distribution (the salt wedge).
   b. The *partially mixed state* in which the local salinity varies vertically a larger amount in terms of the local mean salinity.
   c. The *well-mixed condition* in which the salinity variation over a vertical section varies only a small fraction from the local mean salinity.

   Cases a, b, and c may occur in the same estuary under suitable conditions of tidal and freshwater flows. REPORT NO. 3, EVALUATION OF PRESENT STATE OF KNOWLEDGE OF FACTORS AFFECTING TIDAL HYDRAULICS AND RELATED PHENOMENA, Committee on Tidal Hydraulics, Corps of Engineers (1965). In general the salinity of water in San Francisco Bay varies from that of practically sea water, 30 ppt., in the Golden Gate and South San Francisco Bay proper, to that of brackish water, 10 ppt., in Suisun Bay, and to that of practically fresh water at Chipps Island at the Western end of the Delta. Strictly speaking, salinity in the Bay is dependent upon the tidal stage and the volume of freshwater inflow. TECHNICAL BULLETIN NO. 17, ESTUARIAL NAVIGATION PROJECTS, Committee on Tidal Hydraulics, Corps of Engineers (1971).

the river and pushes salt water further downstream. In a dry year, salt water may be found as far inland as the Delta area. The strength of the tides and winds on a given day may also affect the ratio of salt water to fresh. It is impossible, therefore, to determine with the certainty required for an international rule of law just where sea water will cease to flow in the system at any given point in time.

Considering the impossibility of determining the exact point at which salt water will cease to run, as well as the fact that tidal action may occur sixty and seventy miles beyond the bay proper, it is difficult to imagine that the drafters of Article 7 could possibly have envisioned the inclusion of such an extensive water system within an area described as coastal indentation, as Beazley suggests. Noting the complexity of an actual tributarial system as was represented in Figure 5, the Shalowitz suggestion of drafting a new provision limiting the width of a river which might be considered part of the primary indentation also appears arbitrary and unwarranted by either the purposes or express language of Article 7.

What, then, *did* the drafters intend? Article 13 of the Territorial Sea Convention describes a river flowing "directly into the sea" as having its own baseline between points on the low-tide line of its *banks*.[84] It is clear from this language that Article 13 does not apply to rivers which flow into a bay or estuary. The French text of Article 13 is even more explicit than the English version in this regard, beginning with the phrase, "If a river flows directly into the sea" and adding, "without forming an estuary."[85]

The first text of Article 13 adopted by the International Law Commission contained a second paragraph which read:

---

84. Territorial Sea Convention, Article 13. Originally, the language of this section placed the baseline at a "line drawn *inter fauces terrarum* across the mouth of the river." Many objections were lodged against this wording. Alternate constructions included replacing *inter fauces terrarum* with "natural entrance points" or "mouth of the river." The United States proposed the wording that was finally adopted by the Convention, which draws the baseline "between points on the low-water line on the *banks*." It was never suggested that a river might have a "shore." *See* 3 United Nations Conference on the Law of the Sea, First Committee (Territorial Sea and Contiguous Zone) (1958), A/CONF. 13/39, at 240–45.
85. *See* P. BEAZLEY, *supra*, Chapter I, note 24, §6.11, at 14.

2. If the river flows into an estuary the coasts of which belong to
   a single State, Article 7 shall apply.[86]

This paragraph was deleted because the word estuary was thought
to be too hard to define. Nonetheless, the legislative history
makes it clear that the drafters intended an estuary to be judged
according to the same standards set out in Article 7.[87]

Beazley contends that the draft article above implies not only
that in an estuarial situation Article 7 shall apply, but that all the
water in the estuary as well as the river which created it shall be
measured to make the semi-circle comparison. This conclusion
may not be warranted. The Convention language and the legislative history might be read with equal logic to say that when a
river flows directly into the sea, it will have its own closing line
under Article 13. But when the river flows into a bay or an estuary, that river is no longer an arm of the sea nor an indentation
into the coast. It is then the bay or the estuary itself which constitutes the coastal indentation and, therefore, it is that indentation alone which must be measured. Arguing most persuasively in
favor of such an interpretation is the fact that a river which does
not flow into the sea has no relevance whatever to the coastal
indentation baseline issue, and since the river is already internal
waters by definition, it makes no sense to include the area of the
river in making the critical determination as to whether the
waters of a coastal indentation shall be enclosed as internal.

The Hodgson and Alexander approach would seem most in
keeping with the intent of Article 7 to create a special baseline
for coastal indentations. If one accepts their conclusion that all
water surfaces which do not conform to the general configuration
of a bay should be geographically detached from the bay area
before measurement,[88] one effectively deletes rivers, streams, and
other un-baylike features which run into the bay from the land,

86. United Nations Conference on the Law of the Sea, First Committee (Territorial Sea
    and Contiguous Zone) (1958), A/CONF. 13/39, at 256.
87. *Id.,* at 193–194. Pearcy has defined an estuary as "no more than a wide river mouth
    subject to tidal action." He maintains that since an article relating to estuaries was
    proposed by the Committee of Experts but failed to gain approval in the final Con-
    vention vote, estuaries must legally qualify as bays in application of the baseline rules.
    Pearcy, *supra,* Chapter II, note 6, at 8.
88. R. HODGSON & L. ALEXANDER, *supra* note 6, at 4–6.

but includes for paragraph three measurement purposes subsidiary bays, coves, lagoons, and other bay-like water areas that extend directly from the primary bay and therefore are a valid part of the water area which is created by the indentation in the coast.

Natural Entrance Points

In order to apply the measurement rules of paragraph three, one must determine the *natural entrance points* of the indentation. The term refers in general to those points along the shore at which the sea turns inward toward the land, thus forming a well-marked and landlocked indentation. The location of these points is critical under Article 7, because their determination is necessary not only in completing the areal measurement prescribed by paragraph three but, if a bay *is* found to exist, in drawing the final closing line as prescribed by paragraphs four and five.

The term "natural entrance points" is relatively new in international prescription,[89] other terms being preferred prior to 1951. *Inter fauces terrae* or *inter fauces terrarum* were used consistently by early writers and decision makers and were favored in modern times by the Committee of Experts advising the International Law Commission[90] and by contemporary writers such as Jessup.[91] By far the most commonly used term has been "headlands," a word used by the Tribunal in the *North Atlantic Coast Fisheries Arbitration*[92] in 1910 as well as by numerous other national and international judicial bodies and almost all twentieth-century legal scholars.

Despite this widespread usage, the terms *inter fauces terrae* and "headlands" were eschewed by the International Law Commission in its draft articles in both 1955[93] and 1956.[94] From the lan-

89. The term appears to have been first used in a submission by the United Kingdom appended to their argument in the *Anglo-Norwegian Fisheries Case* (U.K. v. Nor.), [1951] I.C.J. 116, 120.
90. *See Report of the Committee of Experts* (1953), *supra* note 18.
91. *See* P. Jessup, *supra*, Chapter II, note 41, at 430–36.
92. North Atlantic Coast Fisheries Case (Gr. Brit. v. U.S.), Hague Ct. Rep. (Scott) 141,144 (Perm. Ct. Arb. 1910).
93. [1955] 2 Y.B. Int'l. L. Comm'n 251.
94. Report of the International Law Commission to the General Assembly, 11. U.N. GAOR, Supp. (No. 9) at 15–16, U.N. Doc. A/3159 (1956) [hereinafter cited without cross reference as *Report of the I.L.C.* (1956)].

guage used in these drafts, it is clear that the Commission intended to favor a more functional, descriptive approach to identify the entrance of an indentation.[95] It was not until 1958, however, that the actual term *natural entrance points* was introduced into the Convention by way of a series of amendments proposed by the United Kingdom. The phrase was used in three of these amendments, the exact wording of which was eventually adopted by the full Convention as paragraphs three, four, and five of Article 7.[96]

Even though the drafters specifically rejected the use of "headlands" to describe the entrance points of an indentation, the term is still used frequently by commentators as a synonym for natural entrance points. Shalowitz indicates that the natural entrance points for most bays will be mainland headlands, which he defines as either the apex of a salient of the coast, the point of maximum extension of a portion of the land into the water, or a point on the shore at which there is an appreciable change in the general direction of the coast.[97]

Although one may agree with this definition as it relates to headlands, it is not sufficient to define *natural entrance points,* a much wider, more functional concept which may well include headlands as a subcategory but which may include any number of other geographic features as long as they clearly mark the natural entrance to an indentation. For example, it is clear from the second sentence in paragraph three and related legislative history that the drafters envisioned islands as creating natural entrances to an indentation:

> Where, because of the presence of islands, an indentation has *more than one mouth,* the semi-circle shall be drawn on a line as long as the sum total of the lengths of the lines *across the different mouths.*[98]

---

95. Phrases such as "a semicircle drawn on the mouth of that indentation" and "the semicircle drawn at the entrance of that indentation" indicate an intent to focus on the entrance as the key concept.

96. *See* U.N. Doc. A/CONF. 13/C.1/L.62, in 3 United Nations Conference on the Law of the Sea (1958), *supra* note 84, at 227–28.

97. 1 A. SHALOWITZ, *supra,* Chapter I, note 20, 63–64.

98. Territorial Sea Convention, *supra* note 10, Article 7, para. 3, sent. 2 (emphasis added). The word "mouth" in sentence two is used throughout the Convention Records as synonymous with "entrance" in describing the seaward opening of the bay. The original wording of sentence two read, "If a bay has more than one entrance, this semi-

It seems equally clear that the word "natural" was not inserted to preclude the recognition of harbor works and other artificial structures as natural entrance points. Article 8, as noted, indicates that such facilities are to be regarded as a part of the coast, and the I.L.C. Commentary goes further to state that permanent structures erected on the coast and jutting out to sea (such as jettisons, protecting walls, and dykes) are assimilated as harbor works.[99] Thus, one must conclude that such coastal features are not to be considered as nonnatural for baseline purposes and can themselves serve as natural entrance points if they clearly mark the entrance into an indentation from the sea.[100]

In most cases, an indentation which is landlocked and, particularly relevant to the entrance point issue, well-marked will have entrance points of whatever nature which are readily discernible. A special problem arises, however, in the case of an indentation which has a well-marked entrance point on one side but a gentle slope or featureless coast on the other, as in Figure 7. To interpret natural entrance points as synonymous with headlands, as Shalowitz and others have defined the term, would lead to an anomalous interpretation of the Convention which would in effect hold that Article 7 requires two distinct headlands, and when only one occurs in nature, no juridical bay can be deemed to exist. This is an extremely conservative reading that would violate the policy which Article 7 is intended to serve, because an indentation with only one clearly defined "headland" would fail the measurement test automatically even though the indentation might well lie within the land territory of the coastal state and

---

circle shall be drawn on a line as long as the sum total of the length of the different entrances," and the Commission explained this provision in its 1955 Commentary thusly: "If, as a result of the presence of islands, an indentation. . . . has more than one entrance, the sum total of the length of the different entrances will be regarded as the length of the bay." *See* [1955] 2. Y. B. INT'L L. COMM'N 36–37. See also United States V. Louisiana, 394 U.S. 11, 54-66, where the Court concludes that "No language in Article 7 or elsewhere positively excludes all islands from the meaning of the 'natural entrance points' to a bay." *Id.*, at 61.

99. *See* Report of the International Law Commission to the General Assembly, 9 U.N. GAOR Supp. (No. 9) at 15, U.N. Doc. A/2693 (1954); *see also* [1954] 1 Y.B. INT'L L. COMM'N at 88–89; [1955] 1 Y.B. INT'L L. COMM'N at 74; [1956] 1 Y.B. INT'L L. COMM'N at 193; 3 United Nations Conference on the Law of the Sea (1958), *supra* note 84, at 142; United States v. Louisiana, 394 U.S. at 37 n.42.

100. P. BEAZLEY, *supra,* Chapter I, note 24, at 16. The meaning of "natural" in the United Kingdom has been defined by the judgment in Post Office v. Estuary Radio, Ltd., [1968] 2 Q.B. 740, 755, as synonymous with "clearly identifiable."

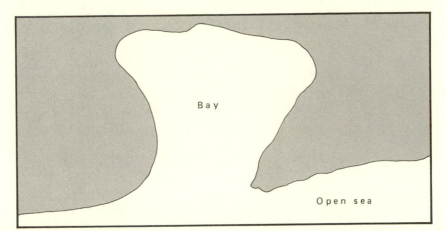

Figure 7. A natural entrance point facing a gently sloping coastline.

thus warrant an exclusive regime. The wisdom of focusing on the natural *entrance* to the indentation rather than its so-called headlands becomes particularly clear in such circumstances.

All commentators agree that an indentation which encloses landlocked waters and is well-marked but which has only one prominent entrance point should be afforded juridical consideration. Yet, the problem remains: How to choose a point on the opposite shore which can reasonably serve as the terminus of a line drawn from the well-marked entrance point for paragraph three measurement purposes?

Several commentators[101] have proposed that in the case of a gently curved shoreline with no obvious entrance point, two tangents should be drawn based on the general direction of the coast on both the seaward and landward sides. At the point of intersection, a line bisecting the angle formed by the tangents would then be drawn to the shore. The point at which the line meets the shore would be deemed the natural entrance point of the indentation. This procedure, adopted by the United States Supreme Court in *United States v. California*,[102] seems quite workable and is illustrated in Figure 8.

---

101. R. HODGSON & L. ALEXANDER, *supra* note 6, at 10–12; 1 A. SHALOWITZ, *supra,* Chapter I, note 20, at 64.
102. The Supreme Court has recognized that where there is no readily identifiable natural entrance point, an objective test must be employed to select one. In its Supplemental Decree in United States v. California, 382 U.S. 448 (1966), the Court stated:

The Juridical Bay

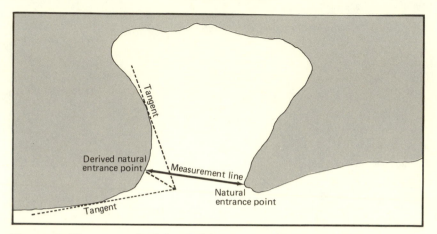

Figure 8. Bisector method for deriving a natural entrance point on a gently sloping coastline.

Another measurement problem arises in the case of a well-marked entrance point facing an absolutely featureless shoreline. It has been suggested that a line be drawn from the easily identifiable entrance point to that point on the opposite coast where the angle formed by the line and the shoreline is not less than 45°.[103] This is to assure the selection of natural entrance points

---

In drawing a closing line across the entrance of any body of inland water having pronounced headlands, the line shall be drawn between the points where the plane of mean lower low water meets the outermost extension of the headlands. Where there is no pronounced headland, the line shall be drawn to the point where the line of mean lower low water on the shore is intersected by the bisector of the angle formed where a line projecting the general trend of the line of mean lower low water along the open coast meets a line projecting the general trend of the line of mean lower low water along the tributary waterway. 382 U.S. at 451.

See also United States v. California, 447 U.S. 1, 8 n.8 (1980), where the Court acknowledges the existence of the "bisector of the angle test" in citing its inapplicability in the case of San Pedro Bay.

103. P. BEAZLEY, *supra*, Chapter I, note 24, at 17. Hodgson and Alexander propose the same 45° test as a more objective way to determine *all* natural entrance points. The test (which is fully described in their work, *supra* note 6, at 10–12) is based on the trigonometric principle that an angle of 45° represents the mid-line between two lines of opposite direction. Thus, the 45° test applied to bays would lead to the universal selection of entrance points at the place where the direction of the shore changes from one facing inland to one facing the sea. This method seems quite reasonable when applied to the featureless coast problem; but because most natural entrance points are easily discernible and problems arise only in special circumstances such as those described above, one cannot agree that such a process should be required for *all* indentations under the specific terms of the Convention.

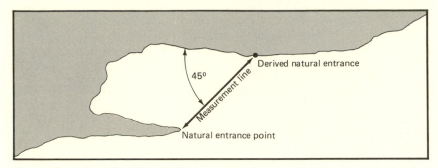

Figure 9. 45° method for deriving a natural entrance point on a featureless coastline.

which retain the land-related character of the indentation. The process is illustrated in Figure 9.

After an exhaustive study of world charts, Strohl was unable to find any indentations with a gentle slope on both sides leading to a true bay inland. He did, however, find many as described above with a well-marked entrance on one side and a featureless curve on the other, such as the Gulf of Cutch in India.[104] Strohl contends that the most logical method for drawing a line between entrance points would be to locate its origin on the side having the well-marked entrance point and to locate its terminus at the closest point of land on the opposite side, as is illustrated in Figure 10.

As can be deduced from Figure 10, the use of the "closest point" method proposed by Strohl will in most cases result in a smaller area of water being enclosed within the bay than if the measurement line were drawn using the 45° test. Although the Strohl method enjoys the benefit of simplicity and perhaps seems more in keeping with general community policies favoring maximization of water area reserved for inclusive use, certainly nothing in the language of the Convention would lead to the conclusion that a given state, in asserting its claim to water areas expressly reserved to the coastal states under Article 7, must draw a measurement line under paragraph three which maximizes community interests at the expense of the state. Although no specific rule is promulgated for the special circumstance of a featureless shoreline, one may deduce a general policy from the express language of Article 7, paragraph five, which grants the

104. M. STROHL, *supra*, Chapter II, note 42, at 62–63.

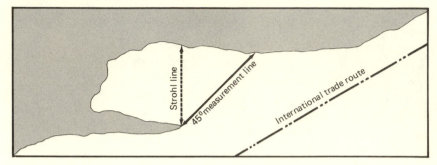

Figure 10. A comparison of the Strohl method and the 45° method.

coastal state the option of enclosing the *maximum area of water possible* for paragraph five purposes. This express language, read in conjunction with the overall view of Article 7 as an accommodation in favor of the exclusive interests of states, would militate in favor of the adoption of the 45° test rather than the closest point method for establishing an entrance point on a featureless coast.

In addition, there is nothing inherent in the "closest point" method which may serve as a reminder to states that, in keeping with general community policy in regard to bays, an entrance point must be selected which preserves the inland character of the waters thus enclosed. Because an angle of 45° represents the midline between two lines of opposite direction, the 45° test will lead to the selection of an entrance point which best approximates that point at which the direction of the waters change from those facing inland to those facing the sea. The use of the 45° test will not overly prejudice community interests because, as can be seen in Figure 10, major navigational routes are likely to remain unaffected, as mariners not heading for points within the bay will in most cases avoid the area altogether, following the direction of the nonindented coastline. The adoption of the 45° test would allow a coastal state maximum freedom to select as a natural entrance point under paragraph three a point on the featureless shoreline which will result in the enclosure of inland waters, the primary justification for placing the waters under exclusive littoral control.

The adoption of the 45° rule would also serve as a reminder that it is the geographical and mathematical requirements of paragraph two which must be served by the location of the measurement line under paragraph three. Such a reminder may be necessary in order to prevent a coastal state from succumbing to another tendency, all too prevalent among commentators, to jump ahead in Article 7 when special circumstances arise and to use paragraphs four and five to justify constructing a natural entrance point on the opposite shore at the furthest point to which a line of twenty-four miles can be constructed.[105] If this point is so far down the coast that both the underlying policies and the definitional requirements of Article 7 are violated, it is inevitable that states whose interests are compromised by such a decision will vigorously oppose it.

It is for precisely these reasons that the configuration and measurement rules for determining whether or not a juridical bay exists are placed first in Article 7, in paragraphs two and three. Only after the initial determination is made that an indentation is indeed a bay do the closing line limitation rules of paragraphs four and five become relevant. An understanding of this internal structure is critical to the determination of natural entrance points for paragraph three measurement purposes, and becomes even more critical when special circumstances arise. The first order decision in special cases must be to locate as natural entrance points not those which lie at the closest point on the opposite shore nor those which lie as far down the shore as is possible using a twenty-four-mile line, but rather those which best retain the landlocked nature of the indentation. Next, the semicircle test must be applied to determine whether these landlocked waters may qualify as a bay. If they do so, then and *only* then do the twenty-four-mile closing line rules of paragraphs four and five come into play. For all these reasons, the 45° test seems the most workable and least burdensome solution for the selection of a natural entrance point on a featureless coastline.

Islands

Paragraph three, sentence two, sets forth a special measurement rule to be used where, because of the presence of islands,[106] an

---

105. *See id.,* at 63. This tendency seems to result from confusing the measurement line prescribed by paragraph three with the closing line prescribed by paragraphs four and five.

106. It was not until this century that a need arose to define the geographical concept of an island in international legal terms. *See* C. SYMMONS, THE MARITIME ZONES OF

indentation has more than one mouth. In that case the semi-circle required for measurement purposes shall be drawn on a diameter line equal to the sum total of the lengths of the lines across the different mouths, or entrances, of the indentation.[107] In measuring the area of the actual indentation for comparison with that of the semi-circle, however, the water area enclosed by the low-water mark around the shore and a line drawn across the entire width of the bay, including both the lines drawn between islands *and* the islands themselves, is measured. Paragraph three, sentence three, provides that in measuring the water area thus enclosed, islands within the indentation shall be included as if they were part of the water area itself.[108] If the area of the indentation thus measured equals or exceeds the area of the semi-circle, a bay is deemed to exist.

ISLANDS IN INTERNATIONAL LAW 1–11, 18, 93, 252 (1979). In its final draft of Article 10 in 1956, the I.L.C. defined an island as "an area of land, surrounded by water, which in normal circumstances is permanently above the high water mark." [1956] 2 Y.B. INT'L L. COMM'N at 220. At the 1958 Conference, the United States proposed an amendment to Article 10 which defined an island as *"a naturally-formed area of land, surrounded by water, which is above water at high tide."* U.N. Doc. A/CONF.13/C.1/L.112; *reprinted in* 3 United Nations Conference on the Law of the Sea (1958), *supra* note 84, at 242. The United States felt such a change was necessary because the "permanently" and "in normal circumstances" criteria of the 1956 draft were conflicting, and because they wished to exclude the use of artificially created features as a means to extend the territorial sea. *Id.* The Commentary attached to the U.S. proposal points out that unlike other islands under international law, islands located behind the closing lines of bays or rivers do not generate their own territorial sea because their surrounding waters are merged into more extensively sovereign waters, the internal waters of the coastal state. The U.S. proposal was adopted by the First Committee as Article 10(1) of the Territorial Sea Convention. U.N. Doc. A/CONF.13/C.1/L.77, Rev. 2. Article 10(2) continues: "The territorial sea of an island is measured in accordance with the provisions of these articles." UNCLOS retains the language of Article 10(1) of the Territorial Sea Convention in Article 121(1). The remainder of Article 121 reads:

> 121(2) Except as provided for in paragraph 3, the territorial sea, the contiguous zone, the exclusive economic zone and the continental shelf of an island are determined in accordance with the provisions of this Convention applicable to other land territory.

> 121(3) Rocks which cannot sustain human habitation or economic life of their own shall have no exclusive economic zone or continental shelf.

UNCLOS, *supra,* at 48.

107. Territorial Sea Convention, *supra* Article 7, para. 3, sent. 2. For full text of Article 7, see *supra* text accompanying note 10.

108. Territorial Sea Convention, *supra* Article 7, para. 3, sent. 3. For full text of Article 7, see *supra* text accompanying note 10.

This method of measurement gives an advantage to the coastal state, because in drawing the semi-circle a smaller diameter line is used, whereas in measuring the indentation itself a state is allowed to use a line equal to the total distance measured between islands, *plus* the width of the islands themselves, as its axis, as well as to include islands within the bay as part of the water area. Moreover, this advantage was expressly intended by the drafters.

The legislative history of the special rules pertaining to islands is very illuminating and because it will be necessary to refer to this history at several points in the text below, it requires full explication. During its Fourth Session in 1952, the International Law Commission decided that it would need the advice of technical experts in order to draft the rules for bays. The Committee of Experts, which met at The Hague from April 14 to April 16, 1953, at the invitation of Professor François, Special Rapporteur of the International Law Commission on the regime of the territorial sea, had before it the following inquiries:

Accepting the low-water line system as the general rule for measuring the territorial sea, while in bays a straight line across the bay should circumscribe the "inland waters," what technical observations can be made as to

A. the definition of a bay as opposed to a mere curvature in the coastline?
B. any relation between the maximum length (B miles) of the above-mentioned straight line and the width of the territorial sea?
C. the points between which the said straight line should be drawn?
D. the direction of or the points between which this line should be drawn in case different lines of B miles are conceivable?

In reply, the Committee of Experts stated:

ad A. 1. A bay is a bay in the juridical sense, if its area is as large as, or larger than that of the semi-circle drawn on the entrance of that bay. Historical bays are excepted: they should be indicated as such on the maps.
    2. *If a bay has more than one entrance—as indicated sub B— this semi-circle should be drawn on a line as long as the sum total of the length of the different entrances.*

        3. *Islands within a bay should be included as if they were part of the water area of the bay.*

ad B. 1. The closing line across a (juridical) bay should not exceed 10 miles in width, this being twice the range of vision to the horizon in clear weather, from the eye of a mariner at a height of 5 metres (which is the internationally accepted height for hydrogeographical purposes). In cases of considerable tidal differences the low-water lines should be taken as the shore-lines between which the width of the bay should be computed.

        2. *If the entrance of a (juridical) bay is split up into a number of smaller openings by various islands, closing lines across these openings may be drawn provided that none of these lines exceeds five miles in length—except one which may extend up to a maximum of 10 miles.*

ad C. 1. In case the entrance of the bay does not exceed 10 miles in width, the line inter fauces terrarum should constitute the delimitation between inland-waters and the territorial sea.

        2. In case the entrance of the bay exceeds 10 miles, a closing line of this length should be drawn within the bay. When different lines of this length can be drawn, that line should be chosen which encloses the maximum water area within the bay.

ad D. D. has become redundant by the answer to foregoing question.[10]

In 1953 and 1954, the Special Rapporteur submitted to the International Law Commission various drafts of Article 7 which incorporated all of the recommendations of the Committee of Experts, including A(2), A(3), and B(2) above relating to islands.[110] At its Seventh Session in 1955, the Commission adopted a new draft article, which reflected most of the Committee's recommendations, but extended the limit on the closing line for single-mouthed bays to twenty-five miles and deleted section

---

109. *Report of the Committee of Experts on technical questions concerning the territorial sea,* undated, attached as Annex to Addendum to the Second Report on the Regime of the Territorial Sea by J. P. A. François, Special Rapporteur, U.N. Doc. A/CN.4/61/Add.1, May 18, 1953, *reprinted in* [1953] 2 Y.B. Int'l L. Comm'n 75, 77–78 (emphasis added to sections relating to islands).

110. U.N. Doc. A/CN.4/90, at 25; U.N. Doc. A/CN.4/77, at 10.

B(2) which had placed a limitation on the closing lines between islands. That part of the 1955 draft pertinent to islands reads as follows:

> If a bay has more than one *entrance,* this semi-circle shall be drawn on a line as long as the sum total of the length of the different entrances. Islands within a bay shall be included as if they were part of the water area of the bay.[111]

During its Eighth Session in 1956, the International Law Commission adopted yet another draft of Article 7. Except for a change in the recommended length of the closing line for single-mouthed bays from twenty-five miles to fifteen miles, the language of this draft is almost identical to that contained in the 1955 draft article. As pertains to islands, the 1956 draft reads:

> If a bay has more than one *mouth,* this semi-circle shall be drawn on a line as long as the sum total of the length of the different *mouths.* Islands within a bay shall be included as if they were part of the water area of the bay.[112]

The *Commentary* which accompanied both the 1955 and 1956 drafts expressly states the intent of the Commission to design a special legislative scheme for bay-related islands and the multi-mouthed bays which they create. The 1955 *Commentary* reads as follows:

> If, as a result of the presence of islands, an indentation which has to be established as a "bay" has more than one *entrance,* the sum total of the length of the different *entrances* will be regarded as the length of the bay. Here, the *Commission's intention* was to indicate that the presence of islands at the entrance to an indentation links it [the indentation] more closely with the territory, which may justify some alteration of the proportion between the length and depth of the indentation. In such a case an indentation which without islands at its entrance would not fulfill the necessary conditions *is to be recognized* as a bay.[113]

---

111. [1955] 2 Y.B. INT'L L. COMM'N at 36 (emphasis added).
112. [1956] 2 Y.B. INT'L L. COMM'N at 268–69 (emphasis added).
113. [1955] 2 Y.B. INT'L L. COMM'N at 37 (emphasis added). Note the use of "mouth" and "entrance" as interchangeable terms.

Several intentions are clarified in this *Commentary*. First, it is obvious that the Commission considered "mouths" and "entrances" as synonymous terms, as they are used interchangeably throughout the draft articles and the *Commentary*. This usage reinforces the point made above that a variety of geographical features are included within the term "natural entrance points." Since natural entrance points obviously exist at each land terminus of an entrance, islands which form multiple entrances to an indentation by definition form natural entrance points as well.

Secondly, the Commission makes clear that the presence of islands which form separate entrances creates an indentation which is even more landlocked than one whose axis is completely open to the sea. This geographic fact justifies an alteration in the strict application of the semi-circle rule, the purpose of which after all is to guarantee the fulfillment of the well-marked and landlocked criteria.

The third and perhaps most important indication of an intent to create a special regime for multi-mouthed bays is revealed in the Commission's use of the imperative to direct that in such cases, an indentation which without the presence of the islands would not meet the necessary conditions "*is to be recognized* as a bay."

The relevant language pertaining to islands in both Article 7 and the *Commentary* is mandatory:

> Where, because of the presence of islands, an indentation has more than one mouth, the semi-circle *shall be drawn.* . . .[114]

> [A]n indentation which without islands at its entrance would not fulfill the necessary conditions *is to be recognized* as a bay.[115]

It was not the intent of the drafters to create an optional scheme that states might choose to apply if they so desired, as in the case under the straight baseline system of Article 4. The Commission's intent, self-evident from their official *Commentary*, was to create a mandatory scheme to cover the commonly occurring geographical phenomenon of islands creating more than one entrance to

114. Territorial Sea Convention, Article 7, para. 3, sent. 2 (emphasis added). For full text of Article 7, see text accompanying note 10.
115. [1955] 2 Y.B. Int'l L. Comm'n at 37 (emphasis added).

an indentation and thereby locking the waters of that indentation even more closely to the land and marking the entrances to that indentation even more clearly from the sea.

The language of the 1956 *Commentary* reveals the same intent:

> If, as a result of the presence of islands, an indentation whose features as a "bay" have to be established has more than one mouth, the total length of the lines drawn across all the different mouths will be regarded as the width of the bay. Here, the Commission's intention was to indicate that the presence of islands at the mouth of an indentation tends to link it [the indentation] more closely to the mainland, and this consideration may justify some alteration in the ratio between the width and the penetration of the indentation. In such cases an indentation which, if it had no islands at its mouth, would not fulfil the necessary conditions, is to be recognized as a bay. *Nevertheless, islands at the mouth of a bay cannot be considered as "closing" the bay if the ordinary sea route passes between them and the coast.*[116]

The only significant variation from the 1955 *Commentary* is the addition of the last italicized sentence, which was inserted at the insistence of the United Kingdom which wished to preserve the right of innocent passage through areas which previously had been considered territorial sea. Although successful in preserving this right under Article 4, a U.K. Amendment to Article 7 to this effect, introduced 15 April 1958, was rejected by a vote of 28 to 18 with 22 abstentions.[117] Having been rejected in amendment form by the First Committee in 1958, the limitation on the closure of multi-mouthed bays implied in the final sentence of the 1956 *Commentary* above can no longer be considered a part of the special regime for bay-related islands created under Article 7.[118] It is likely that the First Committee resisted placing limiting language into the Convention which is made unnecessary by the fact that islands which truly create multiple entrances to an indentation, in concert with the lines drawn across these entrances, form

---

116. [1956] 2 Y.B. INT'L L. COMM'N at 269 (emphasis added).
117. U.N. Doc. A/CONF.13/C.1/L.62, in 3 United Nations Conference on the Law of the Sea (1958), *supra* note 84, at 146.
118. Likewise, no such limitation on bay closure is to be found in UNCLOS, although the restriction in Article 4 (straight baselines) *is* preserved in UNCLOS, *supra*, Article 8(2), at 4.

the seaward boundary of the internal waters of the coastal state and therefore do not tend to enclose major navigational routes.[119]

Some commentators, apparently aggrieved by the intent of the drafters to grant special status to multi-mouthed bays, have attempted to deny or dilute the regime established under Article 7. In his recent work on islands, Bowett cites the language of Article 7, paragraph three, as well as the 1955 and 1956 *Commentaries* in full and concludes that "[i]n effect, islands are ignored for the purposes of Article 7."[120] Perhaps the concerns of the United Kingdom alluded to above are reflected in this restrictive view. But to read Article 7, paragraph three, as indicating that islands in effect are to be ignored under Article 7 is to seriously misinterpret the intent of the drafters and the purpose of paragraph three.

Far from ignoring islands, the Committee of Experts, the International Law Commission, and the First Committee of the full Conference each expressly adopted rules which grant special significance to bay-related islands. Islands which create more than one entrance to what might in some cases be deemed a mere curvature of the coast have the effect of granting that indentation status as a juridical bay.[121] Paragraph three, sentence two, codifies community recognition of the fact that the presence of such islands creates an even more landlocked and well-marked inden-

---

119. This is not the case, however, with islands off the coast which a state chooses to enclose by the straight baseline system of Article 4. Because these islands do not create separate entrances to bays but merely fringe the mainland, such optional enclosure may well intersect major sea routes and is properly limited by the right of innocent passage.

120. D. Bowett, The Legal Regime of Islands in International Law 30 (1979). It is possible that this language is meant to refer only to the last sentence of paragraph three which reads, "Islands within an indentation shall be included as if they were part of the water area of the indentation." If so, the statement proves too much, as it appears to refer to the whole of paragraph three relating to islands, thereby causing considerable confusion and misapplication among those citing Mr. Bowett's work as authority.

121. For example, the keys along the southern coast of Florida, opposite and south of Miami, give Biscayne Bay a number of mouths and account for its status as internal waters. Without these keys, the Bay would be little more than an elongated, irregular coastal indentaion. Pearcy, *supra*, Chapter II, note 6, at 7. Likewise, there would *be* no coastal indentation without the presence of Long Island, which creates a juridical bay comprised of Long Island Sound and portions of Block Island Sound. *See* United States v. Maine et al (Rhode Island and New York Boundary Case), 469 U.S. 504, 105 S.Ct 992, 83 L. Ed. 2d 998 (1985).

tation than one whose axis is fully open to the sea. Islands which create multiple entrances to an indentation tie that indentation more closely to the land regime and therefore trigger a special relaxation in the areal and geographical requirements for a bay. Islands which create more than one entrance to an indentation, even one which might otherwise be deemed a mere curvature of the coast, have the legal effect of granting that indentation bay status. One may scarcely ignore a geographical feature which has been expressly given such profound juridical significance.

The recognition that islands and the multi-mouthed bays which they create deserve special treatment under international law is not unique to the 1958 Convention. As early as 1805, Azuni wrote:

> It is already established among polished [sic] nations that in places where the land by its curve forms a bay or a gulf we must suppose a line to be drawn from one point of the inclosing land to the other *or along the small islands which extend beyond the headlands of the bay,* and that the whole of this bay or gulf is to be considered as [internal] sea. . . .[122]

Calvo saw the presence of such islands as enhancing the coastal state's ability to defend the indentation which the islands sheltered and therefore as creating a special category for protected waters:

> Gulfs and bays protected *either naturally by islands,* sand bars, or rocks, or by the cross fire of guns placed on each side of their entrances belong to the territorial sovereignty adjoining.[123]

Ortolan, writing in 1893, likewise demonstrated the general recognition of islands as enhancing the defensibility of a bay as well as creating an alternative basis for bay claims:

> We must classify under the same heading as roadsteads and ports, gulfs, and bays and all other indentations. . . when these indentations made in the land of a single State do not exceed in width the

---

122. D. AZUNI, *supra,* Chapter III, note 2, §17, at 254 (emphasis added).
123. C. CALVO, *supra,* Chapter III, note 3, §367 (emphasis added).

double range of cannon or when the entrance may be controlled by artillery *or when it is naturally defended by islands. . . .*[124]

This historical recognition of islands as creating an exceptionally land-related and protected multi-mouthed bay is concretized in paragraph three, and the intent of the drafters to create a special regime for such waters is fully supported in the legislative history. With such a clear indication of intent, it is somewhat surprising that so many questions are raised in the academic literature concerning the nature of this regime and so many answers provided which seem to have no basis in either the language of the Convention, the legislative history, or the historical treatment of bays.

One possible source of confusion may be that, in almost every case, recent scholars have mischaracterized the relevant language of paragraph three as referring to islands which occur *"in* the mouth of the bay."[125] Not only is this unfortunate mischaracterization unreflected in nature, which has not seen fit to arrange islands in a perfect line across the mouth of most indentations,[126] but it is wholly unsupported by the language of paragraph three which sets forth *no* locational requirements whatever for islands which create multiple entrances to an indentation. The Convention does not require that such islands lie "in," "on," "within," or in any other geographical relationship to the mouth of a bay.[127]

---

124. J. ORTOLAN, *supra,* Chapter III, note 50, at 156 (emphasis added); *see also* almost identical language in R. PIEDELIEVRE, *supra,* Chapter III, note 50, §417, at 363.

125. *See, e.g.,* R. HODGSON & L. ALEXANDER, *supra* note 6 at 12; M. STROHL, *supra,* Chapter II, note 42, at 70; 1 A. SHALOWITZ, *supra,* Chapter I, note 20, at 220; P. BEAZLEY, *supra,* Chapter I, note 24, at 18–19 (emphasis addded).

126. *See, e.g.,* the chart of Naragansett Bay in Rhode Island. If islands are formed by silting or are part of a submerged peninsula, they are more likely to be in an orderly row. But if they are the result of independent natural activity, such as volcanic action or erosion from tidal currents, their position will not be logically arranged in a straight line between mainland entrance points. M. STROHL, *supra,* Chapter II, note 42, at 60.

127. Both the 1955 and 1956 *Commentary* refer to islands lying "at" the mouth (1956) or entrance (1955) of an indentation as linking the indentation more closely to the mainland, but this term embodies the concept that islands which create separate entrances to an indentation will by definition lie in relatively close proximity to that indentation. It does not indicate that the islands must lie *in a straight line* between "headlands"(another mischaracterization), as Bowett and others suggest. D. BOWETT, *supra* note 120, at 30–31. The literature is replete with references (e.g., D. AZUNI, *supra* text accompanying note 122) which indicate that islands lying *beyond* bay headlands might create multiple entrances to the bay.

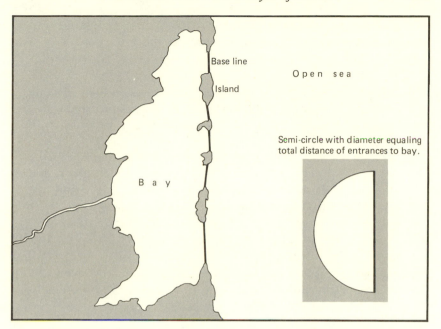

Figure 11. Islands misconceived as "in the mouth of the bay."

In fact, the very language of sentence two expressly states that because of the presence of such islands, an indentation will have *more* than one mouth, not the single one implied by the use of the phrase "in the *mouth* of the bay." The key concept under Article 7 is the *entrance* to the bay, which must be well marked and in such proportion to the depth as to enclose landlocked waters. It is the fact that certain islands factually create *multiple entrances* to the bay, *not* their location, which warrants the application of the special measurement rules of paragraph three, sentence two.

It is a well-settled learning theory that the language initially used to circumscribe a concept determines all further conceptualizations.[128] Having misstated the referent of paragraph three, sentence two, as "islands *in* the mouth of a bay" rather than as "islands which create more than one mouth to an indentation," most commentators proceed to conceptualize the idea *visually* in the same terms. In almost every text surveyed, a slight variant of

128. *See* S. ENGLEMANN, CONCEPTUAL THINKING (1970).

Figure 11 appears as a supposed illustration of the geographical situation envisioned by paragraph three, sentence two.[129]

The results of this conceptual and visual error are two-fold:

1. Those making the initial mischaracterization go further along the same conceptual track and begin to design complicated schemes to handle "exceptions" to the non-rule which they have established.
2. Others reading the texts of *these* commentators incorporate the language concept error, the visual representation error, and the new tests devised to handle "exceptions" to the non-rule into their own research work.

The fact that the original conceptual errors are made by scholars and geographers whose work is respected and whose expertise is well known creates an even greater danger that the errors will be repeated by subsequent commentators, lawyers, and judicial bodies without reasoned analysis of the actual language of the statute or the legislative history.

The Hodgson and Alexander interpretation of the paragraph three rules relating to islands is an example of the problem cited. In a subsection of their work on special circumstances entitled "Islands and the Mouth of the Bay,"[130] the authors contend that islands may occur in three distinct configurations in relation to the *closing line* of a bay:

1. islands situated *in the mouth of the bay* in such a way that the *closing line* bisects them;
2. islands which *screen* the mouth of the bay; and
3. islands which form the *headlands* of a bay.[131]

Serious misconceptions inhere in both the general rule that these authors set forth and the so-called exceptions to which the rule gives rise.

The authors' first premise is that regardless of the natural entrances formed by the islands themselves, a "closing" line must

---

129. The map reproduced herein is taken from R. Hodgson & L. Alexander, *supra* note 66, at 16. *See also* P. Beazley, *supra*, Chapter 1, note 24, at 18; 1 A. Shalowitz, *supra*, Chapter I, note 20, at 221; Pearcy, *supra*, Chapter II, note 6, at 8; D. Bowett, *supra* note 120, at 31-37. Bowett and others have tended to simply reproduce the map devised by Hodgson and Alexander.
130. R. Hodgson & L. Alexander, *supra* note 6, at 12–20.
131. *Id.* Emphasized phrases indicate critical misconceptions.

initially be drawn between the mainland entrance points. If this line intersects an island, that island may be incorporated into the closing line, which will now be measured by the various lines between the "headlands" and the islands. "Islands not intersected by the line between *natural entrance points* should not be utilized in the closing line."[132] One need scarcely point out that no authority is cited for this conclusion and that none exists in either the language of Article 7, the legislative history, or the historical development of the international law of bays.

The most serious structural error in this approach lies in the direction to draw a "closing line" under paragraph three *prior* to the determination of the juridical status of the indentation, a procedure which is clearly contraindicated by the language and structure of Article 7. A final closing line is drawn under paragraph four or five only *after* a bay determination has been made using the definitional and measurement rules set forth in paragraphs two and three. The placement of the special rules for islands within paragraph three indicates that these rules are to be applied as part of this initial juridical determination.

The presence of islands which create multiple entrances to an indentation triggers a certain relaxation in the geographical and mathematical requirements of paragraph two, even to the extent that an indentation which without such islands would fail to meet the "necessary conditions" is nonetheless to be recognized as a juridical bay. It is obvious that if a "closing" line is drawn as Hodgson and Alexander suggest, ignoring the natural entrances created by the islands unless they bisect the premature "closing" line and thus closing the bay prior to juridical determination, the special regime for bay-related islands intended by the drafters is effectively vitiated. The text of Article 7 and the legislative history indicate clearly that, by their very presence, islands may significantly affect the juridical determination of an indentation, while Hodgson and Alexander and their progeny[133] insist that the initial determination take place as if the islands were not there.

Another fundamental error lies in the assertion that although it is mandatory under Article 7 that a state draw lines between islands for semi-circle measurement purposes under paragraph

---

132. *Id.*, at 12.
133. *See, e.g.*, P. BEAZLEY, *supra*, Chapter I, note 24, at 18–19; D. BOWETT, *supra* note 120, at 31.

three, these same lines may not be used as closing lines under paragraphs four and five. Instead, the authors posit the rule that, regardless of the presence of islands, the closing line of the indentation is to be drawn between "entrance points," presumably on the mainland, denying completely the geographical fact expressly addressed by paragraph three, sentence two, that when islands form separate mouths or entrances to an indentation, the natural entrance points no longer lie solely on the mainland but at the land terminus of each entrance, however numerous these entrances may be due to the presence of the islands.

Because the closing line issue has been incorrectly merged into the analysis of paragraph three by Hodgson and Alexander and others, and because the issue is so central to a general understanding of the special regime devised for islands under Article 7, it will be necessary to address the issue at this point, at the same time reiterating that such closing lines are in actuality *not* drawn until the initial bay determination has been made taking all islands which create entrances into the bay fully into account.

Although there is no express directive in Article 7 to the effect that the measurement lines between islands made mandatory under paragraph three are to become the official closing lines of a multi-mouthed bay, one may find implicit authority in the fact that once the indentation has been measured utilizing the lines between islands and a positive juridical determination has been made on the waters enclosed by these lines, it makes no sense whatever to draw the closing line landward of the islands, thereby deleting areas of water already effectively declared internal.

Even more conclusive authority may be derived from the legislative history relevant to the closing line issue. It appears that the Committee of Experts conceived of the measurement lines and the closing lines between islands as one and the same and addressed the question in two separate sections of their 1953 *Report*:

ad A. 2. If a bay has *more than one entrance*—as indicated sub B— this semi-circle should be drawn on a line as long as the sum total of the length of the *different entrances.*
ad B. 2. If the entrance of a (juridical) bay[134] is split up into a

---

134. Note that the juridical determination has already been made by the time the closing line issue becomes relevant (footnote added).

> number of smaller openings by various islands, *closing lines* across these openings may be drawn, provided that none of these lines exceeds five miles in length—except one which may extend up to a maximum of ten miles.[135]

This language is most illuminating for two reasons. First, it is evident that the drafters perceived of the lines drawn across multiple entrances created by islands as closing lines, lines which by their very definition form the seaward limit of internal waters as well as the baseline of the territorial sea. Secondly, and perhaps even more interestingly, this section of the *Report,* read *in pari materia* with the section preceding, proves beyond doubt that even in the earliest drafting stages, it was never intended that the term "islands" was to refer solely to those islands which create multiple entrances by lying neatly "in the mouth" of a bay. In the section of the *Report* just preceding *ad B.2* above, the Committee limited the normal closing line of a single-mouthed bay to ten miles.[136] Yet they expressly did *not* so limit the sum total of multiple entrances created by islands. If the drafters *had* conceived of islands which create multiple entrances to bays as limited to those bisecting a "normal" ten-mile closing line, as Hodgson and Alexander and many others suggest, it is obvious that the sum of the various openings *between* the island and mainland entrance points would then have to total *less* than ten miles. It is evident that, by expressly allowing the closing lines drawn between the various islands and the mainland to measure no more than five miles with the exception of one entrance which might measure ten miles *in and of itself,* the drafters recognized that the sum total of the multiple entrances created by islands *could* exceed the ten-mile limit set for single-mouthed bays. In such circumstances, there is no way that the islands creating these multiple entrances could lie in a straight line across a ten-mile opening.

It must therefore be concluded that the drafters fully realized that islands which create multiple entrances to bays are quite likely to occur geographically seaward of the mainland entrance points and, further, having made it permissible to draw closing lines across the various openings, that the presumptive limit of internal waters would move seaward as well. By placing a mathe-

---

135. *Report of the Committee of Experts,* (1953), *supra* note 18, §ad B(2).
136. *Id.*

matical limit on the length of multiple closing lines, the drafters merely limited the extent of such seaward expansion.

The draft article submitted to the International Law Commission by the Special Rapporteur incorporated the two-tiered approach of the Commitee of Experts and expressly directed that both measurement lines and closing lines be drawn across the entrances to multi-mouthed bays. The 1955 draft article prepared by the Commission, however, while retaining the general measurement rules, deleted the express reference to closing lines "across these openings."[137] The legislative history of this decision indicates that the change was not due to any lack of agreement among the drafters that closing lines should be drawn across multiple entrances. This was an implicit assumption. Rather, the change appears to have taken place within the context of the debate over the prescribed length of the closing line for *single-mouthed* bays.

During its Seventh Session in 1955, the International Law Commission determined that for a variety of reasons the limit on the width of the regular closing line should be increased from ten miles to twenty-five miles.[138] In discussing how the change might affect other sections of Article 7, the islands issue arose; and Mr. Sandström pointed out that the presence of islands actually emphasized, from a geographic point of view, the inland character of the waters within the bay.[139] Special Rapporteur François then drew the attention of the members to paragraph three of his draft text [140] and proposed that the wording be changed to reflect the new twenty-five-mile limitation, i.e., that closing lines be drawn between islands provided that none of these openings exceeded five miles, except for one which might extend up to twenty-five miles.[141]

---

137. *See Report of the Committee of Experts* (1953), *supra* note 18, §ad B(2). *See also* U. N. Doc. A/CN.4/77, at 10.
138. [1955] 1 Y.B. Int'l L. Comm'n at 206–11. See *infra* discussion of paragraph 4 for full legislative history of this decision.
139. [1955] 2 Y.B. Int'l L. Comm'n at 215.
140. U.N. Doc. A/CN.4/93. The language of paragraph three of the draft text is virtually identical to §ad B.2. of the *Report of the Committee of Experts. See supra* note 135.
141. [1955] 2 Y.B. Int'l L. Comm'n at 215, para. 14. Note again that there was no intent to limit the sum total of closing lines between islands to the twenty-five-mile limit placed on single-mouthed bays, nor was there any assumption that such islands would lie "in" the mouth of a bay.

Mr. Krylov objected to such a provision as cumbersome and said it was unnecessary to overload the text with such detailed provisions. He proposed that no provision limiting the length of closing lines drawn across multiple entrances be inserted in Article 7, so as to leave future arbitrators a free hand to decide specific controversies on a case by case basis.[142]

Committee chairman García Amador, agreeing to some extent with Mr. Krylov, stated that paragraph three as proposed by the Special Rapporteur was a further example of adopting arbitrary distances for closing lines without any rational foundation. He proposed an amendment to read as follows:

> 3. If the entrance of a bay is split up into a smaller number of openings by various islands, closing lines across these openings may be drawn.[143]

Mr. Fitzmaurice, a member from the U.K., argued that there were good reasons to retain such a provision since islands lying near the mouth of a bay existed so commonly in nature. However, he stated that he would accept, with reluctance, Mr. Krylov's proposal to delete the provision altogether [144] before he would consider Mr. García Amador's amendment which he felt would be tantamount to removing all limitations, making it possible to draw closing lines from island to island endlessly, enclosing hundreds of miles of open sea.[145]

No consensus on these views having been achieved, Mr. Sandström suggested that the problem might be resolved to the satisfaction of all if a distance of twenty-five miles were specified as the maximum acceptable *sum total* of the various closing lines drawn connecting the islands and the mainland. This would correspond to the twenty-five-mile limit placed on the opening to a single-mouthed bay.[146] It is quite interesting to note, in view of

---

142. *Id.,* at 215, para. 16.
143. *Id.,* at 215, para. 18.
144. *Id.,* at 215, para. 19.
145. *Id.,* at 215, para. 20. In his position, Mr. Fitzmaurice reflected the U.K. concern over closing lines interfering impermissibly with ocean traffic. He failed to note the obvious check on such interference provided by the language of paragraph three, sentence two, i.e., that the relevant islands are those which create *entrances* to the indentation. Obviously, those islands lying hundreds of miles from shore could in no way be claimed to create well-marked entrances to a landlocked indentation.
146. *Id.,* at 215, para. 22.

later analysis, that no support whatever is recorded for this proposal.

At last, Chairman García Amador proposed that in view of so many differing opinions, perhaps the best course would be to withdraw his proposed amendment to paragraph three altogether for the time being, although he would reserve the right to introduce his own draft on the topic at a later stage in the proceedings,[147] whereupon Mr. Krylov's proposal to delete the provision placing a *limit* on the length of closing lines between islands was adopted by nine votes to none with three abstentions.[148] Clearly, it was never intended that the deletion would foreclose the actual drawing of closing lines across multiple entrances created by the presence of islands.

A somewhat detailed summary of the legislative history on the island closing line issue has been included at this point because several intentions are clarified thereby:

1. There was no intent on the part of the drafters, revealed in either the 1955 records above nor in any subsequent session,[149] to limit the referent of Article 7, paragraph three, to islands which lie "in the mouth" of an indentation. Indeed, evidence derived from both the actual language of Article 7 and the legislative record suggests a directly contrary interpretation.
2. There was an implicit assumption among delegates that when islands create multiple entrances to a bay, the proper closing line is one which connects the various islands with the land territory, thus enclosing the full extent of the indentation landward of the islands as internal waters of the coastal state.
3. The drafters expressly rejected the following limitation on such closing lines:
   (a) the "five- and twenty-five-mile" limitation proposed by François;
   (b) the "twenty-five-mile maximum sum total" limitation of Sandström;
   (c) the "no closing lines across major sea routes" limitation of Fitzmaurice.[150]

Since all of the foregoing limitations were expressly rejected by

---

147. *Id.*, at 215, paras. 23–24.
148. *Id.*, at 215.
149. *See* [1956] 1–2 Y.B. Int'l L. Comm'n; 3 United Nations Conference on the Law of the Sea (1958), *supra* note 84.
150. *See supra* note 117.

the drafters, one must conclude that none of these concepts remains implicit in the final language of the Convention.[151] One may also conclude that the rationale of the Krylov proposal, to delete all reference to limitations on closing lines between islands so as to grant decision makers flexibility in deciding future cases, remains an overriding concept. Such a conclusion is consistent with the basic conception of the drafters who recognized that islands which create multiple well-marked entrances to an indentation, and thereby lock that indentation even more closely within the land territory, create a special indentation deserving of a special regime within which the semi-circle test is not so rigidly applied and, therefore, the well-marked and landlocked requirements assume heightened importance.

The Hodgson and Alexander approach to island closing lines has been eschewed by several knowledgeable commentators. Pearcy maintains that when bays have several channels of ingress due to the presence of islands, an individual closing line is to be drawn across each entrance. According to Pearcy, situations of this kind abound along some portions of the coast, the one of most impressive dimensions being Mississippi Sound which is partially enclosed by a series of sandy islands.[152] Strohl likewise states

151. Shalowitz has said that, although the question of whether or not the closing lines between islands must total no more than twenty-four miles was left open by the Convention, we nonetheless may surmise that since the closing line limitation appears in paragraph four following the measurement rules for both single and multi-mouthed bays, the twenty-four mile limit was intended to apply to both. This is a logical approach in terms of the structural analysis of Article 7, but is unfortunately not borne out by the legislative history above, which reveals that such a limit was never intended and was in fact rejected when proposed. Further evidence that paragraph four was intended to apply only to single-mouthed bays may be gleaned from the language of paragraph four itself, which states that "[i]f the distance between the low-water marks of the natural entrance points of a bay does not exceed twenty-four miles, a closing line may be drawn between these *two* low-water marks. . . . " Territorial Sea Convention, Article 7, paragraph four (emphasis added). It seems more likely that when the section relating to limitations on island closing lines was deleted, it left a gap which one must fill in by resort to the legislative history. There is no indication that the drafters intended to place a twenty-four-mile limit on the sum total of island-created entrances, and some evidence that they intended to leave the question open in order to allow flexibility in decision making. *See supra* note 143 and accompanying text.

152. Pearcy, *Measurement of the U.S. Territorial Sea*, 40 DEP'T ST. BULL. 963, 964–66, 969 (1959), *reprinted in* 4 M. WHITEMAN, DIGEST OF INTERNATIONAL LAW 209–211 (1965). Even Pearcy, however, falls prey to the tendency to render the concept visually to include hypothetical islands lying in a straight line between mainland entrance points. *See* Pearcy, *supra,* at 966, Figure 4.

that although a closing line occurs when a boundary line dividing internal waters and the marginal belt is drawn between natural entrance points, paragraph three, sentence two, makes it clear that such a line need not be continuous as in the case of islands which create multiple entrances to the bay.[153]

The problem does not end here, however. In spite of significant evidence to the contrary provided by the language and structure of Article 7, the legislative history, and the work of ancient and contemporary scholars, Hodgson and Alexander and others influenced by their work insist that closing lines may not be drawn between islands unless such islands happen to occur precisely on the line erroneously and prematurely drawn between mainland entrance points. Having posited such a rule, it must quickly become obvious that the majority of island formations which create multiple entrances to an indentation do not conform to this geographical criterion.[154] One would think it reasonable to conclude in light of such coastal reality that the rule posited could not therefore have been intended by the drafters. Instead, these authors maintain that islands which do not fit their general rule, i.e., the majority, are "exceptions" for which exceptional rules must be devised.

The first Hodgson and Alexander "exception" is said to arise when islands occur seaward of the prematurely delimited mouth of the bay. Hodgson and Alexander have devised a new concept to cover such situations, where "a series of islands" which do not lie in a straight line *"in the mouth* of the bay" nonetheless naturally *"screen"* the bay. The exceptional rule devised to apply to such a "screen" is as follows:

> If the islands serve to block more than one-half of the opening of a bay, they may be judged to "screen" the mouth of the bay from the sea.[155]

The authors contend that since more than half of the mouth is blocked by islands, the "screen" should be considered the "dom-

---

153. M. STROHL, *supra,* Chapter II, note 42, at 70. Like Pearcy, however, Strohl is not completely free of conceptual error, as is evident in his description of such islands as lying "*in* the mouth" of the bay. *Id.*

154. P. BEAZLEY, *supra,* Chapter I, note 24, at 19; M. STROHL, *supra,* Chapter II, note 42, at 60.

155. R. HODGSON & L. ALEXANDER, *supra* note 6, at 17.

inant geographic characteristic" of the mouth and therefore serve to enclose the waters within the bay. This screen of islands is the "natural closure" of the bay, even if not situated directly in the mouth, because it forms the "natural line which terminates the conditions of a landlocked or bay-like enclosure." Therefore, the bay-closing line may be drawn by using these "screening" islands.[156]

Hodgson and Alexander cite no authority for their "screening" or "dominant geographic characteristic" concepts; nor do they do so for the rule that in order for such "screens" to be used as a closing line, they must block more than one-half of the "opening." As we have seen, there is simply no justification for arbitrary rules such as these when the so-called exception is no exception at all, but rather lies squarely within the geographical configuration envisioned by the drafters and addressed in paragraph three. Nevertheless, the "screening" concept has been incorporated wholesale into several other works.

Bowett contends that where islands do not lie in "what would be the normal line from headland to headland" and yet block more than one-half of the opening, they operate as a "natural screen" between bay and sea. Therefore the closing line should be drawn using the screen rather than the "natural entrance points." Bowett even goes so far as to reproduce the Hodgson and Alexander map illustrating this supposed exception.[157] Beazley uses similar maps to illustrate the point that in such cases, it *may* be legitimate to treat the outermost islands as the entrance to the bay rather than the "headlands" of the main coast.[158]

In a later work, Hodgson repeats the thesis set forth above and adds the additional rule that when the screening islands continue beyond the "natural entrance points," the closing line should not be extended to include them, unless they are part of a straight baseline system.[159]

---

156. *Id.*, at 17–20.
157. D. BOWETT, *supra* note 120, at 32, Figure D.
158. *See* P. BEAZLEY, *supra*, Chapter I, note 24, §6.26 and Figures 8a & 8b, at 19.
159. Hodgson, *Islands: Normal and Special Circumstances,* in LAW OF THE SEA: THE EMERGING REGIME OF THE OCEANS 168 (Law of the Sea Institute 1974). This last clause indicates that the "screening" theory may be the result of conceptual confusion between island "screens" and the island fringes referred to in Article 4. This confusion is further illustrated by Beazley's comment that when a string of islands forms a markedly concave arc and the only way to meet the semicircle test would be to treat the

Even Shalowitz appears to see islands lying seaward of the "headlands" as an exception not provided for in Article 7.[160] He does not, however, subscribe to the "screening" theory, arguing instead that the closing line should be drawn connecting the islands to the mainland, a conclusion based on the express statement in the legislative history that islands which create separate entrances to an indentation link that indentation more closely to the mainland, and therefore must be considered as part of the seaward boundary of the internal waters of the state.

Each commentator above has in fact accepted the thesis that closing lines may in fact be drawn between islands, but in most cases it is an acceptance based upon an erroneous interpretation of the *Convention* which holds that islands lying seaward of the mainland are not contemplated by Article 7, and thus are exceptions to the rules set forth therein. This misconception in turn has led to the development of rules which are totally unwarranted by the *Convention* but which have begun to be cited as authority by lawyers and law clerks in drafting briefs and opinions related to bays. Arguments under Article 7 now routinely include the issue of whether or not the islands in a particular fact situation do or do not "screen" more than one-half of the bay opening,[161]

---

islands as forming more than one mouth to the indentation, perhaps these islands should be treated under the straight baseline system of Article 4. P. BEAZLEY, *supra*, Chapter II, note 1, at 19. Clearly, this is misguided for two reasons. First, as indicated in the discussion above, such a situation was clearly envisaged by the drafters as falling under Article 7; and second, the language of Article 7, paragraph three is mandatory. There is no option to utilize the straight baseline system of Article 4 when islands form multiple entrances into an indentation.

160. 1 A. SHALOWITZ, *supra*, Chapter I, note 20, at 225.

161. For example, Bowett recently provided an opinion to the U.S. Government in reference to a case in which he appeared, in his capacity as a practitioner, as an expert witness. [*See* U.S. Exhibit No. 62, United States v. Maine et al, (Rhode Island and New York Boundary Case), 469 U.S. 504, 105 S.Ct. 992, 83 L.Ed. 2d 998 (1985)]. In the course of this opinion, Bowett expanded on the "screening" theory and argued that in order for islands to be seen as "screening" a bay, there must first exist a well-marked indentation across the mouth of which the islands may be regarded as a "screen." He contended that no matter how many mouths may be formed by the screen of islands, the rule in Article 7 presupposes a well-marked indentation formed by the *mainland coast*. (*Id.*, at 7.) This is of course an impermissible interpretation in light of the language of Article 7 and the legislative history which clearly indicates that islands *themselves* may create a well-marked and landlocked indentation, even to the extent that an indentation which might not meet the requirements for a bay without the islands *is* to be recognized as a bay when islands

a criterion which should not even be considered in determining whether or not an indentation meets the test for a juridical bay. For this determination, one need only apply the language and underlying policies of Article 7 to a given geographical configuration and decide whether the presence of islands has *in fact* created a landlocked indentation with more than one well-marked entrance. If so, those entrances and the islands which form them constitute the closing line or seaward boundary of the bay, *regardless* of whether the islands "screen" one-half of the opening or lie in any other specific locational relationship to it. It was the intent of the drafters to relax the precise mathematical ratios of Article 7 as applied to multi-mouthed bays, not to impose additional geographical and mathematical criteria as barriers as Hodgson and Alexander and others have done.

An even more ill-conceived rule is devised by the same authors to cover another supposed exception, that of an island "screen" which lies *shoreward* of the main entrance to an indentation. In such cases, Hodgson and Alexander contend that this shoreward screen must also form the closing line of the bay.[162] This is in direct contravention of the language of paragraph three, sentence three, which expressly states that "[i]slands *within* an indentation *shall be included* as if they were part of the water area of the indentation."[163] The plain meaning of this language and its location in paragraph three indicate that islands which lie shoreward of the entrance to an indentation are not considered as creating separate entrances in themselves and thus do not fall within the category of islands to which paragraph three, sentence two, applies. Rather, they are to be governed by their own rule, also in sentence three, which mandates that the area of such islands is to be included as part of the water area of the indentation.

The Hodgson and Alexander approach to shoreward islands,

---

form- well-marked entrances into the indentation. Upon questioning during the deposition phase, Mr. Bowett admitted that he was unfamiliar with the legislative history on this point. Yet, he had purported to present a theory based on the island screen concept which is totally absent from Article 7. When experts use their own theories to apply Article 7 to a given fact situation rather than the language and underlying policies of the Convention itself, a very misleading basis is formed for conflict resolution.

162. R. HODGSON & L. ALEXANDER, *supra* note 6, at 17.

163. Territorial Sea Convention, Article 7, para. 3, sent. 3 (emphasis added). For full text of Article 7, see *supra* text accompanying note 10.

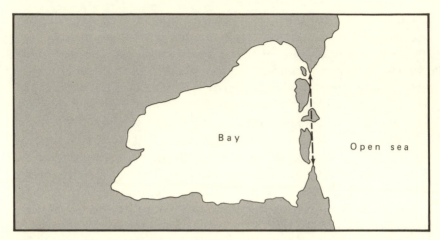

Figure 12. Islands lying imperceptibly landward of natural entrance points.

which has not been as widely accepted as their first "screening" rule,[164] only has validity in a situation where the islands lie just inside the entrance, as in Figure 12, and may in fact create separate entrances to the bay which are indistinguishable from the main entrance. Beyond this borderline situation, the Hodgson and Alexander rule becomes impossible to apply, because it is the main opening which will be perceived by mariners as the natural entrance to internal waters. Drawing a closing line through islands lying to any appreciable degree shoreward of the natural, well-marked entrance, simply because they fit an ill-conceived screening theory, does not conform to geographical reality nor the language of the Convention. Furthermore, such a rule would defeat the purposes of Article 7 by preventing the coastal state from enclosing certain water areas which are well-marked and landlocked within mainland entrance points and therefore well within their right to claim as internal waters, as illustrated by the shaded area in Figure 13.

Such a result is so opposed to the underlying policy which

164. Shalowitz concludes that when islands lie shoreward of the entrance to an indentation, the proper closing line for internal waters is across the major opening, not through the islands. 1 A. SHALOWITZ, *supra,* Chapter I, note 20, at 225. Beazley believes that, in general, if the single closing line satisfies the semi-circle rule there is no compelling reason to treat the islands as anything but islands lying within a bay. P. BEAZLEY, *supra,* Chapter I, note 24, at 19.

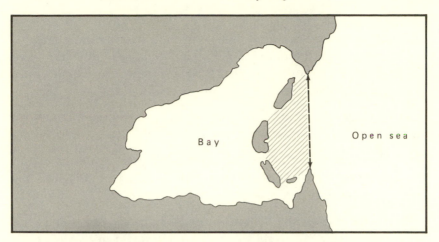

Figure 13. Islands lying landward of natural entrance points.

places landlocked waters within the sovereign authority of the coastal state that it could not possibly have been intended by the drafters, even if it were *not* expressly contraindicated by the language of paragraph three, sentence three.

Hodgson and Alexander perceive yet a third "exception" to their general rule that islands must lie in a straight line between "headlands"[165] to come under Article 7. They contend that in certain situations an island may in itself constitute one of the "headlands" of an indentation. And because they consider this commonly occurring geographical configuration as an exception, more exceptional rules must needs be devised. According to these authors, an island may only be considered as a "headland" if the following "objective" criteria are met:

(1) The island must closely relate to and be associated with the mainland.
(2) The island must form a natural prolongation of the two-dimensional coastline as viewed on a nautical chart.

165. The term "headlands" has been replaced in Article 7 by the more functional term "natural entrance points," a fact which has seemingly eluded many commentators and indeed most courts. A full discussion of the importance of this terminological change to bay doctrine will follow. The term "headlands" will appear hereafter in quotation marks to indicate that the term is now obsolete under Article 7.

(3) The area of the island should be greater than the area of water enclosed between the island and the true mainland.

(4) Ideally, the intervening water area should resemble a *channel* and should not be a principal navigational route, which would serve to isolate the island from the mainland.[166]

In a later work, Hodgson reiterates the criteria set forth above and adds a fifth requirement:

(5) Under normal conditions, an island used as a headland should be relatively small so as not to dwarf the original bay feature and hence change its entire character.[167]

As in the case of the "island screen" rules set out above, the "island headland" criteria devised by Hodgson and Alexander are now routinely cited in the works of other authors as well as in legal briefs and memoranda which purport to interpret Article 7 of the Territorial Sea Convention.[168] Each of these criteria will be briefly analyzed before discussing why the Hodgson and Alexander approach and all current analyses of the "islands as headlands" issue are mere anachronisms, unsupported by the historical development of the international law of bays, made irrelevant by the express language of Article 7, and rendered moot in the U.S. federal/state arena by recent federal court decisions interpreting this language.

Criteria (1) and (2) above are in keeping with the general policies of Article 7 but merely restate the obvious, i.e., that an island which forms part of the coast of an indentation must be closely related to the mainland and must form a natural extension of the two-dimensional coastline. The basic geographical requirement for *all* coastal indentations, whether lying wholly within the mainland or partially formed by islands, is that they be well-marked from the sea and contain landlocked waters.[169] Obviously an island which lies so far from the mainland as to be unrelated to life on the opposite shore of the indentation will not fulfill either of these basic requirements, nor will it conform to the underlying policy of Article 7 to declare as internal those water areas more

---

166. R. HODGSON & L. ALEXANDER, *supra* note 6, at 17–20.
167. Hodgson, *supra* note 159, at 168–169.
168. *See* P. BEAZLEY, *supra*, Chapter I, note 24, at 20; D. BOWETT, *supra* note 120, at 31.
169. *See supra* notes 19–43 and accompanying text.

related to the internal processes of the surrounding land territory than to the open sea. The definitional and measurement requirements set forth in Article 7, paragraphs two and three,[170] comprise the best guarantee that an indentation will meet the community criteria for a juridical bay. Further statement is both confusing and unnecessary.

Criteria (3) and (4) above are simply misconceived. The requirement of criterion (3) that the area of the islands be greater than the area of water enclosed between island and mainland is completely arbitrary and wholly unsupportable. If an island or islands form a part of the coast of a well-marked and landlocked indentation, the semi-circle requirement of Article 7 will serve to regulate the size of the indentation in relation to the surrounding land. There is no necessity for stating the relationship between the area of the island(s) and the intervening water area in terms of yet another mathematical ratio.

Hodgson and Alexander may have derived the idea for criterion (3) from the work of the late S. W. Boggs. In dealing with the geographical situation of islands lying close to the shore and separated by so little water that for all practical purposes the coast of the island is identified with that of the mainland, Boggs advocated this principle: If the area of the water surface between the island and the mainland is less than the area of the island itself, then the island is to be regarded as part of the mainland.[171] This principle was never adopted by the international community; but even more important in this context, the principle was *never* intended to apply to coastal indentations. Boggs devised the principle solely in response to those islands which lie so close to the coast of a state as to scarcely be regarded as islands at all but rather as continuations of the mainland. He specifically referred to Tierra del Fuego at the southern tip of South America and Bubiyan in the Persian Gulf off the coast of Kuwait as examples of the geographical configuration contemplated by his principle.[172]

There is no justification for taking the Boggs principle for offshore islands out of context and establishing it as a rule applicable

170. *See supra* full text of Article 7 accompanying note 10.
171. Cited by Pearcy, *supra*, Chapter II, note 6, at 9.
172. *See* Pearcy, *supra*, Chapter II, note 6, at 9.

to the law of bays. It must be remembered that it is Boggs himself who originated the concept of a semi-circle test to govern the relationship between the water and land of a coastal indentation.[173] It would be an irony to find another Boggs principle, totally unrelated to coastal indentations and intended to cover another geographical configuration altogether, analogized into a coastal indentation rule.

The first requirement of criterion (4) that "ideally," where an island formation serves as one side of a coastal indentation, the intervening water area should resemble a *channel,* is simply too divorced from coastal reality and the language and policies of Article 7 to merit serious consideration. Although situations undoubtedly exist wherein a bay may take on a channel-like shape,[174] there is no authority, ancient or modern, to suggest that a bay *must* look like a channel when, and only when, an island forms a portion of its coast. Whatever the shape of the intervening water area, its proportions will ultimately be judged according to the well-marked, landlocked, and semi-circle requirements of Article 7. *Shape* has been made irrelevant as a test for a juridical bay by the areal standard imposed by paragraph two.

The second requirement of criterion (4), that the intervening water area should not be a principal navigational route, again merely restates the obvious. Any bay, whether formed partially by islands or not, will by virtue of its landlocked nature not serve as a principal route of international navigation.

When one combines the rule of criterion (3) with that of criterion (5), the result is even more anomalous. For if under criterion (5) the size of the island serving as a "headland" must be relatively[175] small so as not to dwarf the original bay feature[176] and change its entire character,[177] and yet criterion (3) requires that the area of this small island must nonetheless exceed the area of

---

173. The Boggs concept formed the basis for the U.S. Proposal to The Hague Codification Conference in 1930 and was used by the Committee of Experts in 1953 as the basis for their semi-circle rule. *See* Chapter III, *supra* notes 139–142 and accompanying text.
174. Long Island Sound, which is created by the presence of Long Island, is an example of a bay which has a "channel-like" shape.
175. to what?
176. the what?
177. into what?

the water enclosed, one may only surmise that one will be left with a small island forming a portion of the coast of an even smaller indentation; and one must then inquire whether such hypothetical configurations exist in nature, and if so, could they possibly fulfill the well-marked, landlocked, and semi-circle requirements of Article 7?

The circumstances in which island-formed "headlands" arise are not as envisioned in the "objective criteria" and hypothetical coastline maps of Hodgson and Alexander,[178] Beazley,[179] and others, but rather as actually exist in coastal configurations such as Buzzards Bay in Massachusetts, Long Island Sound, Mississippi Sound, the Florida Keys, and other similar geographical situations where the islands themselves serve to form an indentation into the coast of a single state, a situation fully contemplated by the drafters as noted above.[180] If the islands are related to the mainland in such a way that an indentation is formed which is well-marked and landlocked, and whose area fulfills the semi-circle test, then that indentation conforms to the underlying community concept of a bay as a body of water more related to the internal processes of the land than to the open sea and, therefore, is an indentation of the type contemplated by the regime established by the drafters under Article 7, regardless of the fact that it is partially formed by islands.[181]

The establishment of additional "objective criteria," unsupported by authority or the language of Article 7, which must supposedly be met before an indentation may be deemed a bay has led to the dilution of the regime established by the Convention and to a confusion of issues in actual controversies. It is now quite common to see argument in briefs and memoranda based *not* on whether an indentation partially formed by an island formation meets the specific definitional and measurement tests set forth in Article 7, paragraphs two and three, but rather whether the configuration meets the "objective criteria" suggested by Hodgson and Alexander, Bowett, Beazley, and others. In many

---

178. *See* R. HODGSON & L. ALEXANDER, *supra*, note 6, at 17, Figure 11.
179. *See* P. BEAZLEY, *supra*, Chapter I, note 24, at 20, Figure 9.
180. *See supra* notes 109–121 and accompanying text.
181. It goes without saying that major sea routes do not normally pass through such waters.

cases, advocates and expert witnesses alike argue that because
one or another of these "objective criteria" has (or has not) been
met, the indentation formed may (or may not) be deemed a juridical bay, whether the indentation meets the criteria concretized
in Article 7 or not. Such an approach aborts the regime established by the Convention drafters and replaces criteria adopted
by the community of states with criteria established by
individuals.

The need for additional rules to cover the exception of "headlands" formed by islands is equally unsupported by the historical
treatment of bays, which reveals that islands have been recognized as "headlands" without issue for many centuries.[182] Such
usage was within the common knowledge of the drafters and thus
may not arbitrarily be read out of the Convention unless
excluded by the express language of Article 7.

Traditionally, the focus of states has been on areas of water
within the coast of a given state which have become so related to
life on shore that they may be subjected to the absolute sovereignty of that state. Whether the surrounding coast has been partially formed by islands rather than mainland has not been seen
as a critical factor in setting aside the enclosed water as internal,
as long as other community criteria for enclosure have been met.
The great variety of land forms historically used by states to
enclose their bays was noted by the German delegation to The
Hague Codification Conference in 1930:

> Hitherto, the methods used have been most diverse. The width of
> the bay may be calculated between the two extreme points of the
> mainland, or *from an island situated off the coast to another island hav-
> ing a similar geographical position, or from such an island to the extreme
> point on the mainland.*[183]

In the United States, islands have been recognized as "headlands" for bays and as natural terminus points for coastal boundaries in general since early colonial and post-revolutionary days.

---

182. *See supra,* Chapter III, note 76; Chapter IV, notes 113, 135–136, and accompanying
text; *see also infra* notes 183–195 and accompanying text.
183. *See* 2 League of Nations Conference for the Codification of International Law
[1930] at 257 (Rosenne ed. 1975) (emphasis added).

This practice is confirmed by the opinion of the New York Court of Appeals in the case of *Mahler v. The Norwich and New York Transportation Co.,*[184] in which the court states:

> That Long Island Sound was included within the territorial dominions of the British Empire . . . is a proposition too plain for argument. It was an inland arm of the sea, washing no shores but those of the provinces, and with no opening to the ocean, except by passing between British *headlands* less than five miles apart. The right of the King . . . rested on clear and fundamental principles of international law. The rule is one of universal recognition, that a bay, strait, sound, or *arm of the sea,* lying wholly within the domain of the sovereign, and admitting no ingress from the ocean except by a channel between *contiguous headlands* . . . is the subject of territorial dominion. . . . *Within this rule, the islands at the eastern extremity of Long Island Sound are the fauces terrae, which define the limits of territorial authority, and mark the line of separation between the open ocean and the inland sea.*[185]

As authority for the use of islands as *fauces terrae,* the court cites several international law treatises[186] and a good deal of case law, including the opinion of the first Circuit Court of Appeals in *United States v. Grush,*[187] which holds:

> [W]here there are islands enclosing the harbour in the manner in which Boston Harbour is inclosed [sic] . . . the whole of the waters must be *considered as included* within the body of the county . . . . *Islands so situated must be considered as opposite shores. . . .*[188]

The Court of Appeals in *Mahler* refers to the case of *United States v. Jackalow,*[189] in which the defendant was indicted for acts of piracy on Long Island Sound and brought to trial in the U.S. Circuit Court in New Jersey. The court was forced to determine

---

184. 35 N.Y. 352 (1866).
185. 35 N.Y. at 355 (emphasis added).
186. H. Wheaton, International Law at 320, 322; E. Vattel, Law of Nations at 130; F. Hautefeuille, Droits des Nations (2d. ed.) at 89; G. Martens, Law of Nations at 170.
187. 5 Mason 290 (1829).
188. *Id.,* at 301 (emphasis added).
189. 1 Black 484 (1861).

whether jurisdiction lay in New Jersey, where the prisoner was found, or in New York, where the crime was committed. Judge Dickerson held that the crime was not committed on the high seas, but in New York, and therefore the prisoner could not be tried in New Jersey. His reasoning was based on the fact that Long Island Sound "was a mere *arm of the sea,* inclosed within *fauces terrae* at its eastern extremity, formed by *headlands* less than five miles apart" and therefore a subject of the territorial dominion of New York.[190] As in the *Mahler* case, there was no question that Long Island formed a portion of the headlands, the *fauces terrae,* of the Sound.

The purpose in quoting extensively from *Mahler* and related cases is not to establish state title to Long Island Sound, but rather to illustrate the complete lack of reluctance on the part of early decision makers to recognize island formations as natural "headlands" of an indentation. There was no question that an indentation formed by both mainland and island coasts was nonetheless *inter fauces terrae* under international as well as municipal law.

Several other cases illustrate the same proposition. In *Martin v. Waddell,*[191] the U.S. Supreme Court declared the waters of Raritan Bay, which had passed directly to New Jersey under a grant from the Duke of York, to be within the internal waters of the state. The fact that the coast of Raritan Bay is partially formed by islands was not considered relevant. Likewise, in *Commonwealth v. Manchester,*[192] and subsequently in *Manchester v. Massachusetts,*[193] the waters of Buzzards Bay were held to be within the territorial limits of Massachusetts,[194] regardless of the fact that one side of the Bay is formed by the Elizabeth Islands. (See Figure 14.)

An early statement by Chancellor Kent also indicates that historically islands were not considered as distinguishable from mainland in determining the major headlands of the coast. Kent declared that given the extent of the American coastline, it might

190. *Mahler,* 35 N.Y. at 357 (emphasis added).
191. 41 U.S. (16 Pet.) 367 (1842).
192. 152 Mass. 230, 25 N.E. 113 (1890).
193. 139 U.S. 240 (1891).
194. *See also* Dunham v. Lamphere, 69 Mass (3 Gray) 268, 270 (1855); 2 C. Hyde, *supra,* Chapter II, note 32, at 471; Hurst, *The Territoriality of Bays,* 3 Brit. Y.B. Int'l L. 42, 42–54 (1922–23).

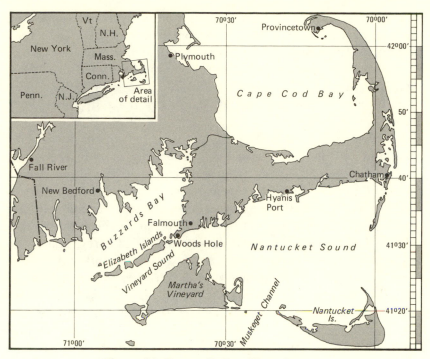

Figure 14. Buzzard's Bay, Massachusetts.

not be unreasonable to assume, for domestic purposes connected with our safety and welfare, the control of waters included within lines stretching from quite distant "headlands," as for instance from Cape Ann (Maine) to Cape Cod, and from *Nantucket* to *Montauk Point,* and from that point to the capes of the Delaware, and from the south cape of Florida to the Mississippi.[195] Again, the relevance of the above statement in this context is not in any sense to justify such an extensive national claim,[196] but rather to illustrate the common historical practice of recognizing the termini of both mainland and island formations as natural "headlands." Quite obviously, Montauk Point was considered by many authorities throughout the nineteenth century as just such a coastal "headland," even though located at the easternmost tip of Long Island.

Modern authorities have continued to acknowledge the fact

195. 1 J. KENT, COMMENTARIES ON AMERICAN LAW 29 (1st ed. 1826) (emphasis added).
196. In fact, such a claim was never seriously proposed.

that islands may serve as bay "headlands" and may in certain instances create bays due to their particular geographical relationship to the mainland coast. Having made an extensive survey of the world's coastlines, Strohl uses a map of Buzzards Bay, Massachusetts, to illustrate a commonly occurring geographical phenomenon, i.e., "how a fringe of islands can make up one side of a bay."[197]

Whether the "headlands" of an indentation are formed by mainland or island has also been treated with indifference by authorities such as Pearcy, who lists Cape Cod Bay, Long Island Sound, Delaware Bay, Chesapeake Bay, Pamlico Sound, Galveston Bay, and San Francisco Bay as "only a few of the many bodies of water which may be enclosed as internal by the drawing of a closing line between coastal headlands."[198] Pearcy makes no attempt whatever to distinguish Long Island Sound and Galveston Bay, whose entrances are partially formed by islands, from the other bodies of water named. In another work, Pearcy reiterates the commonly held view, reflected in the Comments of the International Law Commission in 1955 and 1956,[199] that in addition to serving as "headlands," islands may by their very presence serve to form a landlocked indentation where none might otherwise have existed:

> The keys along the southern coast of Florida opposite and south of Miami give Biscayne Bay a number of mouths and account for its status as internal water. Without these keys it would be little more than an elongated, irregular indentation in the coast.[200]

At the base of the routine treatment of islands as "headlands" in both early and modern times lies the realization that it is the existence of the indentation *itself,* lying within the land territory of the coastal state in such a way that it "retains more the nature of the territory than the open sea,"[201] which warrants the exten-

---

197. M. STROHL, *supra,* Chapter II, note 42, Fig. 19, at 77. *See also* the earlier decision by the United States Supreme Court in Manchester v. Massachusetts, 139 U.S. 240 (1891).
198. *See* Pearcy, *supra* note 152, at 969.
199. *See supra* text accompanying notes 113–116.
200. Pearcy, *supra,* Chapter II, note 6, at 7–8.
201. 1 E. CAUCHY, *supra,* Chapter III, note 3, at 37.

sion of exclusive coastal sovereignty. If an indentation meets the landlocked and well-marked requirements of paragraph two as well as the semi-circle test, then it should be a matter of supreme indifference whether the coasts of the indentation are wholly formed by mainland or partially formed by islands.

In spite of the substantial evidence of customary practice cited above, some commentators suggest that the absence of specific authorization in Article 7 to use islands as "headlands" is evidence of the intent of the drafters to exclude such usage. It could be argued with equal force that the absence of discussion on the issue in the legislative history of either The Hague Codification Conference[202] or the subsequent meetings of the Committee of Experts, the International Law Commission, or the First Committee of the Convention, together with the consistent treatment of islands as "headlands" noted above, is even more compelling evidence that the drafters merely assumed that the commonly accepted practice of utilizing islands as "headlands" would continue and saw no need to devise specific criteria beyond those established for *every* indentation, whether formed partially by islands or not, i.e., that it be well-marked from the sea and contain landlocked waters, the area of which conforms to the requirements of the semi-circle rule.

Further, it must be argued that the express language of the Convention indicates clearly that the drafters intended the focus of Article 7 to be placed on the nature of the *indentation,* rather than the nature of the entrance points. One might assume from observing the amount of analysis devoted to the issues of whether and/or when an island may be considered a part of the mainland and whether and/or when an island may be used as the headland of an indentation, that "mainland" and "headland" must per force be key terms under Article 7. It is important to note at the outset that the words "mainland" and "headland" never appear in Article 7,[203] nor are they used as explanatory concepts in the official Commentaries.[204]

For example, Article 7, paragraph one, reads as follows:

---

202. It was not discussed by the Codification Conference even though clarification of the issue was requested by the German delegation.
203. *See* full text of Article 7, *supra* text accompanying note 10.
204. *See* [1956] 2 Y.B. INT'L L. COMM'N at 268–69; [1955] 2 Y.B. INT'L L. COMM'N at 36–37.

This article relates only to bays the *coasts* of which belong to a single State.[205]

The meaning of this initial paragraph is clear on its face. The drafters did not say that Article 7 was to relate to those bays which "lie within the mainland" of a single state, nor to those "lying inland" or "inter fauces terrae," although all of these terms were within the conceptual repertoire upon which the drafters might have drawn to define the scope of Article 7. States, scholars, and judicial bodies had spoken in such terms from time immemorial. The Committee of Experts had used the Latin "inter fauces terrarum" as late as 1953. Yet the I.L.C. and the First Committee rejected the use of such terms[206] to set forth the first and most basic requirement of Article 7, that it relates only to bays the *coasts* of which belong to a single state.

Although one may argue conclusively, as above, that islands were historically regarded as included within the terms "inter fauces terrae" and "headland," and indeed much scholarly effort has been spent devising and analogizing rules by which islands may be considered "mainland,"[207] *no* such analysis is required to show that an island may form a part of the *coasts* of a state[208] and,

---

205. Territorial Sea Convention, Article 7, para. 1 (emphasis added).
206. An early draft of Article 7 included the word "inland" in the text after the word "penetration" in paragraph 2, to read " . . . a bay is a well-marked indentation whose penetration [inland] is in such proportion to the width of its mouth as to contain land-locked waters. . . ." It was expressly removed by the I.L.C. *See* the 1955 Draft, [1955] 2 Y.B. INT'L L. COMM'N at 36; 1956 Draft, [1956] 2 Y.B. INT'L L. COMM'N at 15; United Kingdom proposal to the First Committee, U.N. Doc. A/CONF.13/C.1/ L.62, adopted at 47th meeting, 15 Apr. 1958, 3 United Nations Conference on the Law of the Sea (1958), *supra* note 84, at 146, 227–28; Final Text of Article 7, U.N. Doc. A/CONF.13/L.52, adopted by the Conference at its 20th Plenary Meeting, 27 Apr. 1958, 2 United Nations Conference on the Law of the Sea (1958), *supra* note 84, at 73,133.
207. *E.g.,* I. BROWNLIE, PRINCIPLES OF PUBLIC INTERNATIONAL LAW 201–02 (3rd ed. 1979); 1 A. SHALOWTIZ, *supra*, Chapter I, note 20, at 161; Boggs, *Delimitation of Seaward Areas under National Jurisdiction*, 45 AM. J. INT'L L. 240, 254, 258 (1951); Pearcy, *supra*, Chapter II, note 6, at 9; Waldock, *The Anglo-Norwegian Fisheries Case*, 28 BRIT. Y.B. INT'L L. 114, 137–59 (1951); *see* M. STROHL, *supra*, Chapter II, note 42, fig. 18, at 76; *see also* The Case of the Anna, 165 Eng. Rep. 809, 815 (1805) for the "portico of islands" language often cited to justify the assimilation of islands to mainland; as well as the Anglo-Norwegian Fisheries Case (U.K. v. Nor.), 1951 I.C.J. 116, 128, for the "a whole with the mainland" language used for the same purpose.
208. The term "coasts" has historically included islands. *See* H. WHEATON, ELEMENTS OF INTERNATIONAL LAW §178 (8th ed. 1866) in H. CROCKER, *supra*, Chapter III, note

therefore, that an indentation whose coasts are formed partially by mainland and partially by island(s) is one which falls squarely within the scope of Article 7, paragraph one. Such an indentation must only be subjected to the same tests required of all indentations which would be juridical bays, i.e., the geographical and mathematical requirements of paragraph two, the measurement rules of paragraph three, and the twenty-four-mile closing line limitations of paragraphs four and five.

Another term conspicuously absent from Article 7 is "headlands" which the drafters expressly replaced with the more functional and far more inclusive term "natural entrance points" in paragraphs three, four, and five. Paragraph three, sentence one, directs that for the purpose of measurement, the entrance of an indentation is to be measured by a line joining the low-water marks of its natural entrance points. If the indentation thus measured fulfills the geographical and mathematical requirements of paragraph two, these same entrance points are used under paragraphs four and five to determine the placement of the final closing line of the bay. We have seen from the analysis of paragraph three, sentence two, above[209] that the drafters recognized that islands as well as mainland may form entrances into an indentation and therefore by definition may form natural entrance points as well.[210] By their use of the term "natural entrance points" rather than "headlands" to circumscribe the entrance(s) of an indentation and by their explicit inclusion of islands within this more functional term, the drafters effectively terminated argument on the issue of whether or not an island may serve as the "headland" of a bay. The presence of "headlands" is simply not required under Article 7; thus, the issue of whether or not an island may serve as one is no longer relevant. All related issues, such as whether or not headlands must lie solely on the mainland and, if so, whether and in what circumstances an island may be considered a part of the mainland in order to become a headland, are blessedly terminated as well.[211]

22, at 472; H. HALLECK, *supra,* Chapter III, note 50, at 130; J. ORTOLAN, *supra,* Chapter III, note 50, §93. *See also infra,* Chapter V, notes 265–270 and accompanying text.

209. *See supra* notes 89–105 and accompanying text.

210. *See supra* notes 98–100 and accompanying text.

211. Of course, the issue of whether or not islands may be considered as part of the mainland is still alive and well in other contexts, such as in situations where the

In answer to the question, "If the headlands issue has been resolved by the language of Article 7, why does argument on the issue persist?" one may only answer "force of habit, and lack of a clear understanding of the requirements of Article 7 and the innovative regime established thereby." The drafters shifted the focus of the rules for the juridical bay from the nature of the entrance points to the nature of the indentation itself. As long as the coasts of the indentation belong to a single state and its natural entrance points enclose a well-marked, landlocked indentation whose area fulfills the semi-circle test, a bay has been formed. The waters are recognized as internal not because it is possible to draw a closing line between mainland headlands, but because an indentation which fulfills the technical requirements of Article 7 is one which the international community has recognized as more related to the internal processes of the coastal state than to the open sea. Having fulfilled these requirements, it is simply irrelevant whether the coasts and natural entrance points of this landlocked water area are composed of mainland or island.

Further discussion of the issue has also been rendered irrelevant under U.S. law by recent federal court decisions which interpret the language of Article 7 and support in large part the analysis set forth above. The U.S. Supreme Court addresses the issue squarely in *United States v. Louisiana*,[212] wherein the U.S. government argues that for a variety of reasons, islands may not serve as the natural entrance points to a bay. The Court examines each of the government's arguments and rejects them, saying in part:

> The United States argues that the Convention on the Territorial Sea and the Contiguous Zone flatly prohibits the drawing of bay-closing lines to islands. A true bay, it is said, is an "indentation" within the mainland, and it cannot be created by the "projection" of an island or islands from the coast. Moreover, the rule of Article 7(3) that the area of an indentation lies between the closing

---

straight baseline system of Article 4 might apply or other situations where islands may form a portico of islands along a nonindented mainland shore. It is within this context that most of the authorities cited, *supra* note 207, were speaking, and their criteria upon which islands and the mainland could be regarded as one are still relevant in that respect. The language of Article 7 makes it unnecessary to analogize these theories into coastal indentation situations.

212. 394 U.S. 11 (1969). The *Louisiana* Case and other United States decisions will be discussed more fully *infra* in Chapter V, *Current State Practice.*

line[213] and "the low-water mark around the shore of the indentation" contemplates a perimeter of dry land unbroken by any opening other than the bay's entrance. Finally, the United States argues, such an opening between the island and the mainland would deprive the enclosed waters of the "landlocked" quality required in a true bay.

. . . No language in Article 7 or elsewhere positively excludes all islands from the meaning of the "natural entrance points" to a bay. Waters within an indentation which are "landlocked" despite the bay's wide entrance surely would not lose that characteristic on account of an additional narrow opening to the sea. That the area of a bay is delimited by the "low-water mark around the shore" does not necessarily mean that the low-water mark must be continuous.

Moreover, there is nothing in the history of the Convention or of the international law of bays which establishes that a piece of land which is technically an island can never be the headland of a bay.[214]

The government's argument that an island or group of islands may not in themselves form a bay is similarly rejected:

The United States argues that since the Convention in Article 7(3) specifically recognizes that islands may create multiple *mouths* to bays, it cannot be construed to permit islands to create the *bays* themselves. Alternatively, the Government argues that if a closing line can be drawn from one side of a bay to an island as the headland on the other side, then it must be continued from the island to the nearest point on the mainland; and the distance to the mainland must be added to that across the bay in determining whether the 24-mile test is satisfied. These arguments, however, misconstrue the theory by which the headland is permitted to be located on the island—that the island is so closely aligned with the mainland as to be considered an integral part of it.[215]

For the proposition that an island may be treated as mainland, the Supreme Court quotes with approval from several of the

---

213. Note that even here, the closing line concept is confused with the measurement line of paragraph three (footnote added).

214. 394 U.S. at 60–62 (footnote omitted and emphasis added). The reasoning of the Court has been cited as authority for the recent opinion of the Supreme Court in United States v. Maine et al (Rhode Island and New York Boundary Case), 469 U.S. 504, 105 S.Ct., 992, 83 L. Ed. 2d 998 (1985).

215. *Id.*, at 62 n.83 (emphasis in original).

authorities cited herein,[216] and goes on to suggest several factors which might be considered in determining whether an island is "an integral part" of the mainland, such as the origin of the island, its size and distance from the mainland, its shape and relation to the configuration of the coast, and the depth and utility of the intervening waters. These factors are suggested, according to the Court, because "there is little objective guidance on this question to be found in international law." [217]

The citation of these factors by the Court undoubtedly resulted from the "island as mainland" issue being thoroughly briefed by both parties who relied heavily on anachronistic juristic arguments without sufficient analysis of the language and intent of Article 7 itself. The best tests for determining when an island may serve as a natural entrance point for an indentation are contained within the language of the Convention itself, i.e., the island must lie close enough to the mainland coast to create a well-marked and landlocked indentation whose area fulfills the semi-circle test. If an island lies so far seaward that no such indentation can be perceived, either from the sea or on two-dimensional maps, or that major sea routes pass between the island and the mainland shore, then it cannot be claimed to form a portion of the coast of a juridical bay. The establishment of separate "factors" such as the size, shape, and origin of the *island* frustrates the intent of the drafters to set forth specific geographical and mathematical requirements for the *indentation*. If these requirements are met, the island which forms part of the coast of the indentation will of necessity be closely aligned to the mainland, and no further inquiry into the characteristics of the island will be necessary.

In *United States v. Louisana,* the U.S. Supreme Court resolves several issues relevant to this discussion of islands:

1. No language in Article 7 or elsewhere positively excludes islands from the meaning of either the natural entrance points or "headlands"of a bay.
2. Waters within an indentation which are landlocked do not lose that characteristic because of an additional opening to the sea created by the presence of an island.

216. *Id.*, at 62 n.82. *See* authorities cited *supra* note 207.
217. 394 U.S. at 66.

3. The Court flatly rejects the following arguments:
   (a) that the Convention prohibits the drawing of closing lines to islands;
   (b) that a true bay is an indentation within the "mainland," and cannot be created by a projection of an island or islands from the coast;
   (c) that the phrase "low-water mark around the shore" contemplates a perimeter of dry land unbroken by any other entrance; and
   (d) that although islands may create separate mouths to bays, the Convention cannot be construed to permit islands to create the bays themselves.

In summary, one must conclude that the "objective criteria" devised by some commentators to cover the so-called exception of island-formed "headlands" are arbitrary and unsupportable both under the language of the Convention and other principles of international law derived from the historical treatment of bays; and therefore, that such criteria should not be applied when interpreting the rules applicable to islands under Article 7. An even stronger case is made for the rejection of such "exceptional" criteria by the fact that the entire issue of whether or not an island may be used as a "headland" has been rendered irrelevant by:

(1) The rejection of the more traditional terms "mainland," "inland," "inter fauces terrae," and "headlands" by the drafters and their replacement by the more functional terms "coasts" and "natural entrance points," which cannot be construed as excluding islands when read *in pari materia* with the whole of Article 7; and

(2) The decision by the U.S. Supreme Court in *United States v. Louisiana* reinforced by their 1985 opinion in *United States v. Maine et al.* (Rhode Island and New York Boundary Case), which reads Article 7 as permitting the use of islands as natural entrance points.

Paragraphs Four and Five

Textual analysis has thus far revealed that paragraph two sets forth the geographical and mathematical criteria for determining whether or not a given indentation is a bay under Article 7, and paragraph three sets forth the measurement rules to be used in determining whether a single- or multi-mouthed indentation fulfills the definitional criteria of paragraph two. Under these rules, if an indentation is well-marked from the sea and contains landlocked waters the area of which meets the semi-circle test, a bay may be deemed to exist, as opposed to a mere curvature of the coast. It only remains to apply the closing line limitation rules of paragraphs four and five in order to determine how much of the bay may be enclosed by the coastal state as internal waters, thus gaining the exclusive sovereignty which that juridical status confers.

It is important to stress at the outset that paragraphs four and five are relevant only to this latter determination. If an indentation fails to meet the geographical and mathematical criteria above, no bay may be deemed to exist under Article 7, regardless of the width of its entrance. Paragraphs four and five relate only to an indentation whose status as a bay has already been determined. The logic of this interpretation is evident in the structural arrangement of paragraphs within Article 7 as well as in the actual language chosen by the drafters. One will note that in paragraphs two and three, the referent noun is "indentation." Once the indentation has been granted bay status under the rules of paragraphs two and three, the proper boundary for internal waters is determined by applying the rules imposed by paragraphs four and five, wherein the referent noun becomes "bay."[218]

Turning to the text, paragraph four directs that if the distance between low-water marks of the natural entrance points of a *bay* does not exceed twenty-four miles,[219] a "closing line" may be drawn between these two low-water marks, and the waters enclosed thereby shall be considered as internal waters.[220] How-

218. Territorial Sea Convention, Article 7, paras. 2–5. For full text of Article 7, *see supra* text accompanying note 10.
219. "Mile" here refers to a nautical mile. In 1929, the International Hydrographic Bureau recommended the adoption of a standard nautical mile valued at 1,852 international meters or 6,076.1033 U.S. feet. The United States adopted the measurement in 1954. Nearly all major maritime countries have adopted it as well. A nautical mile is also equal to 1.60 of a degree of latitude. *See* M. STROHL, *supra*, Chapter II, note 42, at 71; UNCLOS, *supra* Article 10 at 5, expressly includes the word "nautical" to clarify all reference to miles.
220. Territorial Sea Convention, Article 7, para. 4. *See also supra* notes 134–151 and accompanying text for discussion indicating that where the presence of islands cre-

ever, where the distance between the low-water marks of the natural entrance points of a *bay* exceeds twenty-four miles, paragraph five directs that a "straight baseline" of twenty-four miles shall be drawn within the bay in such a manner as to enclose the maximum area of water with a line of that length.[221]

It is interesting to note that only when the entire bay may be enclosed under paragraph four have the drafters directed that a "closing line" be drawn. In paragraph five, where only a portion of the bay may be enclosed as internal waters, a "straight baseline" is drawn to provide an artificial boundary between internal and territorial waters but not a "closing line." Some authors[222] regard the distinction as perhaps inadvertent and in any event confusing, since the term "straight baseline" is also used under Article 4. It would seem to this author that the linguistic variation is not at all inadvertent but rather was specifically intended by the drafters to distinguish between two very different boundary lines.

The term "closing line" is reserved under the Convention for situations in which the entrance to the bay is of such size that the entire bay may be closed off from the sea by drawing a maritime boundary line between its natural entrance points. All of the waters of the bay are then considered as internal waters with the exclusive rights which that juridical status confers. In other situations, a bay may fulfill all the configuration requirements to gain juridical status, and yet be of a size which exceeds the community concept of water areas more intimately related to land than open sea. In that case, a balancing of equities is required. Such a bay clearly lies within the littoral of the coastal state and in all likelihood has become intimately related to the exclusive economic and defense interests of that state. This is particularly true of those portions of the bay which lie furthest landward. Yet, to enclose the bay in its entirety would encroach on equally legitimate inclusive community interests which favor the maintenance of maximum open sea areas.[223]

In response to these conflicting interests, paragraph five rep-

---

ates a bay with more than one entrance, closing lines may be drawn across these entrances, and that there was no intent on the part of the drafters to limit these closing lines to a sum total of twenty-four miles.

221. Territorial Sea Convention, Article 7, para. 5.
222. *E.g.*, M. STROHL, *supra*, Chapter II, note 42, at 71.
223. *See* M. MCDOUGAL & W. BURKE, *supra*, Chapter II, note 8, at 317.

resents a policy decision by the drafters to allow a coastal state to move shoreward and enclose as internal as much of the waters of the bay as might be enclosed by a line no more than twenty-four miles in length. The boundary line which results from this policy choice, however, cannot in any sense be termed a "closing line," which in essence permits the coastline of a state to be continued uninterrupted by the presence of the bay. The term "straight baseline" has been employed by the drafters to distinguish a true closing line from this line drawn within a larger bay to delimit an acceptable boundary between internal and territorial waters.

One must argue, however, that although a separate terminology may be required to distinguish between the boundary line concepts in paragraphs four and five, an alternative term to "straight baseline" might well be devised in order to avoid unnecessary confusion with yet another boundary concept, i.e., the straight baseline system set forth under Article 4. Perhaps the following wording would serve to clarify the concept under Article 7, paragraph five:

> Where the distance . . . exceeds twenty-four miles, an *internal waters boundary line* of twenty-four miles shall be drawn within the bay in such a manner as to enclose the maximum area of water that is possible with a line of that length.

The selection of the twenty-four-mile limitation on the width of bays in itself represents another and much more controversial policy decision on the part of the drafters. Because the substantive configuration requirements of paragraph two may theoretically be met by bays of enormous size, the world community has traditionally attempted to fix some limitation on the width of bays.[224] Many concepts served as a basis for this limitation, including the range-of-vision test, the cannon-shot rule, and others which were derived primarily from the perceived ability of a coastal state to extend its authority and control over adjacent water areas. Prior to the *Anglo-Norwegian Fisheries Case,* the United States and several other major maritime nations regarded ten miles as the maximum permissible length for bay closing

---

224. *See* Chapter II, *supra* notes 39–55 and accompanying text; Chapter III, *supra* notes 73–136 and accompanying text.

lines.[225] The court's holding that this rule had not yet acquired the consistency and authority of a general rule of international law[226] created uncertainty within the world community, particularly since the court did not prescribe an alternative limitation nor did it indicate that there should be *no* limit on internal waters, and yet the ten-mile rule was posited as a "guideline" for bay determination.

The adoption of a twenty-four-mile closing line limitation by the Convention served to remove this uncertainty, but the limitation represented a major departure from past state practice. The legislative history of this policy decision reveals that considerable disagreement existed on this issue for many years, terminated by a most inconclusive final vote[227] of the First Committee in 1958, all of which might lead one to question the viability of the provision were it not for the fact that UNCLOS has preserved the twenty-four-mile rule of Article 7 virtually intact.[228]

The legislative history also reveals widespread confusion as to the proper basis for decision on the closing line limitation issue. The Committee of Experts, expressly eschewing any relationship between the width of the territorial sea and the length of the bay closing line, recommended a ten-mile limit on the closing lines for bays. Their selection of a ten-mile limit was based on "this being twice the range of vision to the horizon in clear weather, from the eye of a mariner at a height of five meters (which is the internationally accepted height for hydrographical purposes)."[229] This recommendation was incorporated into the 1954 draft article submitted by Special Rapporteur François to the International Law Commission,[230] but the Commission substituted a twenty-five-mile closing line limitation in its 1955 Draft.[231] In the official *Commentary* which accompanied the draft, the I.L.C. explained this radical extension:

---

225. 1 A. SHALOWITZ, *supra,* Chapter I, note 20, at 222.
226. 1951 I.C.J. 116, 131.
227. The twenty-four-mile limit was approved by a vote of 31 to 27 with 13 abstentions. *See* 3 United Nations Conference on the Law of the Sea (1958), *supra* note 84, at 146.
228. UNCLOS *supra,* Chapter I, note 19, Article 10 at 5. *See* Brown, *Delimitation of Offshore Areas: Hard Labour and Bitter Fruits at UNCLOS III,* 5 MARINE POL'Y 172, 172–84 (1981).
229. *See Report of Committee of Experts* (1953), *supra* note 18, paras. B(1), C(1), C(2).
230. U.N. Doc. A/CN.4/90, at 25.
231. [1955] 2 Y.B. INT'L L. COMM'N at 36.

The majority in the Commission took the view that the maximum length of the closing line must be stated in figures and that a limitation based on geographical or other considerations . . . would not suffice. It considered, however, that the limit must be more than ten miles. Although not prepared to establish a direct ratio between the length of the closing line and the width of the territorial sea—such a relationship was formally denied by certain members of the Commission—it felt bound to take some account of tendencies to extend the width of the territorial sea by prolonging the closing line in bays. *As an experiment, the Commission suggests a distance of twenty-five miles;* thus, the length of the closing line will be slightly more than twice the permissible maximum width of the territorial sea as laid down in paragraph 2 of Article 3. [232] Since, firstly, historical bays, some of which are no longer than twenty-five miles, do not come under this article and since, secondly, the provision contained in paragraph 1[233] of this article concerning the characteristics of a bay is calculated to prevent abuse, it is possible that some extension of the closing line will be more readily accepted than a widening of the territorial sea in general.[234]

Following the adoption of the 1955 draft, the I.L.C. requested replies from governments to their twenty-five-mile "experiment." Five states registered formal complaints,[235] and the Special Rapporteur noted that the twenty-five-mile limit had found little support among states generally.

At its Eighth Session in 1956, the issue was heatedly debated by the International Law Commission, and the conflict appeared to threaten the adoption of Article 7 as a whole. The Norwegian Government commented in its reply that when the Commission

232. *Id.* The 1955 Draft of the Territorial Sea Convention proposed twelve miles as the maximum permissible width of the territorial sea. This limit was not adopted by the Convention in 1958. However, UNCLOS, *supra,* Chapter I, note 19, Article 3, at 3 establishes twelve miles as the maximum breadth which may be claimed for the territorial sea.

233. Paragraph one of the 1955 draft included the geographical and mathematical criteria which eventually appeared in paragraph two of the final version of Article 7. *See* [1955] 2 Y.B. Int'l L. Comm'n at 36.

234. *Id.,* at 37 (footnotes added).

235. The states were Brazil, Turkey, Israel, the United Kingdom, and the United States. Only China indicated complete approval of the 1955 Draft. U.N. Doc. A/CN.4/99. *See* M. Strohl, *supra,* Chapter II, note 42, at 222 and n.27.

established the twenty-five-mile limitation rule in 1955, they had realized they were not reflecting international law but were dealing with *lex ferenda*. Conflict over the length of the closing line was not, however, a suffficient reason for rejecting the entire article.[236] Noting that the closing line issue had become extremely controversial, Mr. Fitzmaurice of the United Kingdom contended that although the court in the *Anglo-Norwegian Fisheries Case* had rejected a ten-mile limit, this was obiter dicta from which one could not deduce that there should be *no* limit on internal waters as some members had suggested. In view of the enormous indentations which might have the configuration of bays, he believed it imperative to establish a limit and felt that a fifteen-mile limitation would be ample.[237]

Mr. Zourek, the Czechoslovakian member, argued that although the definition of a bay had to be somewhat mathematical, the application of a purely mathematical solution to the question of which waters were to be classified as internal would always prove to be unsatisfactory in specific geographical situations. Fearing that no such limit could ever obtain a majority, Zourek proposed that the mathematical limit be supplemented by other criteria, derived in part from the *North Atlantic Coast Fisheries Judgment*, such as the special economic value of the bay to the coastal inhabitants and its distance from international shipping lanes.[238]

Mr. Fitzmaurice counterargued that the economic criteria proposed were so vague that, if adopted, it would be impossible to determine whether a particular indentation was a bay or not. He maintained vigorously that the only solution was a closing line of definite distance.[239]

Many proposals were subsequently made and rejected in the course of the debate. The Sandström Amendment calling for a closing line of unspecified length was rejected 6 to 4 with 3 abstentions. The Edmonds proposal for a ten-mile limit was rejected 8 to 3 with 2 abstentions. The Faris Bey el-Khouri pro-

236. [1956] 1 Y.B. INT'L L. COMM'N at 190.
237. *Id.*, at 192.
238. *Id.*, at 191, 193, 195–96. *See also* M. MCDOUGAL & W. BURKE, *supra*, Chapter II, note 8, at 300–39, for similar view of supplementary factors which might be considered in enclosing internal waters.
239. [1956] 1 Y.B. INT'L L. COMM'N at 196.

posal for a twelve-mile limit was rejected 7 to 5 with 1 abstention.
The Zourek proposal to supplement any mathematical limitation
chosen with additional economic criteria for internal waters was
rejected 8 to 1 with 4 abstentions. At last, the Fitzmaurice compromise proposal for a fifteen-mile limitation on bay closing lines
was adopted 8 to 5.[240]

This completely arbitrary limitation was incorporated into the
1956 I.L.C. draft of Article 7, and the reasons set forth for the
change in the official *Commentary* were by no means convincing.
The International Law Commission repeated its 1955 rationale
for extending the length of closing lines verbatim and added:

> At its eighth session the Commission again examined this ques-
> tion in light of replies from Governments. The proposal to extend
> the closing line to 25 miles had found little support. . . . While
> appreciating that a line of 10 miles had been recognized by several
> Governments and established by international conventions, the
> Commission took account of the fact that the origin of the 10 mile
> line dates back to a time when the breadth of the territorial sea
> was much more commonly fixed at 3 miles than it is now. In view
> of the tendency to increase the breadth of the territorial sea, the
> majority of the Commission thought that an extension of the clos-
> ing line to 15 miles would be justified and sufficient.[241]

On the recommendation of the International Law Commission
at the close of its Eighth Session in 1956, the United Nations
General Assembly resolved to summon an international conference to consider the legal, technical, biological, economic, and
political aspects of the law of the sea and to embody the results
of its work in one or more international conventions as it might
deem appropriate.[242] Convened in 1958, the First Committee
considered anew the issue of the maximum closing line length for
bays. Despite abundant information compiled by the Secretary
General with the assistance of experts in many fields and made
available to the Committee in the form of preparatory documents,[243] it is clear from the legislative history that the positions

240. *Id.*, at 196–97.
241. *Report of the I.L.C.* (1956), *supra* note 94, at 15–16.
242. U.N. Doc. A/3159, at 3.
243. U.N. Doc. A/CONF.13/7, *reprinted in* 1 United Nations Conference on the Law of
      the Sea (1958), *supra* note 84, at 165.

of the various states on the closing line issue remained much the same as had been reflected in the work of the International Law Commission and in previous Government responses to the work of that body. Several states again pressed for a ten-mile limitation based on long-established state practice and general recognition of the limit in international agreements,[244] while other states argued for the same limitation based upon the normal range of vision at sea,[245] which had been the basis of the original recommendation made by the Committee of Experts.

After much discussion, Mr. Grigorov introduced a proposal jointly sponsored by Bulgaria, Poland, and the Soviet Union, and later supported by a similar proposal from Guatemala, to extend the closing line limitation to twenty-four miles based on three main considerations. Their first premise was that since the maximum breadth of the territorial sea then under consideration was twelve miles, it was logical that the closing line for a bay be twice that distance. Secondly, the International Court of Justice had held in the *Anglo-Norwegian Fisheries Case* that the distance of ten miles was accepted by only a few states and did not constitute a general rule of international law. Lastly, the fact the the International Law Commission had first adopted a twenty-five-mile limitation and then one of fifteen miles indicated that its decision on the length of the closing line did not rest on any very strong basis, whereas a twenty-four-mile closing line would correspond to an established international practice and would protect the vital interests of states.[246]

One might criticize each of these premises as fallacious at worst and arbitrary at best, but miss the most important element in all of these deliberations. Although plentiful authority could have been drawn upon to question *all* of the limitations proposed, not one of the proponents was asked to justify his position on either economic, defensive, or any other rational ground relevant to the size of bays. For example, there was ample evidence to indicate

---

244. The United States, West Germany, and Japan were vocal in this regard. *See* 1 U.N. Conference on the Law of the Sea (1958), *supra* note 84, at 144.

245. The United Kingdom and the United States argued to this effect. *Id.*, at 144–145. The United States would have preferred the ten-mile closing line as traditionally advocated in its foreign relations and as consistent with its three-mile territorial sea claim. *See Hearings before Committee on Foreign Relations on Executives, J to N, Inclusive,* 86th Congress, 2d Session 92 (Question 29) (1960).

246. 1 U.N. Conference on the Law of the Sea (1958), *supra* note 84, at 145.

that technological advancements in the field of navigation had made a ten-mile closing line limitation no longer essential for accurate navigation,[247] thus eliminating the range-of-vision argument from rational discussion. Yet, no one rose to question its use as the basis for a positive rule of international law. In like manner, the twenty-four-mile limitation was proposed as a logical extension of the twelve-mile limit for the territorial sea, even though the logic of such a relationship had never been shown and no such agreement on the breadth of the territorial sea had been achieved.[248] The limitation was purported to correspond to international practice, even though no proof of this practice was asked for or offered; and it was touted as protective of the vital interests of states, even though no delegate was asked to enumerate these interests nor to demonstrate how such interests would be jeopardized by a ten-, twelve-, or fifteen-mile limitation on bay closing lines. The legislative history reveals that the advocates of the twenty-four-mile closing line were never effectively challenged to demonstrate the necessity for this extension of state sovereignty. Yet the amendment submitted by Bulgaria, Poland, and the Soviet Union[249] together with that submitted by Guatemala,[250] supported by no authority and representing perhaps the most significant variation from state practice codified by the Convention, was adopted on 15 April 1958 by a vote of 31 to 27 with 13 abstentions.

H.A. Smith has said that the most difficult task of law is to harmonize principles which may appear to conflict and to define the boundaries within which a given principle is to prevail.[251] If it is generally agreed that the principle of open seas is the most productive of values for all mankind, it is also agreed that a certain

---

247. *See* M. STROHL, *supra,* Chapter II, note 42, at 31–47, for excellent discussion of navigational aids.
248. Shalowitz maintains that the twenty-four-mile closing line limitation was adopted on the assumption that the twelve-mile limit on the breadth of the territorial sea would also become part of the Convention. There were not sufficient votes to support the twelve -mile territorial sea, but the closing line rule for bays was permitted to stand. Hence, the anomaly of an arbitrary twenty-four-mile rule in Article 7 seemingly unrelated to any other limitation on the territorial sea. 1 A. SHALOWITZ, *supra,* Chapter I, note 20 at 222.
249. U.N. Doc. A/CONF. 13/C.1/L.103.
250. U.N. Doc. A/CONF. 13/C.1/L.105.
251. H.A. SMITH, THE LAW AND CUSTOM OF THE SEA 3 (1948).

degree of exclusive use and authority is essential for the protection of the interests of the coastal state.[252] Practical considerations make it necessary that each state have more or less complete jurisdiction over waters enclosed within its land mass. The challenge to those charged with the codification of international law would seem to lie in the framing of a rule which might protect the interests of the coastal state and yet forbid any claims which would unreasonably encroach on freedom of the high seas.[253] One would like to believe that the twenty-four-mile closing line rule is the result of the professional efforts of a group of delegates, informed by the best technical, economic, biological, and political information then available, who carefully weighed the competing equities and determined that a twenty-four-mile line was optimal and necessary in order to preserve the exclusive and inclusive interests of all states. One fears, however, that the twenty-four-mile limitation codified in both paragraphs four and five of Article 7 is merely arbitrary, a manifestation of the desire of many coastal states to gain the greatest amount of sovereignty over water areas which had previously been considered high seas and the prowess of these states in convincing others to vote with them on this issue at the international level.

Can international law be created in this arbitrary and compromisory fashion? Technically, the Convention is only binding on signatories, and surely no claim can be advanced that the twenty-four-mile rule is made more generally binding by the fact that it is a codification of preexisting customary international law. However, it cannot be denied that the rule is a reflection of a general tendency among states to approve an ever increasing sovereignty over adjacent waters and the resources which they provide. This trend will in all likelihood lead to a general acceptance of the rule by states and its consistent application by judicial decision makers. The rule has found few detractors since its adoption, and, in fact, UNCLOS has left it unchallenged and unchanged.[254] The combination of prescription by an international body and wide acceptance and application by states and judicial bodies will

252. M. McDougal & W. Burke, *supra,* Chapter II, note 8, at 316.
253. H.A. Smith, *supra* note 251, at 5.
254. *See* UNCLOS, *supra,* Chapter I, note 19, Article 10, paras. 4–5, at 5.

go far toward establishing the twenty-four-mile closing line rule as positive international law.

One final interpretive issue must be addressed under paragraph five, which directs that, when the entrance to a bay exceeds twenty-four miles, a straight baseline *shall* be drawn within the bay to enclose the maximum area of water possible with a line of that length.[255] Shalowitz maintains that this language leads to the inference that the semi-circle rule must first be applied to the entire indentation and, if it becomes a bay by application of this rule but exceeds the twenty-four-mile limitation on its entrance, a twenty-four-mile line is then to be drawn within the bay without further application of the mathematical criterion. The author claims that there is logic to this interpretation because the semi-circle rule is a geometric expression of the substantive law of bays whereas the twenty-four-mile rule is purely arbitrary, and thus it may be reasoned that if an indentation has met the substantive tests once, that should suffice.[256]

This rational view is completely supported by the foregoing textual and structural analysis of Article 7. Inexplicably, however, Shalowitz goes on to assert that an even more reasonable interpretation of paragraph five might be that the portion of the bay enclosed by the new "closing line"[257] must also satisfy the semi-circle test. Because such an interpretation, if generally accepted, could lead to unwarranted complications in the application of Article 7 and because it is wholly unsupported by the language and legislative history of the Convention, the bases upon which this position is formulated must be challenged.

Shalowitz cites four sources of authority for his view that the portion of a bay enclosed as internal waters by a straight baseline under paragraph five must meet the semi-circle test of paragraph two. Shalowitz claims that this was the original thinking of the Committee of Experts as borne out in the definition of a bay and

---

255. *Territorial Sea Convention*, Article 7, para. 5. For full text of Article 7, *see supra* text accompanying note 10.

256. 1 A. SHALOWITZ, *supra*, Chapter I, note 20, at 223.

257. Paragraph five directs that a *straight baseline* rather than a closing line be drawn within the bay. This confusion between the closing line drawn across the entire entrance in paragraph four and the straight baseline mandated by paragraph five may have led Shalowitz to conclude that the area enclosed by the straight baseline must also meet the semi-circle test.

the ten-mile closing line it recommended to the International Law Commission.[258] Taking portions of the text of these two recommendations out of context and reading them together, the author cites the Committee as first saying, "A bay is a bay in the juridical sense" and then, "The closing line across a juridical bay should not exceed ten miles in width." Shalowitz concludes that identifying the term "bay" with the term "juridical" indicates that the portion of the indentation across which the straight baseline of paragraph five is placed must satisfy the mathematical requirements for a true bay, i.e., the semi-circle test, in order to be considered a bay in the legal sense.

This reasoning appears misguided. First, the combination of two separate portions of the Committee's recommendation is extremely misleading. In response to a specific request for technical observations as to the definition of a bay as opposed to a mere curvature in the coastline, the Committee replied:

> ad.A. 1. A bay is a bay in the juridical sense if its area is as large or larger than that of a semi-circle drawn on the *entrance* of that bay.[259]

It is apparent that the drafters of this recommendation intended that the semi-circle rule be applied by using a line drawn across the *entrance* to the bay as the diameter of the semi-circle. There is no reference whatever in paragraph two or three to the semi-circle rule being applied on a line of definite length.

In response to a different question entirely, i.e., whether there should be any relation between the maximum length of the bay closing line and the territorial sea, the Committee replied:

> ad.B. 1. The closing line across a (juridical) bay should not exceed ten miles in width, this being twice the range of vision to the horizon in clear weather, from the height of a mariner. . . .[260]

258. *See supra* full text accompanying note 109.
259. *Report of the Committee of Experts* (1953), *supra* note 18, at 77 (emphasis added). *See supra* full text accompanying note 109.
260. *Id.*

The use of parentheses to set off the word juridical clearly indicates that once an indentation has passed the semi-circle test, the juridical status of the bay is presumed, provided that the closing line drawn across the entrance does not exceed ten (now twentyfour) miles. If the drafters had seen the two questions and their answers as interrelated, they could easily have used the term "closing line" in place of "entrance" in response to question A. There is simply no indication that the Committee intended the semi-circle test to be applied using any line other than one joining the natural entrance points of the indentation.

As his second source of authority, Shalowitz cites the Bases of Discussion submitted by the U.S. Delegation to The Hague Codification Conference where a semi-circle rule was first proposed.[261] He asserts that the illustration which accompanied the U.S. proposal indicates that the semi-circle test is to be applied to the area enclosed by the straight baseline even though the full indentation may already have met the test. This is an invalid comparison since the scheme embodied in the U.S. proposal, although it did contain a semi-circle test, is very different from the one recommended by the Committee of Experts, incorporated by the International Law Commission, and finally adopted by the 1958 Convention.

The text of the American proposal at The Hague reveals that the drawing of a maximum ten-mile closing line was placed as the *first* step in the determination of a juridical bay. Paragraph one reads:

> (1) On a chart or map a straight line not to exceed ten nautical miles in length shall be drawn across the bay or estuary as follows: The line shall be drawn between two headlands or pronounced convexities of the coast which embrace the pronounced indentation or concavity comprising the bay or estuary if the distance between the two headlands does not exceed ten nautical miles; otherwise the line shall be drawn through the point nearest to the entrance at which the width does not exceed ten miles.[262]

Having first drawn the "closing line," paragraph two of the American proposal directs that arcs of circles with a radius equal

261. *See supra*, Chapter III, text accompanying notes 140–42 and Figure 1 for the essence of the American proposal.
262. U.S. Proposal to 1930 Hague Codification Conference, reprinted in 4 M. WHITEMAN, DIGEST OF INTERNATIONAL LAW 220 (1965).

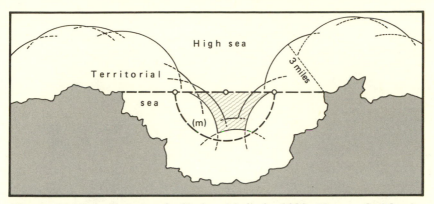

Figure 15. Boggs Arcs of Circles Method, 1930 Hague Codification Conference.

to *one-fourth* of the length of the closing line be thrown from all points along the shore, as illustrated by Figure 15.[263]

One then draws a semi-circle equal to *one-half* of the closing line, as illustrated in Figure 16.[264] Under this plan, if the water area in the so-called envelope created by the arcs of circles exceeds the area of the reduced semi-circle, a juridical bay exists, and the waters enclosed by the closing line may be claimed as internal.[265]

The United States favored this method of comparing a reduced water area because it was thought to simplify measurement. Be that as it may, this mathematical scheme was fully rejected by the drafters of the 1958 Convention, not only in regard to specific details such as the arcs-of-circles methodology but in regard to conceptual framework as well. The substantive requirements for a juridical bay appear *first* in Article 7. After it has been determined that an indentation lying within the coasts of a single state is well-marked from the sea and contains landlocked waters the area of which meets the semi-circle test and is, therefore, deserving of juridical status, then and *only* then do the closing line limitation rules of paragraphs four and five become relevant. Far from appearing as the *first* step in a juridical determination as the United States proposed in 1930, the placement of the closing line

263. *See* Boggs, *supra*, Chapter III, note 137, at 481.
264. *Id.*
265. *Id.*

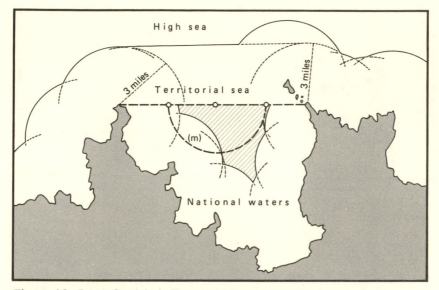

Figure 16. Boggs Semicircle Test, 1930 Hague Codification Conference.

appears as the *last* step in the scheme adopted by the 1958 Convention to draw the boundary of internal waters, after all determinations of "bayness" have already been made. A bay is first
designated; *then* it is delimited. Reference to a completely different and subsequently rejected prescriptive regime cannot provide
support for the thesis that the portion of a bay finally enclosed
by a straight baseline under paragraph five must also meet the
semi-circle test.

The third source of authority cited by Shalowitz is an article by
Boggs[266] in which the semi-circle rule is illustrated by showing the
semi-circle as drawn on a ten-mile closing line at the entrance of
the bay. Boggs was the author of the U.S. proposal to The Hague
Codification Conference. His article merely discusses in detail the
regime set forth above, and as such suffers from the same deficits
as a source of authority for Shalowitz's interpretation of paragraph five.

The fourth source cited is the Report of the Special Master in

266. Boggs, *supra*, Chapter III, note 137, at 541–555.

United States v. California.[267] In its findings in regard to bays, the Master states, "In either case [i.e., indentations not more than ten miles wide at the entrance and those more than ten miles wide] the requisite depth is to be determined by the following criterion,"[268] and then goes on to set forth the semi-circle rule for bays. According to Shalowitz, this statement indicates that the test for inland waters is to be applied to the area enclosed by the paragraph five straight baseline.[269] Such a conclusion is wholly unsupportable. This portion of the *Master's Report* was written in 1952, long before the findings were ordered modified by the Supreme Court under the rules of the 1958 Convention. The Special Master's findings were primarily influenced by the regime proposed by the United States in 1930.

There is no basis of authority to support the Shalowitz thesis that the area of the bay enclosed by a straight baseline under paragraph five must satisfy the requirements of the semi-circle test. Careful analysis of the language and legislative history of Article 7 compels the interpretation set forth in several sections of this work, i.e., that the semi-circle test is to be applied as part of the initial determination of the juridical status of an indentation. Having passed the configuration requirements in the first instance, there is no indication in the language or structure of Article 7 that the semi-circle test is to be reapplied to the area enclosed under paragraph five.

The only rule which *is* relevant to the boundary line mandated by paragraph five is expressly included in the language of that paragraph, i.e., that the twenty-four-mile line shall be drawn within the bay so as to include the maximum water area possible with a line of that length.[270] This provision is independent of any need to locate well-marked "entrance points" to serve as terminus points for the twenty-four-mile line drawn within the bay.

---

267. The Report of the Special Master in United States v. California, 332 U.S. 19 (1947), is identified as No. 6, Original, October Term (1952), and is *reprinted in* 1 A. SHALOWITZ, *supra,* Chapter I, note 20, at 329.

268. Report of the Special Master, No. 6, Original, October Term (1952), at 3.

269. 1 A. SHALOWITZ, *supra,* Chapter I, note 20, at 224.

270. The official *Commentary* to this section makes clear that it was intended to offer direction for those situations where more than one line of twenty-four miles can be drawn. *See* [1955] 2 Y.B. INT'L L. COMM'N at 37; *Report of the I.L.C.* (1956), *supra* note 94, at 16.

Even if such geographical landmarks should exist, there is no requirement that the coastal state use them. Such a requirement would be incompatible with the express direction to enclose the maximum water area possible, since it would be purely coincidental if both conditions could be satisfied by the placement of a single twenty-four-mile line.[271]

Paragraph Six

Paragraph six sets forth two final limitations on the scope of Article 7, i.e., that none of its provisions shall apply to so-called "historic" bays, or in any case where the straight baseline system provided for in Article 4 is applied.[272]

It was never assumed that historic bays, those indentations to which a state is able to establish an exceptional claim by reason of continuous use and the acquiescence of other states, would be included within the scope of Article 7. In drafting their definition for a bay, the Committee of Experts recommended:

> ad.A. 1. A bay is a bay in the juridical sense, if its area is as large as or larger than that of a semicircle drawn on the entrance of that bay. *Historical bays are excepted: they should be indicated as such on the maps.*[273]

The exclusion of historic bays from Article 7 was repeated in all subsequent drafts of the I.L.C..[274] The complete absence of explanatory material on this issue from the official *Commentaries*

---

271. Because the area of the bay enclosed as internal waters under paragraph five will be imperceptible as such to mariners due to the absence of well marked entrance points within the bay, the lack of a charting and publication requirement was a serious omission. UNCLOS, Article 16, now provides such a requirement. *See supra* note 22.

272. Territorial Sea Convention, Article 7, para 6. For full text of Article 7, *see supra* text accompanying note 10.

273. *Report of the Committee of Experts* (1953), *supra* note 18, at 77 (emphasis added). *See* full text *supra* accompanying note 109.

274. *See* [1955] 2 Y.B. INT'L L. COMM'N at 36; *Report of the I.L.C.* (1956), *supra* note 19, at 15. It is interesting to note that in the 1955 draft, the drafters directed that only the provisions of paragraph four (which then contained the twenty-four-mile internal waters boundary line which became paragraph five of the 1958 Convention) "shall not be applied to the so-called 'historic bays,'" whereas in the 1956 draft, historic bays were excepted from *all* foregoing provisions of Article 7.

indicates widespread acceptance of this exclusionary provision.

When the First Committee convened in 1958, they had at their disposal a preparatory memorandum on historic bays,[275] and several delegations, in particular the Japanese, argued that the development of a definition for the historic bay was part of the task of codification and should not be left to arbitral tribunals or the courts.[276] To this effect, Mr. Yokota of Japan introduced an amendment to Article 7, to read as follows:

> 4. The foregoing provisions shall not apply to historic bays. The term "historic bays" means those bays over which [a] coastal State or States have effectively exercised sovereign rights continuously for a period of long standing, with explicit or implicit recognition of such practice by foreign States.[277]

Believing that a definition was needed under the Convention, but that it was unwise to insert one within Article 7 when so little preparatory work had been done on the issue, Panama and India introduced a joint draft resolution which called upon the General Assembly to make appropriate arrangements for a study of the juridical regime of historic waters.[278] This resolution was adopted by the First Committee by a vote of 54 votes to 2, with 10 abstentions.[279] The Japanese amendment was withdrawn, leaving Article 7 free of any definitional criteria for the historic bay.[280]

Paragraph six, therefore, indirectly addresses the question left unanswered by paragraphs four and five, i.e., "what if the distance between the entrance points of a given bay exceeds twenty-four miles and yet a state has historically considered the waters of the bay as internal?" Paragraph six directs that *none* of the foregoing provisions of Article 7, even the configuration requirements of paragraph two, are to be applied to historic bays, and the burden will fall to the coastal state to justify a claim of historic

275. A/CONF.13/1, 1 U.N. Conference on the Law of the Sea (1958), *supra* note 84, at 1.

276. 3 U.N. Conference on the Law of the Sea (1958), *supra* note 84, at 145.

277. U.N. Doc. A/CONF.13/C.1/L.104, *reprinted in id.,* at 241.

278. U.N. Doc. A/CONF.13/C.1/L.158; later revised, *see* U.N. Doc. A/CONF.13/C.1/ L.158/Rev. 1.

279. 3 U.N. Conference on the Law of the Sea (1958), *supra* note 84, at 198.

280. The juridical regime of historic waters remains uncodified in UNCLOS.

use. If proven, such a bay will not be a juridical bay *under Article 7;* but the coastal state *will* be permitted to enclose the waters of the bay as internal and to enjoy the panoply of sovereign rights which attach to that juridical status.[281]

Paragraph six also prohibits the application of Article 7 to situations where the straight baseline system of Article 4 is applied. While both regimes result in the delimitation of the baseline separating internal and territorial waters, Article 4 is much broader in concept and more inclusive in scope than Article 7, which is limited to a single geographic feature.[282] The legislative history indicates that this final scope provision was intended to address the possibility that certain coasts to which the straight baseline system might be applied by states would also contain bays. In that case, the straight baseline would be drawn in such a way as to subsume the entire bay in the larger area of internal waters thus created under Article 4. "In short, the International Law Commission considered that, should straight baselines be drawn covering the coast of the bay, the special rules relating to bays would no longer be applicable."[283]

Summary

The foregoing textual, contextual, and structural analysis of Article 7 has revealed a codification scheme of remarkable innovation and clarity. The *scope provisions* of *paragraphs one and six* limit the application of Article 7 to bays the coasts of which belong to a single state. Historic bays and those which are subsumed as part of a general straight baseline system, drawn optionally under Article 4 to enclose deeply indented coastlines or those fringed with islands, are excluded from Article 7.

If a given indentation satisfies the *definitional criteria* set forth under *paragraph two*, i.e., is well-marked from the sea and contains landlocked waters the area of which equals or exceeds the area of a semi-circle whose diameter is measured by a line drawn

---

281. *See supra*, Chapter II, note 46, for discussion of the proof needed to establish exclusive rights to historic inland waters.
282. *See* Fitzmaurice, *Some Results of the Geneva Conference on the Law of the Sea.* 8 INT'L & COMP. L.Q. 73, 80 (1959).
283. 3 U.N. Conference on the Law of the Sea (1958), *supra* note 84, at 147.

between natural entrance points, that indentation is a bay under Article 7, as opposed to a mere curvature of the coast. The *measurement rules of paragraph three* are to be used in determining whether a single- or multi-mouthed indentation satisfies the areal comparison mandated by paragraph two.

If, and *only* if, an indentation meets the definitional and measurement criteria prescribed by paragraphs two and three and is therefore deemed a bay under international law, one moves forward in Article 7 to the *closing line limitation rules* of *paragraphs four and five*. If the entrance to the bay does not exceed twenty-four miles, the entire bay is enclosed with a *closing line* drawn between natural entrance points, which in turn becomes the baseline delimiting internal waters from the territorial sea. The waters of the entire bay may be claimed as internal by the coastal state, which derives exclusive sovereign authority from this juridical status. Should the entrance exceed twenty-four miles, paragraph five mandates that a *straight baseline* is to be drawn within the bay so as to enclose the maximum water area possible with a line of that length. This water boundary also serves as the baseline delimiting internal and territorial waters. Juridical bay status is thus conferred on only a portion of the bay, and the sovereign authority of the coastal state is restricted in like manner. A publication requirement, now provided in UNCLOS, Article 16, would seem to be a necessary addition to paragraph five in order to clearly mark these partially enclosed waters for mariners; and an alteration in the language, changing "straight baseline" to "internal waters boundary line" would more clearly designate the nature of the line drawn and differentiate it from the straight baseline which may be optionally drawn under Article 4 to enclose deeply indented or island-fringed coasts.

Article 7 also establishes an exceptional regime to be applied where islands have created multiple entrances to an indentation. Because the drafters recognized that the presence of these bay-related islands tends to link an indentation even more closely to the land territory of the coastal state, the strict geographical and mathematical requirements set forth under paragraph two are relaxed for multi-mouthed bays. Special measurement rules under paragraph three provide that the area of the semi-circle shall be measured using the sum total of the measurement lines drawn between islands, whereas the area of the indentation shall be measured taking the full width of the entrance including the islands into account. Islands within the bay are to be measured as part of the water area of the indentation. That a special regime was intended by the drafters is made clear by their express commentary that an indentation which, if it had no islands at its mouth, would not fulfill the necessary criteria, is nonetheless to be recognized as a bay under Article 7.[284] Because the issue of a limitation on the permissible length of closing lines drawn between islands was left open by the Convention in order to provide flexibility for decision makers, it might be argued that a multi-mouthed bay is entitled to a relaxation of the strict application of the twenty-four-mile closing line rule as well, given its exceptionally well-marked and landlocked character and the fact that the drafters clearly did not intend such a limitation.[285]

When one places Article 7 within the context of the Territorial Sea Convention and understands the language, structure, and purpose of each paragraph within the whole, a simple, coherent, and innovative regime emerges which goes far toward concretizing the substantive and procedural international law of bays. By adopting Article 7, the world community, drawing on the historical treatment of bays and balancing the exclusive and inclusive interests of states in the present, has determined that a coastal state may as a presumptive right claim exclusive sovereignty over a bay lying within its coasts which is well-marked and landlocked, the area of which meets the semi-circle test and the entrance of which is marked by a line no more than twenty-four miles in length. A state may claim exclusive sovereignty over a bay whose entrance exceeds twenty-four miles only with extraordinary proof of historic usage. By clearly establishing the substantive and procedural rules for determining the maximum extent of permissible bay claims, Article 7 promotes many of the larger purposes of the law of the sea: to clearly define the rights of the parties, to reduce the likelihood of conflict, to provide clear guidelines for mariners, thereby ensuring that those who use the oceans for navigation and fishing can with certainty determine their location with respect to the reach of coastal power, and to make an equitable allocation of ocean space and resources which may serve both the inclusive and exclusive interests of all states.

284. *See supra* notes 113–15 and accompanying text.
285. *See supra* notes 149–52 and accompanying text.

V

Current State Practice

In General

The principal features of the international law of the sea have been formed through the effort over several centuries to accommodate the exclusive interests of individual states in maximizing areas of maritime sovereignty and the inclusive interests of all states in maximizing freedom of the seas. The legal presumption favoring freedom of the seas remains in place today, but since World War II there has been a radical change in the international context within which that principle gained temporary ascendancy. Many new nation-states,[1] largely poor and conscious of their solidarity, have used their newfound political power to press for a review of traditional international doctrines which do not favor their interests.[2] In addition, the rapid advance of marine

1. In 1945, there were 65 world states. By the end of 1982, that number had increased to 137 [OFFICE OF THE GEOGRAPHER, U.S. DEPT. OF STATE, STATUS OF THE WORLD'S NATIONS 2 (1980). Today, the number is 158 (United Nations verification).
2. Virtually all of the states created after 1945 previously existed as colonies of Britain, France, the Netherlands, Belgium, and the United States; and as such, they mirrored the same conservative maritime policies of their mother countries. As newly independent states, however, most have assessed their increased need for sustenance, liveli-

and undersea technology has precipitated demands by both developed and developing states for increased authority and use of their contiguous waters.[3]

The 1958 Geneva Conventions[4] were adopted in response to the general recognition among states that the time had come to address the problems presented by the radical political and economic changes which had transformed society in the postwar era. By codifying existing law which remained relevant and creating new law to respond to newly perceived needs, the world community sought to place acceptable, if in some cases compromisory, limits on the expansive claims and demands of coastal states. The accommodation between exclusive and inclusive interests achieved in Article 7 of the Territorial Sea Convention[5] represents one of the most successful products of these codification efforts.

The dynamic forces set in motion by rapid change could not be wholly addressed nor checked by international agreement in 1958, however. Since that time, the demand for ever wider sovereignty over ocean space has only intensified and has been joined in its assault on freedom of the seas by a new adversary, the demand by developing states to restrict the use of the seabed of the high seas under a new species of *res communes,* the common heritage of mankind.[6] The adoption of UNCLOS[7] in 1982, a mere fifteen years after Geneva, reflects wide community acquiescence in these demands. Commentators now estimate that as a result of state claims permitted by international agreement,

hood, and security and have concluded that their interests are more closely aligned with those of states favoring expansive offshore claims. *See* Brown, *Maritime Zones: A Survey of Claims,* 3 NEW DIRECTIONS IN THE LAW OF THE SEA 159 (1973); Alexander, *The Ocean Enclosure Movement: Inventory and Prospect,* 20 SAN DIEGO L. REV. 566 (1982–83).

3. Whereas the traditional uses of the oceans, i.e., navigation, fishing, and overflight, required only transitory occupation, new uses such as seabed and subsoil resource exploitation will require relatively permanent occupation of ocean space, with tremendous potential for conflict between exclusive and inclusive state interests.
4. *See supra,* Chapter I, notes 14–17 and accompanying text.
5. *See* full text, *supra,* Chapter IV, accompanying note 10. *See also* Chapter IV, *supra,* for complete textual and contextual analysis of Article 7.
6. *See* Brown, *Freedom of the High Seas Versus the Common Heritage of Mankind: Fundamental Principles in Conflict,* 20 SAN DIEGO L. REV. 522 (1982–83).
7. *See supra,* Chapter I, note 19 and accompanying text.

between 30 and 40% of ocean space has been placed under some form of state control,[8] primarily via claims to expanded territorial seas,[9] claims to legal continental shelves,[10] and claims to exclusive economic or fishing zones.[11] When one further reflects on the

8. *See* Alexander, *supra* note 2 at 561; *see also* Pardo, *The Convention on the Law of the Sea: A Preliminary Appraisal*, 20 SAN DIEGO L. REV. 496, 497 n.30 (1982–83).

9. No agreement having been reached on a maximum width for the territorial sea in Geneva in either 1958 or 1960, the issue was again placed on the agenda for the Third United Nations Conference on the Law of the Sea in 1973. UNCLOS, Article 3 grants states the right to claim a maximum territorial sea of twelve miles. By the end of 1982, of 125 officially recorded claims, 24 states claimed territorial seas of three miles, 4 states claimed territorial seas of six to twelve miles, and 77 states (60%) had entered twelve-mile claims. Even though Article 3 limits such claims to twelve miles, 26 states claim territorial seas over this limit, with 14 of this number laying claims to two-hundred-mile territorial seas. *See* OFFICE OF THE GEOGRAPHER, U.S. DEPT. OF STATE, NATIONAL MARITIME CLAIMS [hereinafter cited as NATIONAL MARITIME CLAIMS], Appendix, Table 1 (1982).

10. National claims to exclusive rights in the continental shelf began with the unilateral Truman Proclamation [Proc. No. 2667, 10 FED. REG. 12303 (1945)], which asserted U.S. jurisdiction and control over the natural resources of its contiguous continental shelf. A second proclamation specified that superjacent waters beyond territorial limits would continue to have the status of high seas, subject only to the right of the United States to establish fishery conservation zones [Proc. No. 2668, 10 FED. REG. 12304 (1945)]. The Truman Proclamation led to a flurry of new maritime claims, with many states in Latin America claiming sovereignty over resources both on adjacent shelves *and* in superjacent waters. See Krueger and Nordquist, *The Evolution of the 200-Mile Exclusive Economic Zone: State Practice in the Pacific Basin*, 19 VA. J. INT'L L. 321, 326 (1979). Such claims were legitimized in the 1958 Convention on the Continental Shelf (*supra*, Chapter I, note 15) and have been significantly expanded under UNCLOS, which defines the continental shelf as the seabed and subsoil of the submarine areas that extend beyond a state's territorial sea throughout the natural prolongation of its land territory to the outer edge of the continental margin (UNCLOS, Art. 76, para. 1). This legal, as opposed to geomorphological, definition includes most of the total continental margin—not shelf alone, but shelf, slope, and rise. Should a state's physical continental margin not extend two hundred miles from the baseline of the territorial sea, a state may nonetheless claim a "legal" shelf of two hundred miles (*Id.*). In situations where the physical continental margin extends *beyond* 200 miles, the Convention text provides a set of alternative criteria delimiting its boundary, but places an absolute limit of 350 nautical miles or 100 miles seaward of the 2,500 meter isobath. (*Id.*, paras. 4,5,7).

11. Much of the concern voiced by states over the breadth of the territorial sea originated in the context of demands for exclusive extraterritorial fishing zones. The 1958 Conventions did not countenance such demands; but even at that time, twenty-three states claimed exclusive fishery zones of twelve miles or less and seven states (Chile, Costa Rica, Ecuador, El Salvador, Honduras, Panama and Peru) claimed fishery zones of 200 miles. By 1973, thirty-two states had made such claims including twelve claims of 200 miles. (Alexander, *supra* note 2, at 569). The sui generis EEZ (exclusive economic zone) created under UNCLOS (*see supra*, Chapter II, notes 9, 29) is closely

fact that all exploitable offshore hydrocarbons, all commercially exploitable minerals in unconsolidated sediments (from sand and gravel to tin), most phosphorite nodules, a significant portion of recently discovered polymetallic sulphide deposits, cobalt crusts, and manganese nodule deposits, over 90% of the commercially exploitable living resources of the sea, nearly all marine plants, and all known sites suitable to the production of energy are to be found in the contiguous offshore areas currently under state control,[12] the magnitude of the policy shift in favor of the exclusive interests of coastal states becomes apparent.

When one turns to the study of current state practice under Article 7 of the Territorial Sea Convention, this shift toward ever widening coastal control becomes particularly apparent. Article 7 is a remarkably unambiguous and generous treaty provision, easily understood and, one would think, easily applied in determining the juridical nature of coastal indentations. Yet, except in federal states where the problem of establishing jurisdiction between dual sovereigns pertains, Article 7 has been eclipsed as the bay provision of choice, primarily due to the tendency of many states since 1958 to draw straight baselines for measuring the territorial

----

related to the fishery zone concept and grants to coastal states exclusive rights to the natural resources of the seabed and subsoil and of the superjacent waters (UNCLOS, art. 56) to a seaward limit of 200 miles, thus incorporating to some extent the rights of the coastal state in an exclusive fishery zone as well as in the continental shelf. In addition, the coastal state is granted jurisdiction with regard to marine research, marine environmental protection and preservation, and the establishment and use of artificial islands, installations and structures (*Id.*). As noted, the EEZ may extend 200 miles from the baseline from which the breadth of the territorial sea is measured (*Id.*, art. 57) but rights of foreign navigation and overflight prevail beyond territorial limits (*Id.*, art. 56). Even though UNCLOS had not as yet entered into force, as of late 1982 fifty-six states had claimed 200-mile economic zones (NATIONAL MARITIME CLAIMS, *supra* note 9, at Appendix, Table 2) and thirty-six states had claimed 200-mile fishery zones (*Id.*, Appendix, Table 3). *See also* OFFICE OF THE GEOGRAPHER, BUREAU OF INTELLIGENCE AND RESEARCH, U.S. DEPT. OF STATE, 36 LIMITS IN THE SEAS 2–7 (4th rev. 1981). The total area enclosed in the aggregate of all 200-mile zones is approximately twenty-eight million square nautical miles, or roughly one-third of the total ocean space of the world (NATIONAL MARITIME CLAIMS, *supra* note 9 at 1). It is further estimated that the ten states with the most extensive coastlines and therefore the largest 200-mile zones (this group includes the United States whose 200-mile exclusive claim measures over two million square nautical miles alone) control one-third of the world's *economic zone* area (*Id.*, at 5), raising serious questions of inequity in resource distribution.

12. *See* Pardo, *supra* note 8, at 497. *See also* Gulland, FAO Fisheries Tech. Paper 206 at 1, U.N. FAO Doc. FIRM/T206 (1980); Alexander, *supra*, Chapter II, note 28, at 76.

sea, regardless of whether or not the configurations of their coastlines are such as to warrant such action under Article 4 of the Territorial Sea Convention.

After the opinion was rendered in the *Anglo-Norwegian Fisheries Case*[13] granting Norway the right to enclose her highly idiosyncratic coasts behind straight baselines, many states drew on the opinion as authority for following the same course of action with regard to their own coasts. In drafting Article 4, the International Law Commission sought to restrict such actions by placing a statutory cap on the *Fisheries* holding, limiting its application to coastal configurations such as those found along the coasts of Norway and a few other states worldwide.[14] Thus, the language of Article 4 unambiguously states that in the case of a state whose coastline is deeply indented or fringed with islands in the immediate vicinity, that state *may*, as an option, enclose the coast at that point with a system of straight baselines which do not depart in any appreciable degree from the general direction of the coast.[15] Because such baselines enclose, as internal, waters beyond the

13. U.K. v. Norway, [1951] I.C.J. 116.
14. It is absolutely clear from the legislative history (*see* [1956] 1 Y.B. INT'L L. COMM'N at 185–190) that the members of the International Law Commission attempted to draft Article 4 adhering as closely as possible to the text of the *Fisheries* case. *See also* Morin, *Some Regional Approaches; Canada,* 3 NEW DIRECTIONS IN THE LAW OF THE SEA 244 (1973).
15. The text of Article 4 of the Territorial Sea Convention, *supra*, Chapter I, note 4, reads as follows:
    1. In localities where the coastline is deeply indented and cut into, or if there is a fringe of islands along the coast in its immediate vicinity, the method of straight baselines joining appropriate points may be employed in drawing the baseline from which the breadth of the territorial sea is measured.
    2. The drawing of such baselines must not depart to any appreciable extent from the general direction of the coast, and the sea areas lying within the lines must be sufficiently closely linked to the land domain to be subject to the regime of internal waters.
    3. Baselines shall not be drawn to and from low tide elevations unless lighthouses or similar installations which are permanently above sea level have been built on them.
    4. Where the method of straight baselines is applicable under the provisions of paragraph 1, account may be taken, in determining particular baselines, of economic interests peculiar to the region concerned, the reality and importance of which are clearly evidenced by a long usage.
    5. The system of straight baselines may not be applied by a state in such a manner as to cut off from the high seas the territorial sea of another state.
    6. The coastal state must clearly indicate straight baselines on charts, to which due publicity must be given.

coastal littoral and thus may more seriously infringe inclusive interests, baselines drawn under Article 4 require publication for effectiveness; and the right of innocent passage must be allowed in enclosed waters which previously had the juridical status of territorial sea.[16]

In spite of these specific textual limitations, many countries have claimed straight baselines in a manner arguably inconsistent with the text of Article 4 since 1958.[17] One result has been that many bay claims which might have been subject to challenge under the mandatory regime established by Article 7 for the designation and delimitation of a juridical bay have instead been incorporated within the expansive areas of internal waters cre-

---

16. *See* Territorial Sea Convention, art. 5.
17. As of Dec. 30, 1983, out of 128 coastal states, 43 or roughly 35%, had officially published straight baseline claims. Robert Smith, U.S. Geographer, reports, however, that a number of states have asserted but have not yet officially published such claims. It is therefore estimated that perhaps as many as 40 to 50% of states worldwide have established straight baselines. Official claims are recorded in OFFICE OF THE GEOGRA-PHER, BUREAU OF INTELLIGENCE AND RESEARCH, U.S. DEP'T OF STATE, LIMITS IN THE SEAS, Vols. 3 (Ireland), 4 (Mexico), 5 (Dominican Republic), 6 (Yugoslavia), 7 (Albania), 8 (Mauritania), 13 (Faeroes), 14 (Burma), 15 (Madagascar), 19 (Denmark), 20 (Saudi Arabia), 21 (Venezuela), 22 (United Arab Republic), 23 (United Kingdom), 27 (Portugal), 28 (Angola), 29 (Mozambique), 30 (Portuguese Guinea), 31 (Thailand), 32 (Turkey), 33 (The Phillipines), 34 (Iceland), 35 (Indonesia), 37 (France), 38 (West Germany), 39 (Svalbard), 40 (Guinea), 41 (Mauritius), 42 (Ecuador), 43 (P.R.C.), 44 (Argentina), 47 (Sweden), 48 (Finland), 51 (Haiti), 52 (East Germany), 53 (Syria), 54 (Senegal), 61 (Oman-Hypothetical), 76 (Cuba), 80 (Chile), 80 Addendum (Chile), 82 (Republic of Korea), 98 (Archipelagic straight baselines of Sao Tome and Principe), 99 (Vietnam). (To date the only state to officially reject the straight baseline option is the United States, where the election of the option would affect federal-state relations.) Some of these claims, such as those asserted by Iceland, Yugoslavia, Chile, Finland, and others, seem geographically justified on the basis of highly complex coastal configurations characterized by deep indentations and/or multiple island fringes along the coast. However, many claims, as for example those asserted by the Dominican Republic, France, and others, would seem to have been asserted in order to enclose some coastal indentations which on the face of it would not appear to meet the criteria of Article 7, *i.e.*, a well-marked, landlocked indentation, the area of which meets the semi-circle test and the mouth of which is no more than twenty-four miles wide. A case-by-case survey of claims is beyond the scope of this work, but having analyzed most of the straight baseline claims promulgated to date, it would appear to this author that a great many claims exceed the limitations imposed by the text of Article 4 and will therefore be subject to challenge in the future. If denied, many questionable coastal indentations will then become open to challenge under Article 7.

ated behind straight baselines established under the optional regime permitted by Article 4.[18]

The importance of Article 7 in international prescription has thus been partially eclipsed by these and other actions taken by states as part of the general thrust toward the establishment of more extensive claims to exclusive authority and control of the oceans. It is believed, however, that the eclipse is merely temporary. In the expansive period of newfound jurisdictional authority, some states have asserted straight baseline claims which appear to exceed the framework established by the drafters of the Territorial Sea Convention and UNCLOS. Some of these claims will undoubtedly be challenged by neighboring states;[19] and as

18. An even more promiscuous use of Article 4 has been the attempt by some states to use a so-called Article 4 straight baseline to enclose a single coastal indentation which has failed to meet the juridical tests imposed by Article 7. *See* Westerman, *The Juridical Status of the Gulf of Tarranto: A Brief Reply*, 11 SYR. J. INT'L L. & COM. 294–306 (1985). The legislative history of Article 4 makes clear that such a use is impermissible. *See* [1956] 1 Y.B. INT'L COMM'N at 192. Referring to the relationship between Article 5 (renumbered 4 in final form) and Article 7, Sir Gerald Fitzmaurice stated that Article 4 was intended to cover only such cases where the character of a particular coast justified the establishment of a general system of straight baselines. If any bays happened to be located on that deeply indented or island-fringed coastline, those bays would of necessity be subsumed within the general straight baseline system. Sir Fitzmaurice emphasized that this interpretation had been made clear in paragraph 5 (now paragraph 6) of Article 7, which specifically excludes from the scope of Article 7 any bays to which the straight baseline system of Article 4 might be applied. Article 7, he continued, was intended to deal with "the totally different case" of bays on a coast where there *was* no justification for the establishment of a straight baseline system. (Obviously, Article 7 would also apply to those bays belonging to coastal states, such as the United States, who have not opted for the Article 4 straight baseline method in delimiting their baselines.) The clear implication of the legislative history is that an Article 4 coastline is one as provided expressly in Article 4, paragraph 1–*i.e.*, a coastline which is deeply indented or cut into or fringed with islands in the immediate vicinity. If such a coast also includes bays, and the coastal state elects to draw a straight baseline along that portion of the coast, those bays need not meet Article 7 criteria to become internal waters, because they will automatically gain that status within the straight baseline. It is equally clear that a single indentation on a coastline which does *not* meet Article 4 criteria can only be designated as a bay under Article 7 criteria. Having failed to meet those Article 7 standards, the presence of this single, failed indentation *cannot possibly* qualify a coast as "deeply indented or cut into", and thus such an indentation cannot be granted "bay" status under Article 4. Such an interpretation would also render Article 7 superfluous, an impermissible interpretative result.

19. A controversy is currently pending in West Africa between neighboring States which have enclosed their entire coastlines behind straight baselines which greatly depart from the general direction of the coast.

these cases come to decision, impermissible claims will be disallowed, thus returning the baseline to the low-water mark along the coast, including the closing lines of truly internal waters. At that point, attention will again be focused on the issues of whether or not a given indentation meets the designation and delimitation criteria established under Article 7, thereby obtaining the status of internal waters on the basis envisioned by the drafters.[20]

In Federal States

The one context in which Article 7 of the Territorial Sea Convention has become increasingly important since 1958 is the federal-state arena, where potential conflict arises between sovereigns competing for resources in coastal waters which lap the shores of both the state and the nation.

Mexico, Brazil, Venezuela, Nigeria

In the federal states of Mexico,[21] Brazil,[22] Venezuela,[23] and Nigeria[24] the potential conflict between federal and state govern-

20. *See supra*, Chapter IV.
21. Carlos Dernal, in his own capacity as a jurist, reports that although the Mexican Constitution, which was modelled on the Constitution of the United States, appears to create a federalist system, in reality all power lies in the central government. De facto, individual states would have no power to exploit internal or territorial waters. Mexico is a party to both the Territorial Sea Convention and UNCLOS. When the Federation signs an international treaty, it signs for the nation as a whole. State law which is not in accord with the new treaty must be modified. All bays and inland waters granted to Mexico by treaty fall automatically under the control of the central government which treats fishing, resource exploitation, and related water issues as federal matters.
22. The Brazilian delegate to the United Nations reports that, like Mexico, federalism in Brazil exists in word but not in fact. States have little power to challenge the federal government. In regard to bays, Brazil applies the rules adopted under the Territorial Sea Convention, *i.e.*, bays wider than twenty-four miles at the entrance become territorial waters. But whether waters are deemed internal or territorial, the federal government remains in control of all national waters of Brazil.
23. A well-informed minister in the Venezuelan Mission to the United Nations reports that the federal government has general competence to draw straight baselines and full control over water resources. States have no power to challenge the federal government as to maritime boundaries.
24. The Nigerian Representative to the Sixth Committee of the United Nations reports that no federal-state disputes arise in Nigeria because, although facially a federation, all power resides in the central government. Mining and resource exploitation are

ments does not arise because the control of coastal resources has been placed solely in federal hands.

Federal Republic of Germany

The Basic Law (Constitution) of the Federal Republic of Germany (F.R.G.), on the other hand, creates a federal system under which every part of the nation is under the dual territorial sovereignty of both the Laender (States) and the federal government.[25] Territory of the Laender may only be reallocated among the Laender; there may be no territory directly controlled by the federal government. This system of dual sovereignty extends into the territorial sea, and there has been a continuing controversy over whether this duality also extends into the continental shelf.[26]

As to the control of coastal resources, the federal government passed the *Federal Mining Act*[27] in 1980; but under the federal system in the F.R.G., the execution of federal laws is attributed to the Laender which provide for the establishment of the requisite authorities and the regulation of administrative procedures.[28] Therefore, the four coastal Laender[29] possess the sole power to establish mining authorities, to issue requisite licenses,[30] and to collect revenues such as royalties or license fees from mining or drilling activities in their internal or territorial waters.[31]

---

under federal control. The federal government then allocates monies received to the states on the basis of a formula which allocates a larger share to that state from whose territory the resource was recovered.

25. *See* GRUNDGESETZ (BASIC LAW) arts. 20, 28, 29. (W. Ger.).
26. For the affirmative position, *see* Seidl-Hohenveldern, *Le Plateau Continental et La République Fédérale d'Allemagne*, 10 ANNUAIRE FRANÇAIS DE DROIT INTERNATIONAL 717, 723; for the negative, *see* Frowein, *Verfassungsrechtliche Probleme um den Deutschen Festlandsockel*, 25 ZEITSCHRIFT FÜR AUSLANDISCHES OFFENTLICHES RECHT UND VOLKERRECHT 1, 3 (1965).
27. Bundesgesetzblatt 1980 I, S.1310.
28. *See* GRUNDGESETZ (BASIC LAW), arts. 83, 84(1). (W. Ger.).
29. Niedersachsen, Schleswig-Holstein, Hamburg, and Bremen.
30. The administrative competence ratione loci is determined among the Laender by the equidistance principle.
31. At present, the F.R.G. claims a three-mile territorial sea. According to the Federal Mining Act, *supra* at note 27, (arts. 30, 31), a licensee must pay to the Laender in whose territory he has operated a fee of ten German marks (DM) for every square kilometer of his field of operation in the first year and another ten DM per square kilometer in each subsequent year, up to a maximum of fifty DM. In addition, he must pay to the Laender ten percent of the market value of resources extracted.

The only offshore area in which the right to the revenues produced by coastal resources remains unallocated, thus creating a
potential area for federal-state conflict, is the continental shelf.
This final allocation is pending special enactment,[32] and at this
writing, agreement on the content of the enactment has not yet
been reached.[33] It may be concluded that until agreement *has*
been reached, no potential conflict under Article 7 exists in the
Federal Republic of Germany due to the special features of their
constitutional and legislative enactments which to date have allocated control over resources to the Laender within whose territory, land or water, the resources lie.

Should the resources on the continental shelf be placed ultimately under federal control, then it is possible that the federal
government might attempt to challenge state authority over certain bay waters under Article 7, in order to overturn their bay
designation and thus gain control over the seabed of any waters
returned to high seas. However, considering the German constitutional and legislative preference favoring state and dual federal-state sovereignty over German territory, together with the
fact that many large German bays have already been deemed high
seas[34] or enclosed behind straight baselines on the Baltic,[35] one

---

These profits, especially from natural gas exploitation licenses, have created controversies between coastal states such as Niedersachsen and noncoastal states such as
Baden-Württemberg, the latter demanding a reallocation of these windfall revenues
among all the Laender. There has been *no* such conflict with the federal government
because the licensing regime allocates all revenues to the Laender.

32. *See* Federal Mining Act, *supra* at note 27, art. 137.
33. It is far from a foregone conclusion that control over the resources in the continental
shelf will be allocated to the federal government. The controversy noted *supra* in note
26 and accompanying text is still ongoing; and those who argue in favor of extending
the authority of the coastal Laender are supported by the fact that the Federal Mining
Act, *supra* note 27, covers the exploration and exploitation of mineral and hydrocar-
bonide resources within the territory of the F.R.G. as well as on its continental shelf.
Thus, say the proponents of Laender control, the licensing regime which allocates
revenues to the Laender must apply to the continental shelf as well. The issue is very
much an open question at this writing.
34. Because the F.R.G. asserts no historic bay claims, large bays such as German Bay,
Heligoland Bay, and Lübeck Bay have already been deemed high seas beyond the
territorial margin.
35. Kiel Bay, Flensburg Bay, Eckenforde Bay, Hohwacht Bay, and the Fehmarnsound
(East and West sides) have been enclosed by straight baselines since 1978. *See* an
Oceana Looseleaf Series, *Western Europe and the Development of the Law of the Sea, Vol.
1: F.R.G. 1925–1977*, at iii, which reprints an "information" reporting the establishment of straight baselines in these areas, effective May 8, 1978. *See also* LIMITS IN THE
SEAS, *supra* note 17, Vol. 38.

must surmise that head-to-head conflict between the Laender and the federal government over bay claims will be unlikely within the F.R.G.. A more likely scenario, considering the German revenue sharing system under which less wealthy Laender are assisted by other Laender[36] from a general fund, would be the enactment of a shared allocation system of some sort, with all revenues from resource exploration and exploitation on the continental shelf being dispersed by way of an equitable formula to all Laender, coastal and noncoastal alike. This, of course, is a speculation; the issue remains unsettled at this writing.

Canada

In Canada, offshore jurisdictional issues have been the source of much federal-provincial litigation and negotiation in recent years. As a result of the *North Atlantic Fisheries Case* and the new maritime powers granted under the Territorial Sea Convention, Canada's internal and territorial waters have expanded greatly since 1958;[37] and the federal and provincial governments have vied actively for jurisdiction, both sovereigns utilizing the same arguments which have been used to support international regimes for coastal jurisdiction over contiguous waters, i.e., that the natural

36. An official at the German Mission to the United Nations reports a current controversy between Lower Saxony, a relatively poor state which has become oil-producing in recent years, and the other Laender, which have contributed to the support of Lower Saxony and who now argue that her oil revenues should be included in the balance so that so much support is not needed from her neighbors. German law, however, gives the right to oil revenues solely to the Laender from whose territory it is recovered.

37. Before World War II, Canada adhered to the rules of the law of the sea which it derived from Great Britain and therefore was a firm supporter of the three-mile territorial sea. Since that time, technological and economic developments have led Canada to perceive its interests, particularly in regard to fisheries and resource exploitation, as more in keeping with those of developing rather than developed states. When the *Anglo-Norwegian Fisheries Case* [1951] I.C.J. Rep. 116, was decided in 1951, Canada realized that due to the special nature of her coastlines, large portions of which are both deeply indented *and* fringed with islands in the immediate vicinity, she could rely on the holding of that case to draw straight baselines enclosing much of her coasts. [See 7 House of Commons Debates 6702 (1956)]. After the Territorial Sea Convention codified this approach under Art. 4, the Canadian parliament issued an order on Oct. 27, 1967, defining straight baselines applicable to Labrador and Newfoundland. [Territorial Sea & Fishing Zones Geographical Coordinates (Areas 1,2, & 3) Order, P.C. 1967–2025 SOR/67 no. 543, 108 CAN. GAZ. 1701]. The lines thus promulgated do not stray perceptibly from the general direction of the coast,

resources of the sea and seabed appertain to the adjacent land mass.[38] Whereas the courts of the United States have relied on federal legislation and international law to settle federal-state maritime boundary issues,[39] Canadian courts have relied primarily on the common law as it relates to historic boundaries,[40]

but the vast bays of Newfoundland are thereby enclosed as internal waters. [Morin, *Les Zones de Pêche de Terre-Neuve et du Labrador à la Lumière de l'Evolution du Droit International,* 6 C.Y.I.L. 91 (1968)]. A second order authorizing straight baselines for Nova Scotia and the Pacific Coast was published May 29, 1969. [Territorial Sea & Fishing Zones Geographical Coordinates (Areas 3,4,& 6) Order, P.C. 1969–1109, SOR/69 no.278, 103 CAN. GAZ. 822]. These straight baselines also do not appear to stray perceptibly from the coast. In 1970, Canada claimed a twelve-mile territorial sea. (68 CAN. STAT., 1969–70). *See* Morin, *supra* note 14, at 243–45. The straight baselines published in 1967 and 1969 remain in force today. Interestingly, an official at the Department of External Affairs, Legal Bureau, Government of Canada, Ottawa, reports that Canadian straight baselines have *not* been drawn under the authority of Article 4 but rather on the authority of Canadian legislation which takes precedence over treaties in the Canadian system. The basis for such legislation has been drawn from historical claims and other sources which are somewhat vague. This official also reports that straight baselines have not as yet been drawn enclosing the Gulf of St. Lawrence or the Arctic Archipelago, but Canada nonetheless claims these waters as internal. Hudson Bay, which Canada has claimed by historic title [*See* N. Nicholson, THE BOUNDARIES OF THE CANADIAN CONFEDERATION 75 (1979)], is included within this Arctic Archipelagic claim. Although Canada has not yet claimed an exclusive economic zone, she has claimed a 200-mile fishery zone. (*See* NATIONAL MARITIME CLAIMS, *supra* note 9, Appendix, Table 3.) The net result of this twenty-year claims process has been a tremendous increase in the area of contiguous seas brought within the authority and control of the Confederation.

38. Charney, *The Offshore Jurisdiction of the States of the United States and the Provinces of Canada: A Comparison,* 12 OCEAN DEV. & INT'L L. J. 312 (1983).

39. *See infra* this section.

40. Charney believes that there are advantages and disadvantages in each approach. Although the outcome of conflict is less predictable under the Canadian method, historic boundaries, once delimited, may be set for all time. If boundaries are set by reference to an international law standard, changes in the international rule may require changes in a federal-state boundary as well. This of course could have deleterious consequences for enterprises who had come to rely on the boundary as originally set. The U.S. Supreme Court addressed this potential problem by freezing the international rule for bays (which it had read into the Submerged Lands Act as the most workable bay definition) as that contained in the then-current text of Article 7 of the Territorial Sea Convention, United States v. California, 381 U.S. 139, 166–167 (1965). One advantage of using international law norms as a basis for decision is that they are not anachronistic, and due to recent codification efforts, especially in regard to bays, they are fairly well-defined. Historic boundaries may be less well defined or may be anachronistically attached to private land boundaries derived from British rule. Perhaps the greatest disadvantage in using international norms to set domestic boundaries is that the placement of a federal-state boundary must always be tested against its foreign policy impact, and a federal court may therefore feel constrained in a decision favoring the state sovereign due to concern over embarrassing

although reference has been made occasionally to international provisions which might prove "indicative" for boundary delimitation purposes.[41] Because of this uncertainty as to the basis for conflict resolution and because there is to date no federal legislation which can provide useful guidelines, the issue of the exact dividing line between provincial and federal jurisdiction in contiguous Canadian waters remains largely unresolved at this writing.[42]

---

the federal government or infringing its interests in international affairs. Charney, *supra* note 38, at 310–313.

41. *See* Re Dominion Coal Co., Ltd. v. County of Cape Breton, (1965) 40 D.L.R. (2d) 593, 602; Reference Re Offshore Mineral Rights of British Columbia, [1967] S.C.R. 792, 800, 807–8, 819.

42. The history of federal-provincial jurisidictional conflict in Canadian offshore waters has been an interesting one. In 1964, the Prime Minister of Canada conferred with the Premiers of Nova Scotia, New Brunswick, Prince Edward Island, and Newfoundland. The Premiers sought federal recognition of provincial offshore jurisdiction and called for federal legislation to settle the issue. No legislation was forthcoming. In 1967, the Governor General referred the issue of offshore jurisdiction to the Supreme Court of Canada, Reference re Offshore Mineral Rights of British Columbia, [1967] S.C.R. 792, requesting the Court to give its opinion on the respective proprietary rights and legislative jurisdiction of Canada and British Columbia in the seabed and subsoil underlying the territorial sea and the continental shelf. British Columbia, which was supported in its petition by every Canadian province except Quebec, Manitoba, Saskatchewan, and Alberta, argued that the historical boundaries of the Province included the territorial sea in 1871, the year British Columbia entered into Confederation. The federal government argued on the basis of the common law and historical boundaries that the boundary of the realm throughout Canada historically ended at the seashore. The Supreme Court of Canada held that as to the lands underlying the territorial sea and those of the continental shelf, both lie outside the historic boundaries of British Columbia; and therefore, all proprietary rights and legislative jurisdiction reside in Canada. *Id.,* at 821. The question of jurisdiction over internal waters was expressly left open. *Id.* (*See infra* note 49, and accompanying text for discussion of this question in reference to the *Strait of Georgia Case.*) Matters were left somewhat unsettled by the fact that the holding of the Reference only applied to British Columbia, although all other coastal provinces had joined in its petition. In 1977, Prime Minister Trudeau proposed a federal-provincial division of revenues and administrative responsibilities in lieu of provincial jurisdiction. A memo of understanding was signed by Trudeau and the Premiers of Nova Scotia, Prince Edward Island, and New Brunswick (*see* Federal-Provincial Memo of Understanding in Respect of the Administration and Management of Mineral Resources Offshore of the Maritime Provinces, Feb. 1, 1977), which was expected to form the basis for federal legislation. Again, no legislation was forthcoming. (Charney, *supra* note 38, at 306). Subsequently, two cases raised the offshore jurisidictional issue but declined to answer it. [Canadian Merchant Services Guild v. Crosbie Offshore Services, Ltd., Canadian Labor Relations Board Decision 291 (Dec. 30, 1981); Seafarer's International Union of Canada v. Crosbie Offshore Services, Ltd., Federal Court of Appeals of Canada, Case A-2-81, Judgment Rendered at Ottawa, Mar. 5, 1982] In February

The only Canadian Supreme Court case which has involved federal-provincial conflict over bay jurisdiction per se has been *Re Dominion Coal Co., Ltd. v. County of Cape Breton*,[43] a 1963 case in which the County of Cape Breton, Nova Scotia, asserted jurisdiction under the Assessment Act to tax the revenues of coal com-

---

1982, Newfoundland submitted a reference to the Court of Appeal of the Supreme Court of Newfoundland on the question of Provincial jurisdiction in the Hibernia area in the Atlantic. (Order in Council No. 135–82, approved Feb. 12, 1982.) In Reference re Mineral and other Natural Resources of the Continental Shelf (1983) 145 D.L.R. 9, 41 Nfld. & P.E.I.R. 211, the Newfoundland Court of Appeal granted Newfoundland jurisdiction over the land three marine miles from shore, reserving the rest of the continental shelf to the federal government. This decision was appealed by both Canada and Newfoundland to the Newfoundland Supreme Court, but neither appeal has been decided to date. In 1984, however, Canada submitted a reference directly to the Supreme Court of Canada as to the issue of the Continental shelf. In Reference re the Seabed and Subsoil of the Continental Shelf Offshore Newfoundland (1984), 5 D.L.R. (4th) 385, the Supreme Court held that Canada was the only entity capable of acquiring rights in the continental shelf after 1949, when such rights became recognized under international law. The issue of Newfoundland jurisdiction over the land and waters three miles from the shoreline is still an open question at this writing. In March of 1982, Nova Scotia and the federal government entered into an agreement for shared management and control of resources from exploitation activities off the northern and eastern coasts of Nova Scotia. The jurisdictional question was left open. (Charney, *supra* note 38, at 306.) On sum, it would appear that Canada is moving piecemeal toward a federal-provincial jurisdictional settlement through a combination of ad hoc court decisions and negotiated settlements. In general, cases to date favor federal jurisdiction beyond the shoreline; but recent decisions by the Newfoundland and British Columbia Courts of Appeal, as well as the Supreme Court of Canada, appear to indicate a new direction toward shared jurisdiction. Even if the federal government does retain jurisdiction in fact, there is a pronounced willingness to negotiate shared resource and administrative allocations with coastal provinces. For example, following the decision by the Supreme Court of Canada cited above which declared Canada the only entity with rights in the continental shelf, Canada and Newfoundland signed the Atlantic Accord (Feb. 1985) which granted Newfoundland equivalent returns on the resources of the continental shelf as if the resources were located on land. The question of internal waters in general and bays in particular is technically open at this writing, although the *Crown Zellerbach* decision (*see* infra note 51 and accompanying text) would appear to state the case that internal waters, hence bays, are considered to be within the jurisdictional ambit of the provinces. An official in the Department of External Affairs, Government of Canada, Ottawa, stated that such decisions are unlikely to be appealed by Canada, although they will continue to be decided on a case by case basis. For further analysis of offshore jurisdictional issues in Canada, *see* Beauchamp, Crommelin and Thompson, *Jurisdictional Problems in Canada's Off-shore*, 11 ALTA L. REV. 431 (1973); Head, *The Legal Clamour over Canadian Offshore Minerals*, 5 ALTA L. REV. 312 (1966–67); Hubbard, *Constitutional Law, International Law, Ownership. . . .*, 2 OTTAWA L. REV. 212 (1967–68); Lewis, *Provincial-Federal Cooperation*, 3 ALTA L. REV. 412 (1964); Martin, *Newfoundland's Case*, 7 OTTAWA L. REV. 34 (1975).

43. (1963) 40 D.L.R. (2d) 593. *See infra* note 51 and accompanying text for recent British Columbia Court of Appeal decision on Beaver Cove, a bay on Vancouver Island.

panies operating under the waters of Sydney Harbour and Span-ish Bay. The Court affirmed the common law principle which holds that, "in defining the boundaries of a municipality which . . . borders on the sea, the Province is entitled to include an area covered by interior or national waters being inter fauces terrae; and the lands thereunder . . . ;"[44] and then proceeded to answer the question of whether or not the waters of Sydney Harbour or Spanish Bay were *inter fauces terrae*. Although Isley, writing for the majority, mentioned in passing that Article 7 of the Territo-rial Sea Convention "is indicative of what has been regarded as a bay,"[45] he declined to apply the tests imposed by Article 7 to the current determination, relying instead on historic case precedent to hold that the waters of Sydney Harbour were *inter fauces terrae,* making the lands under the harbor "lands covered with water" under the Assessment Act. Any coal extraction taking place within Sydney Harbour was therefore assessable by the County of Cape Breton. Spanish Bay, however, was held not to be internal waters and thus not subject to municipal tax jurisdiction.[46] Inter-estingly, *no* international norms regarding bays were applied to this determination whatsoever, not even earlier customary norms providing for a ten-mile limit on bay entrances. Thus, we are left in the dark by the majority as to the exact basis for upholding provincial jurisdiction in one bay area and denying it in another. A vigorous dissent by Currie,[47] relying in part on common law and historic precedent but making specific use of the work of respected commentators in the field of international law as well as the precise criteria supplied by Article 7 for bay designation and delimitation, concludes that both Sydney Harbour and Span-ish Bay meet Article 7 standards and should therefore be declared to be within the jurisdiction of the Province.[48] It seems clear on the basis of this case that provinces are generally granted juris-diction over waters *inter fauces terrae*, on a case by case basis, but to date there has been no attempt to devise a precise basis upon which such determinations may be made.

An official of the Canadian Government in the Department of External Affairs, Legal Bureau, Ottawa, has stated that the issue

44. *Id.,* at 593.
45. *Id.,* at 602.
46. *Id.,* at 593; *see also, id.,* 593–605.
47. *Id.,* at 606–26.
48. *Id.,* at 613.

of federal provincial jurisdiction in Canadian bays is still very much an open question due to the uncertain result in the *Dominion Coal Case,* granting Provincial jurisdiction in one bay and denying it in another without a clear basis for future decision.

There are indications, however, that the jurisdictional issue in regard to bays, and in fact to internal waters in general, may be ripe for decision. In a 1976 case,[49] the British Columbia Court of Appeal held 3 to 2 that the property rights in lands covered by the waters of the Strait of Juan de Fueca, the Strait of Georgia, Johnstone Strait, and Queen Charlotte Strait, belonged to the Province of British Columbia. The Court distinguished the holding by the Supreme Court of Canada in the 1967 *Reference on British Columbia* because that case had applied only to the territorial sea and the continental shelf, whereas these waters were made internal by the fact that the original western boundary of British Columbia had been long recognized as the Pacific Ocean, and several subsequent treaties and acts had distinguished these bodies of water, lying between Vancouver Island and the mainland, from the Pacific Ocean. Both parties appealed; and in *Re Attorney-General of Canada and Attorney-General of British Columbia et al,*[50] the Supreme Court of Canada dismissed the Canadian appeal and held in favor of British Columbia. Once again, the decision was based on Canadian common law rather than international law norms. Reasoning that early documents had set the western boundary of British Columbia at the Pacific Ocean, the majority held the meaning of Pacific Ocean in these acts to be the open sea off Vancouver Island; and therefore the subject straits and submerged lands were part of the Colony of British Columbia when it entered confederation. The Strait of Georgia therefore constitutes internal waters of British Columbia. An official at the Department of External Affairs, Government of Canada, Ottawa, stresses that this decision will have far-reaching implications due to the tremendous increase in internal waters claimed by Canada under her straight baseline system.

In another recent case,[51] the British Columbia Court of Appeal

---

49. (1976) Reference re Ownership of the Bed of the Strait of Georgia and Related Areas, 1 B.C.L.R. 97.
50. (1984) 8 D.L.R. (4th) 161.
51. (1984) R. v. Crown Zellerbach Canada Ltd., 7 D.L.R. (4th) 449.

has held that an attempt by the federal government to assert jurisdiction over Beaver Cove on Vancouver Island in order to
enforce federal environmental law is ultra vires due to the fact
that the bay is part of the internal waters of British Columbia. An
appeal will be taken by the federal government, but it would
appear unlikely at this time that provincial jurisdiction over internal waters will be overturned, although decisions will continue to
be made on a case by case basis as controversies arise.

Australia

As in Canada, Australia has been actively involved in the process
of negotiating an offshore constitutional settlement between the
Commonwealth and her various states. On October 16, 1967, the
parties concluded an agreement relating to the exploration for,
and the exploitation of, the petroleum and certain other
resources of the continental shelf of Australia, as well as certain
territories of the Commonwealth and certain additional submerged lands. This agreement provided the foundation for the
passage of the Petroleum (Submerged Lands) Act of 1967 (Cth)
and the Petroleum (Submerged Lands) Acts of the various states.

The validity of the joint settlement was called into question in
1969 by the decision of the High Court of Australia in *Bonser v.
LaMacchia*,[52] in which the majority, agreeing with the conclusion
reached by the Supreme Court of Canada in *Reference re Ownership of Offshore Mineral Rights of British Columbia*,[53] held that the
Commonwealth of Australia held sole rights in the seabed surrounding Australia.[54]

The future of the joint settlement was further called into question by the passage in 1973 by the Commonwealth Parliament of
the Seas and Submerged Lands Act[55] which vested all rights in the
internal waters of the Commonwealth,[56] in the territorial sea,
including the superincumbent airspace and the seabed and subsoil thereof,[57] as well as in the continental shelf[58] in the federal

52. 122 C.L.R. 177, 43 A.L.J.R. 411 (1969).
53. 65 D.L.R. (2d) 353, 365, 366, 367 (1967).
54. 122 C.L.R. 177, 187 (1969).
55. Seas and Submerged Lands Act 1973 (Cth).
56. *Id.*, §10.
57. *Id.*, §§6, 7.
58. *Id.*, §11.

government. The Act also reserved the power to the federal government to set all maritime boundaries imposed on Australia by virtue of her becoming a party to the 1958 Geneva Convention on the Territorial Sea and the Contiguous Zone and the Geneva Convention on the Continental Shelf.[59]

Sections 14 and 15 of the Act contained certain savings provisions, however, the effect of section 14 being to reserve the rights of Australian states in respect to the waters of the sea of or within any bay, gulf, estuary, river, creek, inlet, port, or harbor which before federation were, and still remained, within the sovereignty of a state.[60] The superincumbent airspace and the subjacent seabed and subsoil of these areas were also included in the saving.[61]

As a result of this federal legislation, all six states of Australia[62] brought actions in the High Court against the Commonwealth, seeking declarations that the Act was wholly or partly invalid. On behalf of the plaintiff states it was submitted, *inter alia,* that both prior and after Federation, they had enjoyed sovereignty and legislative power over the territorial sea adjacent to their coasts up to the three-mile limit, including the seabed, subsoil, and superjacent airspace thereof, as well as over the continental shelf. The defense of the Commonwealth was predicated on the argument that, even if such rights were found to exist prior to the enactment of the Commonwealth Constitution, these rights passed to the Commonwealth upon the commencement of Federation, or at the latest upon Australia's becoming a fully independent nation.[63]

In *New South Wales v. The Commonwealth,*[64] a majority of the Full Court of the High Court of Australia held that the plaintiffs, whether as colonies or states, never in their own right held sovereignty or legislative power over the land and waters of the ter-

59. *Id.,* §§7, 8, 11 and Preamble.
60. *Id.,* §14.
61. *Id. See also* §15 which reserves to the States rights in wharves, jetties, piers, breakwaters, buildings, platforms, pipelines, lighthouses, beaches, navigational aids, buoys, cables, or other coastal structures or works.
62. New South Wales was joined by Victoria, Queensland, South Australia, Western Australia, and Tasmania in New South Wales v. The Commonwealth, 8 A.L.R. 1, 50 A.L.J.R. 218 (1976).
63. *Id.,* at 2.
64. *Id.*

ritorial sea nor over the continental shelf. All rights granted under international law in these areas were vested exclusively in Australia as a nation.[65] Thus, the Seas and Submerged Lands Act of 1973 was a valid exercise of power by Parliament under §§51 pl. (xxix) and 122 of the Australian Constitution.

In a vigorous dissent, Stephen concluded on constitutional grounds that the league seas surrounding Australia belonged to the littoral states.[66] Citing prior case law which had divided authority equally between the nation and the states, Stephen asserted that the Constitution intended to establish two governments, State and Federal, side by side, neither subordinate to the other. This system of dual sovereignty therefore implied a system of shared sovereignty in the league seas.[67]

After the *New South Wales Case* was decided in 1976, discussions took place between the Commonwealth and the states with a view toward reaching a political accord regarding offshore resource allocation. At the conference held June 29, 1979, such an accord was reached. Pursuant to that agreement, Parliament passed the Coastal Waters (State Powers) Act of 1980 under which legislative power[68] (not to be confused with sovereignty) was conferred upon each State with respect to the "coastal waters" of that state, which include any internal waters as well as

---

65. *Id.*, at 2, 3, 11–14, 24, 26, 27, 43–46. [The majority cited *United States v. California, United States v. Louisiana, United States v. Texas* (those versions decided *prior* to the 1958 Convention), as well as *United States v. Maine* and *Reference re Offshore Mineral Rights of British Columbia* as authority for its holding.]

66. 8 A.L.R. 73.

67. A legal officer in the Australian Embassy in Washington, D.C., reports that this constitutional issue is the subject of one of the most heated legal debates in Australia at this time. At the heart of the debate is the question of whether the powers reserved to the federal government under §51 of the Australian Constitution are meant to be exclusive or merely indicative; whether the section reserves a residue of powers to the States or whether the States enjoy an overriding jurisdiction. Still other statutory interpretations may be possible. This question, which is directly related to the offshore constitutional settlement currently under negotiation, is unsettled at this writing.

68. State legislative powers in "coastal waters" include the making of all laws which might be made if the waters were within the actual territorial limits of the State, in addition to specified legislative powers beyond the limits of coastal waters, as for example, the power to enact laws governing subterranean mining which originates within the territory of the State and continues out to sea or laws pertaining to the management of fisheries which extend beyond the three-mile limit. *See* Crommelin, *National Resources Law*, ANNUAL SURVEY OF AUSTRALIAN LAW 1980, 152–173 (1981).

all waters, seabed, subsoil, and airspace three nautical miles seaward from the baseline used to measure Australia's territorial sea as a matter of international law. However, the Coastal Waters Act makes clear that if Australia should follow the international trend toward a wider territorial sea, the breadth of a state's "coastal waters" may not be similarly extended.[69] Federal legislation passed in 1980 and 1981, also pursuant to agreement between the Commonwealth and the states in 1979, established joint authority and administrative power over resources in the continental shelf.[70]

In December of 1981, it was announced by the federal government that the entire package of Commonwealth legislation passed in 1980 and 1981 would come into force on January 1, 1982, because state implementing legislation, though not yet enacted as required by the 1979 agreement, had been introduced in each state legislature.[71] It must be reiterated, however, that this legislative action by both Commonwealth and State Parliaments does not bear upon the issues of sovereignty or jurisdiction in contiguous waters beyond the seashore, which in Australia still reside in the Commonwealth.

As to the more specific issue of federal-state jurisdiction over bays, there seems to be little doubt that under Australian law,

69. The Coastal Waters Act of 1980 preserves the status of Australia's territorial sea under international law and declares that the Act is not to be taken as extending the limits of any State. This provision was inserted to avoid any necessity to seek the approval of the electors under §123 of the Australian Constitution which permits the Commonwealth Parliament to alter State territorial limits only with the consent of the State Parliament and the approval of the majority of electors of that State. Rather, Federal authority to enact the Coastal Waters Act is said to derive from §51 (38) of the Australian Constitution (*see supra* note 67) which allows the Commonwealth Parliament the "power to make laws for the peace, order, and good government of the Commonwealth." *See* Crommelin, *supra* note 68.

70. The Minerals (Submerged Lands) Act 1981, the Minerals (Submerged Lands) (Royalty) Act 1981, the Minerals (Submerged Lands) (Exploration Permit Fees) Act 1981, the Minerals (Submerged Lands) (Production License Fees) Act 1981, the Minerals (Submerged Lands) (Works Authority Fees) Act 1981, and the Minerals (Submerged Lands) (Registration Fees) Act 1981 read together establish the joint Commonwealth-State regime for minerals exploration and production on the continental shelf beyond coastal waters. This legislation is modelled on the Petroleum (Submerged Lands) Act 1967 as amended in 1980 and 1981 to create joint authority. For further details on the joint administration of the resources on the continental shelf, *see* Crommelin, *National Resources Law*, ANNUAL SURVEY OF AUSTRALIA LAW 1981 270–297 (1982).

71. *See* Crommelin, *supra* note 69, at 271. This legislation has come into effect as scheduled, according to a legal officer at the Australian Embassy, Washington, D.C..

states retain sovereign power in their bays, gulfs, estuaries, rivers, creeks, inlets, ports, or harbors which before federation were and still remain with the sovereignty of the state.[72] There has been to date no case in which Australian courts have made use of Article 7 to determine whether or not disputed waters might qualify as a bay.[73] It *is* clear, however, that both Canadian and Australian courts have, to date, been reluctant to tie domestic boundaries to international law norms.

United States

There has been no such reluctance in the United States, where courts have officially applied international norms to federal-state maritime boundary disputes since 1952.[74] The Truman Proclamation[75] on the Continental Shelf in 1945 touched off a flurry of international claims[76] as well as a forty-year struggle between the United States and her maritime states for jurisdiction over offshore resources.

When technological development first permitted oil companies and others to move away from the land mass and into the sub-

---

72. *See supra* notes 60 and 61 and accompanying text.
73. In the special case of South Australia, whose territorial limits expressly include bays, according to historic instruments of confederation, litigation has been necessary to determine which waters may be thus classified. *See* (1977) Raptis v. State of South Australia, 15 A.L.R. 223. In all other cases, the preferred method of federal-state dispute settlement in Australia would appear to be negotiation rather than litigation. Most substantive boundary disputes have been resolved in the context of the offshore constitutional settlement discussed above. Negotiations are underway as of this writing to define with particularity the federal-state boundaries in more complex coastal configurations such as the Great Barrier Reef off Queensland. One of the main reasons that Australia has not yet signed UNCLOS, according to the aforementioned legal officer, is that the federal government is evaluating federal-state responsibilities in several areas in order to apply UNCLOS uniformly throughout the Commonwealth. This overview cannot be completed until several outstanding questions currently under negotiation pursuant to reaching an offshore constitutional settlement have been resolved by the Commonwealth and the states. Naturally, the states favor a jurisdictional division of power, whereas the Commonwealth favors joint administration and allocation of resources with jurisdiction remaining in the federal government beyond the seashore.
74. *See* Report of the Special Master, filed Nov. 10, 1952, United States v. California, 344 U.S. 872 (1952); *see also infra* note 94.
75. Proc. No. 2667, 10 FED. REG. 12303 (1945); Proc. No. 2668, 10 FED. REG. 12304 (1945).
76. *See supra* note 10.

merged lands beneath coastal waters for the exploration and exploitation of resources, these entities sought to secure their interests by obtaining leases from the coastal sovereign who held the rights to the submerged lands, incapable of private ownership under the common law, as the universal occupant.[77] The question presented in a federalist state, of course, is "which sovereign?" Based on the common law view represented in cases such as *Pollard's Lessee v. Hagan*[78] and *Martin v. Waddell*[79] that title to the lands beneath navigable waters had passed to the thirteen original colonies from the King after the Revolution and to states subsequently admitted to the Union on the basis of the equal footing doctrine, most coastal states assumed that they held title to the submerged lands underneath the three-mile territorial sea then claimed by the United States as its international boundary. On the basis of this assumption, California and many other states began, as early as the 1930's, to lease portions of their adjacent submerged lands to interested parties. For many years the Federal Government raised no objection to these claims. However, as it became apparent that the submerged lands off the shores of certain states contained rich and valuable oil reserves and other natural resources, the Federal Government asserted national sovereignty over the same lands.

The United States v. California Case   In 1945, the United States brought an original action[80] against the State of California under Article III §2 of the U.S. Constitution to determine whether the right to exploit the natural resources under the submerged lands off the California coast belonged to the United States or to California. In *United States v. California*, the Supreme Court upset the belief that the states owned the submerged lands beneath the territorial sea, holding instead that the United States possessed "paramount rights" in the land seaward of the line of ordinary low water and of the seaward limit of inland waters.[81]

The Court based its decision on the premise that the assertion of rights in the territorial sea was made by the United States in

77. *See* ANGELL, A TREATISE ON TIDE WATERS 17–21 (1847).
78. 44 U.S. (1 How.) 212, 228–29 (1845).
79. 41 U.S. (1 Pet.) 367, 410 (1842).
80. United States v. California, 332 U.S. 19 (1947).
81. 332 U.S. at 19, 804, 805 (1947).

two capacities transcending those of a mere property owner, i.e., its capacity to assert whatever power and dominion proved necessary to protect the national security and its capacity as a member of the family of nations, responsible for the conduct of foreign relations. The Court concluded that sovereign rights in the territorial sea must therefore be considered aspects of national sovereignty.[82] In 1950, the United States brought similar actions against Louisiana[83] and Texas[84] with virtually identical results.[85]

The Supreme Court's holdings in the *California, Louisiana,* and *Texas* cases precipitated one of the most hotly contested domestic political issues of the postwar decade.[86] The coastal states eventually took their plight to the Congress where a joint resolution in 1952 indicated an intent to "restore" to the states the submerged lands which they believed themselves to own before the *California* decision.[87] In 1953, Congress passed the Submerged Lands Act[88] which gave to the coastal states "title to and ownership of the lands beneath navigable waters within the boundaries of the respective States, and the natural resources within such lands and waters. . . ."[89] The Act defined "lands beneath naviga-

---

82. 332 U.S. at 19, 29, 38–39.
83. United States v. Louisiana, 339 U.S. 699 (1950).
84. United States v. Texas, 339 U.S. 707 (1950).
85. Although *United States v. California, United States v. Louisiana,* and *United States v. Texas* are often referred to as the "Tidelands Cases," tidelands were not actually involved in any of these litigations. In fact, the Government complaints in each case specifically excluded tidelands as well as lands beneath the inland waters of the states from consideration by the Court. The Supreme Court reaffirmed state ownership of these lands under Pollard's Lessee v. Hagan, 332 U.S. at 36. *See* Shalowitz, *Boundary Problems Raised by the Submerged Lands Act,* 54 COL. L. REV. 1021, 1022 (1954). Congress included a provision confirming title in the states to these lands in the Submerged Lands Act, *see infra* note 86, as a safeguard against future federal actions. *See* S. REP. NO. 133, 83d Cong., 1st Sess. 7 (1953).
86. United States v. California, 381 U.S. 139, 185 (1965) (Black, J., dissenting).
87. S.J. Res. 20, 82d Cong., 2d Sess. The legislative history of the Submerged Lands Act leaves little doubt that its object was restorative in that the drafters intended to return to the states the rights which they had enjoyed "since the founding of our Nation and up to the date of the decision in the California case." *See* Hearings before the Senate Committee on Interior and Insular Affairs on S. J. Res. 13 and other Bills, 83d Cong., 1st Sess., 31–32 and in full.
88. 67 Stat. 29, 43 U.S.C. §§1301–15 (1958 ed.). Alabama v. Texas, 347 U.S. 272, 273 (1954), held the Submerged Lands Act constitutional as a valid exercise of the power granted to Congress under Article IV of the Constitution to dispose of the territory and other property belonging to the United States.
89. §3, 67 Stat. 29, 43 U.S.C. §1311 (1958 ed.).

ble waters" as all submerged land lying within the seaward boundaries of a state "as they existed at the time such State became a
member of the Union" but in no event to be interpreted as
extending more than three geographic miles from the "coast
line."[90] "Coast line" was in turn defined as the low-water mark
where the mainland was in direct contact with the open sea and
elsewhere, the seaward limit of "inland waters,"[91] a term inten-
tionally left undefined by the drafters.[92] Congress subsequently
enacted the Outer Continental Shelf Lands Act of 1953,[93] which
deeded to the United States all submerged lands seaward of those
granted to the states by the Submerged Lands Act, the subsoil
and seabed of which appertain to the United States and are subject to its jurisdiction and control. Unlike offshore settlements
reached in other federal states, such as Canada and Australia,
which have to date involved some form of joint authority under
federal ownership, the legislative scheme enacted in the United
States grants absolute ownership and control to each sovereign
in its reserved waters.

The Submerged Lands Act and the Outer Continental Shelf
Lands Act, read together, would appear to embody an effective,
forward-looking regime for federal-state offshore resource allocation. Certainly, this legislation, coming years before a resolution of competing interests by other federal states, does seem
near visionary. At the very least, one might have hoped that it

90. §2(a)(2), 67 Stat. 29, 43 U.S.C. §1301(a)(2) (1958 ed.).This limit was extended to
    three leagues from the coastline in the Gulf of Mexico. §2b, 67 Stat. 29, 43 U.S.C.
    §1301(b) (1958 ed.).
91. §2(c), 67 Stat. 29, 43 U.S.C. §1301(c) (1958 ed.).
92. As originally drafted, the Bill defined inland waters as "all estuaries, ports, harbors,
    bays, channels, straits, historic bays, and sounds and all other bodies of water which
    join the open sea." The Deputy Legal Advisor of the State Department advised the
    drafting Committee that a legislative definition of inland waters might embarrass the
    State Department in its foreign relations if it resulted in different definitions for the
    term being applied by separate departments and branches of the government. It was
    also suggested that to attempt to define the term in a few words might increase rather
    than diminish litigation. Senator Cordon, Acting Chairman of the Committee, rec-
    ommended that since the term "inland waters" had been defined time and time again
    by the courts, no legislative definition seemed necessary, especially if it might affect
    the conduct of foreign affairs. After some debate, this recommendation was accepted
    and the foregoing definition was removed from the Bill. *See* United States v. Califor-
    nia, 381 U.S. 139, 150; and 189–97 (1965) (Black, J., dissenting).
93. 67 Stat. 462, 42 U.S.C. §1331 *et. seq.*, (1958 ed.).

would put an end to federal-state conflict by establishing clear boundaries within which each sovereign could exercise authority and control. Unfortunately, although the Acts do establish an overall zonal division of power, the boundary delimitation guidance in both Acts is, perhaps necessarily, vague; and this has resulted in several decades of protracted litigation to establish the exact baseline-coastline from which to measure the respective zones of sovereign authority.

Although there was some movement toward permanently delimiting maritime boundaries after the *California* decision in 1947,[94] the enactment of the Submerged Lands Act restoring state authority to the three-mile or three-league limit made the issue temporarily irrelevant. However, as advances in technology made resource exploration and exploitation beyond the three-mile limit possible, conflict again arose between California and the federal government.[95] California claimed sovereignty over the waters included within the "overall unit area of inland waters" represented in Figure 17, as well as many other coastal indentations. In 1953, the United States filed an amended complaint

94. After the entry of the 1947 decree, the United States asked that the lands awarded it be defined in greater detail in areas of substantial oil exploration activity which California still claimed as lying within inland waters (water areas which had been specifically reserved to the States in the *California* decision, *supra* note 85). The Supreme Court appointed a Special Master to determine, for seven segments of the California coast, the line of ordinary low water and the outer limit of inland waters. These segments included San Pedro Bay, Crescent City Bay, Monterey Bay, San Luis Obispo Bay, and Santa Monica Bay, as well as an "overall unit area" from Pt. Conception to Pt. Loma enclosing two channels and encompassing islands as far as fifty miles from the Southern California Coast. [This overall unit area is represented in Fig. 17, taken from Appendix C, United States v. California, 381 U.S. 139, 179 (1965).] In the Special Master's Report, filed Nov. 10, 1952 [344 U.S. 872 (1952)] and generally favoring the position of the federal government, the Master adopted as his criteria for defining inland waters those applied by the United States in the conduct of its foreign affairs as of the date of the 1947 decree. In regard to bays, these criteria included indentations with closing lines no more than ten miles in length and with sufficient water area to satisfy the Boggs formula introduced at The Hague. (*See supra*, Chapter II, note 35, and Chapter III, note 137.). Using these criteria, none of the five bays nor the overall unit area claimed by California were designated as inland waters. *See* Report of the Special Master, *supra*, at 2–5. *See also* United States v. California, 381 U.S. 139, 142–45 (1965). This Report was neither adopted, modified, nor rejected by the Supreme Court, but was simply allowed to remain dormant. *Id.*, at 149.

95. Valuable oil reserves discovered more than three miles from the coast but within San Pedro Bay gave urgency to the determination of whether these waters constituted inland waters of California. A. SHALOWITZ, *supra*, Chapter I, note 20, at 55 n.50.

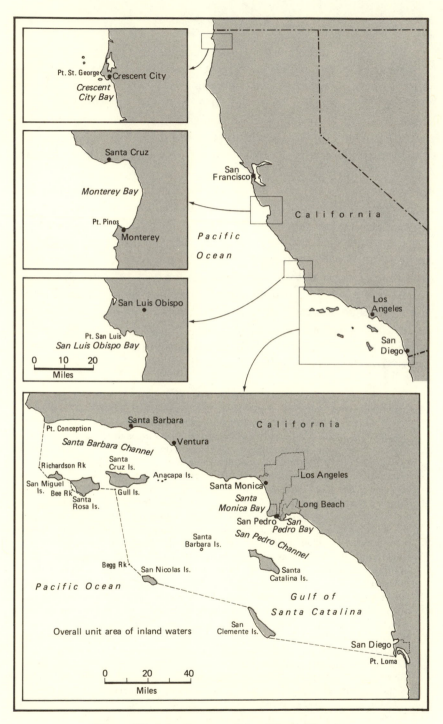

Figure 17. Inland waters claimed by California.

206

reviving the Special Master's Report.[96] In response, the Supreme Court ordered the filing of new exceptions pursuant to reaching a final determination in the case.[97]

In the second phase of *United States v. California*,[98] the Supreme Court had the opportunity to settle many troubling boundary questions which had arisen from 1945. The Special Master's Report, filed in 1952, had made a variety of determinations based on the law as of the date of the 1947 decree. However, the enactment of the Submerged Lands Act[99] and the Outer Continental Shelf Lands Act[100] in 1953 as well as the passage of the Geneva Convention on the Territorial Sea and the Contiguous Zone in 1958[101] raised serious questions as to the continuing validity of these determinations.

The United States contended that the only effect of the Submerged Lands Act on the Special Master's Report was to move the boundaries delimited by the Master seaward a distance of three miles. California contended that the Master had based his determination of inland waters on international norms used by the United States in their foreign relations, whereas the Submerged Lands Act had used the term inland waters in an entirely different sense to mean those waters which the States had historically considered as inland. Thus, California concluded, the lines drawn in the Special Master's Report were drawn according to standards wholly foreign to the Act.[102]

The Court determined on the basis of the legislative history [103] that Congress has intended to leave the definition of inland waters to the courts; and that although the Act had restored state ownership over waters within their historic boundaries, in no case · were these historic claims to extend more than three miles from the Pacific Coast or three leagues into the Gulf of Mexico.[104]

96. *See supra* note 94.
97. United States v. California, 375 U.S. 927 (1963).
98. 381 U.S. 139 (1965).
99. *See supra* note 88.
100. *See supra* note 93.
101. *See supra*, Chapter I, note 14.
102. United States v. California, 281 U.S. at 149.
103. 381 U.S. at 150–54. (*See also supra* note 92.) This conclusion was hotly contested by Justice Black in his dissent, 381 U.S. at 189–212. On balance, it would appear that the majority's reading of the legislative history as well as their interpretation of the express terms of the statute is the more plausible.
104. 381 U.S. at 154–60.

The Court further stated that the 1947 *California* decision had clearly indicated that the term "inland waters" was to have international content since the determination of the outer limits of such waters would in turn define the baseline of the United States for international law purposes,[105] but the Court had given the task of particularizing the definition of inland waters to the Special Master,[106] who had based his definition on current U.S. policy as of the date of the 1947 decree.[107] The United States' position was that these determinations made by the Master in 1952 remained valid, even though U.S. policy had changed significantly with the adoption of the Territorial Sea Convention, because in any event a definition for inland waters must be chosen to reflect the position of the United States as of May 22, 1953, the date of the enactment of the Submerged Lands Act.

The Supreme Court refused to accept the Government's position, however, saying:

> We do not think that the Submerged Lands Act has so restricted us. Congress in passing the Act, left the responsibility for defining inland waters to this Court. We think that it did not tie our hands at the same time.[108]

Concluding that the "baseline" established for international purposes and the "coastline" established by the Submerged Lands Act must be one and the same, the Court held:

> It is our opinion that we best fill our responsibility of giving content to the words which Congress employed by adopting the best and most workable definitions available. The Convention on the Territorial Sea and the Contiguous Zone . . . provides such definitions. We adopt them for purposes of the Submerged Lands Act. This establishes a single coastline for both the administration of the Submerged Lands Act and the conduct of our future international relations.[109]

105. *Id.*, at 163 n.25.
106. *See supra* note 94.
107. 381 U.S. at 163.
108. *Id.*, at 164 (footnote omitted).
109. *Id.*, at 165 (footnote omitted).

However, since future changes in international understanding respecting inland waters might alter the extent of the Submerged Lands Act grant, thus upsetting expectations of definiteness, the Court formally adopted the definition of a juridical bay provided by the express language of Article 7 in force in 1965,[110] i.e., an indentation which is well-marked and landlocked, whose area meets the requirements of the semi-circle test, and whose entrance does not exceed twenty-four miles in length.

Applying this definition to the various bays under contention,[111] the Court held that only Monterey Bay qualified under Article 7 as inland waters,[112] the other indentations becoming disqualified as mere curvatures of the coast when their areas did not pass the semi-circle test. As to the "overall unit area" comprised by Santa Barbara Channel and the Gulf of Santa Catalina,[113] the Court held correctly that none of the waters could be claimed as internal by use of Article 7 criteria,[114] as the islands lay too far from the coast to create truly landlocked waters. As to California's claim that these waters could be enclosed by a straight baseline system as permitted under Article 4 or as historic waters of California, the Court stated categorically that the option afforded under Article 4 lay within the sole domain of the federal government[115] and that California had not carried its burden of proof over a federal disclaimer, i.e., that proof of historic state authority and control must be clear beyond doubt.[116]

The United States v. Louisiana Case As was the case in California, after the enactment of the Submerged Lands Act many issues remained unresolved between the federal government and Louisiana, which continued to license oil exploration and exploitation activities in disputed inland waters. Accordingly in 1956, the

---

110. *Id.*, at 166–67. The Territorial Sea Convention was approved by the Senate May 26, 1960 (106 Cong. Rec. 11196); ratified by the President Mar. 24, 1961 (44 State Dept. Bull. 609); and entered into force in the United States Sept. 10, 1964 (15 U.S.T. & O.I.A. 1606, T.I.A.S. No. 5639).
111. *See supra* note 94.
112. 381 U.S at 170. *See also supra,* map of Monterey Bay at Fig. 2.
113. *See supra* note 94 and Fig. 17.
114. 381 U.S. at 170.
115. *Id.*, at 168.
116. *Id.*, at 175. *See supra,* Chapter II, note 46.

United States was granted leave to file a new suit against Louisiana,[117] whereupon the Court issued an order enjoining both parties from further leasing activities unless by agreement.[118] On October 12, 1956, the parties entered into an Interim Agreement designed to permit further development of the disputed lands while litigation proceeded.[119] And proceed it did, for over two decades of hearings and decrees [120] which spanned the adoption of the Territorial Sea Convention and the holding in *United States v. California,* which incorporated the definition of inland waters provided by Article 7 of that Convention into the domestic law of the United States.[121]

In the major opinion of this twenty-year struggle,[122] the Supreme Court reaffirmed the earlier *California* opinion, asserting that Congress had chosen to leave the definition of inland waters in the Court's hands, and this Court did not intend to tie the definition to the "Inland Water Line" drawn by the Coast Guard in 1895, as had been urged by Louisiana.[123] Rather, the Court held that the terms of the Territorial Sea Convention provided the best and most workable definition of inland waters and therefore reaffirmed its use for the purposes of drawing the federal-state boundary pursuant to the Submerged Land Act off the Louisiana coast.[124]

Applying the terms of Article 7 to specific bay claims, the Court drew four main conclusions:

1. Outer Vermilion Bay, with a closing line from Tigre Point to Shell Keys, does not qualify as a bay under the semi-circle test because it would be part of a larger indentation whose closing line far exceeds the twenty-four mile limit.[125]

2. Ascension Bay, whose headlands [sic] are jetties at Belle Pass on the west and Southwest Pass on the east, includes the inner

117. 350 U.S. 990 (1956).

118. 351 U.S. 978 (1956).

119. *See* United States v. Louisiana, 446 U.S. 253, 256 (1979).

120. For a full history of Louisiana proceedings, *see* 446 U.S. 253, 256–61 (1979).

121. United States v. California, 381 U.S. 139, 165 (1965).

122. United States v. Louisiana, 394 U.S. 11 (1969).

123. *Id.,* at 19–32.

124. *Id.,* at 17–35.

125. *Id.,* at 48–52. *See infra* at Fig. 18, ①, which is reproduced from United States v. Louisiana, 394 U.S. 11, insert at 78.

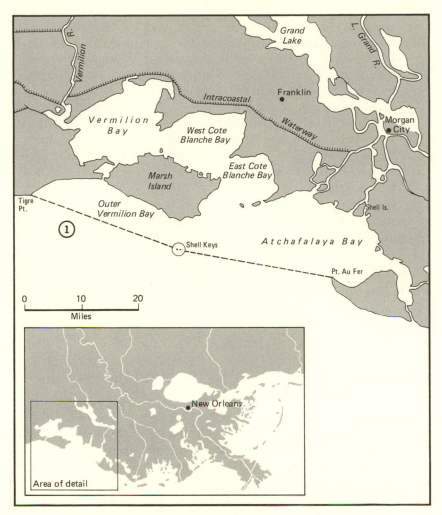

Figure 18. Outer Vermilion Bay, claimed by Louisiana.

bays of the Barataria Bay-Caminada Bay complex, which are separated from the outer indentation only by a string of islands across the entrances to the inner bays. Ascension Bay meets the semi-circle test when the islands are treated (as provided by Article 7(3)) "as if they were part of the water area."[126]

3. Louisiana argued that although East Bay does not meet the semi-circle test when applied on a closing line between its most

126. *Id.,* at 52–53. *See infra* at Fig. 19, ②.

seaward headlands [sic], the indentation qualifies as a bay
because a line could be drawn within the bay which *would* satisfy the test. However, no indentation can qualify as a bay
unless its own features meet all the requirements of Article 7(2)
as well as the semi-circle test therein.[127]

4. Where islands intersected by a direct closing line between the
mainland headlands [sic] create multiple mouths to the Lake
Pelto-Terrebonne Bay-Timbalier Bay complex, the bay should
be closed by lines between the natural entrance points on the
islands, even if those points are landward of the direct line
between the mainland entrance points.[128]

As to the Court's first contention, one may readily conclude on
the basis of visual comparison alone (see Figure 18 at ①) that
the area of the so-called Outer Vermilion Bay would not equal or
exceed the area of a semi-circle drawn on the line joining Tigre
Point and Shell Keys. Louisiana argued, however, that the area
of tributary bays or other subsidiary indentations must be
included within that of the primary indentation in comparing
water areas for the semi-circle test.[129] On the basis of this proposition, Louisiana argued that when the waters of Vermilion Bay
were added to those of Outer Vermilion Bay, the aggregate of
water area fulfilled the semi-circle test.

The United States, while not rejecting out of hand the proposition that tributary waters may be included in calculating the
semicircle test, nonethelesss argued that subsidiary bays may only
be included if they can reasonably be considered a part of the
outer indentation. In this case, Vermilion Bay is linked to Outer
Vermilion Bay by only a narrow access channel between Marsh
Island and the mainland and thus, argued the Government, Vermilion Bay cannot be considered as subsidiary to the primary
coastal indentation.[130]

In answering this question, the Court did not address the issue
of whether or not subsidiary bays might be included in calculating
the semi-circle test, [131] focusing instead on the fact that if Loui-

127. *Id.*, at 53–54. *See infra* at Fig. 19, ③.
128. *Id.*, at 54–60. *See infra* at Fig. 20, ④.
129. Louisiana cited the work of Shalowitz and other experts as well as the U.S. Department of State as authority for this proposition. *See* 394 U.S. 11, 50–51 (1969).
130. *Id.*, at 51.
131. The Court addressed this issue in their discussion of Ascension Bay, which follows.

siana's argument, that the low-water mark must be followed around the entire coast of an indentation no matter where it leads, were taken to its natural conclusion, the Court would have to recognize the whole water complex including Outer Vermilion Bay, Vermilion Bay, West Cote Blanche Bay, East Cote Blanche Bay, and Atchafalaya Bay, with a closing line between Tigre Point and Point au Fer, as inland waters.[132] The Court concluded correctly that since this closing line would far exceed the twenty-four-mile limit imposed by Article 7(4),[133] it followed that Outer Vermilion Bay was neither itself a bay nor was it part of a larger bay complex which met Article 7 requirements.[134]

The Court addressed the subsidiary bay issue directly in holding that the waters of Ascension Bay and those of the Barataria–Caminada Bay complex (see Figure 19 at ②) may reasonably be deemed a single large indentation.[135] The Court reasoned that if the islands separating the inner and outer bays are ignored under the language of Article 7(3) which provides that for the purposes of calculating the semi-circle test "[i]slands within an indentation shall be included as if they were part of the water area of the indentation,"[136] then the aggregate water area enclosed by Ascension Bay, Barataria Bay, and Caminada Bay does meet the requirements imposed by the semi-circle test.[137] The clear purpose of the Convention, according to the Court, was not to permit islands to defeat the semi-circle test by consuming areas of the indentation. The majority therefore concluded:

> We think it consistent with that purpose that islands should not be permitted to defeat the semicircle test by sealing off one part of the indentation from the rest.[138]

132. *See supra* at Fig. 18. Note additional dotted line from Shell Keys to Point au Fer representing, together with the line between Tigre Point and Shell Keys, the closing line of the bay if Louisiana's claim were to prevail.
133. *See supra,* Chapter IV, at notes 218–23 and accompanying text for full discussion of Article 7, paragraph four.
134. 394 U.S. at 52.
135. *Id.,* at 52–53.
136. *See supra,* Chapter IV, full text of Article 7 accompanying note 10.
137. 394 U.S. at 53. *See* dotted line across the whole of Ascension Bay, *supra* at Fig. 19.
138. *Id.* The Court extends its reasoning in regard to Ascension Bay to the waters of West Bay (*see supra* at Fig. 19, ⑤.) whose inner and outer water areas are set off only by a string of islands. *See id.,* at 53 n.71.

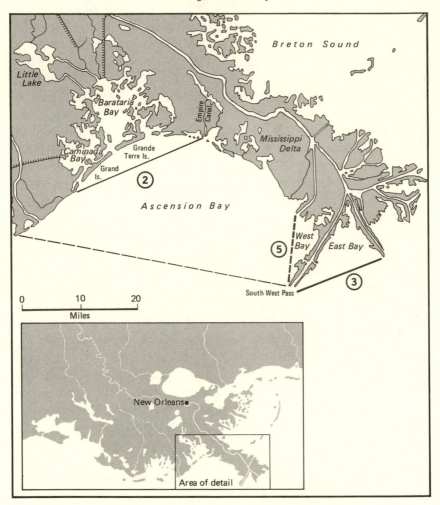

Figure 19. Ascension Bay and East Bay, claimed by Louisiana.

Having deemed the whole of Ascension Bay a juridical bay under Article 7(2), the Court next applied the rule provided by Article 7(5), that "[w]here the distance between the low-water marks of the natural entrance points of a bay exceeds twenty-four miles, a straight baseline of twenty-four miles shall be drawn within the bay in such a manner as to enclose the maximum area of water that is possible with a line of that length."[139] Louisiana

139. *See supra*, Chapter IV, full text of Article 7 accompanying note 10.

had moved inward within Ascension Bay to draw a twenty-four-mile line between Caminada Pass and Empire Canal[140] to enclose the Barataria-Caminada Bay complex along with a portion of the waters of Ascension Bay, and had also enclosed the waters of West Bay (see Figure 19 at ⑤)[141] In holding both of these claims reasonable under Article 7(5), the Court firmly rejected the Government's argument that paragraph five permits the drawing of only one twenty-four-mile line within an oversized bay, as well as the related argument that once a State has incorporated the area of tributary bays in calculating the area of the overall bay for the semicircle test, the smaller bays within the oversize bay but outside the subsequently drawn twenty-four-mile straight baseline lose their status as inland waters.[142] The court concluded:

We find nothing in the Convention or its history to support this contention.[143]

Reading the Court's holding together with the text of Article 7, the following mandatory procedure for bay delimitation may be inferred:

1. First determine whether the configuration of the indentation meets the well-marked and landlocked requirements of Article 7(2).
2. If these are fulfilled, measure the entire bay, including the waters of major indentations and those of any subsidiary bays, including islands lying within the indentation as if they were part of the water area, to determine whether the aggregate area of these waters equals or exceeds the area of a semi-circle drawn across the entrance under Article 7(2) and 7(3).
3. If the semi-circle test is met, a bay exists.
4. Next, measure the width of the entrance. If the width does not exceed twenty-four miles, enclose the entire bay as inland waters under Article 7(4).
5. If the width of the entrance exceeds twenty-four miles, move landward into the bay and draw a twenty-four mile line enclosing the maximum water area possible under Article 7(5).

140. *See supra* straight line drawn at Fig. 19, ②.
141. *See supra* dotted line drawn at Fig. 19, ⑤.
142. 394 U.S. at 49 n.64.
143. *Id.*

6. Should smaller indentations within an oversized bay be "set free" in this process,[144] measure each indentation in turn to determine whether by itself it may qualify as a juridical bay under Article 7.

Since the islands separating Ascension Bay from Barataria and Caminada Bays create extremely narrow entrance and exit channels, certainly no wider than the channel separating Outer Vermilion Bay from Vermilion Bay proper, one may further infer that the Court's holding in regard to Ascension Bay refutes by implication the argument made by the United States that inner bays separated from the main coastal indentation by narrow passageways cannot be included as subsidiary bays in measuring the area of the entire indentation for the semi-circle test. It is consistent with the Court's reasoning in regard to Ascension Bay to conclude that if the waters of Outer Vermilion Bay had passed through the narrow channel created by Marsh Island into Vermilion Bay and *no further,* the Court's holdings in regard to Outer Vermilion Bay and Ascension Bay would have been identical.

Another issue involving the semi-circle test arose in regard to East Bay whose area measured in comparison to a semi-circle drawn on the closing line between the tip of the jetty at Southwest Pass and the southern end of South Pass[145] (see Figure 19 at ③) did not meet the requirements of Article 7. Louisiana argued that it was possible to move inward within East Bay and draw a twenty-four-mile line which would satisfy the semi-circle test. The Court rejected this argument, explaining that by drawing such a line, Louisiana had misunderstood the procedure imposed by Article 7. As noted above, the first determination which must be made under Article 7(2) is whether or not the indentation is well-marked and contains landlocked waters. Next the area of the indentation must be measured against the semicircle test. If the indentation fails to qualify as a bay under these criteria, it is deemed a mere curvature of the coast. It is only when the indentation *does* by its *own* features qualify as a bay[146] but has an entrance which exceeds the twenty-four-mile limit that a State is

---

144. *See supra,* Chapter IV, notes 77–78 and accompanying text.
145. *See supra* at Fig. 19, ③.
146. 394 U.S. at 54.

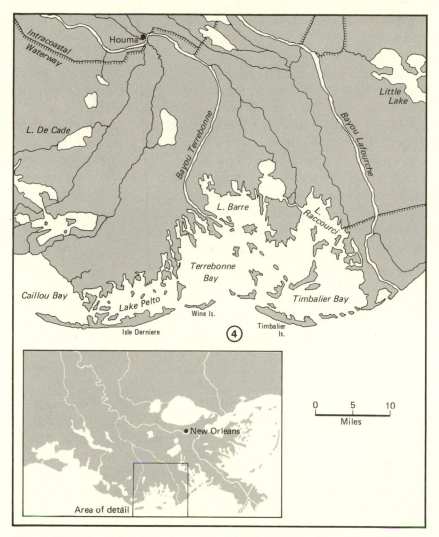

Figure 20. Lake Pelto–Terrebonne Bay–Timbalier Bay Complex, claimed by Louisiana.

permitted to draw a twenty-four-mile line within the bay to enclose internal waters under Article 7(5). The Court concluded:

> We cannot accept Louisiana's argument that an indentation which satisfies the semicircle test *ipso facto* qualifies as a bay under the Convention. Such a construction would fly in the face of Article

7(2), which plainly treats the semicircle test as a minimum requirement.[147]

In regard to the waters in the Lake Pelto–Terrebonne Bay–Timbalier Bay complex (see Figure 20 at ④) which are partially enclosed by islands lying between mainland entrance points,[148] Louisiana had argued that the lines closing the bay should be drawn between the mainland headlands [sic] and the seaward-most points on the islands. This argument was rejected by the Court, which correctly held that under Article 7(3), closing lines between islands must be drawn across the various *mouths* of the indentation. The Court asserted that the mouths created by the presence of islands are to be closed like any other bay, i.e., by lines joining the low-water marks of the bay's natural entrance points, not by lines joining the most seaward points of the islands.[149] In so holding, the Court made clear that the measure-ment lines across the various mouths mandated under Article 7(3) "are to be the baselines for all purposes,"[150] thus refuting the Hodgson-Alexander notion that only those measurement lines drawn between islands which exactly intersect a line drawn between mainland entrance points may be considered as forming the closing line/baseline under Article 7(4).[151]

Louisiana argued in the alternative that even if the closing lines should not connect the most seaward points on the islands, in no event should they be drawn landward of a direct line between mainland entrance points,[152] basing its contention on the lan-guage of Article 7(3) which declares that "[i]slands within an indentation shall be included as if they were part of the indentation."[153]

The Court correctly concluded, however, that islands such as those involved in the instant case which are intersected by the direct mainland to mainland closing line cannot possibly be said

147. *Id.*
148. *See supra* at Fig. 20, ④.
149. 394 U.S. at 56.
150. *Id.*, at 55.
151. *See id.*, at 59 n.79, para. 2. *See also supra*, Chapter IV, notes 130–152 and accom-panying text.
152. 394 U.S. at 56.
153. *See supra*, Chapter IV, full text of Article 7 accompanying note 10.

to be "within" the indentation, nor can an island which forms the *mouth* of an indentation be "within" it.[154] Thus, the Court held that when islands intersected by a direct closing line between the mainland headlands [sic] create multiple mouths to a bay, the bay should be closed by lines between the natural entrance points on the islands even if some of those *points* are landward of the direct line between mainland entrance points.[155]

As to the issue of whether such lines should be drawn landward of the mainland entrance if the islands are not so intersected, the Court implies that the essential question in making such a determination will be whether or not such landward islands lie close enough to the entrance to truly create "mouths" into the indentation under Article 7(3),[156] in which case closing lines for the identation should be drawn across the various mouths. If, on the other hand, such islands lie so far landward from the mainland entrance points that they would not be perceived as creating separate mouths into the indentation, they should be included as part of the water area of the indentation. As to the issue of islands which lie *seaward* of the mainland entrance but create multiple mouths into the indentation, the Court, though not addressing the issue directly, made clear that lines across the various mouths are to be the baselines for all purposes[157], and that Article 7(3) contains no requirement that the islands be intersected by a mainland-to-mainland closing line; rather it speaks only of multiple mouths "because of the presence of islands."[158] One must conclude, therefore, that measurement lines drawn between islands which lie seaward of the mainland entrance points but factually create the entrances of the indentation are to be recognized as the closing lines of the bay under Article 7(4).

In addition to the four specific bay claims discussed above, the

---

154. 394 U.S. at 59.
155. *Id.*, at 60. This holding is limited to configurations such as that presented by the Lake Pelto–Terrebonne Bay–Timbalier Bay complex, *see supra* at Fig. 20, where islands lie directly on a line between mainland entrance points, creating the actual entrances to the bay. *See also supra* Fig. 12, Chapter IV, notes 162–64 and accompanying text.
156. *See supra*, Chapter IV, at notes 162–64 and accompanying text.
157. 394 U.S. at 55.
158. *Id.*, at 59 n.79, para. 2. *See also supra*, Chapter IV, notes 130–152 and accompanying text.

Louisiana Court addressed the general issue of whether or not an island might serve as the headland [sic] of a bay. The United States argued that the Territorial Sea Convention flatly prohibits the drawing of bay closing lines to islands, that a true bay is an indentation into the mainland which cannot be created by the projection of an island or islands from the coast, and that the measurement rule of Article 7(3), which directs that the area of an indentation lies between the closing line and the "low-water mark around the shore," contemplates a shoreline unbroken by an opening other than the bay entrance, otherwise the bay would lose its landlocked character.[159]

The first argument was refuted by implication in the Court's prior assertion that lines across the various mouths created by islands *are* to be considered as baselines for all purposes.[160] As to the remaining Government arguments, the Court rejected them flatly in this now-famous paragraph:

> No language in Article 7 or elsewhere positively excludes all islands from the meaning of the "natural entrance points" to a bay. Waters within an indentation which are "landlocked" despite the bay's wide entrance would surely not lose that characteristic on account of an additional narrow opening to the sea. That the area of a bay is delimited by the "low-water mark around the shore" does not necessarily mean that the low-water mark must be continuous.[161]

Having so held in complete accord with the language and intent of Article 7, however, the Court proceeded to answer a question made irrelevant by that very language, i.e., "may an island serve as a headland to a bay?" As suggested by the extensive discussion of this issue above,[162] the Court may have erred in maintaining that "the general understanding has been—and under the Convention certainly remains—that bays are indenta-

159. 394 U.S. at 61.
160. *Id.,* at 55.
161. *Id.,* at 61. The reasoning of the Court on all issues cited above has recently been approved in the 1985 Supreme Court Opinion, United States v. Maine, et al (Rhode Island and New York Boundary Case) 469 U.S. 504, 105 S.Ct. 992, 83 L.Ed. 2d 998 (1985).
162. *See supra,* Chapter IV, at notes 182–253 and accompanying text.

tions in the *mainland*."[163] Historical evidence indicates that it was the indentation itself, whether formed wholly by mainland or partially by island coasts, which was the focus of the early rules and decisions on bays. In fact, early versions of Article 7 which included the phrase "indentation *into the mainland*" were rejected by the drafters, as was all reference to the anachronistic terms "headland" and "inter fauces terrae." Rather, the drafters opted for the more functional and more inclusive term *natural entrance points* which was intended to incorporate, in addition to mainland "headlands," islands, low-tide elevations,[164] jetties, wharves, and other land forms and artificial structures which factually create natural entrance points into an indentation.

Misperceiving the change in international prescription wrought by the new terminology, but nonetheless believing that no language in the Convention had established that an island could never serve as the "headland" of a bay,[165] the Court proceeded to establish an exceptional rule: an island may be treated as a "headland" when it is so closely linked to the mainland as realistically to be assimilated to it.[166] Deriving this rule from the view of other courts and text writers, all of whom were speaking in the context of island fringes lying off an *unindented* coastline,[167] the Court set out various factors which might prove relevant in determining whether or not an island is to be treated as a part of the mainland, i.e., its size, its distance from the mainland, the depth and utility of the intervening waters, the shape of the island, and its relationship to the configuration or curvature of the coast.[168] The Court then added further imprecision by suggesting yet a second version of the test stated above,[169] i.e., whether the islands designated as "headlands" are so integrally related to the mainland that they are realistically parts of the "coast" within the meaning of the Territorial Sea Convention. There is of course no indication in the language of the Convention or the legislative history, nor in the two-hundred year history

163. 394 U.S. at 62.
164. *Id.*, at 60 n.80.
165. 394 U.S. at 61–62.
166. *Id.*, at 66.
167. *Id.*, at 64 n.84, and 65 n.85.
168. *Id.*, at 66.
169. *See supra* note 165 and accompanying text.

of the international law of bays, that islands were ever excluded from the term "coasts."[170]

The most difficult problem created by the Court's holding in regard to island "headlands" is that it has established an extra-textual test which must now be met before an indentation partially formed by islands may obtain juridical bay status in the United States. It is submitted that no other test is needed in this situation than those mandated by Article 7.

The first requirement of Article 7(2) is the existence of a well-marked indentation.[171] It has been suggested above[172] that the well-marked test is met if an indentation lies between clearly defined natural entrance points in such a way as to signal mariners that inland waters may be enclosed. The Court has clearly stated that islands may form natural entrance points;[173] thus it must be possible for an indentation having an island as a natural entrance point to be well-marked.

The second requirement of Article 7(2) is that the indentation contain landlocked waters. The Court has stated that the presence of another opening around the shore of the indentation would surely *not* cause the indentation to lose its landlocked characteristics.[174] If this is so, then the analysis applied above to the determination of landlocked waters[175] would apply with equal force to an indentation partially formed by an island or islands. The key test is whether or not the *waters* of the indentation are more clearly linked to the land mass by geography and the use of the waters by the shore inhabitants than to the open sea. It matters not whether the shores are formed by mainland or island. It matters only whether the *waters* of the indentation are so closely related to the interests of the coastal state as to warrant their inclusion under exclusive state control. The geographical factors listed by the court, i.e., the depth and utility of the intervening waters and the relationship of the island in the overall configuration of the coast, are relevant as a part of this landlocked inquiry but not as separate tests in and of themselves.

170. *See supra,* Chapter IV, notes 204–212 and accompanying text. *See also infra* notes 267–278 and accompanying text.
171. *See supra,* Chapter IV, full text of Article 7 at note 10.
172. *See supra,* Chapter IV, notes 19–24 and accompanying text.
173. 394 U.S. at 61.
174. *Id.*
175. *See supra,* Chapter IV, notes 24–43 and accompanying text.

The third requirement imposed by Article 7(2) is that, even should an indentation partially formed by islands be deemed well-marked and landlocked, in no event may it obtain bay status unless the area of the waters enclosed meets the semi-circle test. Since Article 7(3) gives specific rules for calculating the semi-circle test in the presence of islands, it surely cannot be argued that indentations partially formed by islands are excluded from this test.

The final test, imposed by Article 7(4) and providing perhaps the best governor on an island's distance from the mainland, requires that the entrance to a bay not exceed twenty-four miles. The Court in the *Louisiana* case was no doubt concerned that states might use islands to justify unreasonably wide claims to inland waters; and therefore, the Court imposed tests guaranteeing the proximity of those islands to the mainland. But the "factors" delineated by the *Louisiana* Court suffer from the same vagueness and difficulty of application as did the "factors" laid down by the Tribunal in the *North Atlantic Coast Fisheries Case* and by the I.C.J. in the *Anglo-Norwegian Fisheries Case.* The concern of the Court is better served by the precision offered by the semi-circle test and the twenty-four-mile limit, read together with the landlocked requirement of Article 7. It is suggested that these express Article 7 criteria provide the best test for whether or not an indentation partially formed by islands should be granted juridical bay status, a possibility clearly contemplated by the drafters. It is suggested that the "island as a headland" or "island as mainland" inquiries are anachronistic, irrelevant, and unnecessary under the express terms of Article 7.

The Federal Baseline Committee After the *Louisiana* case was decided, the federal government established the Federal Baseline Committee, which undertook during 1970–71 to produce a series of 155 charts depicting the U.S. baseline, territorial sea, and contiguous zone in keeping with the provisions of the Territorial Sea Convention.[176] All federal departments and offices with an interest in the law of the sea were invited to appoint representatives to the Committee. Representatives from the Departments

---

176. United States v. Alaska, 422 U.S. 184, Supp. Materials, Vol. 1: Appendix, No. 73–1888, Testimony of Dr. Robert D. Hodgson, Geographer, Dept. of State, at 298 (October Term, 1973).

of State, Justice, Interior, Treasury, and Commerce attended Committee meetings regularly over the two-year period.[177]

It is clear that aside from its general purpose to bring U.S. maritime boundaries into line with the new Convention, the Committee was formed at least in part in order to formulate the federal government's position which would be used in federal-state maritime boundary litigation, both existing and pending.[178] For example, at the very time the case was pending before the Supreme Court which would determine the jurisdictional fate of Cook Inlet in Alaska, the Baseline Committee was officially delimiting the waters of Cook Inlet as high seas on U.S. charts. Naturally, these charts were used as evidence against Alaska by the Government, thus raising serious questions of propriety.[179] Not

177. *Id.*, at 300.
178. In his deposition, Dr. Hodgson was asked whether or not the Department of Justice was to be represented on the Committee because, as reflected in an interdepartmental memo, it has its "lawsuits against most of the coastal states." Dr. Hodgson replied that this was certainly part of the reason, but that his interest in having "justice on board" was their knowledge of the early Supreme Court cases which had applied the Convention. In more direct questioning, Dr. Hodgson was asked, "But was it in part because of the pending litigation, would you say?" Dr. Hodgson answered, "I would say that it was in part because of litigation exisitng and pending." *Id.*, at 301.
179. The special purpose of the charts prepared by the Baseline Committee is evidenced by one official document, which states that "it is not intended that the charts resulting from the Committee's work will be circulated throughout the Government even as a provisional position but rather will be available for use when current or pressing problems arise." *Id.*, at 307. During his deposition, Dr. Hodgson was questioned in part as follows:
    Q. Did the Committee consider among other aspects of the coast of the United States the location of the coastline in Cook Inlet, Alaska?
    A. It did.
    Q. Did you know when you were on this Committee that either at its inception or at any time subsequent during its existence and before the distribution of these maps that there was pending litigation between the State of Alaska and the U.S. Government relative to the status of Cook Inlet as inland waters?
    A. I knew there was a difference of opinion between the State and the Federal Government . . . I don't know whether I knew before the Committee started that there was pending litigation, but I certainly knew during the period of the litigation.
    (With refreshed recollection as to dates, Dr. Hodgson surmised that he did know of the litigation by the time discussions of Cook Inlet began. *Id.*, at 310.).
        In further questioning, Dr. Hodgson was asked if he agreed with a memorandum written by Dr. Chapman, Fish and Wildlife Department, to Dr. Boggs, Dr. Hodgson's predecessor as U.S. Geographer, which stated, "There may be some question of propriety for a Federal Agency to publish such an overprinted line with a case turning upon the position of this line now in litigation with the Government as a

party to this suit." Dr. Hodgson replied that he didn't know if there was a question of legal impropriety involved, but he believed there was no bureaucratic impropriety. The questioning then continued at 312:

> Q. Are you aware that the chart drafted by the Baseline Committee has been submitted by the U.S. Government in this case [United States v. Alaska] as an exhibit?
>
> A. I was not aware of it, but I would expect it to be.
>
> Q. Would you expect that it would be the function of the Committee through the drafting of the chart . . . to attempt to influence the Court relative to any decision it might reach in this litigation . . .?
>
> A. I would say that the function of the Committee and the manner in which the Committee proceeded was not intended to exert any influence on the Court or upon any questions at hand.

Hodgson continued at 313:

> . . . if it is a question of legal propriety, again, I am not in a position to answer this. In a question of bureaucratic propriety, we were in the process of evolving or devolving a set of baseline charts for the United States. The series of charts did not have their genesis because of the Court cases. They had their genesis in the need for these charts by the Coast Guard and by the Department of State to give to foreign fishermen. Consequently, the production of the charts and their ultimate use by the Department of Justice in this suit, I don't think is bureaucratically improper. If we were to produce a series of charts specifically for that purpose, then there might be a question of impropriety.

Dr. Hodgson's remarks are lent an air of unreality, however, by three factors: 1) The charts were originally not scheduled to be published (*Id.*, at 307), thus their genesis could not have been in the need to publish baselines for foreign fishermen; 2) an ex-Justice Department official told this author that the Committee was organized at the insistence of Justice to assist the department in its claim against the States; and 3) the way the Committee worked, according to Dr. Hodgson, was that he would formulate the baseline on the basis of hydrographic and geographic data and present his conclusions to the Committee, which would then be free to challenge his report. Political or legal concerns of other departments often influenced the final decision on the baseline, as for example when the Committee convinced Dr. Hodgson to change his mind on Long Island Sound after he had concluded that Long Island Sound was a juridical bay under Article 7 between Montauk Point, New York, and Watch Hill, Rhode Island. The remainder of Dr. Hodgson's testimony is very instructive in this regard:

> A. The mass of the Committee did not agree with my presentation unless it was agreed by myself that East River was indeed a river. And I said that East River was not a river. It was a tidal estuary; whereupon the whole geographic case collapsed and then it went back to the point that the only line that could be drawn was one drawn on the basis of a historic bay. *And the case*, as I recall, specified Orient Point on Long Island and Fisher's Island which was at New York on the northeast extremity of the Sound and then I drew a line between Orient Point and Fisher's Island . . . " *Id.*, at 325 (emphasis added).

One cannot say with certitude that the "*case*" referred to by Dr. Hodgson above was the case certain to come between the Government and New York; but one *can* say that official baselines affecting state interests were drawn by federal officials with an eye toward federal-state conflict. When one reflects on the fact that the federal prosecutor on all the major federal-state cases through *United States v. Alaska* sat regularly on the Baseline Committee, having major input in baseline decisions, the ques-

surprisingly, the Supreme Court held in favor of the federal government in *United States v. Alaska,*[180] despite an enormously detailed presentation of evidence by the state purporting to show that open, effective, and notorious sovereign authority had been exercised by Alaska continuously for many years with the acquiescence of foreign states. The Supreme Court took this opportunity to establish an extraordinarily high standard of proof[181] for states attempting to establish jurisdiction on the basis of an historic bay claim, leaving considerable doubt as to whether such a claim, though technically possible under U.S. law, could possibly prevail.[182]

Having disposed of most of the federal-state boundary disputes on the Pacific and Gulf coasts, the Federal Government filed suit in 1969[183] against the thirteen states bordering on the Atlantic Ocean—Maine, New Hampshire, Massachusetts, Rhode Island, New York, New Jersey, Delaware, Maryland, Virginia, North Carolina, South Carolina, Georgia, and Florida.[184] Asserting that the

---

tion of propriety cannot be easily brushed aside. When one reflects further on the probable impact of official baseline charts as evidence in these cases, one fears for the concept of the Federal Government as a state trustee.

180. 422 U.S. 184 (1975).

181. *See supra,* Chapter II, note 46.

182. A similar state claim was denied by the Special Master in United States v. Florida, October Term 1973, No. 52 Original, who determined on the basis of United States v. California, 381 U.S. 139, 175 (1965) that a disclaimer by the United States bars state jurisdiction unless the state claim is clear beyond doubt. The harshness of all these decisions may have been significantly softened by the recent holding of the U.S. Supreme Court in United States v. Louisiana (Alabama and Mississippi Boundary Case), 470 U.S. 93, 105 S.Ct. 1074, 84 L. Ed. 2d 73 (1985). The Court held Mississippi Sound to be an historic bay even though there had been no particular acts of enforcement of U.S. sovereignty in the area. The Court reasoned that since foreign states had little reason for interest in the shallow waters of the Sound, they had no doubt acquiesced willingly in the express assertions of authority by the United States. The Court concluded that the absence of any overt exclusionary act supported rather than disproved the state claim to historic title in this case. The Court also made clear that having traditionally claimed the waters under historic title, the United States could not then disavow such a claim in the context of federal-state litigation.

183. The Supreme Court granted leave to file at 395 U.S. 955 (1969).

184. The State of Connecticut was not made a defendant because that State borders on Long Island Sound which according to the Court in United States v. Maine, 420 U.S. 515, 517 (1974) was considered inland water rather than open sea. This contention was later disputed by the Government in United States v. Maine (Rhode Island and New York Boundary Case), discussed *infra.*

United States was entitled to exercise sovereign rights over the seabed and subsoil underlying the Atlantic Ocean lying more than three geographical miles seaward from the coast,[185] the Government alleged that each of the states were at present claiming right or title over portions of these waters. The defendant states answered, each state except Florida claiming for itself as successor to certain grantees of the crowns of England or Holland the exclusive right of dominion and control over the seabed of the Atlantic Ocean to the limits of U.S. jurisdiction.[186] The states offered voluminous evidence to establish the fact that, despite the Court's prior decisions in the *California, Texas,* and *Louisiana* cases, which held that waters and lands beyond the seashore lay within federal jurisdiction, they had acquired dominion over the offshore seabed prior to the adoption of the Constitution and had not relinquished it at Union.[187] The several states asked the Court to overrule the prior cases or in any event to refuse to apply their holdings in the present case.

The Court, however, following lengthy proceedings before a Special Master,[188] refused to reexamine the rule announced in the *California* case that paramount rights to the offshore seabed inhere in the Federal Government as an incident of national sovereignty.[189] The transfer by the Government to the states of rights in the seabed underlying the territorial sea in the Submerged Lands Act[190] was merely an exercise of this paramount authority.[191] The Court observed that the view of the several states was squarely at odds with the declarations by Congress in both the Submerged Lands Act and the Continental Shelf Lands Act,[192] which expressly granted power to the state to the three-mile limit but reserved power to the federal government from that bound-

---

185. United States v. Maine, 420 U.S. 515, 517 (1974).
186. *Id.*, at 518.
187. *Id.*, at 519.
188. Hearings were held in the case from May 27, 1971 through Jan. 24, 1973. The Master commended both parties for their professionalism and for the outstanding quality of their historical research. *See* Report of the Special Master, filed Aug. 27, 1974 (No. 35, Original, October Term 1974), printed on microfiche by the Government Printing Office, card 1 at 6.
189. 332 U.S. at 34.
190. *See supra* note 88.
191. 420 U.S. at 524.
192. *See supra* note 93.

ary out to the limit of the continental shelf. Although the Court acknowledged that the several states on the Atlantic were not precluded by res judicata from litigating the issues decided in prior cases, the Court nonetheless refused, on the basis of stare decisis as well as the enormous amount of federal legislation and commercial activity undertaken on the basis of those decisions, to overrule them. The Court added that because of the prior notice provided by the *California, Louisiana,* and *Texas* cases as well as the Submerged Lands Act, neither the defendant states nor their putative lessees had been in the slightest misled; and therefore held in favor of the United States.[193]

In the succeeding decade, the United States has proceeded to press its claims against the states, primarily in regard to disputed areas of inland waters. In two of these cases, *United States v. Louisiana (Alabama and Mississippi Boundary Case)*[194] and *United States v. Maine, et al. (Rhode Island and New York Boundary Case),*[195] Special Master's Reports have been issued; and because these reports offer an opportunity to study the most recent applications of Article 7 of the Territorial Sea Convention,[196] they will be analyzed in some detail in light of the interpretation of Article 7 presented in Chapter IV above.

The Alabama and Mississippi Boundary Case   The sole issue raised in the *Alabama and Mississippi Boundary Case* is whether the coastlines of the states are the line of ordinary low water along the southern mainland and around certain islands adjacent thereto (known as the "barrier islands"); or whether the waters of Mississippi Sound, which lie north of these islands,[197] are inland waters, and the coastlines of the states are therefore the line of ordinary

193. 420 U.S. at 528.
194. No. 9, Original, October 1979.
195. No. 35, Original, October 1983.
196. The Long Island Sound and Mississippi Sound cases have just been decided at this writing. *See* United States v. Maine et al. (Rhode Island and New York Boundary Case), 496 U.S. 504, 105 S.Ct. 992, 83 L. Ed. 2d 998 (1985), and United States v. Louisiana (Alabama and Mississippi Boundary Case), 470 U.S. 93, 105 S.Ct. 1074, 84 L. Ed. 2d 73 (1985). Because the report of the special master was essentially approved by the Supreme Court in each case (*see infra* notes 237 and 310), a detailed analysis of the Master's findings in each instance remains relevant to this study of the juridical bay.
197. *See infra* Fig. 21.

low water along the southern shore of those islands together with the line marking the seaward limit of those waters.[198] If the waters of Mississippi Sound are found to be inland waters, then they and all the lands beneath them belong to the states under *Pollard's Lessee v. Hagan.*[199] If the waters are deemed marginal waters and open sea, then the states may only claim rights in these waters to the limit provided by the Submerged Lands Act,[200] which fixes the seaward boundary of the states involved at three geographical miles from the coastline.[201]

Brushing aside the claim of the states that the United States by its actions in the area has adopted a system of straight baselines which would include Mississippi Sound as internal waters,[202] the Master proceeds to analyze the state's claim to Mississippi Sound as a juridical bay, concluding, quite correctly, that the Sound fulfills all necessary criteria to obtain the status of internal waters under Article 7. Several points of the analysis appear misguided, however, and deserve closer scrutiny.

The Master correctly lists the four basic requirements which must be met in order to obtain juridical bay status: (1) there must be a well-marked indentation, (2) its penetration must be in such proportion to its mouth as to contain landlocked waters, (3) it must have a closing line of twenty-four miles or less, and (4) it must meet the requirements of the semi-circle test.[203]

Turning first to the twenty-four-mile closing line test,[204] the Master addresses the issue of whether or not Isle au Pitre on the

---

198. *Report of the Special Master,* United States v. Louisiana (Alabama and Mississippi Boundary Case), No. 9, Original, October 1979 [hereinafter referred to as Mississippi Master's Report], at 2.

199. 44 U.S. (1 How.) 212 (1845).

200. *See supra* note 88.

201 Mississippi Master's Report, *supra* note 198, at 2.

202. *Id.,* at 4–8.

203. Mississippi Master's Report, *supra* note 198, at 8. The ordering of these requirements may indicate a minor lack of understanding of the procedure mandated by Article 7. First, an indentation must be found to be well-marked and to contain landlocked waters. If it is so designated, *then* the indentation must pass the semi-circle test. If the area of the well-marked, landlocked indentation meets this third test, a *bay* exists. Then and only then does one proceed to delimit a closing line, not to exceed twenty-four miles.

204. Mississippi Master's Report, *supra* note 198, at 8. In beginning his analysis by drawing the twenty-four-mile closing line, the Master appears not to have perceived the special order mandated by Article 7. *See supra* note 203.

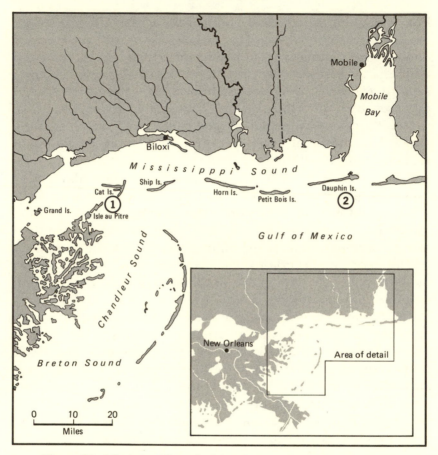

Figure 21. Mississippi Sound, claimed by Alabama and Mississippi.

western extremity of the Sound,[205] as illustrated in Figure 21 above, may serve as a natural entrance point under Article 7. Even with admissions by both parties and indisputable factual evidence to this effect, the Master feels bound to analyze the issue on the basis of the language of the *Louisiana* opinion noted above[206] and in so doing, aptly illustrates the difficulty attending such an analysis. Applying the factors established by that Court to determine whether an island may serve as a headland [sic], the Master holds *not* that Isle au Pitre *factually* forms the natural

205. *See supra* Fig. 21 at ①.
206. *See supra* notes 166–75 and accompanying text.

entrance point into the Sound at its western extremity, but rather that "Isle au Pitre may be properly *assimilated to and considered as an extension of the mainland* for all purposes here pertinent."[207] These of course are tests and conclusions which are completely foreign to Article 7, under which the proper test is whether or not the island forms a natural entrance point into the Sound. Clearly, in the case of Isle au Pitre, this is physically so. The waters of the Gulf turn inward at the tip of Isle au Pitre, away from the sea and toward the land, forming the natural entrance point at the western extremity of the Sound. What purpose is served by an extratextual test, which per force will require massive proof of "assimilation" in future cases and which focuses on the nature of the *land* rather than on the geographical configuration of the *waters* within the land?

The difficulty intensifies in the Master's next procedure, which is to determine the natural entrance point on the eastern extremity of the Sound, so obviously formed by Dauphin Island.[208] Having acknowledged that Article 7 and the *Louisiana* case both expressly provide that islands may create natural entrance points into an indentation, and having found by use of the measurement rules provided in Article 7(3) that the combined distances across the multiple entrances formed by the barrier islands do not exceed the twenty-four-nautical-mile limit, the analysis required by Article 7 is complete. Nonetheless, because of a serious conceptual error, made by several commentators and now enshrined in the *Louisiana* opinion, which holds that Article 7 requires that an indentation must have two mainland [sic] headlands [sic][209] and therefore an island can serve as a headland [sic] only if it can be considered a part of the mainland, the Master feels compelled to analyze whether Dauphin Island is different enough from the other barrier islands forming entrances into the Sound that it can realistically be considered a part of the mainland. Then and only

---

207. Mississippi Master's Report, *supra* note 198, at 9 (emphasis added).
208. *See supra* Fig. 21 at ②. As in the case of Isle au Pitre on the West, the open waters of the Gulf turn inward away from the sea at the western tip of Dauphin Island, forming a natural entrance point on the East. Actually, the presence of Dauphin Island creates *two* natural entrances into the Sound, one as described and the other from the internal waters of Mobile Bay into the Sound. *See supra* Fig. 21.
209. Neither word is present in Article 7, both words having been expressly eschewed by the drafters. *See supra*, Chapter IV, full text of Article 7 accompanying note 10.

then, it is believed, may Dauphin Island be deemed the natural entrance point at the eastern extremity of the Sound.[210]

Whence comes this tortured analysis? It would appear that from a combination of early judicial opinions and the writings of

210. The imprecision of the test imposed by the *Louisiana* decision is amply illustrated in the Master's analysis of Dauphin Island as mainland. Believing that Dauphin Island must somehow be differentiated from the other barrier islands in order to serve as a headland [sic], the Master attempts to discriminate on the basis of distance from the mainland, degree of habitation (conceded to be irrelevant), connection to the mainland by a bridge (held to be nondeterminative in itself) and location in the mouth of Mobile Bay. Mississippi Master's Report, *supra* note 198, at 10. As to the distance of the island from the mainland, it is stipulated to lie 1.60 nautical miles from Cedar Point. Then the thorny questions posed by this criterion must be answered: Is this too far? Not far enough? Is it further distant than any other case we know of? Is it further distant than the distance envisioned by the Court in *United States v. Louisiana*? Without apparent authority, the Master surmises that it is (*Id.*, at 11), but does not use this supposition to deny Dauphin Island a "mainland" designation. It is the Master's last contention, that Dauphin Island may be considered mainland because it is "directly in the mouth of Mobile Bay" (*Id.*, at 11–12), admittedly a juridical bay of Alabama, which is most flawed. By a leap of logic, the Master contends that since Mobile Bay constitutes inland waters of Alabama and since inland waters are considered the equivalent of mainland, then Dauphin Island is, quoting from Pearcy who was speaking solely in the context of island fringes off *non-indented* coastlines, "near, separated from the mainland by so little water that for all practical purposes the coast of the island is identified as that of the mainland." (*Id.*, at 12–13.) The Master then goes on to completely misinterpret and miscite "as a general rule derived from Article 7 Section 6 of the Geneva Convention and the Court's interpretation thereof in United States v. Louisiana" (*Id.*, at 13), that "where islands lie within [sic] the mouth of a bay they are to be considered as part of the mainland for all purposes." (*Id.*, at 13.) (What the Court in *Louisiana* actually said was that when islands created multiple entrances to bays, then for purposes of the semi-circle test "lines across the various mouths are to be the baselines for all purposes." *See* 394 U.S. at 55.) This conclusion in regard to Dauphin Island is misguided in several respects. First and foremost, it is completely irrelevant under Article 7. Second, the theory is unauthorized except by the most tenuous reasoning by any known rule of international law. Third, it leaves the Master open to attack by the Federal Government, and throws doubt on the validity of his conclusion that Dauphin Island is the natural entrance point on the eastern extremity of Mississippi Sound. The best argument that could be made in regard to Dauphin Island and Mobile Bay is that Dauphin Island forms a natural entrance point to Mobile Bay and, due to the change in the direction of the shore at that point *also* forms two natural entrances into Missisippi Sound. *See* Fig. 21 at ②. Further analysis by the Master under the remaining *Louisiana* "factors," i.e., size of the island, depth and utility of the intervening waters, shape of the island, and the island's relationship to the configuration and curvature of the coast, (which includes detailed geomorphological analysis) leads the Master to conclude (*Id.*, at 15) that Dauphin Island *is* an extension of the mainland and thus may serve as a natural entrance point. It is submitted that this final conclusion, which is correct, could have been better and more simply reached on the basis of the tests provided in Article 7 alone—i.e., does Dauphin Island factually constitute a well-marked entrance into the landlocked waters of Mississippi Sound?

various commentators, all concerned with the existence of island fringes off a nonindented coastline,[211] the proposition was derived that in order to enclose waters between an island or islands and the mainland as internal, the islands had to be so connected to the mainland as to be considered mainland themselves. This proposition, used to enclose waters not truly within the coastal littoral as internal, was *not* the conceptual basis of the international rules on bays, which have always applied to *indentations* in the coastal littoral, the coasts of which may be formed entirely by mainland or partially by islands.[212] As is amply illustrated in the foregoing textual and contextual analysis of Article 7, particularly the rules pertaining to islands, no differentiation is made in Article 7 between "islands" and "coasts,"[213] nor between islands which form natural entrance points by lying at the mouth of an indentation and islands which form natural entrance points by constituting a part of the coast of an indentation. The focus of Article 7, fully intended by the drafters and reflected in their adoption of the functional term "natural entrance points," is the physical existence of an indentation lying

---

211. Many of these authorities are cited in the *Louisiana* case, 394 U.S. at 62 ns. 82, 83; 64 ns. 84, 85. (The Master's Report repeats much of this authority, *supra* note 198, at 12–13. In neither case is there an awareness that the authority cited has been taken out of context and misapplied to coastal indentations. There is indeed, according to many authorities such as Sir Humphrey Waldock, a "considerable body of state practice" to support the principle that under certain conditions islands may be treated as part of the mainland. (*See* I. BROWNLIE, *supra*, Chapter III, note 37, at 201.) Such an approach rests on considerations of geographical association and appurtenance, and was the basis for the "a whole with the mainland" language in the *Anglo-Norwegian Fisheries Case* (1951 I.C.J. 128). The International Law Commission failed to produce a draft article on the question in Geneva; but in a comment annexed to Article 10 (Islands), the Commission pointed out that the straight baseline system of Article 4 might be applied in such a situation. (*See* I. BROWNLIE, *supra*, at 202.) Likewise, the cases often cited as authority for the concept of islands as mainland, such as the early British case of *The Anna* [165 E.R. 809 (1805)], apply to situations where islands form "a portico of the mainland" (*see* C. SYMMONS, *supra*, Chapter IV, note 106, at 1), and usually deal only with the issue of whether or not a state may assert jurisdiction in the waters in question, not whether the waters are inland, territorial, or open seas. *None* of these authorities nor those cited in the *Louisiana* case were speaking in the context of *true* internal waters created by coastal indentations to which the rules of Article 7 apply.
212. *See supra,* Chapter IV, notes 113, 135–136, 183–212 and accompanying text for documentation and discussion of this assertion.
213. *See supra,* Chapter IV, notes 204–212 and accompanying text; *see also infra* notes 268–275 and accompanying text, which demonstrates that the convention makes no distinction between these terms.

within well-marked entrance points of *whatever* nature, the waters of which are landlocked, the area of which meets the semi-circle test, and the entrance of which is no more than twenty-four miles wide. To confound this simple, coherent test with an "island as mainland" requirement can only lead to absurdly complicated proof of assimilation and to judicial inefficiency.

Having correctly determined that the waters of Mississippi Sound meet the requirements of the semi-circle test and the twenty-four-mile closing line rule,[214] the Master then proceeds to what should have been the first order decision under Article 7: is Mississippi Sound a well-marked indentation which contains landlocked waters, or is it a mere curvature of the coast? The Master first posits the following definition: "Apparently a 'well-marked' indentation is one which has clearly distinguishable 'natural entrance points,' within which the waters lie *inter fauces ter-rae.*"[215] Then, noting the language of the Court in the *Louisiana* case, that "no language in Article 7 or elsewhere positively excludes all islands from the meaning of 'natural entrance points' to a bay,"[216] the Master holds, somewhat inconclusively, that *if* Isle au Pitre and Dauphin Island are accepted as headlands [sic], Mississippi Sound is a well-marked indentation in the coast.[217]

As has been noted, the Convention provides little clear guidance for an analysis of the term "well-marked." However, the definition posed somewhat tentatively by the Master confuses the well-marked requirement with the landlocked requirement. To say that a well-marked indentation is one which contains landlocked waters, (i.e., waters which "lie inter fauces terrae") is to imply that one must first determine whether the waters are landlocked and *then* one may conclude that they are well-marked as well. This analysis requires the conclusion that the two terms are in fact synonymous, a conclusion common among commentators[218] but one which is not approved in statutory construction.

The correct interpretation of the term "well-marked" requires

---

214. Mississippi Master's Report, *supra* note 198, at 15. *See also* comments in regard to the proper ordering of analysis, *supra* note 201.
215. Mississippi Master's Report, *supra* note 198, at 16.
216. 394 U.S. at 22.
217. Missisippi Master's Report, *supra* note 198, at 16.
218. *See supra,* Chapter IV, note 19 and accompanying text.

a secondary inquiry: to whom? Because there is no publication requirement under Article 7, the existence of a bay must be sufficiently obvious that a mariner approaching the indentation from the sea may be placed on notice. Using the analysis set forth above,[219] an indentation is well-marked from the sea if its existence behind clearly defined entrance points as represented on a seaman's two-dimensional coastal chart is such as to give notice that internal waters are likely to be enclosed, even if no official boundary has been recorded. This test is more than fulfilled by the configuration of Mississippi Sound whose terminal entrance points are factually marked by Isle au Pitre and Dauphin Island and whose mouth is further marked by the barrier islands, giving even more notice to those approaching from the sea that internal waters are likely to be enclosed.

As to the second requirement imposed by Article 7(2), that the penetration[220] be in such proportion to the width of its mouth as to contain landlocked waters and constitute more than a mere curvature of the coast, the Master correctly denies the contention of the states that if an indentation meets the semi-circle requirement, the landlocked requirement is automatically fulfilled.[221] The landlocked requirement constitutes a separate empirical test which must be met before the remainder of Article 7, including the semi-circle test, becomes relevant.[222] The Convention does not provide unambiguous guidelines for decision makers in this regard, however, as the Master's analysis of this issue clearly illustrates.

In order to determine whether Mississippi Sound contains landlocked waters the Master considers five factors: (1) the width-depth ratio of the indentation, (2) the presence of islands at the mouth of the indentation, (3) the "island screen" test devised by Hodgson and Alexander, (4) a memorandum from the Coast and Geodetic Survey authorizing an extension of the coast to embrace an island portico, and (5) language in the Reply Brief of the Fed-

---

219. *See supra*, Chapter IV, notes 19–25 and accompanying text.
220. It is perhaps worth noting again (*see supra*, Chapter IV, note 206; *see also infra* note 274) that the Convention eschewed such earlier wordings as "penetration *inland*" or "penetration *into the mainland*" in order to provide more flexibility in the designation of juridical bays.
221. Mississippi Master's Report, *supra* note 198, at 17. This contention was specifically rejected in the *Louisiana* case, 394 U.S. at 54.
222. *See supra*, Chapter IV, notes 46–58 and accompanying text.

eral Government in the *Louisiana* case, which appears to be an admission that Mississippi Sound is landlocked.[223] The Master concludes correctly that the waters of Mississippi Sound are by their nature landlocked;[224] but the evidence cited as authority for this conclusion reflects lack of clarity as to the nature of the requirement imposed by Article 7.

The language of Article 7(2) plainly implies that some comparison of the width and depth of the waters be made as one factor to be considered in the landlocked determination. Discovering the ratio of depth to width to be .4167:1, the Master concludes that "this is enough to constitute more than a mere curvature of the coast, and I so find."[225] One searches in vain for a future standard in such a finding. What would *not* be enough to constitute more than a mere curvature of the coast? What would be *more* than enough? Although a width-depth comparison is implied, it would seem preferable to look at the nature of the waters enclosed in more than width-depth ratio terms *before* concluding that the waters are not a mere curvature of the coast.

The Master notes further that "the problem is even more complex when there are islands in the mouth of the putative bay."[226] Actually, the problem is made a good deal simpler. Acknowledging the following language from the International Law Commission's 1956 *Commentary:*

> . . . the Commission's intention was to indicate that the presence of islands at the mouth of an indentation tends to link it more closely to the mainland, and this consideration may justify some alteration in the ratio between the width and the penetration of the indentation.[227]

the master fails to take note of the concluding sentence:

> In such a case, an indentation which, if it had no islands at its mouth, would not fulfil [sic] the neccessary conditions *is to be recognized as a bay.*[228]

---

223. Mississippi Master's Report, *supra* note 198, at 16–18.
224. *Id.,* at 18.
225. *Id.,* at 17.
226. *Id.,* at 17.
227. [1956] 2 Y.B. INT'L L. COMM'N at 269.
228. *Id.* (emphasis added). Note the imperative.

Obviously, the presence of islands which create multiple entrances to an indentation creates an inland water area which is even more land-related than one which is fully open to the sea. Rather than complicating the landlocked issue, the presence of islands which create multiple entrances would seem to be near-determinative.

The Master indicates his lack of appreciation of the significance of islands in two additional ways. First, he applies the Hodgson and Alexander "island screen" test[229] and, finding that the islands do in fact "screen" more than 50% of the entrance to Mississippi Sound, concludes that the islands form the limit of landlocked waters.[230] Although it is true that the configuration created by the barrier islands at the mouth of the Sound does satisfy the "island screen" test, as well as the "island portico" test supplied by the Coast and Geodetic Survey memorandum,[231] *neither* of these tests deserves any place whatsoever in an analysis purporting to apply Article 7 of the Territorial Sea Convention. Islands which create more than one entrance into an indentation create an inland water area which is even more land-related than one without such islands. That was the clear conceptual base from which the Article 7 rules pertaining to islands were derived. Such islands, according to the drafters, tend to create an especially landlocked indentation whether they screen 50% of the entrance or not. The Hodgson and Alexander test is totally misconceived and may have been derived from the island portico theory which, as noted above,[232] was devised in order to enclose waters not truly within the coastal littoral but lying between a group of islands and a nonindented coastline, as internal. Such a theory has no relationship whatsoever to the truly inland waters of a coastal indentation; and its use in this context merely confuses the meaning of the landlocked requirement.

How, then, should such a determination be made? Returning to the analysis set forth in Chapter IV above,[233] it was suggested that the phrase "landlocked waters" may best be understood as a

---

229. *See supra*, Chapter IV, notes 155–159 and accompanying text.
230. Mississippi Master's Report, *supra* note 198, at 18.
231. *Id.*, at 18.
232. *See supra* notes 209–210 and accompanying text.
233. *See supra*, Chapter IV, notes 37–43 and accompanying text.

legal conclusion which in effect is a shortened form of this sentence: "We have carefully evaluated the interests of the coastal state in this water area as well as the interests of the community as a whole and have concluded on balance that the interests of the coastal state are paramount."[234] One first evaluates the geographical configuration of the coastal indentation in question because over several hundred years of balancing the inclusive and exclusive interests of states in coastal waters, the world community has recognized that the more deeply an indentation penetrates the coastal littoral, the more intensely the security, economic, societal, and defense interests of the coastal state are likely to be affected; the more enclosed these waters are within the land mass, the less likely it is that the interests of the international users of the ocean will be implicated.

Thus, one studies the geographical configuration of the indentation first, including the relationship of the depth of penetration to the width, because the geographical configuration presented may be so compelling in itself that it may warrant the conclusion that the waters in question are more related to the land than the open sea. In other cases, the inference drawn from geographical configuration alone may not be completely determinative and must then be confirmed or rebutted by actual patterns of human use. One must then proceed to answer the factual questions which underlie the geographical inferences: Have the economic, political, and social processes of life on shore *in fact* become entwined with these waters? Are those who enter the waters from the sea bound primarily for inland ports rather than continuous voyage? Will the security interests of the state be threatened if the waters are deemed marginal or high seas? Will vital international trade routes be infringed if such waters are enclosed as internal by the littoral state?

Applying this analysis to determine whether the waters of Mississippi Sound are landlocked, one first studies the geographical configuration of the waters. Four factors appear relevant in that regard:

1. Mississippi Sound is a well-marked indentation lying between clearly defined natural entrance points at Isle au Pitre and

234. *See supra,* Chapter IV, note 40 and accompanying text.

Dauphin Island[235] where the waters of the Gulf turn abruptly away from the sea and inward toward the land, giving Mississippi Sound the configuration of a bay.

2. Although the penetration of the indentation is somewhat shallow in comparison with its width,[236] the presence of islands which create multiple entrances into the Sound tend to lock the indentation even more closely to the land territory than if the Sound were fully open to the Gulf. Since the plain intent of the drafters was to recognize as a bay an indentation which might fail to qualify were it not for the presence of islands which create multiple entrances, then Mississippi Sound which is almost completely surrounded by land due to the presence of the barrier islands must surely be recognized as such.

Both of the geographical considerations above lead to the inference that the waters of the Sound are closely related to the economic, social, and political processes of shore inhabitants and not essential to the international users of the oceans.

3. The actual water *depth* in much of the Sound measures approximately six feet, leading to an inference that major international traffic routes do not traverse the Sound.

4. The waters of the Sound lead only into the internal waters of Mobile Bay and Lake Borgne justifying the inference that mariners entering the Sound do so only in order to reach inland ports and the further inference that the waters are therefore used primarily by shore inhabitants.

It would appear that on the basis of geographical configuration *alone,* Missisippi Sound is a well-marked coastal indentation containing landlocked waters, i.e, those waters which the world community has recognized as more intimately connected to the land territory than the open sea and therefore subject to exclusive

235. It follows logically, as well as from the language and structure of Article 7 which requires the existence of a well-marked indentation containing landlocked waters, that once clearly defined natural entrance points have been designated to meet the well-marked requirement, these in turn become the first geographical factor to be considered in the analysis of the landlocked requirement.

236. By the Master's reckoning, the ratio is .4167:1 if one measures the width by the length of the entrances between islands (Mississippi Master's Report, *supra* note 198, at 17), but the ratio is much lower if one measures the entire entrance between terminal entrance points.

state control. In the context of the present litigation, this preliminary conclusion would no doubt be subjected to challenge. In
the event that the challenge was permitted over such compelling
geographic evidence, actual proof of human use would become
relevant. There is plentiful evidence in this case to indicate that
the waters of Mississippi Sound are *in fact* vitally entwined with
life processes on shore, that the waters are not utilized as a high-
way for international trade, and that the creation of small enclo-
sures of high seas within the Sound would, in addition to producing an absurd result, greatly infringe the economic and
security interests of the coastal state while not perceptibly bene-
fitting international users. Thus, one may only conclude that the
waters of Missisippi Sound are *in fact* landlocked.

To continue the analysis to the end, only after an indentation
has been deemed well-marked and landlocked does the semi-circle test of Article 7(2) become relevant. As the Master has demonstrated by using the special measurement rules for islands mandated under Article 7(3), the area of the Sound exceeds the area
of a semi-circle drawn on a diameter line equal to the entrances
between the barrier islands. At this point in the analysis, a bay
exists and (it is *now* appropriate to conclude) not a mere curvature of the coast. The only remaining question is how much of
the bay may be enclosed as internal. Since the measurement lines
between islands may become the closing lines, and since these
lines do not total more than twenty-four miles, all of the waters
of Mississippi Sound may be enclosed as internal under Article
7(4). This analysis better represents the coherent scheme
intended by the drafters under Article 7.[237]

The Rhode Island and New York Boundary Case.   The issue to be
decided in *United States v. Maine, et. al.* (Rhode Island and New
York Boundary Case) is the location of the legal coastline of the
United States at the eastern end of Long Island Sound and Block

---

237. In their recent decision in United States v. Louisiana (Alabama and Mississippi
     Boundary Case), 470 U.S. 93, 105 S.Ct. 1074, 84 L. Ed. 2d 73 (1985), the Supreme
     Court held the waters of Mississippi Sound to be an historic bay; and thus, there was
     no need to address the findings of the Special Master that Mississippi Sound also
     qualified as a juridical bay under Article 7. Because the Report of the Special Master
     will no doubt be used as a resource for other such federal-state determinations, the
     above analysis of the Master's findings under Article 7 remains relevant.

Island Sound. The resolution of this issue turns specifically on whether Long Island Sound and Block Island Sound comprise a bay under the terms of the Territorial Sea Convention.[238]

This supplemental proceeding arose out of the decision by the U.S. District Court in *Warner v. Replinger*[239] and the subsequent affirmance by the First Circuit in *Warner v. Dunlap.*[240] At issue in *Warner* was whether or not pilots of foreign flag or American vessels were required to have on board a pilot licensed by the Rhode Island Pilotage Commission. Both courts found that the waters of Long Island Sound and Block Island Sound comprised a juridical bay in accordance with Article 7 and, therefore, that the Rhode Island statute was valid pursuant to federal law which authorizes states to regulate pilotage "in bays, inlets, rivers, harbors, and ports of the United States. . . . "[241]

A petition for a writ of certiorari was filed in the *Warner* case; but because a final decision in that case would of necessity determine the legal baseline in the area, the United States filed a motion for Supplemental Proceedings under *United States v. Maine, et.al.,*[242] urging that Court as the proper forum for deciding whether or not the waters in question constitute inland waters of Rhode Island. On June 29, 1977, a Special Master was appointed.[243] In September 1981, New York filed a Motion to Intervene; and on October 8, 1981, this leave was granted.[244]

Rhode Island and New York assert that the waters of Long Island Sound and Block Island Sound landward of closing lines connecting Montauk Point on Long Island [245] to Block Island[246]

---

238. Report of the Special Master, United States v. Maine (Rhode Island and New York Boundary Case), issued Jan. 13, 1984, No. 35, Original, October, 1983 [hereinafter referred to as New York Master's Report], at 1.

239. 397 F. Supp. 350 (D.R.I. 1975).

240. 532 F.2d 767 (1st Cir. 1976).

241. 46 U.S.C. §211.

242. No. 35, Original.

243. 433 U.S. 917 (1977). In January, 1977, the United States and Massachusetts moved jointly for supplemental proceedings to resolve a controversy regarding the Massachusetts coast. The June 29, 1977, Order of Reference referred both disputes to the Special Master, but the Rhode Island and Massachusetts proceedings were separated when it became clear that the two disputes involved different issues. New York Master's Report, *supra* note 238, at 2 n.2.

244. *Id.,* at 3.

245. *See infra* Fig. 22, at ①.

246. *Id.,* at ②.

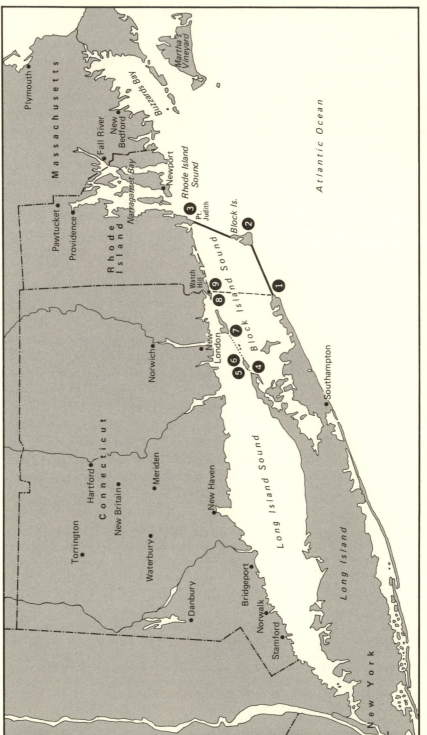

Figure 22. Long Island and Block Island Sounds, claimed by New York and Rhode Island.

and from Block Island to Point Judith, Rhode Island,[247] as illustrated in Figure 22 above, comprise both a juridical and an historic bay, and therefore constitute internal waters.[248] The United States concedes that the waters of Long Island Sound are historic inland waters but argues that these waters are closed by baselines from Orient Point on Long Island[249] to Plum Island[250] and from Plum Island[251] to Race Point, Fisher's Island[252] and from Fisher's Island to Napatree Point, Rhode Island.[253] The Government asserts, however, that the waters of Block Island Sound do not comprise an historic bay nor do the waters of Long Island Sound and Block Island Sound together comprise a juridical bay. In the alternative, if waters of Long Island Sound and Block Island Sound are found to comprise a juridical bay, the Government argues that it should be closed by a line between Montauk Point and Watch Hill, Rhode Island.[254] The Government having conceded historic bay status to Long Island Sound, if the waters of Block Island Sound were found to be historic inland waters, it would not be necessary to proceed with an analysis of whether or not the combined waters form a juridical bay under Article 7. Accordingly, the Master first examines the states' historic bay claim to Block Island Sound.

Utilizing the historic bay analysis derived from the *California, Louisiana,* and *Alaska* cases,[255] the Special Master determines that since the United States has disclaimed historic title to Block Island Sound,[256] the burden is on the states to prove by evidence

247. *Id.,* at ③.
248. New York Master's Report, *supra* note 238, at 4, 7.
249. *See supra* Fig. 22, at ④.
250. *Id.,* at ⑤.
251. *Id.,* at ⑥.
252. *Id.,* at ⑦.
253. *Id.,* at ⑧.
254. *Id.,* at ⑨.
255. *See supra,* Chapter II, note 46.
256. As to this issue the master states: "In 1971, the United States published a series of charts of the United States coastline delimiting the baseline and the territorial seas. . . . These charts included one which covered the entire Long Island Sound and Block Island Sound area . . . . It is apparent that the position of the Government in 1971 is identical to the position of the Government in this proceeding." New York Master's Report, *supra* note 238, at 11. This statement is an apt illustration of the cynical process described above, *supra* note 179 and accompanying text, wherein the federal government, anticipating and in some cases actually involved in litigation

that is clear beyond doubt that Block Island Sound is historic inland waters of the states.[257] Not surprisingly, the Master finds that state evidence of fishing regulations, pilotage statutes, and Rhode Island–New York boundary agreements is insufficient to carry this extraordinary burden;[258] and, holding that Block Island Sound is not an historic bay, turns to an analysis of the waters of Long Island Sound and Block Island Sound under Article 7 of the Territorial Sea Convention.

Brushing aside two alternative theories upon which the states had argued that the waters of Long Island Sound and Block Island Sound comprise a juridical bay,[259] the Master proceeds to analyze the main argument of the states, i.e., that the presence of Long Island serves to enclose the waters of Long Island and Block Island Sounds, thereby forming a single juridical bay which

---

with the states, establishes a federal Baseline Committee to delimit federal boundaries in ways antithetical to state interests. A few years later these so-called "official charts" are used as evidence against the states, with all the damning weight which these "official" federal charts were intended to carry in federal courts. It is little availing for the states to claim, several years after the fact, that these charts merely represent the position of the Federal Government in a suit in which that Government is a party. In this case, the evidence is particularly damning since the "official chart" of Block Island Sound is accepted by the Master as evidence of a federal disclaimer to an historic claim, which in turn raises the burden of the states to produce evidence clear beyond doubt, a level which few state claims could carry over the deference usually accorded to federal claims. To avoid the fact as well as the appearance of impropriety and unfairness, courts should require the Government to provide proof that a federal disclaimer of historic title was issued prior to the period in which these suits began in earnest in the mid-1960's, or at the very least prior to the preparation of "official" charts by the Baseline Committee in 1970–1971. This appears to be the approach taken by the Supreme Court in the *Alabama and Mississippi Boundary Case* (*see supra*, note 182).

257. New York Master's Report, *supra* note 238, at 11.
258. *Id.*, at 12–19.
259. New York and Rhode Island made two alternative arguments: 1) Using the Beazley theory of the "two-headed bay," the states argued that two bays originate from the two sides of the western end of Long Island, the south side forming New York Harbor and the north side forming Long Island and Block Island Sounds; and 2) utilizing the Hodgson & Alexander "island screen" theory, the states argued that Long Island and Block Island are screening islands across the entrance of a bay which stretches from Throgs Neck, N.Y., to Pt. Judith, R.I., apparently the theory adopted by the First Circuit in *Warner v. Dunlap. See* New York Master's Report, *supra* note 238, at 22 and 22 n.16. The Special Master concludes, "[W]hen Long Island is viewed strictly as an island, there is no indentation into the coast that will satisfy the requirements of Article 7(2). The coast in this area is only a mere curvature. This conclusion eliminates two of the juridical bay theories offered by the States." *Id.*, at 28.

satisfies Article 7 criteria. Taking note of expert testimony and the opinion of the Supreme Court in the *Louisiana*[260] case, the Master concludes that Article 7 permits a single large island such as Long Island to form an indentation where none might otherwise exist,[261] as long as the island can realistically be considered part of the mainland.[262]

The Master then proceeds to determine whether or not Long Island may be considered a part of the mainland and, after evaluating massive amounts of evidence regarding the navigability and nature of the East River, the complex estuarine system of the Hudson River estuary, the geographical, geological, social, economic, political, and historical connections between Long Island and the continental land mass, and other matters totally unrelated to the nature of the *waters* enclosed by the indentation (that is to say, the actual focus of the regime established under Article 7), the Master concludes:

> If there is ever a situation where a large coastal island will be considered a part of the mainland so the water enclosed between the island and the coast can be a juridical bay, this is it.[263]

However correct the conclusion, one must repeat with equal force the question posed above: "Whence comes this tortured analysis?"[264] The answer is the same in each case. *United States v.*

---

260. 394 U.S. at 60–66.
261. In so holding, the Master specifically rejects the argument made by the Government that the exception created by the *Louisiana* case for islands which may serve as the "headlands" of a bay applied only to the particular deltaic formations there at issue, or to small, marshy, deltaic islands of that nature. The Master also rejects by implication the Government's argument that islands can only be considered part of the mainland in four limited situations: 1) where the island is separated from the mainland by a river, such that the island creates a bank; 2) where the island is connected to the mainland by a causeway; 3) where the island is connected to the mainland by a low-tide elevation; and 4) where the shoreline is deltaic, actually consisting of innumerable small islands.
262. New York Master's Report, *supra* note 238, at 35. *See also id.*, at 36 n. 25, where the Master refers to the now-familiar authorities whose language is often cited to justify treating islands as mainland. As demonstrated above (*supra* notes 211–213 and accompanying text), these authorities were speaking for the most part in the context of islands lying off a nonindented mainland coast.
263. New York Master's Report, *supra* note 238, at 47. *See also id.*, at 37–46, for summary of evidence presented on the "island as mainland" issue.
264. *See supra* notes 208–213 and accompanying text in reference to the *Alabama and Mississippi Boundary Case.*

Louisiana has placed a tremendous burden on subsequent tribunals to sift through hundreds of hours and thousands of pages of irrelevant testimony, all because of this seemingly innocent passage:

> We have concluded that Article 7 does not encompass bays formed in part by islands which cannot realistically be considered part of the mainland.[265]

As if in explanation of this conclusion, the Court continues in the next sentence:

> Article 7 defines bays as indentations in the "coast," a term which is used in contrast with "islands" throughout the Convention.[266]

This statutory interpretation of the Convention is not supported by the facts. The legislative history reveals that the normal baseline rule embodied in Article 3 fully contemplates islands as forming a part of the coast.[267] In 1958, the United States submitted a proposed amendment[268] to the draft of Article 3. Retitling the Article "Mainland Baseline," the United States proposed that the wording be changed to read: "Subject to the provisions of the present rules, the baseline is the low-tide line on the *mainland* . . .," rather than "the low-tide line on the *coast.*" In their comment to the proposed amendment, the United States explained that the word "coast" was undesirable because the term had been interpreted to include islands and drying rocks and shoals. Such an interpretation, they reasoned, would give an unintentionally wide scope to the draft article.[269]

The Yugoslavian delegate responded[270] that the U.S. amendment constituted an unsatisfactory change in the substance of the Article because it made no reference to islands, whereas the International Law Commission Draft specifically used the term

265. 394 U.S. at 67.
266. *Id.*
267. III Official Records of the First Committee 140 A/CONF. 13/39, (1958). *See supra,* Chapter IV, note 3 and accompanying text for full text of Article 3.
268. A/CONF. 13/C.1/2.87.
269. *See supra,* Official Records, note 267, at 140.
270. *Id.*

"coasts" to cover *both* mainland and island coasts. The idea forwarded by the United States found no support at the Conference, and the proposed amendment was not adopted.

The dicta of the *Louisiana* court is also insupportable in light of the historical treatment of bays, which indicates that islands have been recognized as forming the coasts of indentations for several hundred years;[271] by the writings of early and modern commentators who reflect this historical practice and make no distinction between bays formed wholly by mainland or partially by islands;[272] and most importantly, by the language expressly chosen by the drafters in Article 7. By eschewing anachronistic terms such as mainland, headland, and *inter fauces terrae* and opting instead for the more functional, inclusive terms "coasts" and "natural entrance points," the drafters indicated their intent to focus on the waters of the indentation rather than the nature of the surrounding land. Article 7, paragraph one, reads, "this article relates only to bays the *coasts* of which belong to a single State."[273] The meaning of this initial paragraph is clear on its face. The drafters did not specify that Article 7 was to relate to bays "lying within the mainland," or bays "inter fauces terrae," nor even bays lying "inland,"[274] They rejected these familiar terms for "coasts," a term which, as noted above, was intended to include both mainland and island in the normal baseline rule of Article 3. It would be preposterous to suggest that "coasts" was meant to have an inclusive meaning under Article 3 and to have an exclusively "mainland" meaning under Article 7.

This, then, is where the *Louisiana* Court went wrong. Believing erroneously that the term coast "had been used in contrast with 'islands' throughout the Convention,"[275] the Court derived the rule that since bays could only be formed by indentations into mainland coasts, an island could be said to form the coast of an indentation only if it could realistically be considered part of the mainland. Having made the first conceptual misstep, the Court

---

271. *See supra*, Chapter IV, notes 181–217 and accompanying text.
272. *See supra*, Chapter IV, notes 186, 198–201 and accompanying text.
273. Territorial Sea Convention, Art. 7(1); *see supra*, Chapter IV, full text at note 10.
274. An early draft of Article 7(2) read " . . . a bay is a well-marked indentation whose penetration *inland* is in such proportion . . ." The term "inland" was expressly removed by the International Law Commission. *See supra*, Chapter IV, note 206.
275. 394 U.S. at 67.

then looked for authority to close the waters between island and mainland as internal, and relied on the language of early decisions[276] and the writings of commentators,[277] none of which were relevant to the issue of coastal indentations.[278] All of this has produced a rule of law which is incorrect in its application of Article 7 and which has led subsequent decision makers into the tangled thicket of "assimilation" proof, each case producing more tangential and unnecessary evidence than the last. For although parties may argue interminably over whether or not an island may be considered part of the "mainland," to no certain result, *no* such analysis is required to show that an island forms a part of the *coasts* of a single state, the first and most basic requirement of Article 7(1). An indentation whose coasts are formed partially by mainland and partially by island[s] is one which falls squarely within the scope of Article 7. Such an indentation must then be subjected to the same tests required of *all* indentations which would become juridical bays under Article 7(2): it must be found to be a well-marked indentation containing landlocked waters, the area of which meets the semi-circle test, and the entrance of which is no more than twenty-four miles wide.

Perhaps no one understands the basic focus of Article 7 better than the Special Master himself who, after sifting through voluminous "assimilation to the mainland" evidence, appears to reach the conclusion that Long Island may be considered a part of the mainland on the basis of two quite basic factors, which he identifies as most determinative:

1. The geographical configuration of Long Island and the mainland encloses *waters* which "closely resemble a bay;"[279] and
2. The geographical configuration of Long Island and the mainland encloses *waters* which are *used* as one would expect a bay to be *used*.[280]

276. *Id.*, at 64 n.84.
277. *Id.*, at 65 n.85.
278. *See supra* notes 211, 212 and accompanying text.
279. New York Master's Report, *supra* note 238, at 46 (emphasis added).
280. *Id.* (emphasis added). The Master continues at 46: "Ships do not pass through Long Island Sound and the East River unless they are headed for New York Harbor or ports on Long Island Sound. Ships bound for ports not in the enclosed area navigate outside of Long Island and Block Island as they pass up and down the U.S. coast. Long Island Sound is not a route of international passage; ships merely pass into and out of it as one would expect ships to pass into and out of a bay."

Taking a common-sense approach more in keeping with Article 7 than the involuted "island as mainland" approach mandated by *Louisiana,* the Master makes a first order decision on the proper basis when he states, " . . .[V]iewing charts of the area the bay-like appearance of the area is obvious, and it becomes readily apparent that the enclosed water has many of the characteristics of a bay."[281] This statement clearly exposes the irrelevance of the *Louisiana* test. One needn't require that islands be "part of the mainland" in order to ensure that the island will be close enough to the mainland to form a coastal indentation which might be granted bay status. An island which is too far distant from the mainland will not *factually* create an "obvious," well-marked indentation which encloses landlocked waters. Article 7 provides, as the *California* court has held,[282] the best and most workable definition of a bay. If properly applied, no further tests are necessary.

Although the Master quite correctly focuses on the geographical appearance of the waters in question to begin his analysis, the order in which he proceeds thereafter leads one to suspect a lack of understanding as to the proper application of the tests mandated by Article 7. Having turned instinctively to the geographical configuration of the waters and their use, he concludes that Long Island *may be treated as part of the mainland,* whereas he could have quite properly concluded that the first two requirements of Article 7, a *well-marked indentation* whose proportions are such as to enclose *landlocked waters,* had been met. Instead, having concluded that Long Island may be considered part of the mainland "and as such Long Island Sound is a well-marked indentation,"[283] the Master avoids the landlocked requirement entirely and proceeds to apply the semi-circle test. He concludes that whether the measurement lines of Article 7(3) are drawn from Montauk Point to Watch Hill, as the Government had argued in the alternative, or from Montauk Point to Block Island to Point Judith, as the

---

281. *Id.* The Master specifically declares erroneous the conclusion of the Baseline Committee that Long Island may not be treated as part of the mainland because the East River is commercially navigable or because it is a tidal strait. This conclusion, he asserts, ignores the close geographic alignment of Long Island and the mainland and the obvious baylike character of Long Island Sound. *Id.,* at 47.

282. 332 U.S. at 165.

283. New York Master's Report, *supra* note 238, at 47.

states had argued, the waters measured would pass the semi-circle test.[284] Next, the Master proceeds to determine the proper closing line of the bay, and it is within this process that his analysis is most misconceived.

The Master correctly observes that Article 7 directs closing lines to be drawn between natural entrance points and that both Article 7 and the *Louisiana* opinion indicate that islands which create separate entrances into the indentation may be included within the closing lines. Having deduced the correct tests, the Master fails to apply them, seemingly becoming confused by evidence which suggests that alternative tests are also acceptable under the Convention.

For example, the Master cites "three objective tests"[285] which he claims have been formulated to assist in selecting natural entrance points: 1) the 45° test;[286] 2) the bisector of the two tangents test,[287] and 3) the shortest distance test.[288] The use of any of these tests is inappropriate in the present case, as all three tests have been devised *not* to "formulate natural entrance points" in normal circumstances where points exist which clearly mark the natural entrances to the bay, but rather to *posit* an entrance point in a special circumstance where, because of a featureless coastline or a rounded curve on one side of the bay, no *natural* entrance point may be found.[289] By including these "special circumstance"

---

284. *Id.*, at 49.

285. *See* New York Master's Report, *supra* note 238, at 50 n.39.

286. *See supra*, Chapter IV, notes 103–105 and accompanying text.

287. *See supra*, Chapter IV, notes 101, 102 and accompanying text.

288. *See supra*, Chapter IV, notes 104, 105 and accompanying text. The use of this test was rejected by the Court in United States v. Louisiana, 394 U.S. at 55.

289. The bisector of the angle test was adopted by the Court in the *California* case (*see supra*, Chapter IV, note 102) and applies *only* when a natural entrance point on one side of the bay is faced by a rounded shore on the other, making an exact entrance point impossible to determine. The bisector of the angle test, fully described *supra*, Chapter IV, at note 101 and accompanying text, is used to select a point, then *deemed* a natural entrance point, so that a closing line "between natural entrance points" may be drawn in accordance with Article 7(4). The "45°" test and the "shortest distance" test were both devised as methods for selecting an entrance point on an absolutely featureless shoreline. Although Hodgson & Alexander have *suggested* using the 45° test to find all natural entrance points, this suggestion is clearly at odds with the language of the Convention which mandates the selection of *natural* entrance points, i.e., those points which actually mark the entrances into the indentation from the sea, and has not been approved by other commentators. The Strohl "shortest distance" test, also limited to the featureless shoreline situa-

tests within the natural entrance points lexicon, the Master has done injury to one of the most basic concepts of Article 7: that natural entrance points by definition clearly mark the *actual entrances* to a bay.

Many other key Article 7 concepts are similarly confounded. The Master observes that the natural entrance points selected must enclose landlocked waters, and that many authors have attempted to create a workable definition for the term "land-locked." Unfortunately, the Master could not have cited a more ill-conceived definition than that provided by Hodgson and Alexander, who claim that the "semi-circular test . . . may relate also to the character of the waters being land-locked. . . . A semi-circle, by definition, is twice as wide as it is deep. The opening represents the maximum width. Since this definition characterizes the absolute minimum, true land-locked conditions should require that the opening (of the bay) be narrower than a principal lateral axis of the bay."[290] This statement represents a total misinterpretation of the language of Article 7 which imposes the semi-circle test of Article 7(2) *not* as a final limitation on the *proportions* of a bay but as the final limit on bay *area*. The Strohl test cited by the Master is similarly ill conceived.[291] The actual language of Article 7 would seem to imply that well-marked, landlocked indentations of *varying* portions may pass Article 7 criteria as long as the *area* of each indentation satisfies the semi-circle test.[292]

The most confused analysis is undertaken by the Master in regard to the use of Block Island in the closing line of the bay. The United States utilized the Hodgson and Alexander rules discussed above[293] as the basis for their argument that no islands lying seaward of a line connecting mainland [sic] headlands [sic]

---

tion, suffers from several drawbacks even as a special rule, as noted *supra*, Chapter IV, at notes 104, 105 and accompanying text. It was highly improper for witnesses to testify, as the Master seems to suggest, that these alternative rules for special circumstances were to be used to find the line "that separates the landlocked waters from those waters which are not landlocked." New York Master's Report, *supra* note 238, at 52 n.40.

290. Hodgson & Alexander, *supra*, Chapter II, note 24, at 6, 8.

291. New York Master's Report, *supra* note 238, at 52–53, n.40.

292. *See* full discussion of this issue, *supra*, Chapter IV, at notes 24–43 and accompanying text.

293. *See supra*, Chapter IV, notes 130–151 and accompanying text.

could be included within the closing line of a bay. Then, in a fan-
tastic feat of circular reasoning, the Government argued that
because the Baseline Committee had selected Watch Hill, Rhode
Island, and Montauk Point, New York, as the mainland [sic] headlands [sic], Block Island, which lay seaward of these headlands
[sic], could not be included in the closing line.[294]

The states, relying on the express language of Article 7 and
much of the familiar legislative history on this issue cited above,[295]
argued correctly that Article 7 contains no requirement that
mainland headlands are to be selected *first* and that islands not
intersected by a line between these headlands may not be
included in the closing line. Such an interpretation is in direct
contravention of the special rules designed by the drafters to
apply to islands which create separate entrances into a bay and
hence enhance its landlocked quality. The states argued further
that the natural entrance points of Block Island Sound are
formed by Montauk Point, Block Island, and Point Judith, which
factually create two separate entrances into the Sound.[296]

In evaluating the evidence presented by the parties, the Master
relies most heavily on the Baseline Committee's recommendation
that the closing line be drawn from Montauk Point to Watch Hill.
The Master's concluding paragraph is quite illuminating:

> On this question the Special Master agrees with the findings of the
> Baseline Committee and concludes that the closing for the bay is
> a line between Montauk Point on Long Island and Watch Hill
> Point, Rhode Island. Montauk Point is *one prominent point* marking
> the separation between the waters within an indentation and the
> waters outside an indentation. Watch Hill Point *is the first promi-
> nent point on the Rhode Island coast,* it is almost *due north* of Montauk
> Point, it also *marks the separation between the waters within the inden-
> tation and the waters outside the indentation,* thus Watch Hill Point is
> the *logical natural entrance point* on the north side of *the
> indentation.*[297]

---

294. New York Master's Report, *supra* note 238, at 54–55.
295. *See supra,* Chapter IV, notes 109–116 and accompanying text.
296. New York Master's Report, *supra* note 238, at 55–58.
297. New York Master's Report, *supra* note 238, at 59 (emphasis added). Because the
    Master relied heavily on the Baseline Committee's recommendation for a proper
    closing line, it is interesting to note that even *within* the Baseline Committee, opin-
    ions on this matter were not uniform. A Department of State memorandum dated

Each of the italicized phrases above indicates a misperception which must be challenged. First, there is *no* requirement under Article 7 that a natural entrance point must be selected opposite Montauk Point which is "the first prominent point on the Rhode Island coast"; and even if there *were*, who is to say that Watch Hill is the first? To a mariner approaching from the sea, Point Judith, which also serves as a natural entrance point for Narragansett Bay, is both the *first* and the *most prominent* point on the Rhode Island coast.[298] As for Watch Hill lying almost "due north" of Montauk Point, there is no requirement under Article 7 that such a point serve as a natural entrance point. This assertion may indicate that the Master has based his conclusion on the "shortest distance" test proposed by Strohl;[299] but it must be reemphasized that this test, as well as the "45°" test, were devised to apply solely in the event that it became necessary to create an entrance point on a *featureless* coastline. The test was never intended to be applied in a situation such as the present case, where Point Judith provides a prominent and factual natural entrance point on the Rhode Island coast.

Both of these assertions, read together with the last assertion, that Watch Hill Point is the *logical* natural entrance point on the north side of the indentation, indicate that the Master may believe that it is within his power under Article 7 to "choose" an entrance point which "makes sense" on one basis or another, i.e.,

---

July 8, 1971, addressed to a Mr. Stevenson from Donald L. McKernan on the subject of Baseline Charts, reads in part as follows: "We have carefully reviewed the reasoning behind the Long Island Sound baselines on C & GS [chart] 1211, and are not convinced. It is neither reasonable nor logical to consider any waters landward of Long Island to be high seas. In fact, a reasonable approach to the area, in terms of the close linkage between the land and water regimes in the area would be to draw the baselines from Montauk Point to Block Island to Point Judith, rather than the minimum acceptable baseline of Montauk Point to Watch Hill Point. . . . I understand that other agencies are continuing to distribute sets of charts including 1211 with the disputed baselines. I do not consider it proper to distribute charts indicating interagency agreement when this Department, as far as I am concerned, has not concurred in the baselines shown on 1211. I would appreciate it if you would take appropriate steps to ensure that all distribution cease pending drawing of a proper baseline." One can only reflect again on the propriety of using Baseline Committee recommendations within the context of federal-state litigation. (*See supra* notes 176–179, 256, and accompanying text.)

298. *See supra,* Fig. 22 at ③.
299. *See supra* note 284.

because it lies closest to the natural entrance point on the opposite shore or "due north" of it, and then to impose this choice on the claimant state. Nothing could be further from the truth. Article 7 *mandates* that closing lines be drawn between *natural* entrance points when these factually exist, including entrance points created by islands lying seaward of the mainland entrance points, which create separate entrances into the bay.[300]

The Master's remaining contention, that the Montauk Point–Watch Hill line marks the separation between the waters within "the indentation" and those outside, and his parallel assertion in a later paragraph that Block Island lies too far seaward of "this indentation" to create entrances into it,[301] indicate that the Master has simply accepted the Baseline Committee's conclusion that "the indentation" lies between Watch Hill and Montauk Point. Once that erroneous and premature conclusion has been accepted, then *all* waters and islands lying outside this line must by definition be deemed "outside the indentation."

The Master's assertions in this regard are somewhat vague, but he may be attempting to clarify his remarks in a subsequent paragraph when he asserts that the waters lying west of the Montauk Point–Watch Hill indentation "satisfy all the criteria"[302] for being landlocked, including being surrounded on three sides by land and being usefully sheltered and isolated from the sea. Both parties, of course, had agreed to that much. The issue is whether or not the waters *east* of the Montauk Point–Watch Hill line to the limit of the closing lines drawn between Montauk, Block Island, and Point Judith might *also* be deemed landlocked. The Master fails to analyze this issue beyond a cursory remark that viewed on a chart, the waters do not appear to be part of the land rather than open sea.[303]

But this is exactly the ambiguous situation in which further analysis of the landlocked issue is necessary. Utilizing the interpretation of the term posited above,[304] one must first study the

---

300. *See supra*, Chapter IV, 130–152 and accompanying text.
301. New York Master's Report, *supra* note 238, at 60.
302. *Id.*
303. *Id.*, at 59.
304. *See supra*, Chapter IV, notes 24–43 and accompanying text; *see also supra* notes 220–234 and accompanying text for application of the proposed construction in the case of Mississippi Sound.

geographical configuration of the waters of Long Island–Block Island Sounds. By the Master's own admission, the presence of Long Island along the mainland coast creates a water area which has many of the geographical characteristics of a bay. In addition, several other geographical factors seem compelling:

1. Montauk Point, Block Island, and Point Judith constitute clearly defined natural entrance points which well mark the bay and give notice to mariners that internal waters may be enclosed. Point Judith is a prominent point on the coast of Rhode Island which also serves as a natural entrance point for Narragansett Bay. The light marking the entrance to both Narragansett Bay and Block Island Sound is located on Point Judith.
2. The presence of Block Island creates two separate entrances to the bay. The entrance between Block Island and Point Judith is more heavily utilized due to dangerous underwater conditions between Montauk Point and Block Island, the physical nature of which may indicate that Block Island is part of the same terminal moraine which formed Long Island.
3. Compelling geographical evidence indicates that the presence of Block Island creates a "sill" between the Island and Montauk Point which causes the waters of Block Island Sound to have a "different character"[305] than the waters outside Block Island Sound.
4. Thus, the presence of Block Island, an island which *factually* creates two entrances into the bay as contemplated by the drafters, appears to create a more sheltered, land-related indentation; and thus may justify the affirmative desire of the drafters to recognize, as a bay, an indentation which without the islands, might not fulfill all the necessary qualifications under Article 7.

If the geographical configuration of the indentation is not compelling enough in itself to warrant the legal conclusion that the waters are so related to the land territory as to constitute

305. New York Master's Report, *supra* note 238, at 55–56 n.42. An experienced professional pilot, Captain John Neary, testified that nautical charts clearly mark the shallow depth and underwater obstacles between Montauk Point and Block Island. Neary testified that this condition had the effect of "knocking down the swell" in storm conditions, thus sheltering the waters of Block Island Sound. *See* Neary, testimony November 13, 1981, U.S. Exhibit M-1.

landlocked waters, then, as suggested above, in Chapter IV, actual patterns of human use become relevant and must be studied. There is ample evidence in the present case to indicate that the social, economic, and political processes of the shore inhabitants have become vitally entwined with the waters in question. In addition, by the Master's own admission, "ships bound for ports not in the enclosed area navigate outside of Long Island *and Block Island* as they pass up and down the United States coast.[306] Factually, ships entering the bay bound for inland ports pass through the entrance created between Block Island and Point Judith. The shoals between Block Island and Montauk are clearly marked on coastal maps, and seamen by and large avoid this entrance, making the entrance of the bay even more well marked. As noted above, Point Judith also serves as a natural entrance point for Narragansett Bay, and mariners mark the entrances to both water areas by the Point Judith light. International users pass completely by Block Island *and* Long Island on international trade routes.

Geographical considerations and evidence of actual patterns of human use, which after all lie at the conceptual base of the term "landlocked," militate in favor of the conclusion that the interests of the international users of the oceans are secondary in these waters and the interests of shore inhabitants are paramount. Thus, the legal conclusion is warranted that the waters lying west of the lines joining Montauk Point, Block Island, and Point Judith are *in fact* landlocked.

This, it is suggested, is the analysis which should have preceded all inquiry into closing lines and the semi-circle requirement in the Master's Report. Having determined that the waters claimed by the States comprise a well-marked indentation which contains landlocked waters, it would *then* be appropriate to compare the area of the waters enclosed to the area of a semi-circle drawn on a diameter line equal to the combined distances between islands and mainland as provided in Article 7(3). As it was stipulated that the waters of the bay thus measured *do* pass the semi-circle test[307] and further, that the combined distances of the closing lines do

306. New York Master's Report, *supra* note 238, at 46.
307. New York Master's Report, *supra* note 238, at 47–48.

not exceed twenty-four miles,[308] it would appear that the waters of Long Island Sound and Block Island Sound should have been granted juridical bay status.

Instead of this straightforward analysis mandated by the language and structure of Article 7, the Master has engaged in a protracted analysis that appears to place exaggerated importance on a preliminary baseline selected by the Baseline Committee acting on the basis of federal interests.[309] The Master's analysis suggests that because it can be demonstrated that this preliminary baseline encloses an indentation which meets some of the Article 7 criteria and some of the extra textual tests provided by courts and commentators to cover supposed special circumstances, it is *this* baseline which must prevail, even though it is the *state's* baseline claim which has been challenged and which is therefore in issue. It is the indentation enclosed by closing lines between Montauk Point, Block Island, and Point Judith which must be the focus of the Master's analysis. If the indentation enclosed by these lines meets the requirements imposed by Article 7, Article 7 *mandates* that it be deemed a juridical bay, whether or not another closing line also meets Article 7 requirements or appears more "logical."[310]

308. *See* New York Master's Report, Appendix A—Stipulations of the Parties, Attachment I, at 65.

309. New York Master's Report, *supra* note 238, at 41–43, 55, 58–60.

310. In their recent opinion in United States v. Maine et al. (Rhode Island and New York Boundary Case), 469 U.S. 504, 105 S.Ct. 992, 83 L.Ed.2d 998 (1985), the Supreme Court relies heavily on the factors set out in the *Louisiana* case and on the findings of the Special Master in this case to hold that Long Island is an extension of the mainland and that the waters enclosed between Long Island and the mainland comprise a juridical bay under Article 7. The Court also relies heavily on the Master's and the Baseline Committee's recommendation for drawing a closing line between Montauk Point and Watch Hill; and, therefore, the Court's holding is subject to the same criticism as has been lodged against the Special Master's Report in the analysis above.

VI

Conclusion

Article 7 of the Territorial Sea Convention[311] represents the most recent and most successful formulation of the international law of bays. The fundamental policies reflected in its provisions are those which underlie the law of the sea as a whole, i.e., to protect the exclusive interests of coastal states in national security and economic welfare without unduly burdening the international users of the oceans or infringing the inclusive interests of all states in the shared enjoyment of ocean resources. Because the exclusive interests of states are seen to attach most fundamentally to those waters most intimately related to the land, the world community has traditionally recognized claims of exclusive authority over waters which lie within the coastal littoral. Bays, lying both sheltered within the land mass and dangerously open to the sea, have been seen from earliest times as so vitally entwined with life on shore as to be susceptible of such competence.

Yet, the collection of generally recognized principles and not

---

311. The language of Article 7 remains virtually unchanged in Article 10 of UNCLOS. *See supra*, Chapter I, note 19.

wholly uniform policies which served as guidelines in international disputes for over a century failed to coalesce into a coherent, reliable regime for bay designation and delimitation. Recognizing the need for definition and fearing the unlimited claims of states in an era of rapid technological advancement, the drafters reached a historic procedural and evidentiary compromise in Geneva in 1958. In essence, a well-marked indentation, the waters of which are landlocked, the area of which meets the semicircle test, and the entrance of which is no more than twenty-four miles wide, is guaranteed juridical status under Article 7. Once an indentation has been thus characterized, an irrebuttable presumption is raised that the claimant state owns these waters as a matter of right against all states. An extraordinarily high standard of proof will be required, however, to lay claim to waters beyond these limits as internal.

Article 7 of the Territorial Sea Convention, then, provides a mandatory, self-executing procedure for the designation and delimitation of a juridical bay. When the provisions of this lex specialis are correctly interpreted and applied, as is suggested in the textual, contextual, and structural analysis above and in the application of this analysis to two recent federal-state controversies in the United States, a codification scheme of remarkable innovation and clarity emerges which may serve as a reliable guide for future state action as well as an ordered method of conflict resolution for decision makers.

Bibliography

Books

Alexander, Lewis M., ed. The Law of the Sea: Offshore Boundaries and Zones. Columbus: Ohio State University Press, 1967.

Angell, Joseph Kinnicut. A Treatise on the Right of Property in Tide Waters and in the Soil and Shores Thereof. Boston: Little, Brown and Co., 1847.

Azuni, Domenico Alberto. Droit Maritime de l'Europe. 2 vols. Paris: Chez l'auteur, 1805.

Bluntschli, Johann Kaspar. Le Droit International Codifie. Fifth revised edition. Paris: Guillaumin, 1895.

Bonfils, Henri J. F. X. Manuel de Droit International Public. Seventh edition. Paris: A. Rousseau, 1914.

Bowett, Derek W. The Law of the Sea. Manchester: Manchester University Press, and Dobbs Ferry, N.Y.: Oceana Publications, Inc., 1967.

—————. The Legal Regime of Islands in International Law. Dobbs Ferry, N.Y.: Oceana Publications, Inc., 1979.

Brittin, Burdick H. International Law for Seagoing Officers. Annapolis: U.S. Naval Institute, 1956.

Brownlie, Ian. Principles of Public International Law. Oxford: Clarendon Press, 1966.

Bynkershoek, Cornelius van. De Dominio Maris. Text of 1702–03 trans. by Ralph van Deman Magoffin. In The Classics of International Law, ed. James Brown Scott. New York: Carnegie Endowment for International Peace, 1923.

————. Quaestionum Juris Publici Libri Duo. Text of 1737 trans. by Tenney Frank. In The Classics of International Law, ed. James Brown Scott. (Oxford: Clarendon Press) 1930.

Calvo, Carlos. Le Droit International Théorique et Pratique. 6 vols. Fifth revised edition. Paris: A. Rousseau, 1896.

Carnazza-Amari, Guiseppe. Traité de Droit International Public en Temps de Paix. 2 vols. Paris: L. Larose, 1880–1882.

Cauchy, Eugène Francois. Le Droit Maritime International. 2 vols. Paris: Guillaumin, 1862.

Codrington, Robert. His Majesties Propriety, and Dominion on the British Seas Asserted. London: T. Mabb, 1665.

Colombos, C. John. The International Law of the Sea. Sixth revised edition. New York: David McKay Co., 1967.

Creasy, Sir Edward Shepherd. First Platform of International Law. London: J. Van Voorst, 1876.

Crocker, Henry G. The Extent of the Marginal Sea. Washington, D.C.: Government Printing Office, 1919.

Cussy, Baron Ferdinand de. Phases et Causes Célèbres du Droit Maritime des Nations. 2 vols. Leipzig: F. A. Brockhaus, 1856.

Despagnet, Frantz Clément René. Cours de Droit International Public. Fourth revised edition. Paris: L. Larose et L. Tenin, 1910.

Elder, John Rawson. The Royal Fishery Companies of the Seventeenth Century. Glasgow: J. MacLehose and Sons, 1912.

Engelmann, Siegfried. Conceptual Thinking. (Dimensions in Early Learning Monograph Series). Sioux City, Iowa: Adapt Press, 1970.

Fenwick, Charles G. International Law. Third edition. New York: Appleton-Century-Crofts, Inc., 1948.

Fulton, Thomas Wemyss. The Sovereignty of the Sea. Edinburgh and London: W. Blackwood and Sons, 1911.

Gamble, John King, Jr. Law of the Sea: The Emerging Regime of the Oceans. Cambridge, Massachusetts: Ballinger, 1974.

Gentili, Alberico. De Jure Belli Libri Tres. Trans. of 1612 edition by John C. Rolfe. In The Classics of International Law, ed. James Brown Scott. Dobbs Ferry, N.Y.: Oceana Publications, Inc., and London: Wildy and Sons, Ltd., reprinted 1964.

Hall, William Edward. A Treatise on International Law. Seventh edition by A. Pearce Higgins. Oxford: The Clarendon Press, and London and New York: H. Milford, 1917.

Halleck, Henry Wagner. International Law. 2 vols. Fourth edition by Sir G. Sherston Baker. London: K. Paul, Trench, Trübner and Co., Ltd., 1908.

Hautefeuille, Laurent Basile. Des Droits et des Devoirs des Nations Neutres en Temps de Guerre Maritime. 3 vols. Second edition. Paris: Guillaumin, 1858.

Hyde, Charles Cheney. International Law Chiefly as Interpreted and Applied by the United States. 3 vols. Second revised edition. Boston: Little, Brown and Company, 1945.

Jessup, Philip C. THE LAW OF TERRITORIAL WATERS AND MARITIME JURISDICTION. New York: G. A. Jennings Co., Inc., 1927.

Kent, James. COMMENTARIES ON AMERICAN LAW. 4 vols. First edition. New York: O. Halsted, 1826–1830.

Kerchove, Renee de. INTERNATIONAL MARITIME DICTIONARY. New York: D. Van Nostrand Co., 1948.

Klüber, Johann Ludwig. DROIT DES GENS MODERNE DE L'EUROPE. Second edition. Paris: Guillaumin, 1874.

Latour, Joseph Jean Baptiste Imbart de. LA MER TERRITORIALE AU POINT DE VUE THÉORIQUE ET PRATIQUE. Paris: G. Pedone-Lauriel, 1889.

Lauterpacht, Sir Hersch. THE DEVELOPMENT OF INTERNATIONAL LAW BY THE INTERNATIONAL COURT. New York: Praeger, 1958.

Lawrence, Thomas Joseph. THE PRINCIPLES OF INTERNATIONAL LAW. Fifth edition. Boston: D. C. Heath & Co., 1913.

Liszt, Franz von. DAS VOLKERRECHT SYSTEMATISCH DARGESTELLT. Fifth edition. Berlin: O. Hharing, 1907.

Maine, Henry. ANCIENT LAW: ITS CONNECTION WITH THE EARLY HISTORY OF SOCIETY AND ITS RELATION TO MODERN IDEAS. Fourth American edition from the tenth London edition. New York: Henry Holt and Co., 1906.

————. DISSERTATIONS ON EARLY LAW AND CUSTOM. New York: Henry Holt and Co., 1886.

————. LECTURES ON THE EARLY HISTORY OF INSTITUTIONS. London: J. Murray, 1875.

Marsden, Reginald Godfrey. SELECT PLEAS IN THE COURT OF ADMIRALTY. 2 vols. London: Quaritch, 1894–1897.

Martens, Georg Friedrich von. SUMMARY OF THE LAW OF NATIONS, FOUNDED ON THE TREATIES AND CUSTOMS OF THE MODERN NATIONS OF EUROPE. Trans. from French by William Cobbett. Philadelphia: Thomas Bradford, Printer, Bookseller and Stationer, 1795.

McDougal, Myres S., and William T. Burke. THE PUBLIC ORDER OF THE OCEANS: A CONTEMPORARY INTERNATIONAL LAW OF THE SEA. New Haven and London: Yale University Press, 1962.

McDougal, Myres S., and Harold D. Lasswell and James C. Miller. THE INTERPRETATION OF AGREEMENTS AND WORLD PUBLIC ORDER. New Haven and London: Yale University Press, 1967.

Moore, Stuart Archibald. A HISTORY OF THE FORESHORE AND THE LAW RELATING THERETO. Third edition. London: Stevens and Haynes, 1888.

Nicholson, Norman L. THE BOUNDARIES OF THE CANADIAN CONFEDERATION. Toronto: MacMillan of Canada, and Ottawa: Institute of Canadian Studies, Carleton University, 1979.

Nuger, Antoine Louis. DES DROITS DE L'ETAT SUR LA MER TERRITORIALE. Paris: Impr. Moquet, 1887.

Nys, Ernest. LE DROIT INTERNATIONAL. 3 vols. Brussels: A. Castaigne, 1904–1906.

Oppenheim, Lassa Francis Lawrence. INTERNATIONAL LAW: A TREATISE. 2 vols. Seventh edition by Sir Hersch Lauterpacht. London and New York: Longmans, Green and Co., 1948–1952.

Ormerod, Henry Arderne. PIRACY IN THE ANCIENT WORLD: AN ESSAY IN MEDITER-RANEAN HISTORY. Liverpool: The University Press of Liverpool, and London: Hodder and Stoughton, Ltd., 1924.

Ortolan, Theodore. RÈGLES INTERNATIONALES ET DIPLOMATIE DE LA MER. 2 vols. Second revised edition. Paris: Plon Frères, 1853.

Perels, Ferdinand Paul. MANUEL DE DROIT MARITIME INTERNATIONAL. Trans. from German by Leo Arendt. Paris: Guillaumin, 1884.

Phillimore, Sir Robert Joseph. COMMENTARIES UPON INTERNATIONAL LAW. 4 vols. Third edition. London: Butterworths, 1879–1889.

Phillipson, Coleman. THE INTERNATIONAL LAW AND CUSTOM OF ANCIENT GREECE AND ROME. 2 vols. London: MacMillan, 1911.

Piedelievre, Robert. PRECIS DE DROIT INTERNATIONAL PUBLIC OU DROIT DES GENS. 2 vols. Paris: F. Pichon, 1894–1895.

Potter, Pitman Benjamin. THE FREEDOM OF THE SEAS IN HISTORY, LAW AND POLITICS. New York and London: Longmans, Green and Co., 1924.

Pradier-Fodere, Paul Louis Ernest. TRAITÉ DE DROIT INTERNATIONAL PUBLIC EUROPÉEN ET AMÉRICAIN, SUIVANT LES PROGRÈS DE LA SCIENCE ET DE LA PRATIQUE, CONTEMPORAINES. 8 vols. Paris: G. Pedone-Lauriel, 1885–1906.

Raestad, Arnold Christopher. LA MER TERRITORIALE: ÉTUDES HISTORIQUES ET JURIDIQUES. Paris: A. Pedone, 1913.

Riesenfeld, Stefan A. PROTECTION OF COASTAL FISHERIES UNDER INTERNATIONAL LAW. Washington, D.C.: Carnegie Endowment for International Peace, 1942.

Rivier, Alphonse Pierre Octave. PRINCIPES DU DROIT DES GENS. 2 vols. Paris: A. Rousseau, 1896.

Shalowitz, Aaron L. SHORE AND SEA BOUNDARIES: WITH SPECIAL REFERENCE TO THE INTERPRETATION AND USE OF COAST AND GEODETIC SURVEY DATA. (U.S. Department of Commerce, Coast and Geodetic Survey Publication 10-1). 2 vols. Washington, D.C.: Government Printing Office, 1962.

Simmonds, Kenneth R. CASES ON THE LAW OF THE SEA. 4 vols. Dobbs Ferry, N.Y.: Oceana Publications, Inc., 1976.

Smith, Herbert Arthur. THE LAW AND CUSTOM OF THE SEA. Third edition. New York: Frederick A. Praeger, 1950.

Strohl, Mitchell P. THE INTERNATIONAL LAW OF BAYS. The Hague: Martinus Nijhoff, 1963.

Swarztrauber, Sayre Archie. THE THREE MILE LIMIT OF TERRITORIAL SEAS. Annapolis: Naval Institute Press, 1972.

Symmons, Clive R. THE MARITIME ZONES OF ISLANDS IN INTERNATIONAL LAW. The Hague, Boston and London: Martinus Nijhoff, 1979.

Vattel, Emmerich de. THE LAW OF NATIONS OR THE PRINCIPLES OF NATURAL LAW: APPLIED TO THE CONDUCT AND TO THE AFFAIRS OF NATIONS AND OF SOVEREIGNS. Trans. by Charles G. Fenwick. In THE CLASSICS OF INTERNATIONAL LAW, ed. James Brown Scott. Dobbs Ferry, New York: Oceana Publications, Inc., and London: Wildy and Sons, Ltd., 1758 edition, reprinted 1964.

Wenk, Edward, Jr. THE POLITICS OF THE OCEAN. Seattle and London: University of Washington Press, 1972.

Westlake, John. INTERNATIONAL LAW. 2 vols. Second edition. Cambridge: The University Press, 1910–1913.

Weston, Burns H., and Richard A. Falk and Anthony A. D'Amato. BASIC DOCUMENTS IN INTERNATIONAL LAW AND WORLD ORDER. St. Paul, Minnesota: West Publishing Co., 1980.

Wheaton, Henry. ELEMENTS OF INTERNATIONAL LAW. Eighth edition by Richard Henry Dana, Jr. Boston: Little, Brown and Co., 1866.

Whiteman, Marjorie M. DIGEST OF INTERNATIONAL LAW. 15 vols. Washington, D.C.: Government Printing Office, 1963–73.

Wigmore, John Henry. A TREATISE ON THE ANGLO-AMERICAN SYSTEM OF EVIDENCE IN TRIALS AT COMMON LAW. Third edition. Boston: Little, Brown and Co., 1940.

Articles

Alexander, Lewis M. *The Ocean Enclosure Movement: Inventory and Prospect,* 20 SAN DIEGO LAW REVIEW 561–594 (1982–83).

—————. *Offshore Claims of the World,* in THE LAW OF THE SEA 71–84, Lewis M. Alexander, ed. Columbus: Ohio State University Press, 1967.

Beauchamp, K. and M. Crommelin and A. R. Thompson. *Jurisdictional Problems in Canada's Offshore,* 11 ALBERTA LAW REVIEW 431–470 (1973).

Bencker, H. L. G. *Maritime Geographical Terminology Relating to Various Hydrographic Subdivisions of the Globe,* 29 INTERNATIONAL HYDROGRAPHIC REVIEW 78–125 (1942).

Boggs, S. Whittemore. *Delimitation of Seaward Areas Under National Jurisdiction,* 45 AMERICAN JOURNAL OF INTERNATIONAL LAW 240–266 (April, 1951).

—————. *Delimitation of the Territorial Sea: The Method of Delimitation Proposed by the Delegation of the United States at the Hague Conference for the Codification of International Law,* 24 AMERICAN JOURNAL OF INTERNATIONAL LAW 541–555 (July, 1930).

Brown, E. D. *Delimitation of Offshore Areas: Hard Labour and Bitter Fruits at UNCLOS III,* 5 MARINE POLICY 172–184 (July, 1981).

—————. *Freedom of the High Seas Versus the Common Heritage of Mankind: Fundamental Principles in Conflict,* 20 SAN DIEGO LAW REVIEW 521–560 (1982–83).

—————. *Maritime Zones: A Survey of Claims,* in 3 NEW DIRECTIONS IN THE LAW OF THE SEA 157–192. London: British Institute of International and Comparative Law, and Dobbs Ferry, New York: Oceana Publications, Inc., 1973.

Charney, Jonathan I. *The Delimitation of Lateral Seaward Boundaries Between States in a Domestic Context,* 75 AMERICAN JOURNAL OF INTERNATIONAL LAW 28–68 (January, 1981).

—————. *The Offshore Jurisdiction of the States of the United States and the Provinces of Canada: A Comparison,* 12 OCEAN DEVELOPMENT AND INTERNATIONAL LAW JOURNAL 301–335 (1983).

Crommelin, Michael. *Natural Resources Law,* ANNUAL SURVEY OF AUSTRALIAN LAW 1980, 152–173 (1981).

————. *Natural Resources Law,* ANNUAL SURVEY OF AUSTRALIAN LAW 1981, 270–297 (1982).

Dolgin, Janet L. *A Jurisprudential Problem in the Submerged Lands Cases: International Law in a Domestic Dispute,* 90 YALE LAW JOURNAL 1651–1669 (June, 1981).

Fenn, Percy Thomas, Jr. *Justinian and the Freedom of the Sea,* 19 AMERICAN JOURNAL OF INTERNATIONAL LAW 716–727, 1925.

Fitzmaurice, Sir Gerald G. *The Law and Procedure of the International Court of Justice: Treaty Interpretation and Certain Other Treaty Points,* 28 BRITISH YEARBOOK OF INTERNATIONAL LAW 1–28 (1951).

————. *Some Results of the Geneva Conference on the Law of the Sea,* 8 INTERNATIONAL AND COMPARATIVE LAW QUARTERLY 73–121 (January, 1959).

Frowein, Jochen. *Verfassungsrechtliche Probleme um den Deutschen Festlandsockel,* 25 ZEITSCHRIFT FÜR AUSLÄNDISCHES ÖFFENTLICHES RECHT UND VÖLKERRECHT 1–29 (1965).

Gihl, Torsten. *The Baseline of the Territorial Sea,* 11 SCANDINAVIAN STUDIES IN LAW 119–174. Stockholm: Almquist and Wiksell, 1967.

Head, Ivan L. *The Legal Clamour Over Canadian Off-shore Minerals,* 5 ALBERTA LAW REVIEW 312–327 (1966–67).

Hershman, Marc J. *The Seaward Extension of States: A Boundary for New Jersey under the Submerged Lands Act,* 40 TEMPLE LAW QUARTERLY 66–101 (Fall, 1966).

Hodgson, Robert D. *Islands: Normal and Special Circumstances,* in LAW OF THE SEA: THE EMERGING REGIME OF THE OCEANS 168. Cambridge, Massachusetts: Ballinger, 1974.

Hubbard, H. Albert. *Constitutional Law: International Law: Ownership of and Jurisdiction Over Offshore Mineral Rights,* 2 OTTAWA LAW REVIEW 212–220 (1967–68).

Hudson, Manley O., director. *Harvard Law School Research in International Law: Nationality, Responsibility of States, Territorial Waters,* 23 AMERICAN JOURNAL OF INTERNATIONAL LAW 265–74 (Special Supplement, April, 1929).

Hurst, Sir Cecil. *The Territoriality of Bays,* 3 BRITISH YEARBOOK OF INTERNATIONAL LAW 42–54 (1922–23).

————. *Whose Is the Bed of the Sea?* 4 BRITISH YEARBOOK OF INTERNATIONAL LAW 34–43 (1923–24).

Krueger, Robert B., and Myron H. Nordquist. *The Evolution of the 200-Mile Exclusive Economic Zone: State Practice in the Pacific Basin,* 19 VIRGINIA JOURNAL OF INTERNATIONAL LAW 321–399 (1979).

Lapradelle, Albert G. de. *The Right of the State Over the Territorial Sea,* in 5 REVUE GENERALE DE DROIT INTERNATIONAL PUBLIC 264–344 (1898).

Lewis, D. E. *Provincial-Federal Co-operation,* 3 ALBERTA LAW REVIEW 412–423 (1964).

Martens, Fedor Fedorovich de. *Le Tribunal d'arbitrage de Paris et la Mer Territoriale,* 1 REVUE GENERALE DE DROIT INTERNATIONAL 39 (January-February 1894).

Martin, Cabot. *Newfoundland's Case on Offshore Minerals: A Brief Outline,* 7 OTTAWA LAW REVIEW 34–61 (1975).

McDougal, Myres S. *International Law and the Law of the Sea,* in THE LAW OF THE
    SEA 15, Lewis M. Alexander, ed. Columbus: Ohio State University Press,
    1967.

McDougal, Myres S. and Norbert A. Schlei. *The Hydrogen Bomb Tests in Perspec-
    tive: Lawful Measures for Security,* 64 YALE LAW JOURNAL 648–710 (April,
    1955).

Miller, Hunter. *The Hague Codification Conference,* 24 AMERICAN JOURNAL OF
    INTERNATIONAL LAW 674–693 (1930).

Morin, Jacques-Yvan. *Les Zones de Pêche de Terre-Neuve et du Labrador à la Lumière
    de l'Evolution du Droit International,* 6 CANADIAN YEARBOOK OF INTERNA-
    TIONAL LAW 91–114 (1968).

—————. *National Practice: Canada,* in 3 NEW DIRECTIONS IN THE LAW OF THE SEA
    243–252. London: British Institute of International and Comparative
    Law, and Dobbs Ferry, N.Y.: Oceana Publications, Inc. 1973.

Pardo, Arvid. *The Convention on the Law of the Sea: A Preliminary Appraisal,* 20
    SAN DIEGO LAW REVIEW 489–503 (1982–83).

Pearcy, G. Etzel. *Geographical Aspects of the Law of the Sea,* 49 ANNALS OF THE
    ASSOCIATION OF AMERICAN GEOGRAPHERS 1–23 (March , 1959).

—————. *Measurement of the U.S. Territorial Sea,* 40 DEPARTMENT OF STATE BUL-
    LETIN 963 (1959).

Scott, James Brown. *The North Atlantic Coast Fisheries Case,* in THE HAGUE COURT
    REPORTS 141–225. New York: Oxford University Press, American
    Branch, 1916.

Seidl-Hohenveldern, Ignaz. *Le Plateau Continental de La République Fédérale d'Al-
    lemagne,* 10 ANNUAIRE FRANÇAIS DE DROIT INTERNATIONAL 717–725
    (1964).

Shalowitz, Aaron L. *Boundary Problems Raised by the Submerged Lands Act,* 54
    COLUMBIA LAW REVIEW 1021–1048 (November, 1954).

Teclaff, Ludwik A. *Shrinking the High Seas by Technical Methods - From the 1930
    Hague Conference to the 1958 Geneva Conference,* 39 UNIVERSITY OF DETROIT
    LAW JOURNAL 660–684 (June, 1962).

Waldock, C. H. M. *The Anglo-Norwegian Fisheries Case,* 28 BRITISH YEARBOOK OF
    INTERNATIONAL LAW 114–171 (1951).

Walker, Wyndham L. *Territorial Waters: The Cannon Shot Rule,* 22 BRITISH YEAR-
    BOOK OF INTERNATIONAL LAW 210–231 (1945).

Special Documents

Appendix to Exceptions and Brief of the Common Counsel States (submitted as part
    of the U.S. v. Maine adjudication: 420 U.S. 515). Reproduced on micro-
    fiche by U.S. Government Printing Office.

Beazley, P. *Maritime Limits and Baselines: A Guide to their Delineation.* The Hydro-
    graphic Society, Special Publication No. 2, undated.

Bogota: Charter of the Organization of American States; April 30, 1948. 2
    UNITED STATES TREATIES AND OTHER INTERNATIONAL AGREEMENTS 2394.
    Washington, D.C.: U.S. Government Printing Office, 1952.

Brussels: The International Law Association, Report of the Seventeenth Conference (1896).

The Charter of the Royal Fishery of England. Patent Rolls, 29 Car. 2 pt. X (1688).

Charteris. *Territorial Jurisdiction in Wide Bays.* Internationa Law Association Proceedings, Report of the Twenty-Third Conference 103 (1906).

van Cleve, Richard. *The Economic and Scientific Basis of the Principle of Abstention,* 1 UNITED NATIONS CONFERENCE ON THE LAW OF THE SEA 47 (U.N. Doc. A/CONF. 13/3; *in* U.N. Doc. A/CONF. 13/37). New York: United Nations, 1958.

Exceptions and Brief of the Common Counsel States (submitted as part of the U.S. v. Maine adjudication: 420 U.S. 515). Reproduced on microfiche by U.S. Government Printing Office.

Executive Proclamation No. 2667. *Truman Proclamation on the Continental Shelf,* 10 FEDERAL REGISTER 12303, *reprinted in* 59 U.S. STATUTES AT LARGE 884 (1945).

Executive Proclamation No. 2668. *Superjacent Waters,* 10 FEDERAL REGISTER 12304 (1945).

Great Britain and Tripoli: Treaty of Peace and Commerce, 1 BRITISH AND FOREIGN STATE PAPERS 715 (March 5, 1676).

Gulland. FAO Fisheries Tech. Paper 206. (U.N. FAO Doc. FIRM/T206). New York: United Nations, 1980.

Hodgson, Robert D., and Lewis M. Alexander. *Towards an Objective Analysis of Special Circumstances: Bays, Rivers, Coastal and Oceanic Archipelagos and Atolls.* Kingston, Rhode Island: The Law of the Sea Institute—University of Rhode Island, Occasional Paper No. 13 (April, 1972).

League of Nations. *Conference for the Codification of International Law, Bases of Discussion for the Conference Drawn up by the Preparatory Committee, Vol. II, Territorial Waters* (League of Nations Doc. C. 74. M. 39. 1929. V.). Geneva: League of Nations, 1929. *Reprinted in* Supplement to 24 AMERICAN JOURNAL OF INTERNATIONAL LAW (January, 1930) pp. 1–8, 25–46.

———. *Report of the Committee of Experts for the Progressive Codification of International Law;* Shucking, rapporteur. (League of Nations Doc. C. 74. M. 39). Geneva: League of Nations, 1929.

———. *Report of the Second Committee* (Territorial Sea); M. François, rapporteur. (League of Nations Doc. C. 230. M. 117). Geneva: League of Nations, 1930. *Reprinted in* Supplement to 24 AMERICAN JOURNAL OF INTERNATIONAL LAW 234–258 (January, 1930).

McBryde's Map, World Ocean and Seas. (Available through Transemantics, Washington, D.C.) (1982).

Moscow: Treaty Banning Nuclear Weapon Tests in the Atmosphere, in Outer Space and Under Water; August 5, 1963. 14 UNITED STATES TREATIES AND OTHER INTERNATIONAL AGREEMENTS 1313. Washington, D.C.: U.S. Government Printing Office, 1964.

Oceana Looseleaf Series. *Western Europe and the Development of the Law of the Sea* (Vol. 1: F. R. G. 1925–1977).

Parliamentary Debates. Remarks to Commons by a representative of the British Foreign Office indicating that all departments of government then currently applied the six-mile rule for bays. 169 Parl. Deb. (4th ser.) 989 (1907).

Parliamentary Papers. Proces Verbaux of the Convention *(Parl. Papers,* Commercial No. 24, 1882) (Cd. 3238).

United Nations. DRAFT FINAL ACT OF THE THIRD UNITED NATIONS CONFERENCE ON THE LAW OF THE SEA (U.N. Doc. A/CONF. 62/121). New York: United Nations, 1982.

——. Geneva Convention on the Continental Shelf; April 29, 1958. 15 UNITED STATES TREATIES AND OTHER INTERNATIONAL AGREEMENTS 471. Washington, D.C.: U.S. Government Printing Office, 1964.

——. Geneva Convention on Fishing and Conservation of the Living Resources of the High Seas; April 29, 1958. 17 UNITED STATES TREATIES AND OTHER INTERNATIONAL AGREEMENTS 138. Washington, D.C.: U.S. Government Printing Office, 1967.

——. Geneva Convention on the High Seas; April 29, 1958. 13 UNITED STATES TREATIES AND OTHER INTERNATIONAL AGREEMENTS 2312. Washington, D.C.: U.S. Government Printing Office, 1963.

——. Geneva Convention on the Territorial Sea and the Contiguous Zone; April 29, 1958. 15 UNITED STATES TREATIES AND OTHER INTERNATIONAL AGREEMENTS 1606. Washington, D.C.: U.S. Government Printing Office, 1964.

——. *Juridical Régime of Historic Waters, Including Historic Bays.* 2 YEARBOOK OF THE INTERNATIONAL LAW COMMISSION 23 (1962) (U.N. Doc. A/CN. 4/143) New York: United Nations, 1964.

——. *Report of the Committee of Experts* (U.N. Doc. A/CN. 4/61/Add. 1, 18 May 1953: International Law Commission Fifth Session, Addendum to *Second Report of the Regime of the Territorial Sea* by J. P. A. François, Special Rapporteur) (1953).

——. *Report of the International Law Commission,* Eighth Session (U.N. Doc. A/3159). New York: United Nations, 1956.

——. *Report of the International Law Commission,* Seventh session (U.N. Doc. A/2934). New York: United Nations, 1955.

——. UNITED NATIONS CONFERENCE ON THE LAW OF THE SEA. Vol. 1 of 7 vols., PREPARATORY DOCUMENTS (U.N. Doc. A/CONF. 13/37). New York: United Nations, 1958.

——. UNITED NATIONS CONFERENCE ON THE LAW OF THE SEA. Vol. 2 of 7 vols., PLENARY MEETINGS (U.N. Doc. A/CONF. 13/38). New York: United Nations, 1958.

——. UNITED NATIONS CONFERENCE ON THE LAW OF THE SEA. Vol. 3 of 7 vols., FIRST COMMITTEE (TERRITORIAL SEA AND CONTIGUOUS ZONE) (U.N. Doc. A/CONF. 13/39). New York: United Nations, 1958.

——. UNITED NATIONS CONVENTION ON THE LAW OF THE SEA (UNCLOS) (U.N. Doc. A/CONF. 62/122). New York: United Nations, 1982.

——. VIENNA CONVENTION ON THE LAW OF TREATIES (U.N. Doc. A/CONF. 39/27). New York: United Nations, 1969.

——. YEARBOOK OF THE INTERNATIONAL LAW COMMISSION, 1953. 2 vols. (U.N.

Pub. A/CN. 4/SER. A/1953 with Add. 1). New York: United Nations, 1959.

————. YEARBOOK OF THE INTERNATIONAL LAW COMMISSION, 1954. 2 vols. (U.N. Pub. A/CN. 4/SER. A/1954 with Add. 1). New York: United Nations, 1959, 1960.

————. YEARBOOK OF THE INTERNATIONAL LAW COMMISSION, 1955. 2 vols. (U.N. Pub. A/CN. 4/SER. A/1955 with Add. 1). New York: United Nations, 1960.

————. YEARBOOK OF THE INTERNATIONAL LAW COMMISSION, 1956. 2 vols. (U.N. Pub. A/CN. 4/SER. A/1956 with Add. 1). New York: United Nations, 1956, 1957.

————. YEARBOOK OF THE INTERNATIONAL LAW COMMISSION, 1962. 2 vols. (U.N. Pub. A/CN. 4/SER. A/1962). New York: United Nations, 1964.

United States and Great Britain: Special Agreement Relating to North Atlantic Coast Fisheries. *Reprinted in* Supplement to 3 AMERICAN JOURNAL OF INTERNATIONAL LAW 168 (1909).

United States Army Corps of Engineers. *Explore 5; The California Coastline: San Francisco Bay* (a Bulletin of the San Francisco District U.S. Army Corps of Engineers) (undated).

————. *Report No. 3, Evaluation of Present State of Knowledge of Factors Affecting Tidal Hydraulics and Related Phenomena* (Committee on Tidal Hydraulics) (1965).

————. *Technical Bulletin No. 17, Estuarial Navigation Projects* (Committee on Tidal Hydraulics) (1971).

United States Congress. Approval of the *Territorial Sea Convention.* 106 CONGRESSIONAL RECORD 11196 (May, 1960).

————. *Hearings Before Committee on Foreign Relations on Executives, J to N, Inclusive.* 86th Congress, 2d Session (1960).

————. *Hearings Before the Senate Committee on Interior and Insular Affairs on S.J. Res. 13 and other Bills.* 83d Congress, 1st Session (1953).

————. *Outer Continental Shelf Lands Act,* 67 U.S. STATUTES AT LARGE 462 (1953).

————. *Proceedings in the North Atlantic Coast Fisheries Arbitration.* 12 vols. 61st Congress, 3d Session. Senate Doc. No. 870 (1912).

————. *Submerged Lands Act,* 67 U.S. STATUTES AT LARGE 29 (1953).

United States Geographer. LIMITS IN THE SEAS 104 vols. Bureau of Intelligence and Research, United States Department of State (1981).

————. NATIONAL MARITIME CLAIMS. United States Department of State (1982).

————. *Sovereignty of the Sea,* 3 UNITED STATES STATE DEPARTMENT GEOGRAPHIC BULLETIN 11 (1965).

————. STATUS OF THE WORLD'S NATIONS. United States Department of State (1980).

United States Naval War College. INTERNATIONAL LAW SITUATIONS WITH SOLUTIONS AND NOTES—1937. Washington, D.C.: U.S. Government Printing Office, 1939.

————. INTERNATIONAL LAW TOPICS AND DISCUSSIONS—1913. Washington, D.C.: U.S. Government Printing Office, 1914.

————. INTERNATIONAL LAW TOPICS—NEUTRALITY PROCLAMATIONS AND REGULATIONS—WITH NOTES—1916. Washington, D.C.: U.S. Government Printing Office, 1917.

————. *Note Between Sweeden and the Soviet Union;* July 18, August 21, 1951. 1948 U.S. NAVAL WAR COLLEGE 496.

————. *Note of Protest, United States to Mexico;* January 14, 1948. 1948 U.S. NAVAL WAR COLLEGE 481.

Name Index

Abreu, 48n, 50
Alexander, L., 21n, 22n, 76n, 77n, 81n, 84, 86, 94n, 99n, 107, 111, 115n, 116n, 128n, 130–33, 137–39, 141–45, 147, 182n, 183n, 184n, 218, 235, 237, 250n, 251
Amador, Garcia, 135, 136
Azuni, D., 32n, 44, 45n, 127, 128n

Baldus, 42n, 48
Bartolus, 42n, 48n
Beauchamp, 194n
Beazley, P., 10n, 14n, 15n, 75n, 79n, 81n, 84, 85n, 86, 93, 94n, 97n, 98n, 105–7, 110, 111, 114n, 116n, 128n, 130n, 131n, 138n, 139n, 140n, 142n, 144n, 147, 244n
Bencker, 102
Black, Hugo, 207n
Bluntschill, J., 33n, 36n, 37n, 38n, 43n, 45n, 61n
Bodin, 48n
Boggs, S. Whitmore, 25n, 69–72, 84, 95, 145, 146, 154n, 173, 174, 205n
Bonfils, D., 45n, 59n, 62n
Boroughs, John, 44n, 45n
Bowett, D., 126, 128n, 130n, 131n, 139n, 140n, 144n, 147
Bracton, 36, 39n
Bradley, 59n
Brierly, 50n
Brittin, B., 53n
Brown, 163n, 182n
Brownlie, I., 41n, 154n, 233n
Burgus, 45n
Burke, W., 16n, 17n, 22n, 26n, 76n, 161n, 165n, 169n
Bynkershock, Cornelius Van, 49–51

Cabbett, W., 33n
Calvo, C., 33n, 43n, 57n, 127
Caraseg, 50
Carnazza-Amari, G., 37n, 45n, 61n

Cauchy, E., 33n, 45n, 46n, 58n, 152n
Charney, 192n, 193n, 194n
Charteris, 24n
Codlerington, 42n
Colombos, C., 38n
Cordon, 204n
Coringius, 45n
Creasy, F., 45n, 55, 84n
Crocker, H., 37n, 43n, 45n, 48n, 50n, 66n, 154n
Crommelin, 194n, 199n, 200n
Currie, 195

D'Amato, A., 11n, 12n, 20n
DeCussy, F., 45n, 57
de Fratas, 45n
de Kercheve, Rene, 86
de Lapradelle, A., 46n, 61n
Dernal, Carlos, 188n
Despagnet, F., 46n, 62n
Dickerson, 150
Digges, Thomas, 42n, 44n
Drago, Luis M., 66n

Edmonds, 165
Elder, 42n
Engelmann, S., 129n

Falk, R., 11n, 12n, 20n
Faris Bey al-Khouri, 165
Fenn, 32, 36n
Fenwick, 53n
Fitzmaurice, Gerald, 10n, 79n, 135, 165, 166, 178n, 187n
Flaherty, David H., 38n
François, J. P. A., 81n, 121, 122n, 134, 136
François, M., 68n
Frowein, 189n
Fulton, T., 32n

Galliani, 45n, 52n
Gentili, Albert, 42n
Gentilus, 45n

Case and Statute Index

Subject Index